# Train

## of Thought

Drawdy, Larry
Train of Thought: Stories from On and Off the Rails

ISBN: 978-0-578-94891-1


1. Biography & Autobiography/ Memoir.  2. Transportation/ Railroads.
3. Travel/ Special Interest

Book design and publishing management:
Bryan Tomasovich, The Publishing World


Distributed by Ingram

Printed in the U.S.A.

# Train
## of Thought

### Stories from On and Off the Rails

*To my friend D.L. Lois*

*PEACE* ☺

*Hi. yah!* ✗✗✗✗✗ *EOBF 77*

# LARRY DRAWDY

*Larry 11-14-22 Drawdy*

# Train
## of Thought

Introduction

**Part One**

## Part Two

## Part Three

## Part Four

For My Beloved Wife, who somehow has managed to love me unconditionally through all the years.

That said, she has asked me to warn readers that this book contains some raunchy passages, which is not her cup of tea—nor may it be yours.

# Introduction

*They say old age plays tricks* on your mind. While writing the many stories in this book, I had a revelation: should one wait until getting on in age to write a nonfiction book featuring stories from their youth? There may be some unintended fiction mixed in. I have done my best at being truthful.

Many people suggested that I should write a book about my career at Amtrak as a passenger train conductor, focusing on what many perceived as my insane politically incorrect behavior pushing the envelope and ruffling feathers, leading to countless office visits for reprimands. As I wrote, I realized I must include stories that showed that out of all the character defects I possessed, being an unsafe train conductor was not one of them.

I went into railroad history mode and wrote start-to-finish my forty-year career, starting with the Burlington Northern Railroad freight train days in 1977 when women or minority locomotive engineers and train conductors were a rarity and diversity was just a word in the dictionary. I wrote all the way to my Amtrak passenger train days and to retirement in 2017. I wrote stories about characters I worked with, such as "Dare Devil Dave," "Hot Tub Dave," "Main Line Dave," and many others. Also included are off-color stories and quotes from lady coworkers—many making me look like an angel.

I then wrote some very serious railroad history (from my perspective) of the rampant drug and alcohol use by rails back in the day and have included stories of averted train wrecks that have never been written about and only a few are aware of.

Then I thought, *readers will have a difficult time understanding my career and peculiar mentality unless they know my early life,* most of it buried and not volunteered for decades. And so I felt compelled to write it, and as I wrote, it became therapy resulting in a spiritual awakening of a different kind. Should it help one person, then it will have been well worth it.

My first twenty-six years on earth had a few ups and downs, including my dear father's battle with Satan's piss, most likely resulting in my three stints in reform schools. Then I began drinking and drugging my way through life with several near-death experiences. I then served in the Army for three years in West Germany, smoking hash and drinking stout German beer almost 24/7. I came back to America continuing the same lifestyle, landing in jails, hospitals, two treatment centers, a failed marriage, and to my bottom. I'm still making amends. Along the way in the '70s, we lost my dear brothers, Darryl and Mark, from accidents after indulging too much.

I have not written detailed stories of ladies I got lucky with and not so lucky with and chose to only mention them in a few sentences, while guarding those relationships out of respect for all who would appreciate it; those tales, mostly of a fond nature, are embedded in my memory, and you can read between the lines. I lived and tried to grow up (still trying) in the era of sex, drugs, and rock and roll—and free love! That is not all that was free, as I caught free crabs, free clap, and free Hepatitis A, somehow managing to dodge free Hepatitis C and AIDS—a few of my friends passed away that way.

After some serious thought, I decided not to write about the low-life evil pedophiles that I encountered in my youth, as well as the ones later in life hiding in fraternal and religious organizations. I pray they get what God thinks they deserve and not what I think they deserve. All said, this book contains a glimpse of my early life so readers might better understand my legendary railroad career...to some (and not so legendary to others).

As if that wasn't enough, I wrote about my last thirty-eight years of a mostly happy marriage and helping my sweet wife raise our five children and a nephew, all being confirmed in the Lutheran church and graduating from high school. I also wrote about the many not-so-traditional events and adventures through the years, some that I am not exactly proud of, but have learned to accept.

The last couple of years when taking a break from writing I have been studying humility and ego—one which I am lacking and the other that I am not. I am now searching for the happy medium. My life story lacked humility, but I learned to write it with humility. Well...sort of. As I heard at a meeting once, *when you think you have humility? You just lost it.* It has been a work in progress at best, and more will be revealed.

# PART ONE

# 1958 to 1967
# Not Enough Sunday School

*As long as I can remember*, my parents indulged in refreshments that contained alcohol and I was even allowed to take sips from their drinks. When they weren't looking, I took extra sips. My father was one of the nicest men in the world until inebriated, which usually turned into a two or three-day binge staggering home with lipstick on his collar, black eyes, and reeking of booze and urine—horrifying and disgusting all. That, my friend, is the sugar-coated version. I eventually emulated him. He repented, however, and stayed away from Satan's piss his last ten years on earth while making amends. I forgave him. I miss him, and I love him.

My mother had a few harmless character defects, but giving up on family was not one of them. She was the nicest person I have ever known. I miss and love her. I was the first child born to my parents, Quincy and Louella Drawdy, in Seattle, Washington in 1954. I was followed shortly thereafter by my brother Darryl in 1955, sister Denice in 1957, brother Mark in 1959, and a bonus brother, Jeffrey, arriving later in 1965.

Growing up as a toddler, I heard my mother tell the story many times that they were married in June of 1951 and tried and tried to have a baby. After two years, the doctor told my mother to stand on her head for at least ten minutes after love making while having my father assist. I was born about nine months later. My dear Aunt Marilyn, who is also my godmother, tells me that while changing my diaper as an infant I peed in her face. I heard my father tell the story of when I had a double hernia as a toddler, which was somewhat rare, as most only involve one testicle. He would laugh, telling people

1

I had nuts down to my knees for a couple weeks until I had them medically corrected. I still have the scars today—more so in my mind.

As I grew up, many of the children in my neighborhood indulged in secretive activities such as smoking cigarettes in the woods and playing doctor—and it was not always a little boy that initiated those activities.

1958 is about the earliest I can date things. I remember hearing the neighbor man tell my father the school levy did not pass and there would be no kindergarten next fall. So I never got to go to kindergarten in 1959. I started the first grade in 1960 at the West Seattle elementary school named Fauntleroy for the first of six grades. Six years I attended Fauntleroy, but I was no Little Lord Fauntleroy. *I was Larry, Larry quite contrary.* I developed an inverted whistle with my lips, making a high-pitched sound that irritated the class room. When the class was quiet studying, I would put out the whistle while everyone looked around trying to figure out where it was coming from. Eventually, I would tire and give it up until another day. The whistle was undetectable even with someone looking straight at me. I can still do it today, irritating my dog and family members.

I found that by vibrating my leg in class as if it were in a spasm it would eventually cause the wood flooring to vibrate the book cabinet that would vibrate its glass sliding doors, causing them to rumble, sounding like the start of a earthquake. When the teacher and kids would start looking around nervously, I stopped. One of my classmates caught on but kept it a secret. Then one day as the rumbling started he ran to the window, looked out, and yelled earthquake! He slid under a desk as the class screamed with panic.

Yes, I went to Fauntleroy, but I was no Little Lord Fauntleroy.

In the spring of 1962, I was one of the two eight year olds out of fifteen that made the baseball team sponsored by Century Construction—we were the *2x4s*. I had a B- average without trying very hard in the second grade.

Not long ago, a dear friend convinced me to either move the next story deeper into the book, allowing readers to warm up a little before putting them into shock, or at least warn them beforehand that several stories in this book, though not intended to be offensive, are unavoidable. So, sorry. There are stories that are politically incorrect, inappropriate, and considered racist; however, I'm just telling the truth as I recall. Brace yourself, here comes a big one...

You can't grow up in America and not be at least a little bit racist. In the summer of 1962, when still eight years old, our family took the Great Northern Empire Builder passenger train from Seattle, Washington to Willmar, Minnesota, where my mother's dad (my grandpa) met us and drove 60 miles to visit the rest of the family who still lived at home on a farm in Clements, Minnesota. One day, my two youngest uncles (Neil, 12 and Gary, 14) took me fishing at a country creek. The two of them, for whatever reason, started talking about colored people. I listened as the two of them started arguing about the color of a colored person's ass. I guess neither had ever seen one, and neither had I, yet. Neil said that they had to have black asses, seeing as how they are all black

"No, no, no!" Gary insisted. "Have you ever seen the palms of their hands? They're white! So, their asses have to be white."

Well, over the years I have now seen a few colored people's asses and what I have surmised is that only a small percentage of them are black. The majority are various shades of brown, and yes, I saw a few that paled in comparison to the rest of their skin color. The next time I visit my uncles, I will have to tell them that after many years of investigating that neither was right or wrong, and that both of their theories have merit.

I met most my other aunts, uncles and grandparents several times before—very nice people. My Grandpa Earl, whom I got my middle name from, was a little different, and I grew to resemble him some. He was a good man, but a bad bad boy—meaning he was a great loving man, working hard and caring for all his family, even changing diapers on his mother-in-law while she lay on her death bed. All those virtues proved helpful to me later in my life.

The flip side of Grandpa Earl was he liked to hug all the ladies, and you never knew what was going to come out of his mouth, which proved at times not exactly helpful in my later life. That summer, I heard him talk about women and breast sizes the first of many times. He liked to say, *if it is more than a mouthful it goes to waste.* After all these years, I had a revelation: I never heard my grandma say that. I told you what my grandpa Earl said around me as an eight–year-old, so by the time I was twelve, between my father and him, I had heard as much as a most sailors.

I had a good baseball season in 1963, batting 400 and got a B- average at school.

The summer of 1963, at the age of nine, our family went on vacation to South Carolina to visit my father's side of the family. I met my uncles, Alver and Herman, and my grandfather, Joe Dick, who was a wet brain by then and made my Grandpa Earl look like an angel. Joe Dick had some very bad history, including being jailed for shooting his brother–in-law dead with a shotgun, and suspicion of being involved in numerous other despicable activities. I never met his wife, my grandmother Hattie Bell, my Uncle Gilmore or Aunt Zelma, who all tragically passed away years earlier, much too young, under suspicious circumstances that my cousin Genia and I have yet gotten to the bottom of.

I met my uncle George several years later. It was 1963 before the peak of the Civil Rights Movement. Most references made by my South Carolina clan pertaining to colored people were much more derogatory than my Minnesota clan. It was a very sad culture shock, now deeply ingrained forever. I have been down there five times since, and in some of the communities, the only thing that has changed? *They took down the signs.*

Recently in 2020, I met up with a third cousin, Genia, for the first time who I connected with on the internet in the '90s. She knew my Grandpa Joe Dick back in the '60s. We met in Olar and she drove me around town, telling me the history of the south along with stories of our family, then took me to several cemeteries.

I had a great baseball season in 1964, hitting three home runs and pitching five shutouts, but did not make the all-star team on account of my manager. There were to be three players taken from our team. The players were to vote for their three choices on a piece of paper and put it in the manager's hat. The manager assembled us together for the vote. I had the best pitching record, most home runs, and second best batting average on the team—and I was one of the best two fielders. I got along well with my teammates, but I did have a anger problem.

While pitching, when the umpire did not make the calls my way, I sometimes cried and displayed body language that many disproved of—my manager being the most critical. As we assembled for the vote, he delivered a speech about how a boy who cries while playing baseball when things do not go his way, regardless of his skills, does not deserve to be voted in on the all-star team. He fixed it in order for his son to be get voted in, who had much inferior baseball skills. This kid never seemed to like me, nor did his father. I am still pissed, and it is one of only a few resentments that I still hang on to today—accepting it only comes and goes. I will pray the manager gets what God thinks he deserves, not what I think.

That year I was the only fourth grader to make the track team, taking 4th in the softball throw at the district track meet, out-throwing several 5th and 6th grade boys. I had a B- average for grades at school.

That summer of 1964, at age ten, I was involved in a rock fight with neighbor kids one block over. I remember low-crawling in the tall grass up a small hill, sneaking up on them, when a huge rock landed on the top of my head, clomping my teeth together and nearly knocking me out. The lump and swelling left on my head was huge, with slight bleeding. I had a splitting headache, while my mother nursed it a few days.

And all was well, sort of, as shortly thereafter, spiritual

warfare increased and the battle between good and evil intensified for no rhyme or reason—or was there a reason? So many times in my life, people have asked me, *what's wrong with you? Did someone hit you in the head?* I was soon caught shoplifting for the first of five times, and a short time later, I was car prowling before going on to house burglaries. Some said I was a kleptomaniac. After all these years, I now agree that I was, as a great many of my family and friends learned.

I had a good year at baseball in 1965, subpar to the previous year, but I took first place in the softball throw at the district track meet. I got a B- for grades at school.

That summer of 1965, I read the dictionary and remembered all the words that an eleven-year-old should not, my favorite word being succubus. I also talked the whole Sunday school class into skipping class.

1966 was a very good year at baseball, I made the all-star team, going 2 for 5 in two games, while taking a disappointing 2nd place in the softball throw at the district track meet. The boy that took first, Scott, said to make sure you note he only took first because I had just had my arm taken out of a sling from a internal elbow injury from over throwing—they diagnosed that back then as *little league elbow.* I got good grades, a B- average, while girls were starting to look better than candy—and that, my friend, is sugar coated.

During the summer of 1966, at the age of twelve, I started becoming a parent's worst nightmare by getting drunk in the woods and passing out for the first time. I became involved in several delinquent activities, fighting being one of them. I learned that there were no rules in a street fight and that simply not being maimed or giving up during the despicable event were the goals—if one could call them goals. In my lifetime, I was in about fifty fights where actual swinging and kicking took place, resulting in blood and injuries. I can recall two fights where weapons were pulled out.

My first street fight was conjured up in a pool hall in an area near Seattle by the name of White Center, also known as "Rat City." Several older boys, fifteen or sixteen, thought that a guy named Gary and me would make for some good entertainment if we were to fight each other. They theorized that we would be evenly matched, as I was taller than him, standing at nearly six-foot even at twelve years old, while Gary was older, at fourteen, but only about 5 foot, 7 inches tall... evening things out.

We went to a parking lot across the street from the Epicure Restaurant and the half-dozen older boys circled us, egging us on. Gary was mean and scary, and in less than a minute he had me on the ground. He was yelling at me and tried kicking me in the head a few times as I blocked most the attempts with my arms. He did connect once before he was pulled off.

After that fight, I bought a stiletto knife and became an expert at flipping it open to scare people off, but never came close to using it on anyone. I kept track of the boys present at that fight through the years and know that most of them died at an early age from careless events. I heard that one is in prison today for rape. Gary became addicted to sniffing glue, succumbing to death from glue blockage in his organs at a very young age.

By the start of the 7th grade, I was deep into self will run riot, refusing to get a haircut or listen to any words of wisdom. On my first day of the 7th grade in junior high school, I saw a pretty, 9th-grade girl wearing a shirt that said *'69 breakfast of champions*. I wonder where she is now.

My mother always said that I was handsome, and I was very tall for my age, but for some reason I believed the older bully kids who said I was ugly and made fun of my height. I was an athletic kid, and excelled in baseball and other sports from eight to twelve. I got good grades at school without having to try real hard. At first glance, it appeared that I was a nice boy. But beneath the surface was one of the most confused kids there ever was.

# Miss Clark

*In the school year of 1965-66*, my sixth-grade teacher was Miss Clark. After fifty-four years, I now realize she is one of the greatest examples of humanity I have ever personally known. She was a Negro, or colored—a person of African heritage. She was black. She was the only black employee or student at Fauntleroy Elementary School that was nearly 100 percent white. I recall only one other person not totally white—a student said to be part Indian.

She had a deformity causing her to be a hunchback, and thus, the brunt of many cruel racist jokes; despicable as it was, she was referred to by many as the *nigger hunchback teacher lady*. I am ashamed to admit that I engaged in those conversations, even though I knew and felt that it was wrong... please forgive me.

She was neither weak, nor arrogant, being a true example of humility. She was strict, but not overly so. She was wise, smart, and witty. She knew from my delinquent behavior that my home life was not exactly the American Dream. What I find amazing today is that she cared enough to reach out in attempts to help or console me. I refused her help by sugarcoating the truth of what was going on; she saw right through me, however.

At the time, I felt close to her, but didn't know why. I recently took out my yearbook and there she was, all pretty and smiling. And I had a spiritual awakening. I realized the reason I felt close to her was because I respected and loved her, and still do.

# 1966 to 1970
# Reform Schools

*In December of 1966*, at the age of twelve, I was busted for burglary and taken to the Georgetown Police Precinct in South Seattle, where they did a *good cop, bad cop rough up* routine on me. I eventually confessed to thirty burglaries, although I did about forty. I did not confess to about ten of them because they were the homes that we hit the jackpot in, and I thought I was going to have to pay the people back.

I was then transported to the Seattle Youth Detention Center, where I spent Christmas with black boys from the ghetto who wore ladies nylons on their heads to keep their hair down after processing it with chemicals to make their kinky hair straight. I met white boys from the white ghetto who talked like gangsters in the movies, and a whole host of other nut cases, many that made me look like an angel.

I ended up in isolation, the *pokey*, a cell by myself for a couple days as a result of what *I do not recall*. I thought ripping the zipper off my pants and friction rubbing wounds on my left arm would get me out of that cell and to the hospital. *Wrong.* They had somebody bandage the wounds up. I still have the scars.

After four weeks of them studying me, I went to court and the judge struck his gavel and said, *I commit you to the State of Washington Department of Institutions Correction Center, "Cascadia," in Tacoma, Washington for a six week diagnostic stay*. That was a lot of wording for reform school. Another boy and I were transported the next day in a station wagon with no handles on the inside doors, with a screened cage behind the driver and one behind our heads.

9

A day or two later, a short, attractive, miniskirt-wearing, twenty-something psychiatrist lady diagnosed my personality as borderline "schizoid disorder." I crossed paths with her again on my next visit, as well. After thinking all these years about our visits, today I would diagnose her personality as borderline *cougar disorder*, although I will partially agree with her assessment of my personality disorder, as many years later in adulthood a blood sample taken from me for genetic reasons proved that my Chromosome number 15 had spilt in pieces. As I think about being alone with her in the office, watching her crossing and uncrossing her legs in that miniskirt, I definitely have a split personality. *I wonder where she is now?* Please forgive me—I know that is not exactly humility.

I learned how to pop electrical sockets in order to smoke pencil shavings rolled up in Bible paper. If you strip the plastic off the wire used to twist the end closed on plastic Langendorf bread sacks, you end up with a piece of wire about three inches long. Twist that wire onto the end of a rubber or plastic hair comb so the two ends are pointing out. Wad some toilet paper onto the wire and slip it close to the comb. Have someone distract the staff worker or wait for the right time, stick the two wires into the wall socket, and the socket will short circuit, causing the lights to flicker and the toilet paper to catch fire in order to quickly light the pencil-shavings joint. Each of us boys would get a drag or two, searing our lungs before the staff member—fancy name for *guard*—could break the event up. Lot of work to get sick and dizzy while risk being locked up in isolation.

One evening, they took us boys to a small stage and seating area where they held church services and other events for us. That evening they had a group of boys and girls from a local junior high school perform some dances while singing, and then to my astonishment they brought up a girl contortionist in leotards, split eagle on stage ten feet in front of us. Even as sick as I was, I thought that was wrong. I hope she is well.

I think a good lawyer could sue the state of Washington on

behalf of all of us children present for the split-eagle event on account of child sexual abuse. Those boys interviewed by the miniskirt psychiatrist lady would be entitled to a bigger split.

# Square Needle in the Left Nut

*The Washington State* Department of Corrections Center for Juvenile Delinquents, "Cascadia," was an institution in Tacoma, Washington that performed a four to six- week diagnosis to evaluate a young person's mental fitness and determine the next institution they would remain at until parole. The delinquent girls were locked up in a separate newer building behind the larger original building, where the delinquent boys were locked up.

I was incarcerated there three times as a young man: twice in 1967, and once in 1970. As you can imagine, the young men I was living with at those times were mostly of a devious nature. When arriving from other parts of the state after being committed, new arrivals were held for a day or two before being given a medical examination. During this holding period, the other inmates would always warn the newcomers about the last step of their impending appointment; they would B.S. the newcomer that the doctor finished up his examination by giving them a shot of juices with a square needle directly in the left nut to stop the spread of any possible diseases they had. I, and most of the other young men, would reason the hoax out and not be alarmed. I am a bit ashamed to admit, however, that I kept quiet as a couple boys freaked out awaiting the square needle in the left nut.

# 1967
# Echo Glen Reform School

*After my six-week evaluation* at Cascadia, I was sent to the Echo Glen reform school in Snoqualmie, Washington, nestled in the foothills of the western Cascade Mountain range and situated on a lake-like swamp. The girls were on the other side of the compound and when mingling at school or other activities, a supervisor kept any hanky panky from happening.

One day, a Sioux Indian boy and I "escaped" from the compound and rambled around the forest for twelve hours until the police captured us, took us back, and locked us up in the pokey—solitary confinement. We were each in a cell of our own for two or three days. I had my first successful encounter in the pokey with Rosie Palm, and would soon be meeting her five sisters. I got a bottle of black India ink, some sewing thread and a sewing needle, and tatooed *L.S.D.* on my left arm. Last I heard, my rambling partner was still alive in Wolf Point, Montana. I was paroled in June, serving a total of about six months.

# Summer of Love

*It was the summer of love*, 1967. My parole officer came to my house for a counseling session, another short, sexy, twenty-something lady in a mini skirt...I wonder where she is now. I remember that she was not impressed with my goal of traveling to Haight Ashbury in San Francisco, where all the hippies were gathering, and she advised against it.

That summer, I became friends with a guy named Tim, a year older than I and taller. We were two peas in a pod. We ventured downtown most everyday, panhandling along the streets and sneaking into the Embassy adult theater—it was hard to find a seat that was not sticky. After that cheap thrill, we went on to hanging out at the Seattle Center, where the 1962 World's Fair took place, with the the 600-foot Space Needle, when erected the tallest structure west of the Mississippi. While at the Center, in between panhandling we would pick up girls, asking if they would like to see a statue in a secluded area with trees and bushes all around. I don't recall who the man was, the statue, or why he was famous; once we were there, we would try to make out with them, being mostly successful. Then they would have to get back to their parents they had slipped away from. One day we made out with three different sets of girls. I know this is getting old, but...I wonder where they are now.

That summer, the hotline was one of my pastimes. Back then in the Seattle area there was a glitch in the phone system. When you called a wrong number, the line would make a signal similar to a busy signal, sounding like *eee ahh eee ahh eee ahh*. In the split second between *eee* and *ahh*, kids would communicate with other kids, mostly giving out their name and phone number. It went something like this: you called a number you knew was wrong, and it would go into the busy/ wrong number signal mode,*eee ahh eee ahh*. You could hear kids on there: *eee* "Jill" *ahh* "my" *eee* "number" *ahh* "is: *eee* "9" *ahh* "3" *eee* "5" *ahh*.... After one put their name and number out there, they would hang up and wait for a call or make a call, depending on the situation. Most of the time, the calls I received or made became dead-end conversations. There were three times, however, that I got lucky, sort of....

The first time, I took a bus to north Seattle and met a girl whose parents were not home. She gave me a complete tour of the house, including her bedroom, where we looked at her photo album and then she said her parents were due home at any time, so I politely left on good terms, to never go back. The second time, I conversed with a girl and made arrangements to meet her at her house. That didn't turn out to be nearly as fun, as her two brothers were there blocking any potential hanky panky. Now, the third hotline encounter, the girl invited me over to where she was babysitting. She said to come over after eight, since the baby would be sleeping. The third time was a charm, as we put on a 45 record playing the recent hit song, "My Baby Does the Hanky Panky." *Hi yah!* I wonder where she is now.

September of 1967, I enrolled in the eighth grade at a Seattle junior high cchool, and by October I was violating parole by not attending school. I was caught shoplifting and released, then before the impending court hearing, I tried hitchhiking out of the state, only to be picked up by the police in Spokane, Washington while loitering and being a runaway.

I was locked up again in detention and returned to Seattle where I was again sent to Cascadia, this time for a four-week diagnostic stay. Then on to the Naselle Youth Forest Camp, which is another name for *reform school* located in Naselle, Washington. I actually had a mostly positive experience while incarcerated at Naselle. I became a model prisoner, one of the hardest workers with an axe and later, a chainsaw. There were no girls there, except for a couple ladies who worked in the kitchen. We were allowed to smoke tobacco products and read *Playboy* magazines. On the inside of my closet door, I had a pin-up poster I could see while lying in bed of a pretty naked lady wading in a pond. I wonder where that poster is now.

One day, they took several of us—including a boy who is now a street person—in two vans to the girls reform school in Chehalis, Washington called Maple Lane for a dance. I remember that the lady counselors had chalkboard sticks they used to poke in between the couples slow dancing too closely—to keep any poking from going on. The counselors at Naselle were mostly nice, as were the work crew foremen.

I was paroled in late August of 1968 and enrolled in Denny Junior High School in Seattle and was placed in a special class for rowdy kids taught by a very nice man by the name of Mr. Don Voris. I took half my classes in his portable classroom, and the others, such as wood shop and history in regular classrooms. It appeared that I had made a change in my life for the good, getting my best grades ever with a 3.33 GPA, while holding down a couple different part-time jobs. I did manage to skip one period a day and one day a week alternating the periods and days so as to not get caught.

The summer of 1969, however, I started reverting back to minor criminal activity and that fall started high school at Chief Sealth in Seattle. I actually made the junior varsity football team and played in one practice game before quitting and going down the wrong path again by hopping a freight train to Minnesota with my friends Mike and Larry, drinking, drugging, and stealing along the way. I came back from Minnesota and a couple weeks later hitchhiked to South Carolina and visited with my Uncle Alver, who had twelve toes, six on each foot. My parents flew me back to Seattle.

A short time later, a friend and I were busted for burglary and I was sent to Cascadia in the spring of 1970 for the third and final time, and then on to the Spruce Canyon Youth Forest Camp near Colville, Washington in the northeast corner of the state. I never rambled from there, but did end up in the pokey one day for sniffing a gasoline rag, that being the last time I ever sniffed gasoline—but would soon be sniffing something more interesting, not exactly being humble, sorry. They trained us to fight forest fires, and we were sent out on a few. We would work twelve hours on and twelve off. Some very hard work cutting firebreak trails in the earth with a pulaski tool. On one of those adventures, they mixed us in with adult men prisoners for a couple days from the Loomis prison facility. It was during these couple days that I decided that when I got paroled I was going to do my best to stay out of trouble because I was nearing the age I would be going to prison should I continue my lifestyle. You might be wondering what brought this new attitude on.... Well, it was the manner in which these adult men prisoners were treating me—they were using all the charm they could muster to get close to me, the same way I would try to get close to girls. I started re-thinking a life of crime.

I was paroled early on account of good behavior, just in time to enroll for high school at Chief Sealth in the fall of 1970. That was the last of my reform school days, however drinking and drugging my way into jail a few times and a couple alcohol treatment centers was on the horizon.

To sum up my twenty-two months in reform schools, the experience did open my eyes in respect to one becoming a productive member of society. It would still be a rough road many years ahead, however, before that true desire would arrive. The boys I lived with during that time came from family life and upbringings that made mine seem tame. Some of them belonged in mental institutions or homes for retarded children. They told me stories of abuse they received that should have landed their parents or caretakers in jail. The main topic among us boys, however, almost 24/7, was the exaggerated stories of sexual conquests we had in our past. Most I think were untrue.

It has been a while now, and most of the confused lost souls that I did time with, I do not know where they ended up or how they turned out. I ran across one—a successful lawyer who indicated he knew me, but did not want to converse about it. I ran across another man who was a somewhat successful safety consultant but he flatly refused to acknowledge it ever happened. In my late twenties and early thirties while working as a brakeman on freight trains, we spent many hours in sidings and I always had a newspaper to pass the time. Almost every month I would read in the crime section about boys that I knew in reform school being arrested, charged, or sentenced for some very despicable crimes, including kidnapping, rape, and murder.

Most of the state employees those twenty-two months seemed to do a decent job. I did have a staff worker man at Echo Glen slap me pretty hard across my face after I smarted off and refused an order during kitchen duty, but that was the only time I was physically abused. I would like to express my appreciation for some of the employees who went above and beyond the call of duty trying to help us kids by treating us as human beings, instilling in us a small ray of hope: Mrs. Latterdale and Mr. Peyton from Cascadia, and at Echo Glen, a Miss or Mrs. Bennett, and a shop teacher by the name of Mr. McMillan. At Naselle, I cannot think of one bad adult worker experience. My personal counselor, Mr. Rugo, never failed me. At Spruce Canyon, I recall no incompetent supervisors, but only one I bonded with, his name being Mr. McCaffery.

I would like to honor someone that greatly reduced my early groomed racist views—some that still pop up and haunt me occasionally. I have never spoken or written of this experience until now. Mrs. Latterdale, from Cascadia, was a "colored" person, about to become "black," and one of the greatest examples of a human being I have ever known. It was 1967, I was twelve years old, locked up behind bars in solitary confinement away from the other boys for violating some rule. I was angry, lonely, confused, worried sick, and lost when she appeared like an angel and gave me a warm embrace, telling me everything was going to be okay and said she would pray for me, then smiled and left. If anyone sees her? Please tell her I said *thank you!*

# 1970 to 1973
## School of Hard Knocks

*I drank and took any drugs* I could get my hands on—snorting, eating, popping, smoking, shooting up, and even dabbled with sniffing lighter fluid and gasoline (back in reform school). So, though I can recall most of the events between 1970 and 1973, the order in which the events took place is guess work.

I had a great parole officer, a Mr. *something,* and I needed a driver's license since I was already sixteen and a half. I had a problem from when I was fourteen, when I got a traffic ticket riding a Cushman motorcycle, plus tickets two other times, all for minor infractions, but each ticket included being cited for driving without a license. The third time I went to court, the judge suspended the age I could apply for my license until the age of eighteen.

I was now going to school most of the time and doing pretty well. I asked my parole officer if he would write a letter to the Seattle court system and see if they could overlook my driver's license suspension application age on account of good behavior. He wrote the letter and within a couple weeks I was cleared. I needed to take driver's education as per requirement and no classes were available at my high school until spring quarter. I would be seventeen by then.

I begged my parents to pay for private driver's education, to which they agreed. The quickest one I could get in was in North Seattle in the evening, so most every evening for three weeks I drove my 1958 Ford to within a couple blocks of class, parked it, and walked to class. Did I mention I never did stop driving? Anyhow, I passed with 90 percent or better on all tests and had my driver's license a month before my seventeenth birthday, *hi yah!*

A month later, I carefully cut a zero out of the phone book and carefully glued it over the *4* on *1954* of my driver's license, making it *1950*—old enough to purchase booze. For whatever reason, I decided to get the word *ovary* engraved on my cigarette lighter. I hopped freight trains from Seattle to Minnesota four times, and to Montana and Canada once. I also hitchhiked from Nevada to South Carolina and from Los Angeles to Seattle once each, on top of other thumbing trips across the country and in the city. On one of those thumbing trips in Wyoming, a Volkswagen van, or *bus,* as they called them in the day, with three girls picked me up. While two of them rode in the front, I rode with the third in the rear. I wonder where she is now.

On a thumbing trip in the South, many of the men who gave me rides flipped me shit for my long hair, plus when finding out I was from the north, called me a *nigger lover*. On one of those rides, I was near Jackson, Mississippi when an old hearse with three older teenage white boys picked me up. The hearse had not been in service for many years, at least I don't think it had been. The boys started giving me a bad time about my long hair and being from the north where we tolerated *spooks*, saying those kind of people should be hanged. I was scared and starting to freak out when they stopped and said, *time for you to get out boy, we are turning off here.* They let me out and as they turned off the highway and pulled away up a country road, I heard them howling with laughter as the car went out of sight and disappeared. Thank god! For a few minutes I thought it was me that was going to disappear.

I told you my fondest favorite ride while thumbing from the girls in the van and my least fondest ride from the boys in the hearse. There were a thousand other rides that I can only begin to remember, some that are just as well forgotten, such as drivers being intoxicated, or the lonely old gay men that had a difficult time accepting *no* for an answer.

I hopped freight trains several times it was always a very dangerous adventure, as I nearly fell off a couple times. It was equally dangerous riding in box cars with other nutcases, one time with twelve other suspect characters in the only open box car on the train.

In 1971, I attended the last *bona fide* rock festival in Satsop, Washington, where many at the time simply emulated Woodstock. Reminiscing about that event after all these years is mostly surreal. It was the largest gathering of crazy people that I was ever involved with—mostly of friendly spirit. When you throw drugs such as LSD in to the mix, however, topped off with alcohol and the endless smoking of grass, some of those friendly spirited people became very delusional and were hauled off in stretchers to the hospital.

As you can imagine, there were a fair amount of evil-minded troublemakers, the most common being the rip-off drug dealers, along with plenty of low-life pickpockets among other thieves waiting for opportunities to steal, such as when people stepped away from their belongings where they were camping. There were some bullies that were there to cause grief, though there were more than enough good Samaritans to keep them at bay. There was not much they could do with the rampant borderline pedophile piece of shit men taking advantage of confused and high young girls.

Did I have any fun? Not much, as I mentioned earlier I never understood why I took LSD more than the first time. After, it made me paranoid and I tried to alter that feeling with heavy doses of grass and alcohol. It did not help, until I blacked out or passed out, if you can call that help. I did have some enjoyable experiences while attending, though, one being the great performance of the English rock group Wishbone Ash, and the many frolicking naked girls with flowers in their hair.

I shortly thereafter crossed over from abusive drugging and drinking to out-of-control abusive partaking, leading to several near-death experiences for the following nine years, *and* managing to significantly reduce my IQ in that period.

I was in seven of what could have been fatal car crashes when the cars were totaled. Some of them I was the driver, and others I was not. There may be a couple more wrecks I do not recall. With most of those wrecks, the realization that it was going to happen was a split second before impact. The fact that I walked away from all of them might be considered a miracle by some. Actually, I ran away from the scenes before the cops arrived and if I was the owner of the car? Reported it stolen.

One wreck, however, had a fifteen or twenty-second build up before the final impact. Four of us had just left a keg party late at night heading for another party in an old 1950s four-door automobile. The driver was a young man named Vern who had two or three of his fingers cut off in an industrial work accident and kept them in a jar of formaldehyde to show people. I was the passenger in the back seat with my friend Larry, and I can only guess who was riding passenger in the front. We were in West Seattle, on 35th Street SW heading north, the speed limit 35 mph. Vern pulled the jar of fingers out of the glove box and waved them around and said, *I get stink finger whenever I want*, while laughing. He put them back in the glove box and told us he was going to see how fast this car would do, as he floored it.

For the next half mile I watched the speedometer slowly go from 40 to 70 as we approached the crest of a steep hill, starting just before the water towers above the High Point community. At the towers, it was a half-mile descent to the bottom at Morgan Street, where it leveled out. I raised my large plastic cup of beer and made a quick announcement, *I better have one last drink before I die.* I mostly spilled it all over on myself while getting a gulp. Halfway down the hill was a section of street that leveled out for a couple hundred feet where another street cut in. We were going 100 mph. When we hit the flat section, the car bottomed out and became slightly airborne for a moment and as we landed Vern slammed on the brakes. We veered to the left, sideswiping several parked cars, which at least helped us to slow down, and started a 360-degree spin to the right side of the street. While going backwards, we sideswiped more cars and continued turning until we were facing forward. Vern crashed into a parked car on the left side of the street head-on, at about 30 mph. We all jumped out and ran. About a block away, Vern yelled, *I forgot my fingers! I gotta go back and get them.* When he did, the cops got him.

In the fall of 1971, I met a young, rowdy chapter of AIM: the American Indian Movement, an organization advocating equal rights for American Indians. I have not thought about that meeting for a long time and the drugs and alcohol present blur most of the experience. I was at a party of fifteen or so people, a couple of them friends, getting wasted. Down the street was a party going on of people belonging to AIM. I do not recall if we were invited, however I remember going down there and being greeted by two ladies that took turns trying to break full bottles of beer on my head as I was trying to watch my back, dodging not-so-friendly men. The first bottle to my head almost knocked me out, but the others only fazed me. After two or three more swings at my head, one did finally break. I left and went back to our party, only to return to the AIM party a few minutes later with a few guys. As we approached their house, a shotgun blast hit the street thirty or so feet in front of us. We retreated back to our party and a short time later the police came and broke both parties up.

# Joined Army

*After three stints* in reform schools, it was strongly suggested that I join the military. Serving my country would be a slight upgrade from reform school, and women would be more available. My friend John and I went to the Navy recruiter and they wanted to have me interviewed by a psychiatrist before they would consider letting me join, which would take a few days. I did not want to wait because I feared the law was about to get me, so we went down the street and joined the Army.

That was December of 1972, and a couple weeks later, on January 3rd, 1973 we reported to the Interbay Induction Center in Seattle. After formalities, we took the enlistment oath, which in part meant we swore to obey orders from our superiors, so help us God, and we started our service. One of the first things we did for our country was wait in a large room of twenty of us men recruits, wearing nothing but underwear. We were ordered to bend over, one by one, with our shorts down, as a doctor and a soldier standing closely behind him assisting went down the line and fingered our bungholes. The doctor would put on a latex glove and dip his right middle finger in a jar of gel his assisting soldier was holding, then probe the bunghole of a recruit and when done pull the used latex glove off and deposit it in a bag his assistant was holding, then grab a clean latex glove and proceed to the next. Homosexuals were not allowed to join the service, however the service doctors could finger our bungholes while others watched. And no! I am not making this up.

We then took a bus forty miles to the Fairchild Air Force Base and flew to the U.S. Fort Ord Army Base in Monterey,

California, arriving late in the evening. The next morning, I received a very short crew cut and John got away with a longer cut—not sure how that worked. I remember this fairly well, as I was now without booze and drugs for twenty-four hours. I was in basic with the last soldiers to ever be drafted in the U.S.A. The draft had just been terminated after many years of protest from citizens. The Vietnam War ended a couple weeks later while I was in basic training. We had one soldier go AWOL, stating, *if I can't fight in Vietnam I'm going home.*

I met young men from all walks of life, from all parts of the country, and of all different races—with all different perspectives on just about everything, I became friends with a few. The drill sergeants made an impression on me that will never be forgotten, some of it good and some not so good. They liked to single me out, calling me *big man: big man drop and give me twenty push-ups, big man do this, and big man do that.* I met recruits who had never been away from home, who broke down and bawled like babies from being homesick. I met others who were seasoned con artist degenerates off the street who made me look like an angel. One of the things that baffled me at the time was that many of these recruits must have came from homes without indoor plumbing facilities, because many times I went into the latrine to find all the commodes filled and not flushed. January and February, even in California, were cold and wet months and the recruits from Hawaii became very sick with pneumonia. There was also some sort of meningitis outbreak and many of us went to the infirmary and received immunization. I went as insurance.

The drill sergeants taught us crude songs to sing and march to: *if I die on the Russian front, bury me with a Russian c-nt,* or, *if I die on the Cuban shore, bury me with a Cuban who--.* Yes, the U.S. Army was making men out of us. One day, they took us out to an area with a couple tents and gave us gas masks and a little instruction on how to wear and use them. I was instructed to put mine on and get acclimated to it for a few minutes and then a big, tall thirty-something black drill sergeant marched me into a tent full of tear gas. He said, *take off the mask*, so I sucked in a huge breath and took my mask off. He then started asking me questions through his mask, and I answered back with very quick, short answers. After about three minutes, I ran out of air and took in a breath. It was scary as hell, as I dry heaved and started choking. He led me out of the tent to where I stumbled to the ground and lay snotty, red-eyed, and gasping for air. That was fun. Another day, they had us all gather outdoors on some bleachers and they pulled a rabbit out of a bag and clubbed it on the head, instantly killing the poor creature. They stated that it was done in order to make us tough.

The physical training we were put through was the only thing that I truly respected. The rest of the training went against most of my beliefs. I conformed, however, and became a soldier. And had I been called to die? I would have. That's the conflicting turmoil most soldiers have—you are taught all your lives to live and let live, and then it is all thrown out the window and you're supposed to forget your upbringing and think *kill kill kill*. Okay, I'm done ranting and raving....

I did experience a little fun while serving. One day while standing in formation, the drill sergeant asked for volunteers, and one man raised his hand. The drill sergeant said, *report to the first sergeant for a weekend pass,* and off he went. Then the drill sergeant asked again for volunteers, to which several raised their hands. *Great, report to the kitchen for weekend KP duty.* There was one drill sergeant who while leading physical training, while we all struggled to do push-ups with two arms, he would do them with one arm. I admired that and eventually was able to do twenty of them...and think I might still be able to manage one.

What basic taught me was discipline I could use in all areas of my life. One time during a barracks and locker inspection, the drill sergeant found my *Hustler* magazine I had tucked out of sight. As he held it up for all to see, he said, *we know what Drawdy does in his spare time.* Some things have not changed.

A couple weeks into training, however, the first sergeant summoned me into his office. He was holding paperwork pertaining to the results from my initial scholastic tests we were given.

"You scored pretty good. We want you to test for your GED. You take your tests tomorrow. You're excused."

The next day, I was transported somewhere a short distance away and arrived at an old brick building, joined by a few soldiers from other companies. I think I took five tests, about a half hour each. When I was all done, someone handed me the results and said, *congratulations you passed*. I was happy and felt proud. I could hardly wait to tell my parents—this was my first real accomplishment since getting my driver's license. I studied the results of the tests, arranged in a graph showing where I was average in some areas and above average in others.

We graduated from basic training and John and I got our orders for Fort Sill Oklahoma, home of the Artillery Lawton Oklahoma. We were to be trained for the fire direction center (FDC), which entailed coordinating positions of both the enemy and our troops on a chart, then computing data received from our forward observers, converting that data to calculate the amount of gunpowder to be put in the shell of a canon round, and then relay that information to the soldiers manning the canons so they could fire successfully on the target. I was a little overwhelmed with the slide ruler instrument used to compute data pertaining to the amount of gun powder that would be put in the shell of the round in order to hit the enemy, but eventually I got it.

The transition from boot camp to advanced individual training was a welcomed change. The young men I was now training with were pretty much a mellower group of mostly higher IQ individuals than the majority of those in basic training...more educated, but not without their character defects. The atmosphere was a little too mellow, so John and I went out on the town to the local establishments in Lawton, ending up one evening with a couple black girls for my first taste of brown sugar. Neither had a black ass or a white ass, one being a dark shade of brown, the other a lighter shade of brown. One day, they drove about fifteen of us in several different cars ten miles out of town to the *mountains*...ha ha. Yep, they were rocks about 150 to 200 feet high, spread out for a mile or so, but the local people called them *mountains*.

It was just about time to graduate when my good friend Mike from back home drowned in the ocean off the coast of Oregon. I flew home for his funeral. After the funeral and upon returning to Fort Sill, John was graduating ahead of me, and I stayed another week. I caught up to him in Seattle at home, as we were given thirty days leave before being shipped overseas to West Germany. Of course, all we did was party. I did have a girlfriend, sort of, but she had to be in early, being sixteen years old. I wonder where she is now...actually I do know where she is now. I vaguely remember flying to Fort Dicks in New Jersey and being held there a couple days before heading off for West Germany.

In West Germany. I spent the majority of my time smoking hash and drinking stout German beer, while causing havoc and chasing *frauleins*. I ended up in the hospital infirmary twice for alcohol poisoning, at the time blaming it on the flu. As you can imagine, many soldiers in their spare time indulged in practical jokes on each other, I was involved in my fair share, and the one being the funniest—at least to me—happened by a fluke. I was walking down the barracks hallway and saw something that looked like a tea bag. I picked it up and gave it a little sniff, expecting to smell some sort of tea fragrance, and almost gagged as it was some sort of used German tampon. I dropped it, but then an idea came to me and I picked it up by the strings and walked upstairs to the day room where the pool table and beer combination soda machine was. I put it in the coin return slot and waited for a victim. After a few minutes, there were two of us waiting for the third soldier to get stinky fingers, eventually adding up to several before it was all over.

I had a sergeant who loved to give me a bad time. He was

about 5-foot, 6 inches, and always giving me orders and calling me out in formation for little things like my hair being too long or the shine on my boots was inadequate—anything to belittle me. One day, we were in the NCO Club getting boozed up.

He leaned over and said, "Drawdy, what do you really think of me?"

"I think you're a sawed-off little fart," I responded.

"Let's go outside and we will see about this."

So we went outside and faced off and the sawed-off fart hit me in the face twice real quick, then slowly tackled me as he dove into my mid-section, reaching around me with both his arms holding back my arms tightly, pushing me backwards. I lost my balance and fell on my back in the gravel, but after a minute I managed to pull my arms free and started banging on the top of his bald head with my fists while he was still holding on. Somehow, I managed to stand up still banging on his head, but he let go and ran back into the NCO Club.

I regained my composure after about thirty seconds and chased in after him. I was blocked from entering the club by two sergeants, however, and told I better go to the barracks... *this fight is over.* When he hit me with those two quick punches, he got me good in the mouth and I was bleeding pretty bad. So it appeared that he had gotten the best of me. This was Friday night, so all day Saturday and Sunday I was taking a lot of crap from everyone about getting whooped by the little sawed-off fart. I was somewhat humiliated.

Monday morning it was raining outside so the captain called for formation inside the barracks. We were all in formation with our hats off, per the rule—no hats on during inside formation—except the little sawed-off fart sergeant still had his on.

The captain says, "Sergeant, what is wrong with you? Take off your hat!"

The sergeant hesitated, but he took his hat off and what should have been a bald white head was a deformed swollen black and blue head. He kind of looked like an alien. Many were snickering and soon apologized for giving me such a bad time—a vindication of sorts.

Three different times I slapped men soldiers across their face when they had pissed me off. As I look back, they may have been irritating me, but did not deserve it. Should I ever run across them, I will make those amends, which may not seem exactly humble, but the best I can do.

I had a roommate who was nice enough, though I had a little bit of resentment toward him since he was always trying to get a early discharge for some bogus reason. The *real* reason was, I think, that he was gay and the army wasn't working out for him. I developed another resentment when he would slide his slippers across the linoleum floor, making a sliding sound that drove me nuts, like people who can't stand the screeching chalk on a chalkboard. I hated sliding slippers on the linoleum floor, and I kept warning him to stop. One day as he slid across the room, I got up and I held out my left hand to the right side of his face and said, *you see that?* As he turned his head to look, I slapped him hard on his left side and said, *you didn't see that!* He then ran behind the wall lockers, but as I gave chase a little black roommate got between us and talked some sense into me and I left. When I came back after a few minutes, my roommate was gone and later everyone said he was in the day room upstairs sitting in the corner on a chair staring at the walls and would not respond to anyone. All night he sat there and finally the medics put him on a stretcher and took him away. My middle name is Earl, and that's what I went by in the army. For the next day, all I heard was, *don't mess with Earl 'cause he will slap you into a coma.*

I was scared that I might have really injured him seriously, but a short time later he came back to our room with a story. The story was that when I slapped him he had a flashback to his youth when his dad slapped him as a child, resulting in him going into shock. I thought it was another failed attempt at getting some sort of early mental discharge. I was relieved he appeared to be himself and I was never even reprimanded—

nor did he slide his slippers anymore. Just the other day, I was walking across the kitchen in my robe and slippers and my wife said, *pick up your feet or I'll slap you into a coma, Earl!*

I was in an NCO Club one evening getting boozed up once again and going outside now and then to smoke some hash. I remember talking with a young black man at the bar and things went bad. I do not recall what was said, but I thought what I said was cool. Apparently he did not, as he slammed a bottle of Boone's Farm strawberry wine across my face, slicing me up above and below my left eye, luckily missing the eye itself. All hell broke loose, and the melee spilled outside with about five or six of us white guys facing off with as many black guys, with one big white guy joining them. He was trying to talk everyone out of fighting, but he fled the scene when the real action started. Both sides were wielding weapons ranging from belts to metal bunk bed adapters. A man I knew well from Puerto Rico walked into the middle of the scene and was hit with a metal bunk adapter, re-shaping his head for life.

As we were facing off, hollering at each other, a man pulled a knife and lunged at me. Luckily, before he was able to reach me, my friend to my right slung his motorcycle chain link belt across his left cheek, stopping him cold in his tracks. An instant later, the military police showed up and we all ran. About an hour later, I got a ride to a military hospital. The man that tried to stab me, the man that got hit in the head with the bunk adapter, and I all got stitched up in the same room, with myself taking seven above my eye and six below. There was very few words said between us and no investigation. The man that was hit with the bunk adapter was seriously hurt, as his head swelled up larger than it should have been. His balance, among other things, was never the same.

I was involved in many other altercations—none that I am proud of.

I lost my brother Darryl in the summer of 1975 when the car he was driving slammed into a telephone pole. The root cause of his death being that he was impaired from indulging too much in drugs and alcohol. I was numb, my parents and siblings were devastated. I flew home for his funeral. I dream about him often and miss and love him. I visit his grave several times a year.

# Fuck Him Up, Sir!

*While serving in the U.S. Army* in West Germany during peace time, we went on alert due to a possible war with Iran. This 48-hour period was the only time outside of training at the shooting range or pulling N.A.T.O. Guard that I ever carried live ammo while in the service. Carried it 24/7 while on that alert.

We were in a company inspection formation as a one-star general, along with our commanding officer, a captain, was inspecting us soldiers. As they went down the line, the general would ask random soldiers hypothetical questions.

When he got to me, he asked, "Soldier! Your buddy next to you has a stomach wound and he is begging you for water. Do you give it to him?"

"No sir!" I snapped back.

"Why not, soldier?"

"Because it will fuck him up, sir!"

The general looked at me for a moment then turned to the captain. "As good of an answer as any."

# Vietnam Veterans

*I was in the army* three years during peace time, and as I mentioned, the Vietnam War ended while I was in basic training. While in uniform traveling from duty to duty in the public transportation terminals, I got a little taste of the disrespectful treatment those great Vietnam War Veterans received from some of the American public, since civilians treated me as a symbol of that not so popular war. I heard only a few short accounts from soldiers who served in Vietnam, even though I worked, partied, and bunked in tents with many of them. I spent three years with them, but most would not talk about the experience.

My thanks to all the men and women who served. Thank you Uncle Gary, thank you Uncle Dave. My heart goes out to all those who became disabled and all who did not come back. I pray for all their loved ones. Thank you, Vietnam Veterans for keeping us free.... Peace.

# Returning Home
# Discharged from Army

*In December of 1975*, I returned home from West Germany after serving three years in the U.S. Army. For the following sixteen months, I collected unemployment and played a lot of pick-up basketball in the daytime and after thousands of attempts, successfully stuffing the hoop one time in my life. At night in the bars, I chased ladies and had slightly better luck at stuffing.

One night, I met a nice Indian lady at a White Center bar and we gravitated to a Chinese bar and restaurant across the street and indulged in a midnight dinner on me.

"What are you going to do with the leftovers?" she asked.

"Feed them to my three-legged dog, Snodle.

"Could I have them?"

"Sure."

After dinner, we went to her house in a nearby housing project. Upon entry, she put the food on the kitchen table, told me to make myself comfortable, and she went down the hallway. I was sitting on the couch anticipating some teepee crawling when a bigger-than-me Indian man came out of the hall, ignoring me, and sat down at the kitchen table, devouring the leftover Chinese food. He then went back down the hall and I went out the front door, home to my three-legged dog Snodle.

One time after an all-night date at my place, I took the nice lady back to her home in the morning and her ex-boyfriend was there pointing a .357 magnum at me. Another time, I was invited to a lady's house and when I arrived, there was another man being my competition. After a while, he left and I stayed.

In the morning, I got in my truck and while going down the freeway my left front wheel came off. Someone had loosened the lug nuts.

I could go on and on about the sixteen months between the army and the railroad, but I think one gets the idea. I worked a few jobs that did not keep me around. The main reason being I was inept at whatever the employer was trying to train me for—mostly on account of being under the influence of some form of mind-altering substance or from being severely hungover and spaced-out from the night before.

That behavior would find a bottom and be eliminated five years later.

# Hiring on the Railroad

*It was a Sunday night* in late March 1977 and I was filling out my last unemployment card for my last unemployment check on my last unemployment extension when the phone rang. It was a lady from the Burlington Northern Railroad offering me a job as a section worker, a *gandy dancer*. Section work is hard labor—pounding spikes with a spike maul and lifting creosote railroad ties. The job entailed helping to build and repair railroad tracks, considered backbreaking work by most. I reported the next day to the third floor of Seattle's King Street Station for formalities and paperwork. The following day, I reported for a company physical, and by midweek I was working on the railroad at Interbay Balmer Yard in Seattle with sixty other young men, a few of them being freshly paroled from state prisons.

That summer was the hottest summer on record up to that time, as the temperatures reached over 100 degrees several days in a row. I made a few friends at work and kept track of every worker I hired out with that day. During the first few weeks, I saw guys quit, disappear, and walk off the job almost every day for one reason or another. The main reason that people left was that it was very hard labor. There were men who showed up every day who had to be told everything over and over again. Some of them were *challenged*, or *'slow,'* or back then they were called *retarded*. And there were others not retarded, but who would play a game to get out of work that we called *weasels*. I worked with a weasely parolee who would pick up railroad ties by himself and do a weight-lifting routine with them, but had to be instructed over and over to do anything else.

If you were still working after 60 days you joined the union, at which point it would take a federal case to get rid of you. On the 59th day, foreman Vern came onto the property and handed paperwork to several of my coworkers. The paperwork informed the workers that they were no longer employed by the railroad due to a lack of initiative. The weasels were let go and the retarded fellows who had shown up every day and worked hard remained. We were now down to about thirty of the original sixty and were becoming a productive work force.

One day, we all stepped back in time when the job site became a scene out of Johnny Cash's hit song, "Legend of John Henry's Hammer." If you haven't heard it, the song is about an incredibly strong black man who worked the section on the railroad decades earlier, pounding spikes like no other. There were a couple of old black guys on our crew who we were about to find out could swing a hammer just as well as the mythical John Henry. Mack, an old black man operating a bulldozer, got off of his machine, and the section foreman, Mitch, joined him to put on a show for about ten minutes.

"We're gonna show you boys how it's done!"

They hollered at us and told us to get out of the way and positioned about twenty spikes each in the tie plate holes. The old gandy dancers had two spike mauls, one in each of their hands, and they hammered in the spikes with alternating strikes as they moved down the line of ties. Swinging one arm after the other, they sort of looked like windmills. A machine could not have done the job better. When finished, Mack got back up onto his bulldozer, and Mitch went back to supervising, while the rest of us struggled along in awe—at a much inferior pace than the impressive feat we had just witnessed.

During this summer, my brother Mark passed away at the age of seventeen as a result of drowning while being impaired by drugs and alcohol. I miss him, I love him, and I visit him several times a year.

While pounding spikes, I would see the trains go by with the switchmen riding the shove of box cars—one was a *split tail*—and brakemen waving from the cupolas of cabooses. I could only dream of the job of a passenger train conductor as the silver streak blew by. I decided that I would not rest until I became a passenger train conductor. Every Friday after work, I would go see Connie, the well-preserved employment lady, and try to land myself a position as a switch man. She would ask if I was willing to work weekends, nights, out of town, holidays, and short calls. I would answer yes to all of her questions, give her a smile, and go back pounding spikes on Monday morning.

In the fall, I was bumped out of Seattle and bumped onto the Auburn section for a few weeks. I was bumped again up to the Everett section and worked until early November and got bumped once again with nowhere left to bump to. I worked for seven months on the section and kept track of every man I hired on with. One by one, they quit, got fired, or were injured. After twenty years, there were only two of the original sixty I hired out with left, the two of us that had became conductors— my friend Ken making thirty years and myself forty years. In late November, Connie from the employment office called me up to offer me the trainman job and I jumped on it.

# Trainman Class

*Again, I reported* to Seattle's historic King Street Station with the clock tower, which was once the tallest man-made structure west of the Mississippi River. At King Street Station, along with nine other potential trainmen I began three weeks of instruction in the classroom run by a semi-retired conductor working as a trainmaster from Montana. This man definitely would have been deemed politically incorrect in today's world. The class consisted of ten people: two ladies, one of whom was black, and eight men, one of whom was also black. At that time, railroads were under great scrutiny by lawmakers and equal rights organizations to hire women and blacks. It was the '70s, in the midst of the Virginia Slims revitalizing era of the women's rights movement, and blacks were still not deemed equal by many. The gentleman's agreement was that each hiring class was to be about 20 percent women and 20 percent black. I surmised that by hiring a black woman, the company was killing two birds with one stone.

The class consisted of a lot of stories by the instructor about different train wreck scenarios that could occur if rules were not followed, the colors of signals and their meaning, and adding a few stories of trainmen and locomotive engineers who had lost limbs and their lives in accidents. Over my career, I came to know a few. Every day, we went to lunch and some of us had a beer or two and puffed on a little reefer.

One day, our instructor and a couple classmates drove all of us to Balmer Yard in Seattle and we watched switching operations from the parking lots. Back then, a switch crew consisted of four people: the locomotive engineer, the switch foreman, the head man, and the field man. One common switching scenario was a locomotive connected to twenty or more cars with the locomotive at one end, the field man on the ground well behind the cars on the other end, the foreman on the ground near the end of the cars, with the head man on the ground between the foreman and the locomotive. The twenty cars, locomotive, and crew are strung out on what is called a *switching lead track* with several other tracks connecting to the lead. We watched as the foreman holding a switch list gave a hand signal and the locomotive engineer quickly pushed the string of cars along. The head man would pull the cut lever at the spot corresponding to the list to get the pin up, and the foreman would give the hand signal to stop the train. When the train stopped, the car or cars that the head man had pulled the cut lever on would separate from the others and go down the lead into the designated track that the foreman or field man had lined up. The field man, or sometimes the foreman, would then catch the rolling cars as they rolled by and climb up the ladder, applying a handbrake if necessary, slowing it down to avoid any hard impacts. We watched switching operations for a while, covering the basic things that day, but very soon after completion of our classes, we were going to start to learn the more complex practices that they didn't want us to see that day, such as the double pin moves, drop moves, and gravity drop moves. All of these maneuvers are pretty much forbidden today.

After observing switching operations, we had knuckle insertion class, where a healthy veteran switch man showed us how to replace a knuckle in a draw bar. A *knuckle* is an iron piece of the coupler unit at the end of draw bars used to connect and disconnect trains, weighing somewhere in the neighborhood of seventy-five pounds and slightly resembling a human's closed fist. After the veteran switch man showed us with ease the insertion procedure, we were then asked to demonstrate the procedure ourselves, while being observed by the train master. Not one of us completed the procedure easily, and some of us could not even lift the knuckle off the ground. That was my first experience in train service of a trainmaster looking the other way. The next day during the final rules test I would observe my second. To be honest with you, some of why I survived keeping my job on the railroad for forty years I can attribute to train masters looking the other way. After writing this book, I realize that toward the end of my career, I turned my head the other way a few times in order for a trainmaster to survive keeping their job.

I kept track of every single one of my nine classmates. The black guy, Ed, became a switch man in Seattle's Stacy Street Yard for several years before giving it up. The black lady, Wendy, quit her position after about a year. I heard that she had found a job more to her liking. One guy gave it up right away—his wife was not fond of the extra board. Another fellow made it twenty years before getting a disability. A fellow named Mike made thirty-plus years, and like I mentioned earlier, my friend Ken made thirty years and myself forty. The other three all eventually moved on to different careers: one in the computer field, one lady became a fireman, as did another guy in the class who was the first person I gave a nickname on the railroad—"Fog Horn Leg Horn." His voice was deep with a slight southern draw and it reminded me of the cartoon rooster character I grew up watching.

# Fisher Flour Mill Job

*Early in my freight railroad* switching career, I worked the Fisher Flour Mill Job on Harbor Island in Seattle. It was not my favorite job. I never did quite figure it out. As I recall, the switch list was provided by the mill and unlike anything I had ever tried to decipher. The mill seemed to be a flour dust bowl and where we spotted the hopper cars it was dark and dingy. Even a little reefer added in did not seem to help.

The crew did get a big break where they could sleep in a room adjacent to a Fisher Flour Mill employee locker room, but the only couch was taken by the switch foreman, Ben. During our break, I would sometimes do a little *sitting on the dock of the bay*—Elliott Bay—near the locker room and throw flares into the water. Did you know that they burn underwater and under the right conditions have a psychedelic effect?

One memorable afternoon shift during our coffee break in the mill guard shack we watched the last quarter of the 1979 Larry Bird vs Magic Johnson NCAA finals basketball championship game as Magic Johnson of Michigan State won over Larry Bird and Indiana State.

# Choke Hold

*I was working* on the Burlington Northern Railroad, Trainmen Extra Board, in 1979 and didn't make it in to work one night. Long story short, I wrecked my car, leading to my arrest. The cops at the Seattle jailhouse put me in a baton choke hold resulting in a near-death experience.

It started when I smarted off to an officer as I was being booked into jail for suspicion of DUI. A tall mild-mannered (I thought) black policeman asked me to blow into a breathalyzer tube. I pulled the tube out of the machine and said, *I don't blow anything!* Well, he was not mild-mannered anymore and informed me that I was going to be charged with obstructing a police officer. He called for three more officers and they manhandled me into an elevator and up a couple floors to the drunk tank. That's where they put me in the baton choke hold.

I remember thinking that they were going to kill me, so I decided to play dead to get them to let go. I remember my body going limp, and I was just about to lose consciousness when they dropped me to the cement floor of the jail and added another charge of resisting arrest.

I was lucky. It was proven a few years afterwards that several people had died up there when being given the same treatment. Their families were awarded damages and the offending officers were prosecuted.

# F-Word

*In September of 1979*, I was in a Tacoma alcohol treatment facility that was once the thriving Puget Sound Hospital many years earlier. I drove by about a year ago, and the building was condemned and fenced-off, ready to be bulldozed. I parked my car and got out, reminiscing about the twenty-one days I spent there, my fellow patients, the counselors, the nurses, and the bottom I had found back then. Not *absolute* rock bottom, but close to it. My counselor was a lady who had done time for killing her abusive drunken husband in self-defense. One of the nurses gave me back rubs while I was in bed.

I am not sure exactly why—it might have been because of the rough neighborhood we were in—but the staff would drive us patients five or six miles south to attend A.A. meetings in Parkland, a slightly less rough neighborhood. On one of my first nights there, a few of us were driven in a van to the Blue Spruce Motel in Parkland. It's still there today. We assembled in a fairly large, open room adjacent to the office for my first meeting. There were about seven people from outside of our group of five for a total of about a dozen people. Most of us were chain smoking.

My head was spinning; I was in a fog, lost, confused and at the end of my rope. As the meeting started, people were sharing, but I heard nothing. I was there, but I wasn't. It was all a blur. *Why am I here?* I thought. *Get me out of here! These people are crazy. What is this language they are talking?*

Then I heard the *F-word* and I snapped out of my daze, looking across the room at a man who was staring at me.

He said, "I never heard a word anyone was saying until I heard *fuck!*

I started listening.

I often say at meetings that almost every worthwhile thing I have learned in my adult life came out of the mouths of people at meetings. Many of those words were from the God of my understanding. Now, sometimes the words were not so pious. I have a little bit of sobriety now, however, and can almost always decipher what words have the flavor of God and those that do not. I hear the *F-word* at almost every meeting I attend, and sometimes the overuse of it offends and disturbs me.

That said, hearing the *F-word* at that meeting was my first spiritual awakening in the program. You might say that this was unusual, as far as moments of enlightenment go, but it paved the way for many more spiritual awakenings of a different kind.

Forty years later, I was at a meeting in the exact same neighborhood—a thousand feet from the Blue Spruce Hotel— when a lady off the streets barely three days sober was rambling and spewing off her story to her bottom.

"I don't have to get drunk and fuck people I don't want to anymore."

I rarely laugh at a meeting. Though as soon as I began, I stopped and it grew into a spiritual awakening of a different kind. I rarely regret the past, nor wish to shut the door on it, but this was the exception to the rule. *I don't have to get drunk anymore* I had heard said thousands of times, and had practiced that without fail. Her saying, *I don't have to get drunk and fuck people I don't want to anymore,* however, was the missing wisdom I had yet to hear. Had I heard those words forty years earlier, the temptation and urge to fuck people I didn't want to anymore would not have haunted my sobriety with so many ups and downs.

I could finally relax. I thanked her after the meeting.

# Mount Saint Helens

*On May 18, 1980*, I was living in Seattle when Mount Saint Helens erupted. I remember hearing the news on the radio that she blew, so I took several hard looks many miles south, but didn't see much other than a darkened sky barely visible to the naked eye.

Early the next day, my beeper went off and I called the crew desk. I was instructed to report to work as the head brakeman on a freight train going south to Portland. I don't recall any of the other crew members, nor the first leg or the last leg of that trip, but what happened in between I remember, even though I was still in my toxic phase, in a fog and short on sleep.

When we rolled south out of Centralia, Washington and started up the hill toward Napavine, it looked like fresh snow on the ground; it was volcanic ash, however, and as we crested Napavine Hill and descended down the other side into Winlock on toward Vader, the ash appeared much heavier, some places a couple inches deep or more.

The volcanic eruption was the largest and most destructive in US history. By the end of its fire and fury, fifty-seven people had died.

We had train orders to stop and not to pass over the Cowlitz or Toutle Rivers until receiving permission from the flagger in charge. The eruption had caused massive volcanic mudslides that pushed trees, rocks, and everything else in their path into the rivers. The banks were overflowing and taking down more trees downstream, causing more destruction along the way. Several homes were washed away.

My engineer called the flagger in charge of the Cowlitz River bridge and we received permission through his limits. A couple minutes later, he called the flagger in charge of the Toutle River bridge and we were instructed to hold back of the bridge. He told us to be ready at *a moment's notice* when to make a run for it. I'm not sure where the flagger was positioned, however I got the impression he had a view of the bridge and some of the river upstream, watching out for objects that could take out the bridge.

My engineer put the train into a crawl at about 10 miles per hour as we approached, keeping in constant radio communication. Then the flagger said, *okay to come across, looks clear for now.*

I remember before we crossed looking east upstream and west downstream, and the river being wider, higher, and running faster than one could imagine, scary as hell. What was even scarier was when I looked at the river beneath us as we crossed—the water was clearing the bridge by only a foot, or less.

When our locomotives got to the other side, I continued to worry until the caboose a mile behind us made it across. I have thought about that adventure many times since and now believe that running trains during those conditions was not in the best interest of safety.

# 1980
# The Bottom Year...
# and on to Sobriety

*The king of drugs* is alcohol, that's what I believe (and many others). While many believe it's not a drug, most will agree that some people should not drink.

I was sipping drinks while at family functions with and without permission as long as I can remember—my drug of choice, alcohol. At the age of twelve, I sniffed lighter fluid on a rag several times, leading to sniffing gas on rags several times— and none of those experiences was fun, only scary, something I eliminated early on. I was introduced to criss-cross speed when very young, and until I found sobriety, had several on-and-off short addiction periods as short as a few days and as long as two weeks—again, none of those experiences exactly fun, just scary. I took barbiturates twenty-five times? Not sure, though I can remember it was like being stupid drunk leading to black outs. I took mescaline a few times, recalling part of that first trip as fun, but the rest of the trip and the others to follow as scary. I took LSD ten or fifteen times and really did not enjoy it, not even once. I shot heroin up one time, one time too many. I snorted cocaine several times, though I do not recall ever buying it; I may have in some sort of trade with other drugs, as it was way too expensive. I ate mushrooms and drank mushroom tea several times, not really liking it, as it always made me paranoid. I smoked hash almost daily for three years while in West Germany, serving in the Army. I do not recall the first time I smoked marijuana, however I smoked it whenever offered, or available. The same went for consuming alcohol. I took animal tranquilizer once and like heroin, it was one time too many.

Yes, I tried just about everything there was to get high on before I hit my bottom. A mellow night consisted of consuming a bottle of M.D. 20/20 loganberry wine. Most called it *Mad Dog*. The *M.D.* actually stands for Mogen David, the producer, and the *20/20* for 20 ounces and 20 percent alcohol. One bottle of that could cause serious effects, and if the mellowing quality of the weed that evening was subpar, one became a mad dog.

I was at a Seattle Rat City bar in early June of 1980, getting inebriated as I had grown accustomed to, when I became involved in a fistfight. As a result, I ended the night with my right ring finger knuckle being broken. I was to report to work the next morning, but in a drunken stupor I concocted the devious plan to call the crew desk assignments clerk and report a phony on-duty injury from my trip earlier in the day. I claimed that I broke my knuckle during a switch move in Bellingham, Washington, and was marked off as having been injured while on duty.

The next morning, my morality got the best of me and I called the crew desk to come clean. I told them that I had been drunk the night before, that I was very sorry for the report, and that I would like to mark off as sick. I even admitted to them that I had actually broken my knuckle in a bar fight. The phone went silent and, long story short, I was pulled out of service pending an investigation with charges of immoral conduct, to name one of the few.

I had been a bad employee; missing calls for work, showing up impaired, and engaging in verbal confrontations with co-workers. The list of my offenses went on and on. I had more than my fair share of chances to straighten up. The B.N. had even sent me to treatment for drug and alcohol abuse in September of '79, but now they wanted me gone, and it looked as if they were going to make that happen.

My Stacy Street union representative, B.J. Smith, implied that my chances were less than nil to keep my job. I was put in contact with the B.N. counselor, Bob Franzen, and even Mr. Franzen more or less said that I was done. Mr. B.J. had the investigation postponed, and we waited. I called every day and said that I would do anything to get my job back. I was at my wit's end. Rock bottom. My wife had left me, and the only one in my corner was my mother.

Miraculously, a deal was struck like no other I have ever heard of before or since. At the investigation, I was to plead guilty of all charges and terminated from employment with a 120-day negotiated deal that the B.N. could allow me back to work if certain conditions were followed. The deal being I would check into treatment once again. After treatment, I would attend meetings and report to Mr. Franzen what I was doing to change my life to become a productive member of society. Should he feel that I had indeed changed, I would get my job back and even retain seniority.

Nobody in the whole world thought that I would ever work on the railroad again—except my mother. It was a long shot. I tried to talk my way out of treatment by telling Mr. Franzen that I would go to extra meetings, but the answer was a firm *no*.

I remember meeting B.J. and getting set for the investigation. He had me take my pimp hat off and remove my earring before heading in to face my judgment. It was short, over in twenty minutes, and the next day I drove my 1968 Mercury Cougar to Monroe, Washington to check into treatment.

One of my counselors was a pretty little lady, being a very fine example of sobriety—a direct contrast to one of the nurses who may have needed treatment herself. The fog started to lift after three weeks of meetings on top of meetings, while making a few friends of the female variety, and a few that were not, one being Emil Oscar Sommer.

Emil was my roommate and was admitted about the same time as I. He was a near *wet brain*, with one foot in the grave at about sixty years old. He was out of touch with reality, *incoherent*, as they say, and whenever anybody tried to converse with him? *Nothing*. He lay in bed in a stupor, but did manage to get out when needing to use the bathroom...most of the time. About the second or third day, in the middle of the night, he scared me when he came to life bitching and moaning about what, I could not decipher. I observed him and watched him pull his foot out of the grave. About all I could get out of him, verbally, was *I am Emil Oscar Sommer*, nothing more.

We were having an A.A. meeting chaired by an outside source one day and I was asked and agreed to read "How it works," a formality to opening up meetings. After the meeting, a treatment counselor took me aside and said that he felt that he had indeed witnessed a spiritual awakening. He explained that when I read the words I was given that Emil came out of his stupor and paid close attention to every word I read. Emil did come around some—that is to say, he communicated and interacted pleasantly with all, but he still had a long way to go.

Finally, I drove my Cougar back home to Federal Way. Waiting for me there was my fourteen-year-old brother, who had come to live with me shortly before I went to treatment, which is an interesting story in itself. He had been in continuous trouble with the law and spent time at the Echo Glen reform school. Part of his condition for parole was that he live in a new environment. Unbeknownst to the parole board, that would include experiencing my despicable spiral to the bottom *and* my uplifting start to recovery.

I mainly went to meetings in the Western Washington area at Serenity Hall in Renton, the Fremont Hall meetings near Lake Union in Seattle, meetings at the Easy Does It Hall in Burien, meetings in Everett, Auburn, Tacoma and many in the basements or sanctuaries of churches—and even a few in people's homes. Almost every day and sometimes twice a day I went to meetings, as it was suggested *90 meetings in 90 days* while reporting to Mr. Franzen. I worked out of the Millionaires Club, a charity organization, for $30 a day, plus a free lunch for the next four months.

My first year of sobriety was unusual in many respects, but the most unusual thing was that I actually managed to stay sober. In my first year of sobriety, I was fired from the railroad, left by my wife, thrown in jail, and I caught the clap. The only things I did right during the first year was not drink or use and go to meetings and not drink or use in between. It was the summer of 1980. I was out of work for four months while the union appealed my termination.

# Spiritual Awakening:
# No More Pot

*I was at a meeting* and a man by the name of Dallas said that changing from alcohol to pot was like changing rooms in the Titanic—even if you survive, you will be haunted for the rest of your life. Before I left for treatment, I had marijuana plants growing in my backyard and now—there they were, a few very small ones a little over a foot tall. Every time I ever quit drinking and drugging, it was smoking pot that led me back to the gates of insanity.

I pulled them up, put them in the oven, and baked them on low to dry them out. They didn't amount to much; I rolled them up into one little pinner joint just enough to get wasted.

I was listening to hard rock on the radio. I put the joint in my mouth and was just about to light up when an outside vacuum from the open front door seemed to suck the air out of my living room. I turned the knob on the stereo tuner and it went from hard rock to easy listening. I fell to the floor on my knees, my head in the red shag, dog-scent carpet, and I prayed for a minute, got up, flushed the joint down the toilet, never to be seriously tempted again.

# Jailed for Fishing

*I was checking in* with Bob F., the railroad counselor, every week concerning what I was learning at meetings. The main topic was that if i stayed sober and changed, he would try to get my job back. I stayed sober, but change came slowly.

I was married on paper, but I was dating a nice Indian girl from the Tulalip Indian Reservation who I had met in treatment. When I would visit the reservation, the men weren't very friendly, but the ladies certainly were. My girlfriend had a brother—we will call him "the Chief"—who fished for a living. Being Indian, he had certain fishing privileges that allowed him to sell fish to the cannery for top market value. Now, I was also a fisherman back before I started railroading. My friend— we will call him "Tall White Man"—and I would take his boat, motor, and gill net into the Duwamish River at a secluded spot near the Boeing airplane plant in Seattle late at night, catch ten or so salmon, and go around town to sell them for a quarter of the market price through the back doors of certain restaurants early in the morning.

Now that I knew the Chief had a cannery card, a scheme started to develop. I called Tall White Man, told him about the Chief and his cannery card, and let him in on a plan to team up with him to make some fast money. Tall White Man was game, so I talked to the Chief. He agreed, and brought in his Indian friend—we will call him "Scout". The four of us formed a crew; the Indians had the card, Tall White Man had the equipment, and I had the plan.

One night, the four of us showed up at a secluded place near the Boeing plant and into the river we went. The Chief and I shoved off in the boat, with Tall White Man and Scout posted up on the bank as lookouts. We set the nets and started pulling them back in, filling the boat with King Salmon. It was the mother lode! We filled the 12-foot boat twice to the hilt. We put the seventy-two salmon in the trunk of my '68 Cougar, covered them with ice, and headed fifty miles north to a cannery. The front of the car was high in the air as the rear was weighed down low to the ground. We were lucky that the cops didn't pull us over.

Up north, we met a man at the cannery and sold our catch off for $1.60 per pound. The Chief and Tall White Man got bigger cuts, because one had the card and the other had the equipment, but Scout and I walked away with $500 each, which went a long way in 1980. Such a quick payday went to our heads, and we developed "gold fever" just like in the old Bogart movie, *The Treasure of the Sierra Madre,* where the characters began plotting against each other in order to get bigger cuts of gold. This was not gold fever, it was salmon fever!

The very next night, the four of us planned to repeat the success of the previous evening. The Chief and I were in the boat when the fisheries patrolmen put the spotlight on us from their boat. I tried to gun the outboard motor, but the prop kept popping out of the water, and the patrol was soon right on top of us. We were handcuffed, standing in a 12-foot boat in the middle of the Duwamish river, fully dressed. I became meek, as to fall in could be fatal.

The Chief and I went to jail. It was very early Saturday morning, and there was no court until Monday. The Scout and Tall White Man dodged the situation by being on shore. The Chief was bailed out by his sister, and I sat in jail. My one phone call could have been to my parents, as they would have certainly bailed me, but I was much too ashamed to call them after all the grief I had put them through. Instead, I called a friend who I knew had money. However, it just so happened that he had just run out, or so he told me. I sat in jail until Monday morning and was appointed a public defender who got me out, contingent on me returning the following week to court.

I was still barely sober. I guess I was what you could call a *sober fish thief*. I went to court the following week, and the judge grilled me some about what and why we were in court. Judging by my responses, he ascertained that I was clean and sober trying to change my life. *You did this sober?* he asked incredulously, shaking his head.

The public defender was able to strike a deal with the court that all charges would be dropped if I agreed to relinquish the confiscated boat, motor, and nets for auction, with the proceeds given to the city. I readily agreed and was released. Tall White Man was not exactly happy about losing his equipment, and my relationship with the Tulalip clan ended—although through the years I heard tales of my sweet cinnamon girl now and then, the most recent one being that she has now gone to the spirit in the sky.

# Dancing at a Ladies Club

*I was still going* to meetings and sober when I heard that there was an amateur night at a ladies club by the name of *Papa Bear's* in the Ballard district of Seattle. Male dancers would compete, strutting their stuff, and the winner would take home one hundred dollars. For preparation, I tanned myself in the sun, went on a five-day diet, and practiced dancing to the tune of the Rolling Stones 1980 hit, "Miss You'."

The night came, and I showed up to "Papa Bear's" standing 6'3" tall and weighing in at a lean 212 pounds. I wore my brown cowboy "pimp" hat, brown Jockey shorts, and a matching tan. I am sure that all of the other contestants were high as a kite. One even offered me something to snort, and when I turned him down he asked me what I was jazzed up on. When I told him I was sober, he said something to the effect that I was crazy. He got that right.

We were introduced in a group then danced one by one. They asked what tune I wanted to dance to, so I told them "Miss You," by the Stones. My turn came, and they played something off the album that I was completely lost on. I had never heard it before! I was out of sync, and it was one of the longest few minutes in my life. I felt the stare of the ladies observing me and met eyes with a few, only to turn away instantly and pray that it would end soon. Had it been a song I knew, it would have been fun.

The dancers did their thing one by one for about half an hour. One dancer that could possibly have won ("The Snorter" from earlier) was doing well right up until he, in one swift motion, turned around, bent over, pulled down his shorts and spread his cheeks with his hands while the girls screamed. I am not sure if it was good or bad screaming, but it lasted for about ten seconds until the lights went off and "The Snorter" was bounced out of the building.

At the end of the night, the five or six of us dancers left came out one by one, and the ladies applauded, with the loudest reception to be considered the winner. It was not even close, as one man clearly outdid the rest of us. At that point, I decided to retire from dancing.

# Got My Job Back

*So, I have told you* the stories of the crazy things I did in my first year of sobriety—the tale of how I got fired, the botched fishing plan that landed me in jail. It paints a pretty good picture about why my wife left me. The details of how I managed to get the clap will not be volunteered at this time.

In November of 1980, Mr. Franzen gave the B.N. the okay to let me back to work contingent on a couple things: I had to pass a physical examination and a railroad rules test. I had been diagnosed with Hepatitis type A from drinking too much, and I thought that could be a problem. I was worried about it heading into the exam, but my vision tested at 20/10 in my left eye, and 20/15 in my right, with no sign of hep. Now the General Code of Operating Rules (G.C.O.R) was the next hurdle. I studied like no other time in my life, and the fact that I was clean and sober was paramount. I took the test with rules examiner, Bud Johnson; when he checked the answers he double-checked them, then triple-checked them. He was in shock that I did so well. I may have even aced it—I never saw him mark the test paper. All he said was that I had passed, looking me straight in the eyes, without turning his head.

Thank you, B.J. Smith and Bob Franzen! Forty years clean and sober. Thank you, mother, for the prayers. After writing this turn of events, describing the bottom I hit and the recovery I made with the help of so many people, after forty years I just now had a revelation: if it had not been for a trainmaster in Bellingham who refused to look the other way, my bottom could have been oh, so much lower. Thank you, sir.

I had been "running against the wind," but the wind had now subsided.

*Merry Christmas and a*

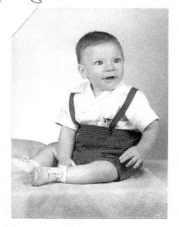

*Happy New Year*
*Queenie Lou & Larry*

Top: First Christmas, 1954. Bottom: Easter at Echo Glen, 1967.

Top: Happiest Christmas Moment Ever, 1968. Bottom: Last Time All Together, 1974.

# FAUNTLEROY
## ELEMENTARY SCHOOL

MISS CLARK
Room 1

Humblest Teacher Ever, 1966.

Left: Photo Booth Snuff Shoot, 1969. Top: Naselle Reform School, 1968.
Bottom: 3 German ladies I met while in the Army, 1974.

Top: Mom never gave up on me. Bottom: With two Army buddies, 1974.

Top: Being questioned by military police, 1973. Bottom: Uncle Duane back in the day.

# PART TWO

# Auburn, Washington
# 1980

*By Thanksgiving 1980,* I was back to work on the Burlington Northern Railroad, retaining full seniority in Auburn, Washington. I was five months clean and sober. There was a yardmaster in Auburn who was instrumental in my early sobriety by the name of Dale. *Thank you, sir!*

The Auburn yard was a maze of several yards rolled into one. At the time I worked there, it was the busiest rail yard I had ever worked in before or since, supporting thirteen switch engine jobs each day and several local road jobs, as well. It was a major through-line for freight trains to Yakima and a passenger train each day, one heading east and one west. There was almost always something rolling 24/7, with a main yard, ice house yard, class yard, and the B.S. yard. The B.S. yard was not much more than a couple of tracks that was used to put cars going nowhere.

# Wenatchee Waylon Jennings

*On one of my many* freight train runs from Seattle to Wenatchee, Washington, before sobriety, I spent some of my rest time in a downtown bar called "The Silver Spur" having a few beers. One weekday in the middle of the day, one of the booze hounds in there insisted that he was Waylon Jennings, and he sure looked like him. He convinced the owner of the bar to get the house band to come in and back him up, so that he could prove that he was the real deal.

About an hour later the band shows up, Waylon steps on stage, and takes the microphone. Lo-and-behold—Wenatchee Waylon can't sing.

My next time through town, I asked about old *Waylon*. Turns out that he got pinched for check fraud and a few other things.

# Booze Stops

*I remember being* in the caboose on a southbound train from Seattle to Portland, Oregon. The conductor spotted the caboose at a tavern somewhere on top of Napavine Hill, in Napavine, Washington hopped off, and scampered inside to get a six-pack of beer.

The same procedure was employed going east out of Seattle, stopping in Skykomish, WA to get booze. This went on every day somewhere and was just part of the old culture.

# Virgin Trip

*In October 1978* before sobriety, I worked a freight train I caught off the Seattle Stacy Street switchman's extra board to work from Seattle to Wenatchee, Washington. The hotel we stayed at in Wenatchee for our rest was across the street from Joe's Log Cabin, and that is where a lot of us gathered to indulge in spirits. Needless to say, I did not get a lot of rest.

We were called for a mainline change early one morning to work a train back to Seattle. At that time, the engineer pool did not line up with the trainmen's pool, meaning you would go over to Wenatchee with one engineer (aka a *hoghead*) and return to Seattle with a different one. When I showed up to the crew room, my conductor and rear brakeman were there with a very young guy I had never seen before. We got our train orders, and I learned that the new guy was a student engineer. The working engineer was drunk somewhere.

Our westbound train arrived from Spokane, Washington and the conductor told the kid and me to get on the power and wait. I say *kid* because I swear he looked like he was still in high school, and being on the short side only made him look younger. We got on the power and waited. About twenty minutes later, I see the rear brakeman Roy and conductor Andy dragging the drunk, older-than-dirt hoghead up on to the second locomotive behind us. The conductor then came into our cab and grilled the kid about how many times had he been over the mountain and if he thought he could manage operating the train by himself. The kid insisted that he could handle it.

"Okay, I am going to ride the second unit and babysit numbnuts," the conductor said. "The rear brakeman will catch the caboose."

The rear brakeman, using his portable radio, had the kid pull the train up a half mile or better before having us stop. We then swapped caboose crews and headed on our way. Over the course of the next four or five hours, we were to climb a 2.2 mountain grade, go through the eight-mile Cascade tunnel, then down a 2.2 mountain grade with a long-ass freight train. This was a lot of responsibility for a kid. I remember him barely being able to see over the console, but he did a good job.

As we were descending the 2.2 mountain grade somewhere between Icicle Creek and the east end of Skykomish, the drunken hoghead that had to be carried aboard—now 90 percent sober—came up from the second unit into the lead locomotive with us in full uniform: striped railroad coveralls, matching coat and hat, and a red handkerchief around his neck. He acted as if he had done nothing wrong, took the throttle, and got us home safely.

Thirty-five years later, I was the conductor on a passenger train headed north out of Seattle, and the kid was a Sounder hoghead, deadheading on my train. We started talking about that night he had to fill in for the drunk hoghead and I said, "You know what Doug? I was with you on your virgin trip!"

We both got a big laugh out of that.

# M.P. 85 Near Fatal Crash

*A new engineer* or trainman hiring onto the railroad takes at least two years to have a good, safe understanding of the various parts of train operations. If they are *toxic*, as I was during my first three years, they will never live up to their potential and will be a risk to themselves and others. When I hired on, there were four and five-person crews on all trains and yard jobs. To expect a whole crew to be clean and sober was wishful thinking. The older guys liked booze; the younger guys had pot, speed, and God knows what else. I worked on crews where everybody was some combination of drunk or stoned. The common goal of many railroad employees was to maintain a nice buzz and earn a good living while doing it. If you could walk without a stagger and talk without slurring your words, you were left alone. Even if you slurred or staggered, your fellow employees would hide you from the higher-ups and do your share of the work. Most of those fun times and not so fun times came to a crashing halt in 1987 after a horrific accident that I will cover later in this book.

Sometime in 1978 before my bottom, I was called off of the Burlington Northern R.R. Stacy Street switchman's extra board in Seattle to work a brakeman's job south to Portland, Oregon. My locomotive engineer, a man from Skykomish, Washington, was one of the few men on the railroad who made me look like an angel. It was daylight and we were southbound on main track #1 just past Vader, Washington on a long freight train. I was the head brakeman riding on the fireman's side in the locomotive with Mr. Skykomish. On the adjacent left main track #2, we could see the red marker in the distance of the caboose of another train heading south, the same direction as us. Mr. Skykomish buried the throttle in notch eight as we caught up to the caboose on main #2. He got onto the radio and contacted the train dispatcher, requesting to be lined up at junction M.P. 85 in five or six minutes southbound on main track #1.

The dispatcher called the train next to us and asked if they were making track speed, as well as their location. Charlie, the engineer on the other train, answered back, informing the dispatcher that he was at track speed and at mile post 80. Mr. Sky got back onto the radio and told the dispatcher that we would reach mile post 85 first. We were passing them now, and our head end started to overtake theirs. I could see total fear in Charlie's eyes just ten feet away, but Mr. Sky had an unhinged look of pure madness on his face. Sky again picked up the radio handset and shouted to the dispatcher that we would arrive first, but the dispatcher did not answer.

We passed them all right, but we were now barreling down on a red signal a mere three-quarter's of a mile away. I should have pulled the emergency brake valve right then, but as soon as I began to shout in horror, Sky dynamited the train, the brakes locking our wheels and sending us sliding to a stop. We finally ran out of momentum just one hundred feet short of the red signal. On the other side of the junction on main track #1 sat a train facing us. Charlie rolled by on his train on main track #2 to main #2 southbound. When they cleared, the train on main track #1 ahead of us crossed over main track #1 to main track #2 northbound through the junction. Then it was our turn to proceed southbound.

Not long after that, on a different trip, a rock slide hit Charlie's train near Ridgefield, Washington, derailing several cars behind the locomotives and rupturing a large tank of poisonous anhydrous ammonia. Sadly, the fumes killed Charlie and the lady brakeman working with him. They were both very good people who didn't deserve their fate. Mr. Sky, on the other hand, went on to crash his train into another near Everett, Washington a few months later with no serious injuries reported. I crossed paths with Mr. Sky at the Monroe alcohol treatment center a short time later.

# Ferndale Near Fatal Crash

**Sometime around 1979**, I worked up north with an older-than-dirt hoghead. He called everyone "partner" and liked his booze as much as I did. One day we worked north and tied up in Vancouver, BC for our layover and rest period, though we really didn't get much rest due to a long night of heavy drinking. We got onto a new train the next day and left Vancouver heading south over the Fraser River across the Canadian border. Back then, there was no such thing as an alarm to put the train into emergency mode should the head end crew neglect to do their duty for whatever reason, most common being that they had fallen asleep. There was a dead man's pedal that the engineer had to keep his or her foot on at all times that would cause the brakes to apply if it had been released for more than a few seconds. During my early career, I recall only once or twice ever seeing a dead man's pedal that wasn't jerry-rigged with a bent air hose to keep the pedal applied. So much for safety.

We came over the border through Blaine, Washington, both of us falling asleep shortly before Ferndale, Washington.

Both my partner and I were jolted awake by the sound of someone screaming at us over the radio. *Stop your train! Emergency! You're gonna kill someone!* My elderly partner dumped the air as fast as he could, and we came to a screeching halt just a short walking distance from a train and crew on the mainline switching in Ferndale. I say a short walking distance because "White Center Danny," one of the local crew members, was on our engine within a couple minutes of us stopping. Just before Danny made his way into the cab, my old

77

partner looked at me and said, *If anyone asks, all of the signals were green.*

For the next thirty-seven years, I would cross paths with Danny on occasion, and I think he might have still harbored a little bit of resentment toward me. I can't say that I blame him.

# 18 Fatalities

*The last day I worked* on the railroad, our passenger train while traveling at 50 mph struck a man walking near the tracks just south of mile post 68 in Mount Vernon, Washington. The locomotive engineer hollered over the radio, *Emergency! Emergency! Emergency! We just hit someone!* as the train began sliding to a stop.

I was at the conductor's desk in the bistro lounge and made my way fifty feet to the P.A. The moment we stopped, I made a quick announcement: *If there are any medical professionals on board, please report to an employee.* Then I opened a door, hit the ground, and rushed to the scene.

When I found him, it was obvious that there was no reason to make an attempt at first aid; the lady medical professional passenger who showed up a minute later agreed. From the previous seventeen fatalities I had witnessed, I had learned one thing for positive—we were not going anywhere until the coroner sanctioned it. I asked every policeman, medical person, and railroad official who showed up if they had called the coroner.

As we waited for the coroner, my mind raced back, tracking over the previous forty years of incidents. Fatalities on the railroad happen mostly by trains running over people who are walking on or near the tracks, or while people are driving vehicles over or near railroad tracks, mostly at crossings. Sometimes, it's a matter of people not paying attention, and many are impaired from drugs or alcohol. A fair amount of these fatalities are suicides, while some being purely accidental, such as the heartbreaking ones involving children.

My first fatality was Thanksgiving evening in 1978 or 1979. I was a young brakeman on a freight train northbound from Portland, Oregon to Seattle and as our train came into downtown Puyallup, Washington, a lady who appeared to be crossing the tracks on foot in front of us suddenly lay down across the rails. When the elderly coroner showed up and attempted to go under the train to remove her body, I could see him struggling. I asked if he would like me to do the deed. He stepped back and I went under the train. I picked up the woman's severed arm and put it in her coat sleeve, then pulled the hood of her coat over her disfigured face. Out from under the train, I lifted her up and carried her to a stretcher, where I lay her down and said a prayer.

The second fatality that I was involved with was in 1992 near King Street station. I was the switch foreman on the daylight passenger train switch job. At that time, we would shove our southbound trains from the coach yard at Royal Brougham street up the northbound main track a third of a mile into the King Street tunnel. Once in the tunnel, we would get signal indication into one of the station tracks and hand the train over to the outbound crew going south to Portland. On this particular move, a person would be mounted high on the rear of the train in the coach with one hand on or near the emergency brake valve. To be clear, the locomotive was on the south end of the train and the person watching the shove (me, in this case) was on the north end. On that day, as we were shoving north on the northbound main track at about 20 mph, I saw a man to my left on the other side of the southward main track rapidly walking towards our track; he was eyeballing up and down the tracks, first to the left then to the right, taking great care in his footing with his eyes on the path.

At first, it appeared to me that he was in a hurry and wanted to cross in front of us, but suddenly he hesitated, and it seemed as if he had changed his mind, realizing that it was not safe to cross. When we were about two hundred feet away, the man suddenly bolted into our path. I yanked the emergency brake valve as fast as I he could, right as he dove onto the tracks, laying his neck across the east rail in front of us. The wheels locked up, and we slid into the man and over him for another hundred feet. I raced down the stairs, jumped off the train, and ran back to the mangled man, but there was nothing I could do. Had I not applied the brakes, it would have been a less horrific scene—instead of a clean decapitation, he had a mangled, broken neck as the wheels were locked up and sliding on impact. The poor man jerked around in spasms for two or three minutes before finally succumbing to his wounds.

I was the first to the scene of these horrific events too many times. On one incident, the spindly bartender, "Lemon Drop Erik" and I rushed out to the scene as I pulled a young man's corpse from a river. On another incident, I gave a young man failed resuscitation attempts while his buddy wailed in the background. I will spare you the details of the other fatalities, but suffice to say that they were not fun. There were many other times the train was fortunately put into emergency braking fast enough to allow the potential victim to escape or only be injured. It is never a fun experience holding injured people's hands until the ambulance arrives. A thousand times I heard the train's air brakes exhaust into emergency and waited for the locomotive engineer to state the reason. Most commonly, they would say we just missed someone—they were called near misses and were much better than the alternative.

But going back to my last fatality, the coroner showed up, did the investigation, and released the train. We received all the authorities and permissions required to continue southbound, so we performed a train air brake test and departed. When I went to put the delay time into the delay device, it came up at one hour and nine minutes, which might be some kind of record for delays of that type—usually it would be about three hours or more. The locomotive engineer, "Coalition Sniffa," on the northbound passenger train we soon passed in the siding told us to get onto the yard radio channel. When we did, he told us that there was still some DNA on the front of our engine. I had our engineer, "Trench Coat Sam," stop the train in a wooded area before the Everett station stop. I hopped out with some water bottles to clean up the remaining viscera. I apologized to the deceased with a prayer before continuing into my home terminal, that day being my last day on the railroad.

# The Old Milwaukee Road Railroad

*My first couple years* on the Burlington Northern Railroad railroading as a brakeman I do not recall clearly, as it was over forty years ago and most of that time I was in *la la land* as I've explained. What I do remember is that just a few months after I hired out we started hiring a few ex-Milwaukee Road Railroad trainmen and enginemen who were fairly young. Their opinion was that the Milwaukee was on the verge of going under water, out of business, down the tubes—and they were getting jobs with the B.N. before that happened, ahead of all those that were sure to be trying later.

When going south from Seattle to Portland there were some junction points associated with the Milwaukee, one being Black River between South Seattle and Orillia, that the B.N. and Milwaukee interchanged at. The Milwaukee ran between Chehalis, Washington and North Portland Junction about eighty miles on our tracks. When working on the south end, I recall my old head co-workers snickering at the sight of their older inferior locomotives smoking and struggling along.

They went bankrupt in 1980 and thousands of employees were without jobs—but a handful landed on the B.N. in the Northwest. One of them was a conductor by the name of Mike N who was very instrumental to me in achieving sobriety. There were many conductors, engineers, and other employees that became truck drivers, among other occupations, but many traveled to wherever they could to work on a railroad.

In 1987, a new railroad was formed in Montana, the "Montana Rail Link," or the M.R.L. Just a year or two before I retired, I was working as a passenger conductor on the

Empire Builder between Spokane, Washington and Seattle. We had some B.N. deadheaders we were taking to Wenatchee and I started talking with one man who was originally off the Milwaukee and had been booming for thirty-five years from one railroad to the next; now with a few years on the B.N., he was close to retirement as I was. He told me that at that time there were still twenty or so former Milwaukee guys on the Montana Rail Link, the M.R.L. Then he smiled and said they called it, *Milwaukee Road Lives.*

# Rules Classes

***Railroad operation*** rules classes are very important, since not complying to some rules can be deadly, such as going past a red signal, sleeping or being intoxicated on the job, not slowing down for a slow order, moving the train without a signal, not applying hand brakes on unattended cars, and many others. Most railroaders understand those rules and comply nearly 100 percent of the time.

Back in the day, there were rules pertaining to sixteen different whistle signals, before everyone had a portable radio. I was called into Seattle's King Street Station to attend my first rules class since my hiring out class. I was hungover and struggling with the test, not marking any of the answers concerning whistle signals. One by one, the fifteen other people in the class had their tests scored, all of them passing and then leaving. The rules examiner came over to my desk and reviewed the answers to questions I had completed; I had done pretty well, however there were several that I did not answer and he read them to me one by one. They were all multiple choice, mostly concerning whistle signals. He would ask a question and wait for me to answer. I would make my guess and if I was right, I marked the test; if I was wrong, which I was on about half of them, he would tell me the correct answer and explain the signal to me until he was sure I understood, then I would mark the test. At the end of the test, he told me, "I can see you had a long night and it might be wise to study and rest up before you get tested next time." *Thank you, sir!*

I soon after got sober and the following thirty-eight years I took about a hundred rule tests concerning train operations, passing them all without hoping or expecting any spoon-feeding from an examiner. For many years working passenger services, we had what they called *block training* where they would bring employees from other crew bases in the Northwest of all crafts together for classes such as diversity and first aid training, then separate us for individual craft training—the train conductors and locomotive engineers having train operation classes and tests together. One year, the rules instructor for train operations, who was from the locomotive engineer craft, did the formalities class with all the crafts explaining the week-long block training process and introducing each employee to the class while requesting they say where they were from, their craft, and years of service...and anything else they would like to add. After introductions, he says on the passenger railroad the locomotive engineer is the most important person on the train, as he puffed out his chest a little bit.

He looked at me and said, "Wouldn't you agree to that?"

I looked him straight in the eye and responded, "In theory that is correct, however I can tell many stories when that was not the case."

A few years later, I was attending the customary rules class with the same instructor. While there were usually two or three ladies in class from the passenger train conductor craft and passenger train locomotive crafts, that year there were none. We took three tests concerning train operations and safety rules governing our crafts and it was the one and only time I aced all three—100 percent correct.

As the rules instructor looked over the third test, he looked up and said, "This is not like you. You usually miss two or three questions."

"Look around this classroom," I replied.

As he did, he said, "What?"

"Do you see any ladies?"

He came right back with, "No distractions."

# Time Slips for Pay

*Many years before* I hired out in 1977, and until about the turn of the century, trainmen and enginemen had all the records of time for pay purposes kept on a time slip with a carbon copy for each slip. On every road crew, the engineer had his own book for the engine crew and the conductor for the train crew. On a yard switch job, the switch foreman had one for the whole crew. Each employee had an ink pay stamp with their name and employee number on it and would *stamp in* on the appropriate time slip. The crew member in charge of the slip would fill in all the particulars, sign it, and put it in the designated company time slip box.

Most the road jobs back in the day were paid by the mile. For example, it was about 191 miles from Seattle to Portland, which paid a conductor and locomotive fireman about a dollar a mile, a locomotive engineer a little more, and the brakeman a little less. Now, there were lots of ways a crew could earn extra money on these trips—though it would take me a month to even begin to explain all of them.

There were arbitrations the unions had negotiated over the years—and I will tell you one little story of many that I was involved in where we earned extra pay that was not exactly forthcoming. I was on a local road switcher and we were switching cars out in the Orillia yard near Kent, Washington at the crack of dawn. I was the pin puller, the head man high on the lead. I pulled the pin on the last car, an empty flat car, and watched it as it rolled down the lead toward the old prior right's N.P. conductor. The car was intended for a track beyond him, but when it was passing by him he suddenly threw the switch under it, causing it to derail, *WTF!*

He did not seem concerned at all, as he motioned to the engineer to bring the locomotive down to the derailment, stopping just short of the derailment. The rear brakeman showed up as the hoghead threw some wood blocks and chains down to us on the ground. The conductor started blocking up the wheels of the derailed car as the rear brakeman started wrapping a chain around the draw bar on the locomotive. I was standing around, still dumbfounded by the derailment, when the conductor looked up from his kneeling position while adjusting a wood block and said, *we get an extra hour's pay to re-rail our own equipment; just got to add it to the time slip.*

# Mr. White Oldsmobile 442

*We were still* in the midst of the, *getting a buzz was okay* era—if you could talk and not slur and walk and not stumble, you were all right. I found this out quickly one night while I was the switch foreman on the Auburn, Washington night lead job. We were all extra board that day, with the exception of the locomotive engineer. My head man was a black man and pulled the pins on the wrong cars a couple of times, resulting in the cars going down the wrong tracks and requiring us to reach back in and couple up to them, pulling them back out before kicking them again. This created a lot of extra work and time lost. He smelled of alcohol when he approached me on the lead to ask when we were getting a coffee break.

I told him that we would have been to coffee a long time ago if he had been pulling the pins at the right spots. I admit that I was being a smart ass, but what came out of his mouth was much worse.

He said a couple of vulgar things, adding that he was going to, "cut my heart out as sure as my momma was white," and that I had better watch out for his white Oldsmobile 442 because he was gonna get me.

This argument went from the lead into the switch shanty, and for thirty minutes he would say something mean and I would respond with, "F--- you, boy!" That is the only response I gave him, as he continued his threat to "cut my heart out as sure as my momma was white."

Someone called the trainmaster, who came down and removed him from service for violating *rule G*, meaning that he was found to be drinking or intoxicated while on the property.

The investigation was to be held a couple of weeks later, and there was talk that the NAACP was going to represent Mr. 442. I was concerned, but I do believe I was by far the lesser of two evils in this case. At the investigation, there was nobody at all representing Mr. 442; he chose to represent himself. He pleaded insanity, agreeing to go to treatment for substance abuse and keep his job. My union rep, Mark, represented me well and did most of the talking for me, which was a good thing.

The railroad official that held the investigation took me aside afterward, hinting that there had been some inquiries from another organization. He told me if I had said anything more than what I had said to Mr. 442, I would have been fired. I crossed paths with Mr. 442 for a few years after that and later heard that he had made some choices that resulted in him losing his railroad career. I hope he is well.

# Miracle Hall

*In 1981, I had been clean* and sober about a year. I was attending meetings in Renton, Washington at "Serenity Hall," an old building with a lot of old crusty sober people (like I am now). There were a few younger people who came and went and a few who stayed, taking sobriety seriously. I remember talking with a young man my age with a considerable length of abstinence from drugs and alcohol, Bobby T. I asked him if he knew of any meetings where the people were mostly younger... and he said *yes*.

I then started going to meetings in an old house in Pacific, Washington named "Miracle Hall." In later years, it would be referred to as "Miracle Hall Number One." I will be forever grateful for the friends that I made there sharing our experience, strength, and hope. Miracle Hall moved a few times over the next several years to buildings in and around Auburn, Washington, each time becoming larger in membership, with mostly short-term members.

When speaking at meetings years later, I carried a message, in part: "Many of the ladies and men I drank and drugged with pursued it into the gates of insanity or death, others have one foot in the grave, while some started making better choices and live on, and there are a few of us who found sobriety."

After writing and saying that many times, I had a sad revelation. I realized that many of the friends that I'd made early on in the halls of sobriety relapsed, and they also went on to pursue it into the gates of insanity or death. My wife, having heard me convey that message a few times, would become a little disheartened thinking about those who relapsed most of the time, not ending well.

She would say, "What about the ones who are still sober? Our friends? They should be mentioned in the book."

I am going to make mention of everyone whom I can recall clearly that attended Miracle Hall meetings back in the day; regardless of the outcome, they were all inspirational: #1 Jeanine, my wife. Julie & Al. Indian Ed. Little Joe. Neil. Jeanie. Mike R. Maple Valley Rick. Michael H. Bobby T. Katie. Lonny. Jerry B. & Andrea. Debby. Tucker. Dean C. Mark C. Susan C. Red Head Pat. Larry & Rhonda. J.W. & Rhonda. Red Head Jim. Dwight. Frankie & Johnny. Fred, higher power were his chickens. Karen & Mother Carla. Kelly & Sally. Dean & Kathy. Scott & Laurie. Little Mark. Ray. Owen. Mike W. Mike & Montana. Mama Rose. Max & Carla. Dan B. Paul S. Kenny & Laurie. Rachelle. Connie N. Terry N. Kim & Dean. Bud H. Tall Joe. Eugene P. Short Lonnie. Robin & Mother. Chrissy R.

You never knew where the next words of wisdom would be coming from at those meetings. One day, a man named Dallas shared, "If you take a drunk horse thief and sober him up? What do you get?"

The room went silent for a moment, then he answered himself, out loud. "A sober horse thief," as he gave me a hard stare.

I had never stolen a horse, however I got the message: I may have been sober, but I still had some character defects. As old age settles in, most of those behaviors are approaching extinction.

# Wishram Stories
# 1982 and 1983

*From midsummer* of 1982 to the fall of 1982, and summer/ fall the following year, I worked in Wishram, Washington, across the Columbia River from The Dalles, Oregon. In the summer of 1982, I put my motorcycle in the back of my 1972 Suburban and drove to Wishram and marked up on the Wishram Brakeman's Extra Board while renting an apartment at the Horseshoe Apartments from George Bunn, who owned a lot of property in Wishram.

I was working as the head brakeman on a run from Wishram to Bend, Oregon. As we were going up the mountain grade, winding along the Deschutes River, the hoghead said to me, "Hey, come over here and run this thing while I take a leak."

He got up and had me sit in the running position. After a few simple instructions, the hoghead headed down to the nose of the cab to pee, leaving me to sit at the controls. The throttle was set on notch 8, keeping us at right about the 20-mph speed limit.

As we rounded a bend, three deer suddenly appeared on the track. With a rock wall on the right and a sheer, vertical cliff on the left, the deer had no option but to run ahead of us. You do not want to stop on your way up a mountain, as you may not be able to get started again. In that case, you would need another locomotive to give you a push, if there was one available. If not, you may even have to roll back down to the bottom of the slope to start over. Not wanting to stall out the train by slowing down, I whistled like you have never heard someone whistle before. For the next ninety seconds, I mowed the deer down, one by one. I sometimes shed a tear thinking about it. The engineer rushed back into the cab, having peed all over himself in his haste to see what all the whistling was about.

Speaking of peeing, I have another story of a different day on the same route, traveling northbound. We were pulled into a siding to meet a southbound. As the rules regarding passing trains required, I got off of our locomotive and crossed over the main line to the outside of the soon-to-be-passing train. Those trains were close to a mile long and going about 20 mph. I figured taking a leak during the roll-by was better than in the nose of one of those smelly old engine bathrooms.

When the head end went by, I whipped it out and start peeing while observing and inspecting the passing train. I figured that I had at least four minutes before the caboose would come by, carrying someone who might see me. Who I did not expect was the hobo woman standing in the doorway of a boxcar, grinning from ear to ear as she whizzed by.

# Vancouver, Washington
# 1982 and 1983

*I worked two stints* in Vancouver, Washington on the B.N.R.R. switchmen's extra board. The first stint, I lived in a boarding house about a mile from the Vancouver yard from the middle of October 1982 until January 1983. The next stint, I lived in my travel trailer near the Vancouver B.N. yard office from October 1983 until January 1984. I have many stories from those two stints, but I couldn't tell you exactly what stint they occurred. This was a while back. There was and still is the B yard, main yard, roundhouse, rip shed, as well as several industries *still smoking till this day* to switch out. The caboose track is still the caboose track, just without cabooses.

The extra board was long, and I don't think that I made forty hours in a week but a couple times. Almost all the jobs I worked were night switch engines, so I had a lot of free time during the day. I mostly spent it by going to meetings, playing my harmonica, reading, and taking long walks. On one of those walks, I saw a sign on a house in the business district of downtown Vancouver that read, *Fortune Teller Palm Reading.*

Curious, I knocked on the door, and a forty-something heavy lady with dark eyes, wearing a headdress straight out of the movies, answered the door and invited me in. After asking a few questions, I determined that I couldn't really afford to get my fortune told at that time; the lady seemed to be eyeball-screwing me. Before making my exit, however, she convinced me to help her rearrange a couple of large pieces of furniture.

By this point in my career, I was very conscientious in my work and do not recall any near misses, injuries, or blatantly unsafe coworkers. There were, however, the normal cast of characters spewing nonsense, but nothing I hadn't heard before. Overall, my stays in Vancouver were very mellow.

It must have been during my first stint that the trainmaster wanted to qualify me as a switch foreman. When I asked about the qualifications, he said that three trips as a helper were enough to qualify me. I thought it was odd, but did not argue, and was assigned a few jobs as foreman. There was a yardmaster by the name of Jeffries who loved to talk about the top of a mountain he owned, and there were three laid-off switchmen from Seattle in the same position as myself.

I met a clerk while working in Vancouver who was a man at the time and later became a lady by operation. She eventually died of AIDS. The twist to this story is that in 1992, shortly after my mother's funeral, I was discussing the family tree with elder relatives. It turns out that the Vancouver clerk was my third cousin who I recall meeting once in my very early youth, long before we worked together in Vancouver.

Twenty-five years later, I was a passenger train conductor working out of Seattle. They hired a new baggage lady at the King Street station, humping and throwing bags, who later became a trainmen and enginemen clerk; as I got to know her, I found out that she had worked in Vancouver at the same time as I did. I had a few years of interaction with her concerning everyday operations and overtime work. Eventually, I nicknamed her "Gayle with a Y." I would talk with her occasionally about Vancouver, not really remembering her, although I was positive she worked there as a crew caller during the same time as I had, knocking on my door a time or two to give me a work assignment—some of us fondly referred to them as *call girls*. There was an old SP&S railroad rule that if you lived within a mile of the crew office and did not own a phone, a crew caller would come to your residence and give you your work call in person.

One day in 2016 as I was talking to her I had a flashback. It was her in 1983—a young pretty little thing knocking on my door.

"I remember you now! You were a lot younger then." I told her bluntly.

"We all were."

# Locomotive Engineer Strike 1982

*It was September of 1982*, and our train arrived in Bend, Oregon. The locomotive engineers went on strike, and no trains were going to move until it was over. My conductor and rear brakeman saw the strike as an opportunity to go on a bender in Bend.... They invited me along, but I politely declined. Our locomotive engineer took a Greyhound bus back to Wishram right away.

The strike went on for about three days. After the first day, the two boozers asked me if I wanted to take the Greyhound bus back to Wishram with them. Once again, I opted not to join them. I had no desire to go back to Wishram at that time. I was currently staying comfortable in the Cimarron Hotel with all the amenities that the horseshoe apartment in Wishram lacked, passing my time by blowing my harmonica, heading to the YMCA to work out, and making it to a meeting or two. Besides, nobody from the railroad had called me.

The strike ended, but I still hadn't gotten a phone call from the railroad so I called the crew dispatcher.

"You're still in Bend? Why?"

"I've been waiting for instructions. Have you received any?"

"No. Let me call you back in a few minutes."

When the dispatcher called back, he instructed me to deadhead back to Wishram on the bus.

In the end, I got paid to work the train up to Bend, about a day and a half pay, plus eight hours pay for the layover, and another day and a half to ride the bus back to Wishram. Not too shabby, all things considered: four days pay while actually working on a train ten hours, eight of those hours with my feet up observing the scenery. I put in time slips for two more days of pay, accounting for the layover, but the railroad declined to pay me for them.

I started to complain about what I ended up with, but my union rep said, "I think you did better than anyone would have thought."

# Hobo Rides Free

*On another trip* from Wishram to Bend we had stopped to do some work in Madras, Oregon. While pumping up the air brakes and getting ready to leave and continue our trip, our engineer struck up a conversation with a hobo on the ground from the window of his seat. The hobo wanted to hop our train; he was trying to get to Redmond, Oregon. We were on a straight shot when we left for Bend, however, and would be rolling much too fast doing track speed through Redmond for someone to try hopping off.

The engineer told the hobo, "Get on one of those empty boxcars back there on the front part of our train. I will slow way down in Redmond and watch you get off."

So, he got on and we headed south. About an hour later we slowed down in Redmond to about 10 mph and watched the hobo hop off before getting back up to maximum authorized speed. That is the one and only time I was ever involved with the pleasure of assisting a hobo in such a deluxe manner in my career, all due to a locomotive engineer with a big heart for one day.

His heart wasn't so big on other days that I worked with him.

# Bullet Shot

*I was on the head end* lead locomotive of a Westbound freight train from Pasco, Washington to Wishram, Washington, traveling along the Columbia River. I was sitting in the fireman's seat on the side closest to the river when the engineer and I were startled by a sudden loud, crisp noise. It sounded sort of like an electrical crackle when a circuit overloads and blows. We started looking around at the panel on the back wall but couldn't find anything apparently wrong and the units seemed to be pulling and loading as intended.

After a few minutes, we gave up our search. As I settled back into my seat, I noticed a hole in my window just a few inches in front of my head, surrounded by some spider web-like cracks. I slid open the window and ran my finger in and along the hole, scooping up fresh slivers of glass. I think a stray or maybe even intentional bullet from the other side of the Columbia River had smashed into my window—that was the cause of the loud, crisp noise. I dodged a bullet.

# End of Marriage,
# Start of a New Marriage

*I started dating* a nice, smart, pretty lady in February of 1977 and we were married in September of 1978. Unfortunately, that did not work out. In 1981, with over a year of sobriety, we had been split up for close to two years when I tried to win her back, making amends. She said, *go out and fall in love with another girl, break it off, and I might consider taking you back.*

She had endured some of the most despicable treatment a person should not have to experience while with me, and that is a sugar-coated explanation. How I dodged at least a couple nights of going to jail for that treatment can only be described as unjust. I can blame the behavior on alcohol and drugs, but it still hurts; I made the amends, however it still haunts me deeply...and once again, I am sorry.

I was going to meetings and not drinking or drugging in between—that was the only thing I was doing 100 percent correct. The only requirement for membership was a desire to stop drinking; if they had told me anything else in the beginning, such as I had to stop swearing, smoking tobacco products, quit chasing women, or believe in Jesus, I would have been gone drinking and drugging the minute I got my job back on the railroad. One of the suggestions for newcomers was not to have any serious relationships for at least the first year of sobriety, so being as sick as I was, I had many relationships that were not serious.

*Somebody's knockin'. Should I let him in? Lord, it's the devil. Would you look at him? I've heard about him.* But I never dreamed he'd have blue eyes and blue jeans. About one year to the day of my sobriety date, I was at a meeting at Miracle Hall

#1 in Pacific, Washington with Little Joe, Mike R., and a few other nutcases. In the kitchen afterward, I started talking to a little blonde lady.

"My, you're a cute, dainty, pretty-looking little thing," I told her.

She says, "I get dirty, too...."

She was to become my next wife, and to this very day she says that what she meant was that she got dirty doing housework, yard work, and even dabbled with greasy dirty automobile work.

We continued to date and I became close to her daughters, one being about nine months old and the other four years old. I was holding the younger one on a dock on the Puget Sound waterway when she saw a bird and said her first word excitingly: *Birdie!* She is my *bird girl* to this day. The other girl at four years old asked me, *do you love my mommy?* I dodged her a little when I said I love everybody; she accepted that as I love her mommy, her sister, and her. She became *my belle*. We all moved in together and started being a family.

One day we left the older girl, my belle, at a neighbor's for a birthday party for an hour. I went to the door to pick her up.

The gentleman who answered said, "Your daddy's here to get you."

"Oh no, this is not my daddy," she said, "this is my mom's boyfriend. My daddy only comes to get me when we go to see his daddy and mommy."

I got sick thinking of her and her sister having to explain who I was—or was not—while growing up, so after we got home and the kids were in bed, I proposed to their mother as I stood next to her while she sat on the couch.

"Will you marry me?"

She wasn't prepared, and hesitated a few seconds.

I said, Well?"

"Yes!"

I had forgotten to kneel at the proposal, but an hour later when we went to bed I was kneeling all over the place.

Prior to that day, I had been thinking of my soon-to-be ex-wife's statement: *should I fall in love with another girl and break it off, she might consider taking me back.* It might have worked out that way, except I fell in love with three girls.

October 2nd of 1982 we were married and I was given the honor and privilege to adopt the girls in 1984 while my wife was pregnant with daughter #3, *mo jo*, born in 1985, followed by a son, *the duke*, in 1989, and the *bonus daughter* in 1997. When people ask me about my family, I give them mostly the short version: I married a lady with two kids and was fortunate to be able to adopt them, then we banged out three more. Sometimes people would make a comment that I was not the real father of the older two, which were almost fighting words, as I would say I am their real father, just not their biological father.

# The White House

*Railroad deadheaders* are workers transporting from one crew base to another while on the clock—easy money. The passenger train conductors as long as I can remember always accommodated freight engineer and conductor deadhead crews by letting them ride in secluded places on the train—the rear half of a coach car or sometimes even sleeper compartments. This was a real treat, especially on top of getting paid the same as if we were working. For instance, back in the day, a four-hour deadhead trip on a passenger train from Portland to Seattle paid a little less than an eleven-hour freight shift. Needless to say, I enjoyed deadheading.

Later, in 1985, when Reagan was trying to bust all the unions, that deadhead pay was reduced to actual time for the newer people; the old heads got eight hours for a deadhead, however, whether it was four, five, or eight. I still liked to deadhead.

Slowly but surely, the train conductors and locomotive engineers who transferred to passenger service from the Burlington Northern Railroad in the late '80s started to disappear; during the last three years of my career, I was the last conductor in passenger service from Seattle being of prior rights Burlington Northern origin. I was *bulletproof*, a term fondly used by railroaders who were over sixty years old with thirty or more years of service. Once you reached those milestones, you are entitled to your pension period. I retired at sixty-three years old with forty years of service. I didn't want to be fired or anything, however as a joke I would tell people when they called me into the office, *Are you going to fire me? Too late,*

*I just retired!* Believe it or not, several men and a couple ladies I know ended their careers that very way.

For my last three years, I mostly worked a run from Seattle to Spokane with a 24-hour layover in a hotel, of which I was paid for eight hours. My grandchildren lived only eight miles from the hotel, and I was able to visit with them. After my layover, I worked the train back to Seattle, had a day off, then worked a train to Vancouver, B.C., Canada, got paid while I slept and then worked a train back to Seattle; I averaged about sixty hours pay a week, while only being on the property forty-five hours. At the end of this, I had a 74-hour weekend. Sweet job.

When I worked freight in the '70s and '80s, there was a white switch shack on the north end of Seattle's B.N. Balmer yard with lockers and a restroom where the north end switch crews reported to work and took their coffee and *beans*— beans being the slang term on the railroad for lunch breaks. During breaks, some played a card game called pitch. This little shack was painted white and referred to as the "White House." It was eventually converted to a storage and pick up point of oxygen machines for crew members of trains going to pass through the eight-mile Cascade Tunnel. Should the train derail or malfunction in the tunnel, the train would be stocked with enough emergency oxygen to keep everyone alive until they were rescued.

Sometime in the '90s, the main line tracks were reconfigured, adding new junction points, and the White House went away; nevertheless, the White House was a reference point for railroaders for decades after and still is today, even though it is long gone. Any train in that vicinity, when asked by a dispatcher, yardmaster, or other trains where they were would respond with, *coming up to the White House, just passed the White House, going past the White House....* The legacy lived on. I passed the white house legacy story on to many of my retired coworkers, and they all agreed it was pretty close to accurate.

Ever since I could remember, B.N. deadheaders got on the train in Wenatchee, Washington going westbound to Seattle, most hoping to get a sleeper room, and were let off at the White House four miles short of Seattle's King Street station, which saved them the hassle of commuting back to Interbay where their lockers and cars were. This got them home to their families forty-five minutes sooner—and paid the same. In later years, after the passenger railroad took charge of the passenger trains, there was pressure from management not to stop the train at the White House to let deadheaders off, claiming it was dangerous or too time-consuming—and it became an official written rule. Then some of the newer sleeper car attendants took exception to deadheaders riding in sleeper compartments for one reason or another.

Despite this, sometime after leaving Spokane, I would talk with the attendant in charge of the crew car sleeper before arriving in Wenatchee; I could usually convince them to agree to give up three or four rooms for deadheaders, contingent on if called in the office they knew nothing about it—I would take the heat. I would then call the Wenatchee yardmaster half an hour before arrival and ask if there were any deadheaders. I would let them know how many rooms I had available and try to situate them the best I could with what was available. Sometimes they would have to double up, or if we didn't have much room at all, those with the most seniority would be given a room and the rest would have to tough it out in coach. I left it up to them.

During my last three years, I had some fun with deadheaders at Wenatchee and would have a little crew briefing with them trainside before letting them into a sleeper room. I would tell them, "If you don't bother the help, keep your rooms tidy, and refrain from ejaculating on the curtains, I will let you discharge at the White House."

# Leather Gap Bob

*In the '80s,* I caught an eastbound freight train from Seattle to Wenatchee, Washington with a prior rights Great Northern engineer named Bob. Bob wore custom-made dark sunglasses with a combination leather elastic wrap-around band that stretched from ear to ear around the back of his head, including a special piece of leather in the corner eye gaps that hid his eyes completely. Most of us thought it was a pretty weird look; he was the only person I have ever known to wear sunglasses of that nature, covering the corners of one's eyes. Bob expected his brakeman to run the locomotives for him when he needed a break, as I and many others can attest to. We had just penetrated the mouth of the western portal of the eight-mile-long Cascade Tunnel when Bob got up from his station.

"Sit over here for a bit," he strongly requested. "I've got something I want to look at in the second unit."

Operating on the uphill grade in the tunnel required a person to manipulate the throttle very little, if at all. The trains were usually maxed out in tonnage versus the horsepower given, so most the time, notch 8 was the position and pushing the *alerter* button when alerted was all that operating entailed throughout all eight miles of the Cascade Tunnel when heading eastbound. Naturally, it was different westbound, as we would be descending downhill, which required some clear thinking and skill.

Bob came back up from the second unit after about fifteen minutes. When he entered the cab, I thought we had run over a skunk. I put two and two together and realized what he was up to in the other unit. He took control of the train and started jibbering and jabbering as we discharged out the mouth of the eastern portal of the tunnel. We were now at the climax of the climb and in three or four minutes; the entire train was now on a 2.2 mountain grade descending down the eastern slopes of the Cascade Mountain range.

As best as I can remember, the lead locomotive was one of a new series. We had run them only for a couple of months at that point, and many hogheads had not mastered the quirks of them yet. When Bob put the train's locomotive's into dynamic braking, the brakes didn't respond. Instead of setting the train's air brakes right then, Bob began fiddle-f---ing on the back wall, pulling out various electrical panels and re-injecting them. His theory was that by pulling out one of these panels and re-injecting them, eventually the right one would reset the dynamic braking, and they would start working. In the meantime, we were banging around curves much faster than we should have been going. Finally, Bob gave up trying to figure the dynamic braking out and set twenty pounds of the train's air brakes. It took about ninety seconds, but it seemed like forever before the train slowed down. Came very close to being a runaway train.

A few years later, when random pee testing became law, Bob suddenly developed an attention deficit issue concerning a red flag and decided to become a truck driver. Another way of saying that smoking weed was no longer tolerated while working on the railroads, and should you not quit, chances were that you would eventually get fired.

# Hot Tub Dave

**Back in the late-'70s,** I worked freight on the Burlington Northern Railroad with a locomotive engineer off the old Great Northern Railroad, a real nice man who I became friends with. I nicknamed him "Hot Tub Dave" twenty years later. Dave and I shared many of the same interests, some good and some not so good, one being the overuse of recreational drugs and some not so recreational. I was lucky, becoming clean and sober in 1980, and by the grace of God still am today, while Dave battled toxic pollutants the rest of his life. At times, he'd gain some lengthy periods of being clean and sober, however eventually he would relapse and later recover awhile, only to keep repeating that up and down roller-coaster lifestyle.

Dave talked and understood my language, and we always had pleasant interactions. He may have been one of the few people I worked with on the railroad who made me look like an angel, depending on one's perspective. I worked freight over the Cascade Mountain Range in the late-'70s, riding alongside him in the locomotive as his brakeman as we smoked reefer while getting high on the high rail, high up in the mountains. A couple years later, in 1981, we were both clean and sober working an Auburn, Washington transfer job from Auburn to Tacoma, about a fifteen-mile route. We took a small train to Tacoma and when coming back to Auburn we were *caboose hop*; that is to say we only had two locomotives and a caboose as we broke the record time for a train getting from Tacoma to Auburn—at least I am pretty sure we did, while a rule or two may have been violated.

In the late-'80s and '90s, I worked passenger trains with Dave and heard many a story concerning his bending a few rules while operating trains. One night I was on the evening switch engine in Seattle when Dave's train from Portland arrived earlier than his normal early arrival. I was the switch engine foreman and climbed up into the locomotive after Dave had gotten off to make sure it was cut out and ready to be handled as a train we were taking around the wye at Stacy Street yard and then back to Seattle's passenger train coach yard for switching operations. As I was in the locomotive, the Seattle Road foreman of engines, "Air Gap Tommy," climbed in as well to pull the speed tapes pertaining to the trip that was just made. But the tapes were already pulled—or should I say, partially pulled—as they were all mangled and wadded up. Tommy mumbled to himself and took them to his office. Long story short, the bartender had turned Dave in for suspicion of speeding as many of his bar items had slid off the tables and he was scared that the train was going to derail on a curve. The conductor tipped off Dave that he was going to be turned in and someone pulled the tapes, thus tainting them. Tampering with speed tapes is a federal offense. The tapes, being pulled and mangled, were no good—unable to decipher whether Dave had been speeding or not; however, they had the reported times from the station agents between station stops, in addition to the train dispatcher's times recorded between junction points, which indicated he had been speeding. The bartender's statement that started the whole investigation became moot.

I was not at the investigation concerning this matter, however I was in and around King Street Station the day it took place and it was very well attended by government officials, union officials, and passenger train officials. When it was all said and done, some sort of deal was made retaining a job for Dave as a union official back east in some sort of secretary position. I had firsthand knowledge that after a couple years of that job he had a relapse and he came back to Seattle to running locomotives again, but first he had to re-qualify. That is when I gave him his nickname, "Hot Tub Dave."

While working the Canada train, I would be sitting in the bistro lounge at the conductor's desk delegating various duties and closely listening to my portable radio when Dave would always come back and sit in the lounge. Now, there was the question of why he was in the lounge when he was supposed to be in the locomotive qualifying. Had I been called in for an investigation on the matter, I am sure I would have survived, as the locomotive engineer doing the re-qualifying of Dave was still in the locomotive and it could be argued that we were just as safe without Dave in the locomotive as with him in it. Having said all that, Dave would be in the lounge and he liked to visit with the lady travelers. I overheard many conversations in which Dave would bring the subject of hot tubs up, thinking if he could get them talking about hot tubs, maybe he could get them *in* a hot tub. "Hot Tub Dave."

One day Hot Tub was working a train, being re-qualified on the Seattle to Portland run, and a mudslide hit the train at Castle Rock, Washington; it derailed, causing a few minor injuries. I had firsthand knowledge that when this happened, Dave was visiting in the lounge doing his hot tub spiel. I always wondered how he explained not being in the locomotive when that happened. Dave continued his relapsing lifestyle and in order to keep his job a deal was made that he live in a halfway house in California under close supervision.

I lost track of my friend Dave through the years. then I heard he got caught up in the Alaska Airline Miles scandal and retired before they could fire him. I recently received the sad news that he has passed away and is now, presumably, in that great hot tub in the sky.

# Conductor Balls

*I was working freight* in the '80s when I was involved in my one and only drop of a caboose from the main line into a yard. This was a pretty rare move, at least I think it was, seeing as how I only heard of one in my forty years with the railroad. The Seattle to Portland line is about 191 miles long; in the '80s, it paid a conductor $191—about a dollar a mile—to work that run. A brakeman stood to earn a little less, a fireman about the same as the conductor, and the locomotive engineer slightly more than the conductor. The idea was to run like hell, because your money was already made—we got paid by the mile. This was not exactly conducive to safety.

My conductor was a short, thin, red-haired, mustached man off the old Northern Pacific Railway; he reminded me of Pepé Le Pew. He wore a necklace of small Seattle Seahawks footballs around his neck. We left Seattle in the morning heading south for Portland with a long freight train. Three hours later, after working in Tacoma, we were now over a mile long and heading on to Longview, Washington, where after working we were now only a half mile long and continued on. We crossed from Vancouver, Washington over the Columbia River into the Beaver State of Oregon; fifteen minutes later we crossed the Willamette River approaching Lakeyard, which back in the day was a very large and busy rail yard on the west side of the mainline tracks. We received orders on the radio from the train dispatcher to set out our train and pick a track up—a new train—at Lakeyard before taking it to Hoyt Street yard a couple miles farther south, which would be our final terminal.

According to our contract, if we picked up between Vancouver, Washington and Portland, we earned ourselves an extra hour's pay, or should I say...about an extra thirteen miles' pay? Regardless of whether you did it in thirty minutes or ninety minutes, one hour's wage was all the extra you were going to get. A drop of the caboose would save us thirty to forty minutes if successful, and if the drop went bad, who knows how much time we would lose? In this situation, we cut the caboose loose behind the rest of the train a half-mile before the yard switch, sped the train ahead of the caboose with me on the end of that train, and when nearing the switch, I hopped off when the rear of the train was over the yard switch, where I lined up the caboose to roll into the yard on to the rear of our new train. The train and head end crew kept going a little over a quarter-mile, eventually making the set out. Okay...got that? I remember the conductor reassuring the head end crew from the caboose radio that we could do this.

I followed "Conductor Balls" as we went to the caboose platform between us and the train with a broom in his hand. He reached the broomstick handle down low across the draw bar between our caboose and the rear boxcar of our train and was able to manipulate the rear angle cock of the train closed from that position, cutting off the air to the caboose. He then plugged the air to the caboose with one of the emergency brake valves and bled the brakes off with the bleeding rod under the bunk bed near the floor. We were now rolling free without air brakes, still coupled to about two thousand feet or more of train about a mile from the north switch at Lakeyard.

"You will climb on the rear of that boxcar," Conductor Balls instructed me, "then I will have the hogger bunch the train, and I will pull the pin. After that, I will tell him to hi-ball, separating the caboose from the train. About a quarter-mile after separation, you will bail off and hand-line the caboose from the main line to the second track over on the engineer's side, towards our pick up."

I climbed onto the rear of the train. Conductor Balls called to bunch the slack, and it ran in. He got the pin, called for a hi-ball, and away I went with the train at about 22 mph and the caboose trailing behind at about 15 mph. Conductor Balls manned the caboose handbrake with all the slack out in the chain in case he needed to crank on it to stop. When we were separated by about three hundred feet, I saw Balls waving and heard him yelling. I knew it was about that time, and I could see the switch ahead. When we were about two hundred feet from it, I bailed off the proper way I was taught. With my switch key in one hand, my legs were not quick enough to keep up with the speed of the train I was hopping off of. As most trainmen learned quick, there was a way to decelerate without killing yourself.

Managing to survive the dismount, but losing the time it took to slow myself down, I was at the switch a split second after the train cleared the switch. I inserted my key, unlocked the lock, and hand-lined the switch toward the new train before running down the lead to throw one final switch.

A couple seconds later, Mr. Balls came rolling by and yelled, "Line everything back, kid!" I watched and listened as he cranked on the brake and guided the caboose to a soft joint on the pick-up.

The head brakeman got the train in a set out, shoving toward us on an adjacent clear track. Mr. Balls watched the shove, using the caboose radio from the cupola as I walked toward the head brakeman to help make the cut and set handbrakes. We then set the remaining cars over to an adjacent clear track, and after cutting away, we applied handbrakes and put our locomotives on the new train.

Conductor Balls said that he and the head man would *get the rest of this* and instructed me to walk up to the main and get ready to line back after we departed.

After the air test was completed, the train pulled out as I waited at the main line switch. When the caboose hit the main, they did not stop. I lined back the switch, locked it, and ran to catch up, barely managing to hop on the caboose. I could hear Mr. Balls telling the hogger to highball before I was even on board! That was a drop that I will never forget.

You know what else I will never forget? The next morning, when we met for breakfast, my conductor asked the waitress if she wanted to see his balls? As we all started to go into shock, he pulled out his Seahawks football necklace.

# Conductor Penicillin

*In the '80s,* I was working the trainmen extra board out of Tacoma, Washington. One day, I was called to work a local freight train that ran the line from Tacoma south to Centralia, Washington, about fifty-four miles, before turning inland and heading west for about another fifty-four miles on the ocean branch line, working all the way through Elma and right up to the Pacific Ocean. The old conductor I was working with was from the Old Northern Pacific Railroad. He was a real nice guy who seemed to forget that he was married while at work, like so many others did. It was a real common part of the culture. The other brakeman was a polite, quiet guy, but the engineer always called everyone a "wormy cockroach," but not usually to their face. I am sure that whenever I stepped out of earshot, I became a wormy cockroach.

We were taking the train to the ocean, stopping every so often at an industry track or siding to switch cars as needed. We were not very long—twenty or twenty-five cars max, with a caboose. Along the way, the conductor started counting the cars down from the caboose radio, spotting the caboose at a dirt road in the middle of nowhere.

"What's going on?" I asked the engineer. He hadn't told me about any work that needed to be done around here.

"Take a look out your side and you will see what that wormy cockroach is up to."

Once we came to a stop, I saw the conductor help two ladies onto the caboose before hearing him hi-ball the engineer on the radio.

"Wow, that guy has got to be nuts!" I said, and the engineer agreed.

We made our way out to the ocean and did a little work in the yard down there before heading to the hotel for our eight hour's mandatory rest. Once our rest was up, we got our locomotives and caboose, built a new train, and hi-balled back to the dirt road before once more coming to a stop. The ladies hopped off the caboose and went on their way. We continued along our route, stopping off to do a bit of work along the way to Centralia, and back up to Tacoma before tying up.

The next time I worked with this crew, we were all on the locomotive lite engine going out to a cranberry company to pull container cars, when I saw the wormy conductor take out a bottle of pills before popping a few into his mouth.

"What are those?" the hoghead asked.

"Penicillin pills."

"Did you catch something?"

"No," the conductor said, gulping down the pills, "but my wife is going to be out of town for a few days, so if I do catch something this will get rid of it before she gets back."

Now, I don't think that his theory holds much water; however, I do agree with the hoghead's opinion that the conductor was, indeed, a wormy cockroach.

# Gay Neighbor Man

*In 1988, we got a new* next-door neighbor man by the name of Melvin—about 30 years of age, nice guy. I had him figured out pretty quick as being gay; he wasn't in the closet. Our family was polite to him and got along well, as far as being neighborly and friendly.

My daughters were four, eight, and twelve at the time and had no idea he was gay, at first—and really didn't understand what it entailed. Well, apparently some neighbor kids with parents not as accepting as my wife and I were making jokes and bad-mouthing the new neighbor man—badly upsetting my two older daughters, as they really liked Melvin.

My wife and I were having a talk with the older two, consoling them that all was well; however, they were not going to settle for a sugar-coated explanation, since they had been hearing some very derogatory things of a vulgar nature pertaining to Melvin's sexual orientation.

Our older daughter asked us, "What does it mean when they call him a faggot, or a queer?"

My wife was in shock, without an answer, so after a little silence I spoke up.

"Those people calling him those names are being mean. They should be calling him *gay.*"

The older daughter then asked, "What does it mean to be gay?"

"Here is the deal, girls..." I explained. "If there were three naked ladies on the couch here, and a naked man in the recliner chair at the other end of this room? Melvin would walk right past those ladies and go kiss the man."

My wife was not exactly happy, but I think I gave a clear answer.

# Minority Locomotive Engineers and Trainmen

*By 1988, ten years* into my freight career, I had worked with around four hundred different trainmen and close to two hundred different locomotive engineers. Thinking about it after all these years, not many of them were minorities—a black person being rare, and I recall only one Asian locomotive engineer, one Asian trainman, one American Indian locomotive engineer and one American Indian trainman. There were also a few Latino T&E, or those who were mixed blood. By the time I retired in 2017, minority trainmen and locomotive engineers were much more common—though I'm not sure if it was yet equal, relative to the total population of T&E. I tend to doubt it.

I worked with a black engineer a few times in the '80s who hired on in the '60s. He and I had a few things in common and got along well. On one trip for a few hours he opened up to me and gave me an education on the hiring practices toward blacks after the Civil Rights Movement in the '60s. The railroad owners and many of their employees were not exactly happy with the new laws governing hiring rules pertaining to blacks and schemed some very underhanded practices to thwart the possibility of a black person attaining a job. The one hiring practice that disheartens and stuns me still today is that they took the applicants who would be least likely to succeed. So, if you could not read and write very well, you had a good chance of being hired so that they could fire you when you took a rules test that you could not pass. They hired physically or mentally unfit applicants and waited for them to quit, or be fired, when they failed to perform as well as their fit white peers. And should a black man make it past all the initial racist shit and stay employed? The battle would still carry on with racial slurs and a whole host of other despicable behaviors toward them.

I am sure I am only touching on a very small fraction of the injustices related to those hiring practices back then. Yes, only a very few of those black men from the 1960s made it thirty or forty years to retirement; my hat's off to them, and to the others not as fortunate. I hope they can find it in their hearts to forgive.

# Women on the Railroad

*When I hired on* the railroad in 1977, there were a few women trainmen; a woman locomotive engineer was rare, and a minority one extremely rare. There was no significant difference in the proficiency or manner in which the work was performed between men and women. When it came to character abnormalities, women and men were equal.

When it came, however, to sexual harassment? Not so equal. The sexual harassment of women by men was common, while sexual harassment of men by women was a rarity. What I will say about the men of those times in relation to sexual harassment is that some of them made me look like an angel--and that is sugarcoating it. Even as bad of a bad boy as I was, some of the sexual harassment I witnessed women receive offended me.

I will convey short stories off retirement fliers I wrote of two ladies whom I worked with from back in the day; both worked many years, making it to retirement. Elle Skyles hired out August 2nd, 1976 in Seattle on the Burlington Northern Railroad as the first B.N. female trainmen in the Pacific Northwest. She marked up first at Stacy Street yard on the Northern Pacific switchman's extra board. In 1976, random drug and alcohol testing was years away and diversity was just a word in the dictionary; it was a man's world and a different era to say the least. Elle survived. Portable radios on yard jobs were nonexistent, so switchman walked on top of moving boxcars at night passing signals with flares or lanterns, risking life and limb. Elle survived. I worked with Elle my first time in 1978 at Stacy yard on a midnight goat; she worked the field and I pulled pins—we were snakes. The Stacy extra board was a catch-all board when the brakemen's board went dry at Seattle. Elle caught road jobs to Portland, Wenatchee, Canada, and everywhere in-between, including passenger train service. Elle rode covered wagon units, helper locomotives, cabooses, and the point of many trains hanging onto the side of a boxcar in the dark, rain, or fog. She worked almost all the yards in the Northwest, including the Burlington Northern King Street coach yard when she was eight months pregnant with the first of her two sons. Elle came to Amtrak in 1987 when recruited, keeping her seniority intact, and tried the relatively safer life of a passenger train conductor. Thank goodness Amtrak had switch engines because she found that being a snake was in her heart. While hand lining the old King Street crossovers for the Empire Builder's reverse move into the station, she made her first contact with her husband of eighteen years, Jack, a 1969 Union Pacific hogger now retired. They eventually worked the 565 switch engine together and the rest is history. Elle is pulling the pin after thirty-seven years of railroad service.

Paula Dennis hired out in train service August 12th, 1976 on the Burlington Northern at Spokane during the era of Virginia Slims and the revitalized women's rights movement of the 1970s. The U.S. Court system at the time ordered railroads to hire women in all positions of employment. Paula was one of the first ever women to hire out in train service. These pioneer women were not welcome by all. Even the nicest men had tainted perceptions and attitudes of women working these traditional men-only jobs. Paula and a very few endured and forced attitudes and perceptions to a gradual change that was more tolerable for women that followed. We heard tales of Miss Paula from across the Cascade Mountain Range all the way to Seattle. I laid eyes on her the summer of 1982 in Wishram, Washington. Paula was furloughed from Spokane and I from Seattle; we worked the former Spokane Portland & Seattle Railroad terminal brakeman's extra board, out of Wishram. We worked freight trains, seniority in the caboose.

It was there the tales began to mellow, as did she. Paula always spoke her mind and supported the underdogs and those who could not help themselves. In the late '80s and early '90s, I had the pleasure of being marked up several times as her helper working on the Amtrak Switch Engine 565 in Seattle's yard. Paula mastered the art of getting on and off moving equipment as safely as anyone I ever witnessed. After many years on extra boards and switch engine assignments, Paula finally was able to hold conductor on the Empire Builder between Seattle and Spokane where she tied up for the last time, December 29th, 2010....*You've come a long way, baby!*

# 1987 Crash

On January 4th, 1987 in Chase, Maryland, a group of freight locomotives went past a red signal and into the path of a passenger train that was traveling at 108 mph. The resulting crash killed 16 people and injured another 164. After the investigation, it was concluded that the two-man freight crew that survived had been smoking marijuana just prior to the accident and most believed that to be the greatest contributing factor to the crash—the locomotive engineer getting nearly all the blame.

As I said earlier in the book, to expect a whole crew to be clean and sober was wishful thinking. The older guys liked booze, the younger guys had pot, speed, and God knows what else. I worked on crews where everybody was some combination of drunk or stoned. The common goal of many railroad employees was to maintain a nice buzz and earn a good living while doing it. If you could walk without a stagger and talk without slurring your words, you were left alone. Even if you slurred or staggered, your fellow employees would hide you from the higher-ups and do your share of the work.

Most of those fun times and not-so fun-times came to a crashing halt in 1987 after the crash in Maryland. I say *most* because thirty years later there were still toxic railroaders and trainmasters turning their heads the other way; the old culture had greatly diminished, however it still lived on, sort of like people who still don't believe in civil rights. Shortly after the accident, random urine testing went into effect. The Burlington Northern Railroad, as well as all other railroads, began periodically sweeping railroad property with dogs, sniffing out lockers for drugs and pulling people out of service if weed and or other drugs or alcohol was found in their locker or car. There was an uproar from employees who contended that it was against our civil rights to search our property without consent—and the matter eventually went to court. It was ruled that on railroad property the owners could do almost anything they wanted.

I worked with a fair amount of coworkers who were very upset now that testing for marijuana could be done randomly and positive results led to being pulled out of service on the first offense with mandatory counseling, and a second offense resulting in termination of employment. Several coworkers quit working on the B.N. after deciding that if they could not smoke weed, they would just find another job. Others continued to smoke weed and most of them were eventually caught, with some surviving to come back to work for many years before retiring and others that could not quit no matter how hard they tried and never coming back.

There were a few that continued to smoke weed and use other drugs, but managed to stay employed for a while by doctoring urine tests results. They would keep something in their wallet or on person that they would drop into their urine sample, foiling the test and buying them time to cleanse their system enough to pass a second test. That took a lot of effort and strategy, and I suspect that all of those people eventually slipped up and were caught, though it wouldn't surprise me to find out some of them managed to elude or foil the testing all the way to retirement. In fact, I knew of one.

With random pee testing in effect, the breathalyzer for alcohol came shortly thereafter. Most did not gamble with their jobs and refrained from drinking during the suggested eight hours before reporting for duty, but there were those who for whatever reason could not help themselves. Eventually, most were caught and pulled out of service. Should they agree to the terms of the company counselor, which sometimes included treatment for substance abuse, they would be allowed to come back to work after a while. A second violation meant termination, but in my forty years, I met two guys who managed to make it back after being nailed twice. They were rare exceptions to the rule. I heard recently that most of the railroads have adopted a stricter policy: one strike, you're gone. During my time, I never saw someone get pulled out of service for substance abuse who wasn't warned to quit a few times before it happened.

Showing up to work with booze on your breath was one thing, but with urine testing in effect, an employee could test positive on Monday after smoking a joint on Saturday and be pulled out of service. Employees complained that there was no way that you could be impaired from smoking a little weed two days earlier. What's worse is that we soon came to find out marijuana stayed in your system up to thirty days after smoking. Some of my coworkers learned that the hard way. I personally knew one conductor and one engineer who tested positive when they were randomly tested after a vacation. I am sure that this situation was widespread, however these particular gentlemen were out of service for only a few days with counseling by claiming that the weed found in their test was the result of second-hand smoke. Of course, they were sternly advised to stay away from second-hand marijuana smoke as a second positive could result in termination.

When a person gets fired off the railroad, the union and that person under the law can request a formal hearing to plead their case and try to get their job back. The railroad and the union must first agree on an arbitrator, then the accused party would bring in a union representative and the railroad would send a representative of their own to the hearing. After hearing both sides of the story, the hearing ended and the arbitrator went home to mull it over. After a short period, the arbitrator would make a decision that the employee would either get their job back with back pay, which was rare, or get their job back without back pay (not so rare); but the most common decision was that the employee was terminated.

The most interesting situation I heard about was from an arbitrator at a union convention many years back. In this case, a man was fired for his second positive test of marijuana. At the hearing, when asked to explain why he tested positive for marijuana, the fired employee explained that he did not use marijuana, but his girlfriend at the time was a heavy user. He claimed that he tested positive because he performed oral sex on her nearly every day and the fluids from that activity is the one and only thing that could have caused him to test positive. Sounds like something I would have tried in the '70s. He was forced to seek employment elsewhere. After thinking about this many years later, his explanation may have been true and a different arbitrator may have given him the benefit of the doubt and ruled differently.

Through the years, I refrained from ratting people in for being impaired while on the property, taking a few minutes to talk with coworkers living on the edge. Several times I smelled alcohol from the night before—just a few hours earlier, possibly less—and tell them, *this is a good job, you might want to change your habits...I gave it up years ago.* I turned in two people in my career for substance abuse issues. In about 1990, there was a laborer at the King Street coach yard who would be drunk or high and move locomotives around, which he was not authorized to do in the first place. I warned him several times, as did several others, not to move them, especially while under the influence and to quit coming to work impaired. One night, he ran a locomotive over a blue flag and derail, so I turned him in. Administration came down to work and pulled him out of service. He went and got some help, and came back a couple months later. Unfortunately, he was unable to keep his nose clean and was pulled out again for substance abuse, ending his career.

The second guy I turned in was later in my career. A hoghead running passenger trains had a noticeable meth or crack habit. Several of us spoke with him about it, but he kept up his dangerous behavior. Eventually, two other coworkers and I met with him in a hotel lobby and voiced our concerns on deaf ears. Reading newspaper headlines in my mind about a train wreck caused my imagination to run wild, and the idea of people being killed in a passenger train crash due to the negligence of an engineer high on crack got the best of me—I decided to turn him in. It was still a while before he was finally nailed, but he is all done now.

# 1971 and 1987 Amtrak

*From what I was told*, and I've read up some on, was that in 1971, a big change took place within the freight railroads governing passenger trains. Prior to 1971, the passenger railroad trains were owned and operated by freight railroads that also owned the tracks they ran on. As a result of losing money for many years, the freight railroads gave up most of the responsibility to run passenger trains to Amtrak. Another big factor was rail fans, referred to by many as *rail enthusiasts* or *foamers*, who repeatedly rallied for funding to keep Amtrak running as it risked budget cutbacks due to a myraid of political agendas. Through the many years, and still to this day, rail fans have been a big influence on keeping Amtrak going. *Thank you!*

The name *Amtrak* came from blending the words *America* and *track*, replacing *track* with *trak*. Founded as a quasi-public corporation to operate many U.S. passenger rail services, it receives a combination of state and federal subsidies, but is managed as a for-profit organization, many referring to it as a *clusterf---*.

The newly formed Amtrak employed all the workers in relation to their trains, with the exception of trainmen, locomotive engineers, and train dispatchers—the operating entity of the trains. I was told that owners of the freight railroads felt they would have better control should their people be operating and coordinating movement of the trains. *Control over what*, you may ask? They would have less opposition putting passenger trains in sidings that netted them little money while running freight trains that made them the big money. This mentality by the freight companies was always a back-and-forth situation heavily influenced by politics and big money; the real answers and reasons may never be known.

As a passenger train conductor, I experienced hundreds of times we were in a siding waiting for a freight train to get out of our way. Passengers would ask me why we were waiting for a freight train and I would tell them that the owners of the tracks, the freight railroad, cared more about making money on the freight than they did about people.

Around 1985, Amtrak started pursuing the idea of having their very own locomotive engineers and train conductors. After a couple years of bargaining between freight railroad owners and unions, deals were struck and Amtrak started taking applications from the freight railroad seniority rosters— this being in 1986 and implemented in 1987, through as late as the early '90s. Most of those that chose to change companies were given six-month trial periods to figure out if the job would work for them. If they decided that they weren't a good fit, they were allowed back to their previous railroad position. Should they stay past the six months, they were protected by the union-negotiated agreement "C-2," ensuring that if ever the passenger railroad should fail to keep them employed, they could exercise their employment rights with seniority back to their former freight railroad; should that not be possible they would receive lost wages. Now, different railroads in different parts of the country had various side agreements that we will not go into; however, the main idea was job protection. Amtrak now had their own trainmen and locomotive engineers, though the freight owners still employed the train dispatchers, who made most of the decisions governing train movements.

# Last Freight Job: Sumas Turn

*My last job working* on the Burlington Northern in freight was as a brakeman on a job out of Seattle in 1988 called the "Sumas Turn." We would be assigned to take a train at about 4 a.m. and operate it north from Seattle, working along the way in Everett and Burlington, Washington. At Burlington, we headed east several miles before stopping to work at Sedro-Woolley, then we headed north up to Sumas, Washington on the Canadian border, where we did our final terminal switching.

At the end of the shift, we would head to the Caribou Hotel around noon for an eight-hour rest. The total distance of this trip was 114 line miles. After the rest, at about 8 p.m., we would reverse our route on a train back to Seattle and hoped to be off duty by 4 a.m. I worked this shift Monday through Saturday with Sunday off and enjoyed it because, as with all the union arbitrates negotiated through the years, that job paid 60 hours of wage for being on the property for only 48. The very best part of the job was that when you got off work at 4 a.m. Saturday, you were not required to be back to work until 4 a.m. Monday. This gave you plenty of time to get some rest at home before spending the rest of Saturday and all of Sunday to do whatever you wanted. Railroad schedules were rarely that nice.

While going north in the morning the scenery was beautiful as we wound slowly along the Nooksack River (*Nookie-Sack* to some, *nut sack* to others). At around 10 a.m., we would pass a small farmhouse where a pretty Indian lady would come out and wave to us. Eventually, she would be on the side of the train I was riding on and only thirty feet away, smiling and waving. I would return her same enthusiasm. For a few weeks, it was always the highlight of my trip. Then one day as we approached the farmhouse my hoghead, Randy, said, *oh oh Larry, you're in trouble now!* The figure along the tracks looked a lot larger than usual. It turned out to be a non-smiling, cross-armed, and cross-looking Indian man. Needless to say, I didn't wave to him, but gave him the peace sign instead.

On a different trip late one night while headed south, we were spotting boxcars at a Sedro-Woolley industry. To do this, we had to block a street crossing for about ten minutes. As I was walking past the crossing after finishing our task, a man in a car started yelling obscenities about us blocking the street at me. I stopped for a moment and calmly explained that I really had no other choice but to block the road with the way that the tracks were configured. He called me a couple of choice things.

"This crossing doesn't even have lights! Where are the *bleeping* lights?"

At this point, I lost my composure and shined my lantern light, with the hot bulb inserted, in his face.

"See this light, buddy?" I said. "This is the only light I need!"

I admit now that I should have kept it quiet, because after putting our train back together and rolling west toward Burlington, the man started stalking our train in his car, pointing a gun at us as we approached crossings. At one point, he climbed onto our locomotive and went up the side with no door to try and get in; thankfully, he jumped back off. The caboose would get over one crossing and he would race a half mile up to the next one and wait. I remember the hoghead crouching and peeking out the windows as he operated the locomotive. The conductor and I were taking cover in the same way, talking with the train dispatcher and other brakemen on the caboose over the radio. We got the license plate number and car description to the dispatcher, who relayed it to the police. A short time later, the dispatcher called and told us that we could relax—the police got him.

I never heard any more about it, but I am guessing that he went to jail for a DUI—or was committed to the Sedro-Woolley Mental Institution. I hope he calmed down and saw the light.

# The Caboose

*Love is a strong word* that I do not use often, but I loved riding and working from the caboose. When I hired out, there were cabooses from several different railroads still in operation from the 1970 railroad merger of four railroads forming the Burlington Northern Railroad, those being the Great Northern Railroad, Northern Pacific Railroad, Spokane, Portland and Seattle Railroad, and the Chicago, Burlington and Quincy Railroad. I don't think I was ever in a caboose exactly like another, especially ones from the pre-merger railroads.

Over the years they had all been modified in one way or another, sometimes by mechanical, and sometimes by crew members in the day when cabooses were assigned. The biggest modifications were from coal-burning stoves to oil stoves. Upon entering a caboose, however, it took a few minutes to figure out the bunks, desks, lockers, cabinets, bathroom, sink, and where the batteries were and whether they were charged. There were plenty of spots to keep equipment and tools associated with fixing problems encountered with air brakes, track defects, and a whole host of other unforeseen situations, including derailments. There was at least one radio, sometimes two handsets for communication with the locomotive engineer, other crew members with portable radios, the train dispatcher, other trains, and workmen on or near the tracks. There was also an oil stove for heat and sometimes a refrigerator that worked...or a cooler with a bag of ice. Yes, I loved being on the rear in the caboose—home away from home.

There was usually the conductor and rear brakeman in the caboose. I heard that before my time on some railroads there was even a flagman assigned to certain jobs who worked out of the caboose; though I never experienced this firsthand I know it to be true.

In the Northwest, on the Burlington Northern Railroad, I worked out of a caboose about five hundred times and almost always enjoyed it—except for a couple times when my conductor was an extreme nutcase, or in later years, when I was the nutcase conductor with an extreme nutcase brakeman. The conductor had a desk on the rear and window both facing the direction the train just came from. The idea was that while looking over paperwork the conductor could also look at the tracks the train had just passed over, observing any possible indications of dragging equipment. There was a caboose spotlight for observation at night.

There was also a cupola in the center of the caboose that one would climb up a couple steps into; it was usually occupied by the rear brakeman. The cupola had windows set in a full circle, 360 degrees, from which to observe the front of the train, mostly in the direction it was moving; you could also look back if need be. There were seats facing forward and backward in some, while others had a pair of seats that flipped. The idea was that one would look forward, and when the train was going around a left-hand curve, sit on the left and observe as much of the train as possible, looking out for shifted loads, smoke coming off the axles or journals, anything that might seem unsafe. When the train would straighten out and go around a right-hand curve, the brakeman would then change sides and observe on the right; in the same manner, the crew on the locomotive would observe the front half of the train while looking back on the curves.

Okay...what I just explained was how things were *most* of the time on a caboose; not everyone was exactly conscientious.

Several times, I was told by the conductor: "I'm going to sleep, so here is what you do...sit in the cupola and observe the front of the train from the left on left-hand curves, and from the right on right-hand curves, and then on straight track jump down and sit at the rear desk and observe the track we are passing over. You got that kid? I'm hitting the rack...wake me up if you need to." That was a fairly common scenario. And then there were the pothead and booze-hound conductors—a few who brought their girlfriends along.

In the mid-'80s, the caboose started to be eliminated from most trains throughout the country on all railroads due to advancements in technology. The caboose era slowly came to an end as the *detector* started replacing the eyes on the caboose. There were several types of detectors. One scanned the trains undercarriage, detecting any warm wheels, axles, or journals, and then reporting over the radio pretty close to where they were so the crew would know where to look after bringing the train to a stop. Should one find a defective piece of equipment, they were required to take the train slow until there was a yard or siding to where the bad order could be set out to be repaired. There also were other detectors that scanned the train for dragging equipment, most of those proceeding bridges on waterways. Eventually, with all the detectors everywhere, the need for eyes on the caboose was nearing history. The unions were strong and argued that should the detectors fail, the crews would save the day. It was a good argument. There was also the need for the locomotive engineer to know when the entire train was moving, as the caboose crew would always convey that on the radio—plus report when the entire train was past a speed restriction so the train could resume track speed. There was also the question of knowing whether the air brakes were working throughout the train, an even more important thing for the engineer and crew to know. All three of these observations were always reported by a crew member on the caboose.

Along came the rear end device—yes, the tool that screwed the rear-end crew, leading to the elimination of most cabooses on trains. It was called the *Rear End Device*, or *RED*. They would be attached—or one could say, coupled—to the rear knuckle of the rear drawbar on the rear car of the train, with an air hose hooked into the train air brakes. There was a sister unit in the locomotive on the front of the train named *Mary* that received communication from *Fred* on the rear on how much air was in the train's air brakes at all times, eliminating a crew member on a caboose having to convey that. The RED could also convey with a signal when the train was moving or stopped and very soon Mary became sophisticated with a counter, so the engineer could punch in the length of the train when the locomotive was going by a slow restriction, thus knowing when the rear would be by, giving the go-head that it was okay to speed up. Yes, the RED became *FRED*—the *Fu- -ing Rear End Device*. So Fred and Mary were eliminating the caboose with the help of track side detectors.

Decades before my era, cabooses had red lens oil or kerosene lamps mounted on their rear; later, they were battery-powered. These lamps were put in place in the name of safety, so crews of approaching trains would see the red lens glowing and govern their train accordingly to hopefully avoid a crash. Fred even came with a battery-powered red light, among all its other features.

The end was fast approaching for the caboose. Steadily, the railroads began eliminating the caboose by not buying any new ones and investing in more detectors—Freds and Marys. The trainmen unions still had some pull, so in order to keep members employed while cabooses went away, they made agreements that kept trainmen employed through attrition; some chose to receive monetary buy-outs to retire, while others took the money and were severed from the railroad to go on to other occupations. Many who declined the buy-out eventually became locomotive engineers, but the majority remained in the trainmen craft.

There are still a few cabooses on local trains on out-of-the-way branch lines where they are used mainly for shoving platforms, but the caboose as it was known back in the day is history. In 1988, I moved on to become a passenger train conductor. Had there still been cabooses operated as they were back in the day? I might have stayed on freight.

# My Favorite Caboose Story

*My favorite caboose story* happened twenty years after they were retired from the railroad and I was a passenger train conductor. I was down in Portland, Oregon one day for a union meeting, or safety meeting, might have been both. After the meeting, I was waiting in the crew room to deadhead home on the northbound passenger train to Tacoma, Washington.

Before departure, "Titlow Doug," the locomotive engineer on the train, saw me in the crew room.

"Hey, I am getting ready to retire in a couple weeks," he offered. "Why don't you come up and ride with me?"

"How about I come up at Kelso and ride to Olympia?"

He said okay and later I climbed up with him at Kelso and rode in the fireman's seat. We talked about the days when we were on freight and the various people who had come and gone–and a little bit about retirement. He said he had enough money saved, and that meant he was retiring.

As we pulled into Centralia, Washington, we observed a man with a grip *like a small work bag* wave to us and come toward the engine.

Doug and I looked at each other, asking the same thing.

"Who is that?"

"You know him?"

Neither of us had ever seen him before.

The man climbed up the locomotive steps, came into the cab, and nodded at us. "Hi, I'm Mike, a new transfer to Seattle, a locomotive engineer, and I am taking head-end trips in order to get qualified on the territory, per the Seattle Road foreman"

Doug looked at his head end pass and said, "Sure."

There was not much room in the cab, as I was spread out on the two tight firemen's seats. Mike said he would stand up against the back wall between Doug and me, and I informed him that I was dropping back to the coaches at Olympia in twenty minutes, and he could have my spot then.

As we rolled along, I asked Mike where he hired out.

"Burlington Northern Santa Fe Railroad in Seattle at Stacy street yard as a switchman, in 1996."

"That's where I hired out in 1977!" I said. "It was still the Burlington Northern Railroad then. Did you know B.J. Smith?"

"No, never met him," said Mike.

""He has been the switchmen's union griever since 1976," I tried again.

Mike thought a moment. "No, don't recall him."

Well, I was a little irritated, as B.J. basically saved my job in 1980, but I let it go.

Mike started in with how he had begun as a switchman and become a conductor on freight, then a freight locomotive engineer.

Puffing out his chest, he finished, "And now I am a passenger train locomotive engineer. I've done it all."

I lost my cool. Pointing my finger at him, I said, loudly, "You ever get a hum job on a caboose?"

Mike gave me a quiet, "No."

"Well, then you haven't done it all!"

# Hiring Out on Passenger Service

*In October of 1988*, I accepted a job with the passenger railroad on the conductors extra board in Seattle. At that time, the train crews were already reduced, with a big change on the yard jobs. Where there used to be three switchmen on a job, there were now only two; the switch foreman job was renamed to *yard conductor,* and the positions of head man switchman and field man switchman were merged into what was now called an *assistant yard conductor.* The passenger trains mostly had only two trainmen: a conductor and an assistant conductor, though a very few had two assistant conductors and a baggage man. Some trains worked with only the conductor.

On the road jobs, there were always two enginemen aboard: a locomotive engineer and a locomotive fireman. The fireman position was eventually phased out—most were surprised how many years it lasted past the steam engine era. There are now assistant passenger train locomotive engineers on jobs that are six hours or longer.

# Passenger Train
# Conductors Extra Board

*I accepted employment* with the passenger train company and through standard union negotiations, carried my seniority to the Seattle Passenger Train Conductors Extra Board. At this time, there were conductors and engineers from all over the Northwest from several different freight railroads: a locomotive engineer extra board, assistant locomotive engineer extra board, passenger train conductor extra board, and assistant passenger train conductor extra board.

I was on the conductor's rotating extra board—first in and first out. There were two or three of us on it guaranteed 40 hours pay a week. You protected the board from 12:01 a.m. Monday to 11:59 p.m. Sunday. If you worked 16 hours in a week, you got paid 40. If you worked 41, you got paid 41. The idea was to work as little as possible, and should that not work out, try for 45 or more hours—at least that was my theory.

There were two downfalls protecting the board: should you refuse a call or miss a call for work, you lost your guarantee. For example, say if you worked 8 hours on Monday and nothing the rest of the week, you would receive 40 hours pay for working 8 hours; however, should the crew desk call you Sunday morning to work an 8-hour shift and you declined for any reason, or failed to answer the call for work, you would receive 8 hours pay for the week. I never lost a guarantee. The other downfall protecting the board was every now and then you would be sitting good on Saturday or Sunday with 8 or 16 hours in, getting ready to collect that 40 and hoping to attend an important weekend family function, when the phone would ring. It would be the crew desk needing you to work. After this happened a couple times and reporting to work while upsetting family members and myself, I marked up on a yard switch engine that was home every day with regular hours and days off that also made a lot of overtime; for about three years I did that, plus I worked a lot of my rest days at the overtime rate in and out of town when to do so did not hamper my family life too much. *Ka ching, ka ching.*

# Driving Cab

*While on the passenger train* conductors extra board, I took a job at the Farwest Cab company of Seattle to supplement my income. After a half-hour test from King County officials proving I could read a map, I was licensed.

I worked with the cab company mostly Friday or Saturday nights throughout the year and a half I worked the guaranteed passenger conductor extra board. On slow weeks, while collecting the guarantee, I would go get a cab and report to the cab company dispatcher on the car radio when I was ready to pick up fares. The deal was the driver paid for the gas and we split the fare money 50/50 with the cab owner. I think the dispatchers had their favorite drivers, but still I was kept busy and brought home about a hundred dollars most nights. Now, I suspected other drivers made about the same, though many depended on driving cab as their only income. They, however, were dispatched to *stable* people as many times I was not. I gave rides to many hookers (a few were stable), pimps, and plain nutcase drug addicts, while losing one fare almost every night I drove: they said they had *no money, sorry* or they said they had *no money, screw you, what are you going to do about it!* I was scared a few times and feared for my safety.

There was one time that I arrived at a home in the Rainier district of Seattle and the parents of their higher-than-a-kite daughter gave me ten dollars and an address in Georgetown a couple miles away to take her to. There was no such address and they may not have even been her parents. I flagged a cop car down and handed her over. Another night in the South Park neighborhood, two men ran me around in circles looking for a house for a few minutes and then tried to take me down an alley; instead, I slammed on the brakes, threw it into park, and jumped out while yelling for them to get out—which they did, and left. Yep, I drove the ones the dispatcher would not give to her buddies.

One night it was slow and I saw a couple cabs parked at an airport hotel parking lot; the drivers were standing around visiting, so I pulled in, got out, and introduced myself. They asked me what else I did besides driving cab and I shot my mouth off about being on the passenger train guaranteed conductors extra board—and I was only doing this for pocket money. Well, I should have answered that a little differently because that was the end of my hundred dollars a night; I was soon lucky to get thirty dollars a night, as they told the dispatchers and other drivers, most of them resenting me.

It did not hurt too bad, as it coincided with my move to the passenger train overtime yard job.

# Passenger Train Yard Operations: Chalking Days

*Throughout the '90s*, I worked various passenger train yard jobs on and off using the #565 switch engine most of the time. I worked a lot with a strange conductor on the shorter side who knew how to switch just fine; however, like the rest of us, he had some serious character defects, always shouting to his coworkers, *All the ladies are mine!* When reminded he was married, he would grin and say, *'Eatin' ain't cheatin'*. He came to be known as "The Little General." Many times when any of us men would be talking to a lady coworker around The Little General, we ended up talking to the back of his head. He also called himself *the loner with a boner*.

There was also a switchman named "Ear Plug Doug" because he wore earplugs most of the time in an era when most us of us did not. Now, I really wish that I had. Earplug gave me my yard nickname: "Harry Tung." Self-explanatory, I think.

One time, The Little General and I went to the Burlington Northern Train Dispatcher's office on Lander Street in Seattle near our yard during our lunch break. The Little General introduced me to the lady dispatcher as "H.T." and she took the bait.

"What does H.T. stand for?" she asked.

I started to squirm a little. and The Little General replied, "Harry Tung!" as quick as he could.

I still remember the lady to this day. She didn't even hesitate for a second.

"You were waiting for that."

I worked with a lady conductor by the name of Janet on and off through the years—nice lady. One day after a coworker called me H.T., she said, "I know what the guys mean when they call you that; I think of it as "Happy Thoughts."

I thought for a moment. "Thanks, Janet. Should there be an investigation, that's what we will use.

While we were working together, The Little General started chalking up all the buildings, pillars, and underpasses in the coach yard and Seattle King Street Station with hairy tongues: yes, a huge tongue with hair on it. One day, I went to see our superintendent about a labor change in the works.

Before I could get a word out, he asked me, "What is going on with all these hairy tongues everywhere? They're even inside the locomotives!"

"You don't think I'm doing it, do you?"

"Maybe not, but you know who is!" he said. "And if it doesn't stop, there will be charges."

He was not happy, and I left without discussing the impending labor dispute. I relayed to The Little General what the superintendent had said pertaining to hairy tongues and him bringing charges should it not stop. For the next two weeks, The Little General doubled his efforts, chalking hairy tongues on every surface he could get his hands on.

Sadly, The Little General passed away in 1996 from playing Russian roulette. I kissed his forehead while he lay in his casket, while saying a prayer and good-bye. In his honor, a fellow conductor named Happy Dave, "H.D.," and I erected and firmly cemented a sign for a new unnamed stub track in the coach yard. The sign read, *Little General Stub*. The Little General had made an impression on me, and for about two years after his death, I carried chalk; when in a siding or yard somewhere, I would chalk people's nicknames.

I was chalking the Royal Brougham Street underpass in the coach yard late one night with "Handbrake Henry," a nickname for a locomotive engineer on a different shift, when the cops shined a spotlight on me from their squad car. One of them got out and demanded to know what the heck I was doing.

"I am glorifying a coworker we work with here with his nickname."

The cop asked a few questions to ascertain if I was really a railroad employee and belonged where I was. When he was sure I was where I belonged, he looked at me as if I was crazy, hopped back into his patrol car, and drove off.

I'll admit it; it was very childish to be chalking things up, but also lots of fun. I had at least a few people egging me on right up until I got the ultimatum. A trainmaster with orders from the superintendent said that if the chalked wall by his office did not get cleaned up and the chalking stopped, there would be charges. Unlike The Little General, I decided to stop.

# Oscar Laboe

*In the early to mid-'90s*, I worked a lot of passenger switch jobs with a locomotive engineer who wrote stories under the pen name, "Oscar Laboe." I never read any of his books, nor did I ever confirm he wrote any, but he did tell me some very disturbing stories about railroaders we all knew.

He said that one of our conductors was trying to run a trespasser off the property one night while working freight in Pasco, Washington. The hobo drew a knife, overpowered the conductor, and bent him over a drawbar between two box cars to have his way with him. He also told me that one of our locomotive engineers was higher than a kite one night, when he decided that having his girlfriend slip a 12-ounce beer bottle up his you-know-what was a good idea. When the bottle became impossible to remove, they had to rush to the Auburn, Washington hospital emergency room.

I got to know those two men eventually, but I never bothered to ask them if these stories were true or not, though after getting to know them, I'm thinking there was some truth to both the stories.

Oscar was all about cheap thrills. He was a good locomotive engineer, but in a lot of ways he made me look like an angel. He sent a Christmas card to my house one year addressed to *Mr. and Mrs. Harry Tung*. My wife was not amused. The more we worked together, the more I grew to like him.

One day, a train fanatic— a "foamer"—was following our switch engine around. We would do our work at the station, and there he was. Then we would be at the bad order track, and there he was. We headed down to the post office, and he was there, too. After a few hours of this, Oscar hopped off the engine and approached the train fanatic.

"Where do you work?" Oscar asks.

"Boeing..." he says.

"Well, how the f--- would you like it if we were to come down to Boeing and follow you around all day?"

The foamer left.

Another time, we were at the coach yard switch at Royal Brougham Street waiting our five minutes to come out with a train; when time was up, we started out, only to see a police car that had gotten caught on the tracks between the crossing gates that had come down .

"Look at that f---ing idiot!" Oscar said over the locomotive radio.

"I have a scanner," the cop responded. "I heard that."

"I don't care! You are still an idiot."

Oscar messed with a lot of people's heads, but none more so than a road locomotive engineer by the handle of "Triple D," or "Dare Devil Dave."

One of our switch moves was to take an unoccupied train from the coach yard to King Street Station a third of a mile away and leave it on the departure track. After that, we would kill a little time talking with coworkers and checking our company mail, as the main office was just downstairs of the station. While down there, Oscar would draw a penis on the back of a seat check card and put it in D.D.D.'s mailbox. This went on for several weeks, until a coworker told me that D.D.D. was about to confront a lady conductor, Janet, he was working with; he figured she was the culprit because she would grin whenever he shouted and stomped his feet after getting his *dick mail*. I told Oscar about it, and we agreed that enough was enough—it was time to put an end to it. For the first time in weeks, no dick mail was delivered. After spotting his train, we found D.D.D.

Oscar asked him, "Did you get any mail today?"

"No...."

"Not even any dick mail?"

D.D.D's face went red as he puffed out his chest and came up shouting at Oscar. I stood in between them for a minute as they quarreled, but they calmed down and ended up laughing about it together.

Around 1993, new licensing for locomotive engineers was being implemented by the Federal Railroad Administration. It was now law that locomotive operators had to be licensed. The license required, among other things, being physically fit and able, and having no police record. It was a big deal, and some locomotive engineers were nervous about it, though I think everyone already employed was covered under a grandfather clause—meaning that they weren't immediately affected by the law, but any new infractions of the law could result in the loss of their license. Fifteen or so years later, licensing became mandatory for train conductors, as well.

I was working the daytime passenger switch job with The Little General and Oscar one morning around six. We were sitting on the 565 switch engine, and it was just starting to get light out. The 565 switch engine we were sitting on was under a repair facility shed with a blue flag on it, and both entrances to the track were covered with derails and blue flags. When you have a blue flag on equipment, you can't move that equipment until the person that put the blue flags and derails up remove them. In later years, that was changed to someone from the same craft, or position, of the person who placed them. The idea for the derail is that if the blue flags go unnoticed while something is being worked on and a train or equipment gets moved, or a piece of equipment accidentally rolls down the track toward the workers, they would be safe, as the derails would knock the rolling objects off of the track before it could hit them.

Oscar called to have the flags removed and a mechanic came along to take down the derails and then the blue flags. Oscar was just about to throttle out of the track when all of us see a black guy who we had never seen before walking fast toward our engine—and then quickly up our stairs. The cab door was partially open, and the man stepped in, pointing his finger at Oscar.

"I need to see your engineer's license."

Without missing a beat, Oscar said, "F--- you! Who are you?"

The man, somewhat shocked by Oscar's response, took a card from his wallet, and handed it to Oscar. *Dennis Morgan, Federal Railroad Administration.*

Oscar then took his license out of his wallet. "Very well," he said pleasantly, as he handed it to him. "Here's my license."

# One-Armed Man

*One dark cold December night* in 1995, I was working a northbound train out of Portland's Union Station to Seattle's King Street Station. We stopped at the Royal Brougham Street crossovers in Seattle just short of the station. The other conductor and I hand lined us from the northward main line track to the southward main line track, then my partner walked ahead a little ways and hand lined us into a station track; he then got on the train and I stayed on the ground, while the hogger pulled the train through the crossovers into the station. I was left to line everything back and walk in.

When lining back, I saw a hobo-type man in the shadows—a trespasser, which was fairly common back in the day. Unless they were stealing, vandalizing, or threatening harm to others, or themselves? They were left alone. Toward the end of my career, however, and especially after 9/11, most every trespasser was reported.

After unloading the passengers from the train and getting ready to go home, it was reported by a freight train crew that one of the switches I lined back was not lined up correctly. The train dispatcher instructed the freight crew to line it up and proceed.

I received several calls the next couple weeks from my supervisors insinuating that it must have been me who neglected lining the switch back. I was a little irritated and told them there was a man in the shadows and it must have been him being devious. They said it had to have been me and there was going to be an investigation unless I signed a waiver admitting guilt, with *fifteen days* hanging over my head.

There was a very popular television show in the '60s called *The Fugitive*, and later, in the '90s, it was made into a big movie. The plot involves a doctor convicted of killing his wife, but he repeats over and over that he had seen a one-armed man leaving the scene of the murder. Nobody believes him until several years later when the true murderer is tracked down and the doctor is vindicated.

I started telling people that the one-armed man threw the switch I was accused of not lining back. I was very upset, but then I got an idea that somehow I was able to get my wife to go along with. She dressed up in my old work clothes, making her appear as a one-armed man, and I took a picture of her from behind in a setting that resembled the railroad. I featured the picture in a flyer I had made:

Wanted by the FBI
Trespassing on railroad property, and for questioning concerning railroad derailments and the opening of mainline switches. Missing left arm.
If you have any information about this person, please contact your local authorities.

I then posted it up everywhere in the Seattle work stations and dropped it in all employee mailboxes. I soon got a call from the trainmaster; he told me that I must show up and sign the waiver or there would be an investigation and that I'd get time on the ground. I showed up at his office and the superintendent was there also. I studied the waiver, looked over at the two of them and said, *I saw a one-armed man*, and then signed the waiver.

# Driving Cancer Patients

*My mother passed away* from lung cancer in 1992. As most would agree, that is not one of the best ways to leave this earth. Keep in mind while reading my favorite story about driving cancer patients that my mother and I shared a very similar sense of humor.

After she had passed, I became a driver for the American Cancer Society, driving patients to their chemotherapy, radiation treatments, and related exams. In the '90s, getting any form of cancer was pretty much a death sentence. As many can attest to, the survival rate today is much better. I drove about once a week for two years. I would receive instructions from a coordinator, go to a person's house, and sometimes have to help them into my car, as most were dealing with being elderly on top of their cancer ailment. We would drive to the treatment facilities and I would assist as needed with getting them into the doctor's office, then take them home when they were done. Usually, this added up to about a two-hour adventure most days.

Some of these patients became short-term friends. That may sound harsh, but the truth is that they were near the end, and I didn't have much time with them. One foot in the grave, so to speak. Because of this, I may have been the only human to ever hear some of the stories that came out of their mouths. I look back at it today and sometimes shed a tear. We have all heard the stories of the lady that nobody ever heard utter a profanity in her whole life until death was knocking on her door or a mental disease was embedding itself in one's brain. Cancer can be the cause for both.

Once a week for two years I heard stories from men and ladies that as many say, *would make a sailor blush*. I'm obligated to keep most of these stories to myself, as they were told to me in confidence when the end was fast approaching. I will, however, relate one gentleman's story, as it later turned out to be an irony of sorts.

This man had clearly lived a great life. As I drove him to and from his appointments, he talked fondly of his wife who had passed on a couple years earlier. It was ever so apparent that he loved and missed her dearly. One day, he told me that as he became older, he could no longer perform as he used to in the bedroom. His wife was not exactly happy about that. She had read about the pump, a medical procedure pioneered in the '60s and '70s, in which a device was surgically inserted that allowed a gentleman to *inflate* his manhood as needed. He went ahead and had it done and his wife was happy for a few weeks. One night, he was raring to go, but she was giving him the cold shoulder.

"If it's not the real thing, I don't want it!"

He told me a couple of other stories, but that is the one I remember most because twenty-five years later one evening, after taking the little blue pill, I crawled into bed, snuggled up to my wife, and was given the cold shoulder. When I asked her what was wrong, she did not answer. I knew exactly what was wrong, however; if it wasn't the real thing, she didn't want it!

# Hearing Loss

*Railroad workers brought* a class action suit against the railroad owners for hearing loss in the late-'80s, and any worker that had been around for a few years was entitled to a settlement—as almost every worker had some degree of hearing loss. I went to an audiologist and had a few hearing tests done, and he determined that I had some "very minimum" high-range hearing loss in my left ear. I put in a claim with the railroad and soon after was contacted by a railroad claims agent to come in to discuss my compensation. I sat across from the claims agent in his office as he studied the results of my hearing test.

"I don't think you have enough hearing loss to warrant any monetary compensation."

I cupped my left hand to my left ear, leaned forward a little and said, "Huh?"

He studied me for a few seconds. "…Okay. Fifteen hundred dollars."

Many workers received upwards of ten thousand dollars in compensation. I personally knew many who deserved compensation, and many who did not. I heard about people training themselves to have selective hearing for the tests, and a few tricks that others used to temporarily deafen themselves. One guy told me that he cleaned his ears out with a Q-tip as well as he could. Then he took a bath and soaked his head under the water for a long while and had his hearing test done while his eardrums were still wet, simulating severe hearing loss and worming him a large monetary compensation.

I could tell you stories of hearsay and speculation pertaining to hearing loss settlements, and there would be a lot of truth to it, but I have one story where the person bragged about worming a large settlement for hearing loss that I have no doubt is absolutely true.

Railroads regularly run load tests on their locomotives. An electrician hooks instruments up to the control components and electrical panels of the locomotive and revs the motor to notch 8 (full throttle), keeping it at the maximum position for as much as ten minutes while reading their instruments to determine if there are any issues that need addressing or parts that need to be replaced or repaired. While these locomotives are in maximum throttle position, they are insanely loud, and the employees performing these tests are required to wear earplugs. The smart ones wear the heavy-duty, over-ear hearing protection.

I know a guy who made an appointment for his hearing test half a mile away from where they performed these load tests. They would perform several of these load tests in the morning hours; one morning he went through the back door of an engine compartment during one of these load tests wearing no hearing protection. When his ears started hurting, he got into his car and drove to the hearing doctor. Just thirty minutes after deafening himself, he had his hearing tested. He settled for ten thousand dollars—a fair amount of dough in 1991.

# Wreck Lawyer Dinner

*I was on a passenger switch job* in the '90s pushing our train toward the station. The idea was to park the train at the station platform for the outbound crew to get passengers aboard before leaving town. We called this "spotting up" an outbound train. We were shoving along with one guy on the end, while the engineer and I manned the switch engine.

The man on the point, Kenny, alerted us on his portable radio of a red signal ahead, and we stopped just short of the King Street tunnel on the northbound track. Something down the line was causing a bit of congestion. While waiting for a more favorable signal, I was shocked to hear a loud whistle coming from directly behind us. The engineer, Jack, and I looked back just in time to see another train coming at us from where we just were. I had just enough time before impact to dive to the metal floor of our engine. The incoming train crashed into ours at about 13 mph, derailing their engine as well as ours. Luckily, there were no serious injuries.

The other crew had gone past a restricting signal with a lunar aspect—in short, requiring them to beware of danger ahead. My engineer and I were sent to the hospital. I was off for three days due to skinning and bruising one of my knees when I dove for cover on the steel floor; I was also being observed for possible whiplash from the impact. The engineer was off for a little longer, as the impact managed to hurt his pelvis.

After returning to work, someone had dropped a news article in my company mailbox about an injury arbitration settlement. In this scenario, a railroad worker had been involved in a near-miss collision, something like what I was just involved in, except the trains had stopped short. No impact. The incident had frightened one of the railroad workers so badly that he couldn't work a shift without freaking out. On top of that, he was having constant nightmares about train wrecks. As a result, the shaken worker won a court battle against the railroad and received a cash settlement and a disability pension. A few days later, I received a phone call from a lawyer. He invited me to Andy's Diner, an old railroad dining car restaurant for dinner. He wanted to discuss the wreck. *Why not?*, I thought.

During dinner, the lawyer and his consultant took turns grilling me about any sort of ailments I may had been suffering as a result of the collision. If I were experiencing any nightmares, anxiety, or apprehension about working they might be able to help me. Of course, they had the right doctor to see. They told me that if I continued to work as normal, but took off one day every month or so because I wasn't feeling up to it due to some residual effect of the wreck, and stretched that out two more years until I had twenty years under my belt, then they could get me a cash settlement and a disability pension.

Not my cup of tea. I worked twenty-plus more years and retired.

# Switch Humper

*In the '90s*, in Seattle for a couple years my job was the night passenger switch foreman with the #565 switch engine. Around this time, we were changing all of the mainline switch locks that had been around since at least 1977. The new locks had a little trick to them; when you pushed the key in you gave it a turn to open it, the lock would trap your key until you reversed the motion. With the new lock, you could no longer get your key back out unless you reversed the motion and locked the lock in the locking position. It had always been a rule that after unlocking a lock and hand lining a main line switch for the route of a train movement, one was to lock the lock into the locking position in the name of safety—the idea being to avert any accidental or malicious hand lining while a train movement was passing over the switch. That leads to a derailment, and some very deadly ones are recorded in history. The new lock was a little finicky, but you'd get the hang of it after a while.

One night, the crew desk called a man on his day off to work as my assistant conductor. Normally, he worked the Empire Builder route to Spokane. He had a lot of seniority, being off the old Milwaukee Road Railroad, but no experience with the new lock and key. We were doing our work using the northbound mainline as a lead at the coach yard over Royal Brougham Street when "Technical Tim," the train dispatcher, called and asked us to get in the clear, as he had a northbound train short on time coming in. We were now *lite engine*, and backed in the clear of the switch points, waiting for the Milwaukee guy to line the switch back. He lined it back without a problem, but was having trouble locking up the new lock. He was one of those guys that keeps all of his keys on a chain attached to his belt. This was a high stand switch, and he was a shorter guy with an even shorter key chain, so he was up on his tippy-toes, just barely able to reach the lock.

The Milwaukee guy was still struggling to get the lock figured out when Technical Tim called and asked if we were in the clear.

"As soon as this guy gets done humping the switch!" I said back.

At that moment he had it locked and looked up and glared at me as he hopped aboard. From then on out, "The Switch Humper" was his nickname.

# Exchange Students

*In the day*, my wife was one of the hardest workers ever, raising our five kids while working several part-time jobs on-and-off through the years. As if that weren't enough, she did her fair share of volunteer work for our church. These days, she is still a hard worker—caring for her challenging, ailing 97-year-old mother who lives with us pretty much 24/7; she still manages to do volunteer work at the bingo hall.

Okay, back to the day...one day she decided with my support to take on foreign exchange students in the late-'90s, reasoning the experience for our family of learning the culture of a different country would be positive–while being compensated a little. We provided lodging and a family atmosphere for three different Japanese college girls at three different intervals—all of a very positive experience, the last being the best.

Her name was Yumi, a very pleasant, cheerful young lady, and always asking questions about American customs, formalities, and the quirks of our society...as the Clinton scandal was constantly in the news. I told her one day that any questions you have of the good things of our society you should ask my wife; any questions of the not-so-good things of our society, you can ask me. She indicated that she understood perfectly, and our relationship grew blossoming into one like no other.

Yumi got her first taste of chocolate milk and really liked it. She asked my wife, "Where chocolate milk come from?"
My wife asked her, "Have you ever seen a field of cows?"
"Yes."
"Well, there are cows that are white, cows that are white

and black, and cows that are just black; that is where chocolate milk comes from."

As Yumi became excited and amazed, my wife told her she was joking.

She came home from school one day and asked me, "Ah, what does *f*--- mean?"

I took my right index finger and cupped my left hand in a fist. I inserted my finger into my fist and said, "F---".

"Ahhhhh...."

Then we changed the subject.

Yes, she was good family while with us.

One day after living with us a few months, she asked me for a ride to another college across town for some sort of activity and I decided to tell her a politically incorrect, off-color joke. First, I set her up a little by asking her, did rich Japanese men have tattoos of dragons on their chest?

She said she had heard that, however had not ever met one, and that those men were rumored to be of a mafia-type mentality and culture.

Then told her I was going to tell her a naughty joke, to which she agreed.

I said, shortly after World War II, when American troops were occupying Japan, there was a Japanese father with three daughters, and he asked the oldest: what kind of man are you hoping to marry? She said a rich Japanese man with one dragon on his chest.

Very good, he says, then he asked the next oldest, and she answered: a handsome Japanese man with one dragon on his chest.

Very good he say's, then he asked the youngest daughter: what kind of man are you hoping to marry? She answered: a U.S. serviceman with one dragon on the ground!

As the car went silent for a minute, I was thinking I may have said too much.

But suddenly, she said, "Well?"

"Well what?" I said.

"What did the father say?"

I let it go and dropped her off at the college.

A couple weeks later, while driving her somewhere else, she said, "My friends say it is impossible."

"What's impossible?"

"I ask all my friends. They say, *one dragon on the ground? Impossible!*"

I miss that girl; our whole family does. One experience that comes to mind while she lived with us was my father-in-law would come visit often and one day he and Yumi were sitting in the living room—visiting, smiling, having a nice time. And I thought, *here is a guy who was fighting her country during World War II.* For a few minutes, it seemed as if that horrendous war had never happened.

# D.D.D.

*Around 1994*, I was the assistant conductor for "Conductor Big Boy," and our engineer was Dare Devil Dave. We worked between Seattle and Portland, spending three nights in Portland away from our home terminal.

Dare Devil Dave had been terminated a few times in his twenty-five-year career—all incidents I was not directly involved in. I had firsthand knowledge of such, however, like when he ran a red signal at M.P. 111 to name just one instance. Conductor Big Boy and I had a full-time job keeping him and us out of trouble. Triple D was as good of an engineer as there was when he wanted to be–the problem being there were many times when he didn't want to be.

One day, coming north, a Federal Railroad Administration (F.R.A.) inspector approached us while doing our Vancouver, Washington station stop. Standing on the platform, he announced that he had permission to ride the locomotive with D.D.D.; he added that our train master, Ed Q., had cleared it. Big Boy walked him up to the locomotive and D.D.D. welcomed him aboard—at least we thought he did. We finished our station work and hi-balled northbound to Centralia, where the inspector was due to get off and return to Vancouver on a southbound train. When the inspector got off and we rolled by, he did not look happy. In Seattle, before we went home, D.D.D. told us that he and the inspector had a disagreement because according to the rule when two persons are in the cab, the engineer is supposed to call out the signal aspect and the other person in the cab is to repeat it, or vice versa. Well, D.D.D. was doing neither, and the inspector asked him, *why not?* D.D.D.

said, *as far as I am concerned, I am usually alone up here and that's how I feel today.*

The next day, before leaving Seattle's King Street Station, we had the passengers loaded and no engineer—as the trainmaster had him in the office chewing his butt for his behavior the day before with the F.R.A. inspector. Finally, he came out—not in a good mood—and we departed southbound. We got stopped at Auburn, Washington and copied a train order over the radio from the train dispatcher to cross over at the hand throws and run against the current of traffic in yard limits from north yard limits Auburn to south yard limits Auburn, and then cross back over at Sumner. There was a switch tender there who hand lined us from the southward to the northward main track; we crossed over going the maximum speed, in this situation 20 mph. D.D.D. throttled up to well over that speed and Big Boy and I just looked at each other in disbelief as we crossed back over to the southbound at the crossovers in Sumner with the help of a switch tender and then on to Portland.

The next day, we worked home to Seattle and upon arrival, D.D.D. was pulled out of service pending an investigation. The train master, "Air-Cooled Tommy," approached Big Boy and wanted a statement of the facts pertaining to the infraction of speeding. Big Boy wrote a statement all right; it said that the train masters knew the engineer in question was speeding everywhere just by looking at his running times from point a to point b—all documented on several years of delay reports. Tommy threw that statement away and after the investigation was held, D.D.D. was fired. Six months later, he was back to work after arbitration between the company and the engineers union; the arbitrator ruled in favor of D.D.D., stating that if the infraction was so serious, you would think they would have at least invited the conductor to the investigation.

I told Conductor Big boy twenty-three years later that his statement the company refused to accept resulted in him not being invited to the investigation, and that in turn resulted in D.D.D getting his job back.

# Fake Federal Railroad
# Authority Inspector

*As the day passenger* yard conductor on the #565 switch engine job at the coach yard in Seattle, my assistant conductor was the Switch Humper and my locomotive engineer, "Hand Brake Henry. One morning, we had a foamer, "Dr. Death," in the crew shack with us, as we always let him ride in the switch engine and foam in exchange for military commissary products—mostly cigarettes, he being a retired twenty-year military man. Dr. Death knew more about railroading than many seasoned railroaders.

We were sitting in the shack and Dare Devil Dave came through the door—yes, the guy who was fired in the previous story.

"The union just won my job back," he said, "and in order for me to get qualified and start running on my own again the trainmaster wants me to work with you guys today."

Hand Brake Henry used to be Dare Devil Dave's brother-in-law; Triple D was married to Hand Brake Henry's sister and that marriage did not end well—neither of these men cared for each other.

"If it's okay with the F.R.A. Inspector," I said to Triple D, "you can work with us today."

I then introduced him to Dr. Death, the foamer, as *Tom Williams the F.R.A. Inspector*—as if it had been planned for months. Triple D took it hook line and sinker and Hand Brake smiled and gave me a wink.

We went out and built a morning train as Triple D ran the train and Hand Brake sat in the fireman's seat, while Dr. Death sat in the fold-out seat in the middle of the cab; the switch humper and I did the ground work. It became time for us to take the outbound train from the coach yard to King Street Station and I was riding in the cab when we stopped for a red signal at King Street station.

At that point, Dr. Death asked to see Triple D's locomotive engineer's license. "I don't have it," Triple D said. "I just got reinstated. It's in the mail, swear to god."

Dr. Death put on one of the greatest shows ever by having a fit. He pointed at Triple D and commanded, "You get out of that seat!"

Then he pointed at Hand Brake Henry. "You get in the engineer's seat!"

The two of them traded seats and when the signal turned green, we spotted the train in the station. We were all standing on the station platform listening to Dr. Death reprimand Triple D.

"I'm not sure what I'm going to do about this serious infraction. I have to talk with my superiors on this matter. I tell you what.... We already had lunch planned at Kettle's; meet us over there in thirty minutes and I will have some answers for you then. Let's hope for the best."

Then we all went to the switch shack, got in our cars, and drove to Kettle's restaurant while Dr. Death and I made a plan along the way. I took the back of a train order and wrote: *I, Triple D, do solemnly swear to abide by all railroad rules in the future, including having on person my locomotive engineer's license when operating a locomotive. I understand that I have just been screwed by a fake F.R.A. inspector. Sign here.* I gave it to Dr. Death, to his satisfaction.

We all met and made conversation while having lunch, and all the while Triple D was sweating it out.

As lunch nears the end, Dr. Death pipes up to Triple D. "I talked with my boss and he has agreed that if you sign a warning letter in acknowledgment that it will not happen again, we will let it go at that."

Triple D is all, "Sure, sure, sure."

"But first," said Dr. Death, "I noticed you didn't ding the bell before you moved the locomotive—can you remember to always do that in the future?

"Yes, yes, yes," said Triple D as he was handed the paper.

He clearly just wanted to get it over with; he didn't even read it. He started to sign the *document* when I grabbed him by his wrist. "Read what you're signing."

An instant later, he's the Triple D we always knew—jibber-jabbing and, surprisingly, admitting he got fooled a good one.

# Inaugural Run, May 24, 1995

*I was thinking* that I would write about the fatal Amtrak passenger train wreck on December 18th, 2017. That happened six months after I retired. It was on its inaugural run near DuPont, Washington where it derailed at 78 mph, resulting in three deaths and many very serious injuries. I hope those that passed and their families find peace; I hope the injured and their families find peace, as well.

After some thought, I came to the conclusion that although I knew all the employees on that train—and for many years was chairman of the Amtrak Pacific Northwest monthly safety committee meeting—that me writing a theory about that wreck would be just that...a theory. I was not there when it happened.

The National Transportation Safety Board (NTSB) concluded their investigation of the wreck, citing just about everyone who had anything to do with the planning, training, safety, and implementation of that train service leading to that deadly event to be at least partly responsible. I concur.

Many other people have studied the facts, situations, particulars, and circumstances pertaining to train crashes, most believing that even when the crews have vast experience, and they possess the highest caliper in safety awareness, for no rhyme or reason train wrecks are going to happen. I was lucky never being in a deadly one. I have several stories about trains on which I was part of the operating crew, on both freight and passenger trains, where we narrowly averted catastrophe. I was equally to blame as the other crew members, and in some cases I was at least partly at fault. I have kept silent about one up to now, an event twenty-five years ago that may have been marred with tragedy on the level of the crash at DuPont, though was averted.

There was a daily passenger train that ran from Los Angeles to Vancouver, British Columbia, Canada for many years, the *Coast Starlight* train. In 1981, the final terminal of Vancouver, Canada was changed to Seattle's King Street Station, no longer running the train north to Canada; passengers could transfer to a connecting bus. After thirteen years of ending the *Coast Starlight* at Seattle, however, interest in reviving a new train service between Seattle and Canada started up. State officials, passenger train officials, northern county officials, and a whole host of other railroad fans in favor of restoring service got it all lined up with the host railroads in the U.S. and Canada, including the U.S. customs and Canadian immigration officials. It was a big deal.

The Burlington Northern Santa Fe freight host railroad from the U.S. would oversee the implementation of the new service, with a lot of help from Amtrak passenger train officials. They had to figure out speed limits on the route, as it had been freight-only for thirteen years. They had to train and familiarize the Amtrak passenger train crews to become qualified on the route. Seattle Amtrak passenger train services had to put up bids for three new crews to work north, plus train them and the extra boards.

I won the bid to be the assistant conductor for the conductor known as The Little General, and our locomotive engineer being Dare Devil Dave, who had just recently returned from being fired for six months. We trained with the new Talgo train equipment from Spain, the train being named *The Mount Baker* after the snow-capped mountain in the Cascade Mountains that was often viewed along the route. The equipment was the most modern equipment of the time any of us had ever seen; it took extra training to learn the safety features and quirks, while getting used to the Spanish technicians who spoke broken English. They were training us and were also assigned to the train to keep the power generator running in the power car, among other things. We had a qualified locomotive engineer road foreman from the Burlington Northern Santa Fe host freight railroad and one from the Amtrak passenger train corporation in charge of the operations training.

Every day for five or six weeks there was training on the route between Everett and Blaine, Washington. Although I do not recall physical training in Canada, we had classes on Canadian rules and became rules qualified, though not fully qualified until making a trip with a crew that was qualified before officially being qualified—the training was a little bit of a cluster, but was done well.

The day came for the inauguration run, operated by my crew along with a pilot freight crew qualified on the route, including Canada. In the body of the train with me and The Little General were two freight train personnel called *pilots,* meaning they would be backing us up in our duties. One being a conductor and the other a brakemen, they were qualified on the whole route, including Canada and Canadian rules. On the locomotive was Amtrak passenger train locomotive engineer Triple D, an Amtrak passenger train assistant engineer off the extra board, our locomotive engineer qualified road foreman train master, and a Burlington Northern Santa Fe pilot freight train locomotive engineer qualified on all the route and rules. We were an operations crew of eight on the train, and the Burlington Northern Santa Fe road foreman was in his automobile shadowing the train with his portable radio.

The inauguration run was not for the general public—it was for all the people who had been instrumental in reviving the passenger train service and their special guests, many of them noteworthy politicians, local celebrities, and news people who are going to get news now that they missed then. The passengers were boarded at King Street Station and we departed after formalities and speeches on to Edmonds, Washington for a station stop. There were more speeches while a small band played music. We then made our way toward

Everett, Washington and a track side detector scanned our train near Mukilteo, Washington, reporting an integrity failure. The Little General insisted we stop the train and communicate to the train dispatcher the integrity failure, as rules pertaining to the report of an integrity failure were new and had been revised more than once; when in doubt, take the safe course.

We stopped the train and the dispatcher agreed it was the safe course. Two of us went outside walking and inspecting the train and after observing nothing out of the ordinary we continued our journey. At Everett, there were more speeches and formalities, then on to Mount Vernon, Washington. At Mount Vernon, our train stopped at the station to the wildest celebration yet: there were twenty-five or thirty adults dressed up like the wild west, including several women dressed as ladies of the night or saloon ladies, all while a band played between formalities and speeches. We were stopped just short of the Skagit River bridge spanning the Skagit River, in between track side signals in the middle of the limits of a *Form Y* work bulletin work area with men and equipment working on or near the tracks. All the while, women were on the station platform enticing or teasing us while acting horny and suggestive.

After about twenty minutes, it was time to depart, so we got everyone back on the train and closed up the doors. The engine crew asked the foreman in charge of the work crew if it was okay to continue through his limits, to which he said: *okay to do so, watching out for men and equipment working, whistling as you see them, while dinging your bell*, Triple D repeated the instructions and got an okay on the repeat.

Triple D said over the radio to The Little General, "You ready?"

"Okay to go, delayed in the block, don't forget the 20 after the 10."

The Little General's informal, but important instructions meant that since we were stopped at the station being delayed, the favorable green signal indication we came in on indicating favorable conditions ahead became moot and conditions ahead could now possibly not be favorable, and to proceed prepared to stop at the next signal; also directly in front of us was a 10 mph slow order on the bridge, followed by a 20 mph slow order after the bridge that was nearly two miles long all the way through the city of Burlington, Washington, with multiple street crossings. We departed and went 10 mph on the bridge and the engine crew called out a clear signal ahead—all was good. When we got off the bridge, we went from 10 mph to 20 mph and suddenly we were climbing upwards of 50 mph.

The Little General jumped up out of his seat. "We're supposed to be doing 20 mph! *WTF?*"

At that moment, we heard the voice of a very alarmed man on the portable radio: *Amtrak, did you guys get that 20 mph slow order?*

We slowed back down to 20 mph and continued through Burlington onto Bellingham, Washington, our next stop, where everything was *hush hush* as the locomotive Amtrak road foreman trainmaster fell on the sword and volunteered himself to be taken out of service for the speeding violation. I was told later that when coming off the bridge at 10 mph, and with a train order to go no faster than 20 mph through town, the four on the locomotive saw the new dual speed limit sign (though not yet in effect) saying 79 mph for passenger, 50 mph for freight, that had been covered up and heavily duct-taped with a black plastic bag during training. They had looked at the train master, who gave the okay to do 79, while all four of them forgot about the mandatory 20 mph speed restriction train order.

Now, it was admirable of the trainmaster to take the fall; however, had it been done according to rules, they could have taken all eight of us operations personnel out of service and held the train two or three hours until they could get a qualified crew from somewhere else to replace us—at least an engineer and conductor; meanwhile, they could have pulled us out of service and transported us somewhere to be pee-tested. Not sure how the big-wig passengers would have been accommodated, however I am sure it would not have been *hush hush.*

Yes, a voice over the airwaves asking, *did you guys get that 20 mph slow order?* I am positive that man averted a potential catastrophe, as I was told that the gates at the crossings those two miles were still set to activate for a train traveling at 20 mph, and there would be no warning for vehicles or pedestrians should a train being doing 79 mph. I also suspect that the workers had been realigning and adjusting the tracks in that two-mile stretch, preparing it for the new higher speed limits, and it may have been only stabilized for a 20 mph train.

When we arrived at Vancouver, B.C. as planned, the train was terminated—all passengers having limos and various other transportation back to the U.S. The seven of us were reprimanded and then deadheaded back to Seattle in a van. Triple D was yapping away as is if he had not a care in the world—as the rest of us sweated it out for a couple weeks....

A few years later, on New Year's Eve, a passenger train out of Canada traveling south ran a red signal and missed a head-on collision by eight seconds with lite power freight locomotives in Seattle at mile post junction number 4; it was almost a reenactment of the infamous Super Bowl Sunday wreck of 1987, except this time it was the passenger train that ran the red signal.

...It was the year 1969, when the first man landed on the moon, the New York Mets won the World Series, and Dave hired out on the Great Northern Railroad as a locomotive engineer. Dave earned some nicknames during his career. He was known as: "Super Dave," "Nine Lives Dave," and most commonly, "Dare Devil Dave." As I said, when he wanted to be, Dave was as good as any hoghead to ever run a locomotive. Many times during his career, Dave received extra time off from railroad duties, though each time, he managed to make it back to the throttle—a record equal to no other.

At the turn of the century, Dave had a spiritual awakening and became that great locomotive engineer we all knew he could be full-time, until 2005 when throat cancer forced his early retirement. I would drive up to Everett and visit him at his home as he was going though treatments and tell him he was a miracle—*anyone else would be dead by now*. He told me a couple years later that the first time I said that, he was not amused; however, he later appreciated it.

Railroaders have been known to tell tall tales, and Dave was no exception. He had a slight limp, and when questioned about it, he would snap that he got it while in the navy on a ship in Vietnam while taking cover during a surprise attack. Dave beat cancer, but succumbed to death from heart failure after the battle. At his funeral, the U.S. Navy surprised us when they showed up and performed a 21-gun salute in his honor.

*I got a call just the other day--da dah da dah-from the crew assignments in p.a.--- da dah da dah----they say you have a new engineer----da dah da dah---I say who might that be?---da dah da dah-- we express sympathy dah da dah-- you have Triple D!---da dah da dah-you have dare devil Dave dah da dah  he's been known to sin da dah da dah --be ready to give up your specimen--dah da dah-mile post 111 dah da dah mile post number 4 da dah da dah he is lucky to have a job anymore--da dah da dah-wah wah dah da dah called up my union man dah da dah say Mr. Flanigan da dah da dah ---you got to double up my bonehead--da dah da dah--I got dare devil Dave on my job----da dah da dah---wah da dah da dah wah!------I got a call a few years later one day dah   da   dah my good friend Dave had passed away-------I got the   dare   devil   Dave   blues   da dah ---da dah........da dahhhhhhhhhhhhhhhhhh.*

# Wabash Cannonball

*One day, our passenger train* departed the Olympia Station stop headed southbound for Portland. I was the conductor in the body of the train. Our next station stop was in Centralia, Washington. About ten minutes out of Olympia, we were doing 79 miles per hour on main track two, getting close to the Wabash junction.

At the Wabash junction, there was a chance that we would cross over from the left to the right from main track two to main track one at 35 mph and travel another two miles before stopping in Centralia. For station work concerning passengers and baggage, main track one was a whole lot better than main track two, as it was next to the station, which eliminated the risk of people having to walk over tracks.

Back to the train...we're doing 79 mph on main track two and, as far as I could tell, we were going to go straight down main track two at Wabash because we were not slowing down. Suddenly, the train went into emergency braking and we hit the Wabash crossover at about 70 mph, twice as fast as we were supposed to.

It felt and sounded like we went off the tracks—and we were stopped on the ground. Scary as hell! I was on the rear of the train high in the rear of the coach by the back door. When we crossed over, the violent movement snapped the lock on the door and it slid open. I shoved it shut and hurried downstairs. Still shaken from the sudden stop, I jumped to the ground and jogged toward the engine, observing the wheels of the train. I was really surprised to see that we were still on the rail. I climbed up onto the locomotive, and the engineer was clearly in mild shock.

He said in a very worried tone, "Anybody hurt?"

"I am not sure," I said, "I hope not."

"...I thought I had a clear signal that we were going straight," he explained sheepishly. "I plugged it when I saw that we were gonna cross over.... What are we gonna do?"

"Tell the dispatcher, if he calls, you had a near miss." I told him. "You ready? Let's go!"

"Okay."

I climbed back down from the locomotive and got on the lower level snack bar car, the second car back, and gave the hoghead a highball hand signal; we then continued down the track. The bartender was making body motions like his neck and back were hurt.

"Knock it off, Don!" I told him.

I got on the P.A.: "Ladies and gentlemen, boys and girls, the engineer put the train into emergency braking to avoid running over a dog. I had a little talk with him, and he won't be doing that again."

After a few weeks, when the engineer had calmed down and was back to his normal self—and we hadn't been caught and fired—whenever we went through the Nelson Bennett mile-long tunnel near Tacoma, I would get on my portable radio with my harmonica and play "Wabash Cannonball," reminiscing of the time that we were...the cannonball.

# Save the Dog

*I was working as conductor* on an Amtrak passenger train in 2003. The hoghead I was working with had an early-1970s seniority date. We were eastbound along the Puget Sound waterway between Seattle and Everett doing track speed at 60 mph when the train came to a very quick stop—unlike a smooth station stop or a rough emergency stop.

I was alarmed, and got on my portable radio to the hogger. "What happened?"

"Just ran over and killed a guy."

I hit the ground and sure enough, the person was deceased. While waiting for authorities, I climbed up into the locomotive and had a talk with the hogger.

"Why didn't you dump the air brakes into emergency?"

"Wouldn't have mattered," he said.

I was stunned and held my breath while the investigation was being done, thinking, *when they figure out he only set 20 lbs. of air, even if it would not have mattered, he would still be in big trouble—and I might be as well, for not ratting him in.* The police, medics, BNSF official, and coroner arrived, did an investigation, and after a couple hours released our train and we continued our journey to Bellingham.

A few weeks later, I was with the same hoghead, and we were doing 79 mph just north of Burlington, Washington when the train went into emergency braking.

I was thinking the worst. I was on the radio while the train was sliding to a stop. "What happened?"

"We almost hit a dog."

A couple nights later in Bellingham, we were having dinner and I looked him in the eye. "Let me get this straight... you don't dump the air for a human being, but you do for a dog. Why is that?"

"Humans know better."

Again I was stunned, and disheartened, to say the least. I was gonna go to the grave with this story...maybe I should have.

# Almost Run Over

*When working on* the Burlington Northern Railroad, I performed a lot of dangerous work as a switchman, brakeman, and conductor. Going in between railroad cars, locomotives, and coupling air hoses, hoping the equipment doesn't move. Riding the sides of boxcars into dark industry tracks and nearly getting scraped off by close clearance buildings, fences, machinery, and box cars on adjacent tracks.

I had my share of cuts, bruises, and scares getting on and off moving trains at high rates of speed in rainy, dark conditions. And there were many times while walking around the ends of cars that were not supposed to move...that did.

Yes, I had my fair share of close calls working freight eleven years, nine of those before random drug and alcohol testing began, when there were known to be a few of the operating craft toxic. When I went to passenger service in 1988, I thought it would be a little safer; not exactly true, as I came to realize. During the twenty-nine years in passenger service, I had three locomotive engineers move the train when not instructed to, coming fairly close to running me over. I say, *fairly close*, because one of the rules I followed without fail was G.C.O.R. Rule. In part, employees must expect the movement of trains, engines, cars, or other movable equipment at any time, on any track and in either direction. The three incidents I am about to relate to you seem to come under the *no-rhyme-or-reason* category, which means to me there were many possible reasons to pick from and we will never absolutely know what happened. To me, it appeared that none of the people involved were high; it was more the combination of complacency, being in a hurry, and plain ignorance being the main culprits—myself being an equally contributing factor.

I was on a switch engine job up in Seattle in about 1990 when the former Great Northern tall, lanky rogue engineer and I walked up to the roundhouse to get the switch engine. When we got to the locomotive 565 switch engine, we both climbed into the cab and he started looking for the automatic brake valve handle and adjusting his seat. I told him that I would be on the point in a minute and went out the fireman's door and proceeded down the running board on the side the engineer could not see, as there was no door to the running boards on his side.

When I got to the end, I did not help matters when I got off on his blind side and stepped into the middle of the track to open the knuckle on the front and slide the drawbar to the middle of the engine to prepare for our first coupling. When I did, the engine started forward and still being young, I jumped into the clear, out the blind side, and climbed up the stairs. I walked across the nose of the engine into view of the engineer and we continued toward the work.

The engineer never had a clue as to what nearly happened, and when we went to coffee, I told him. He just muttered that I *should have known better*, displaying no regret. Thinking about that incident now, many years later, I believe we were both at fault—him for moving the locomotive without receiving verbal instruction or a hand signal, and not dinging the bell before movement; and I was at fault for not telling him I was going to be in the foul, adjusting the drawbar and opening the knuckle.

Had he run over and killed me and the whole truth revealed exactly how it happened? The engineer would have been fired, and as for me, most people would have said: *he was a nice guy, but he should have known better.*

In about 1995 at Seattle, I was working a yard job switching passenger trains out. When they were ready for passengers, we would take them to the station about one-third of a mile away, which in this case meant the train was backed up the main line with me riding high in the rear coach directing the movement by communicating on portable radio to the engineer, a former Great Northern Railroad switchman known for bending a few rules.

While coming up on the King Street tunnel, I said on the radio, *20 cars to a red signal, and then 10 cars, 5 cars, that will do...stop.* Each time, the engineer would acknowledge with clicks of the radio handset.

When stopped at the red signal at the King Street tunnel across from King Street Station, I decided to step off the train. After stepping down, I saw a station worker and stepped in front of my train, looked both ways before crossing the other main track, and started visiting while keeping an eye on the signal.

After a couple minutes visiting, the signal went yellow and I said, *gotta go*, and just as I was walking across the tracks in front of my train to re-board—it started moving. I came fairly close to being run over and I climbed on the rolling train at the lower vestibule where I had gotten off as it was moving and rushed topside up to the position I should have never left.

This was a case of an overzealous engineer who had watched the signal turn more favorable and a yard conductor communication glitch as the conductor—me—should never have left his position without telling the engineer. However, the engineer should not have moved the train.

I never told him he could have run me over, but someone is going to tell him now. Had I been run over and the whole truth revealed? The engineer would have been fired and what most everybody would have said about me: *nice guy, but he should have known better.*

Around 2005, when working a Seattle to Bellingham, Washington passenger run, the three-person crew that I was on had a regular routine twice a week for a few years. The train would come in from Portland and I would hand line it into stub track King Street 4 or 5 and line behind; the Portland crew would go to the hotel for rest, and cleaners would clean the train while commissary took care of the food and beverage.

When it was all ready to go, we would back it out on to the southward main track and pull it forward into King Street track tunnel #3. The reason we did this was that it was much easier to load the passengers on 3 track since it was right out the front door of the station, versus the back door; plus, when departure time came there was no backing out of a stub track, as tunnel track #3 was signal indication straight ahead eastbound. The reason we did not land our inbound into tunnel track #3 to begin with was because the Empire Builder train #8 was there preparing for its departure.

I was told by several station employees that they greatly appreciated the extra effort; my crew, however, was the only crew that made that move. The other crews received passengers and left from the stub track.

One day, I was working short without an assistant conductor and when getting everything lined up for backing out of the stub track—things played out a little differently. Usually, I would get it all lined up, including the tunnel track #3 switch, and then get on the rear and request for the backup move on my portable radio. This time, I got her lined up and was about three car-lengths from the rear of the train double checking the route, switch points, derails, and making sure everyone was in the clear when the train started backing up without being instructed to. Rather than panic, I could see the route was clear, as it was protected by fences and not a person or train within a quarter mile as the rear went by me.

I said on the radio: *looking good, 10 long ones to go, 5 now, stop when you get over the switch.* When I got the switch lined up, I had him pull into tunnel track #3, lined back, and then walked up and climbed onto the locomotive to have a talk with the hoghead.

He was already deep into a crossword puzzle.

"I never gave you a backup to come out of the stub track."

"Huh? I could have sworn I heard one."

# Bible Proverbs

*Had I read the Bible* at age eleven and understood it, rather than the dictionary (as I did), I am pretty certain life would have played out differently for me. I would have managed to stay out of reform school and probably could have avoided abusive drinking and drugging. There is a bit of a Catch-22 here, because the rough road that I traveled down led me to my wife and the mother of our five children, all of whom I love dearly.

Very early in my sobriety, I was at a meeting when an older man made the statement, "If you take a drunk horse thief and sober him up, what do you get?" Answering himself, he said, "A sober horse thief." And he gave me a hard stare.

About a year into sobriety, a preacher was giving me a ride home from a meeting. During our conversation, he said to me, "I think you've got the not drinking and drugging thing down; I don't think you're ever going to drink or drug again."

I started patting myself on the back, but he followed that with, "But you have other problems, boy. The Devil can't get you to drink and drug anymore, so he's working overtime with the seven deadly sins."

"What?" I asked, not sure what he was implying. I was sober, and on top of the world.

"Yeah," he continued, "The Devil is making you indulge in lust, anger, greed, sloth, gluttony, envy, and pride."

I knew and somewhat understood some of those sins, but of the last two, I hadn't a clue. The preacher dropped me off at home and I never saw him again in person. I am pretty sure he has a television show now.

In 1998, after eighteen years sobriety, sixteen years of marriage and twenty-one years on the railroad, I was having marriage and job problems, owing to my *sober horse thief* behavior. At that time, I took a job that worked Sundays—which took me away from the regular 12-step meeting I had been attending for five years; I did not replace it with another one for seven weeks, until the quality of my sobriety nearly resulted in me being fired. Yes, there are a lot of reasons to not attend meetings—but no good ones.

My friends Mark and Jim suggested that I try reading the Bible. I read the *New Testament* of the Bible, but most of it came across to me as a fairy tale. I understood what Jesus was all about, but knew nobody that resembled him for more than a minute at a time. Then I read the *Old Testament*. When I read passages from "Proverbs," I learned lessons, such as, *it is better to sleep with a woman at the house of ill repute than with a wanton woman.* I had a spiritual revelation: I was a sober horse thief, and the Devil was working overtime. I read verses from Proverbs every day and soon learned that I was addicted to cheap thrills. Drinking and drugging were only a symptom of my disease, and my true affliction was the separation of my will from that of God.

I changed jobs back to Sundays off and started attending meetings again, getting back on the right track.

# Pin Up Smoking Car

*Many years before the invention* of the cell phone, there was a device called a *beeper* that one carried while working on the railroad. They usually ran on double-A batteries, and you would clip it into your shirt pocket. They were about the size of a pack of cigarettes. I still have mine. The railroad crew dispatcher, when in need of your service, would call your home number and if there was no answer they would call the number associated with your beeper. The beeper would beep, letting you know that it was time to get to a phone and call work.

Early one day in 1978, my beeper went off. After finding a phone booth, I slipped a dime into the slot and called the crew assignments clerk. He asked me if I had a blue suit jacket, and said that he needed a brakeman for the *Coast Starlight* passenger train from Seattle to the crew change point in Portland to report for duty at King Street Station in two hours.

"Don't worry," I said. "I will be there wearing a blue suit jacket in two hours."

The dispatcher wished me luck and I hung up the phone. I called a friend of mine's dad, and he agreed to loan me a blue suit jacket. When I went to get it, he told me that it was mine to keep, and I thanked him. The jacket was light blue and not a very close match to the dark blue conductor's uniforms of the time. I gave that jacket to the Salvation Army many years later.

What I recall about that first passenger train trip (besides the eye candy) and those fifteen or so trips that followed during that era, was that it took about twenty years seniority at that time to even think about working it regularly as a trainman or in engine service. Most of the men working those regularly assigned positions back then had hired out in the steam engine days. They passed the time telling old war stories about World War II while puffing on fine tobacco products and sipping on their favorite beverage.

On that particular train in the day, there was a locomotive engineer, a locomotive fireman, a baggage man who only threw bags on and off at the various station stops from the baggage car, and a head brakeman who would do any lining of track switches associated with the train movement in the rare instances where that was needed, as well as sell tickets to passengers. That left the rear brakeman and the conductor with not a whole lot to do, as there were train attendants on every coach, porters in the sleepers, and other employees who ran the diner and lounge cars. The conductor could usually be found at one end of the lounge car that was kept private for entertaining his favorite passengers—usually of the female variety. The rear brakeman kept an eye on everything else.

Twenty years later, when I finally could hold that regularly assigned conductor position, times had changed: smoking was supposed to be prohibited on trains; and random pee testing was in effect, eliminating nearly all of the favorite beverage consumption, as well as most of the drug use. Furthermore, there was no locomotive fireman, no baggage man, and no rear brakeman. This meant that most of their responsibilities were now the conductor's; that meant having a private conductor's office area in the lounge car a challenge that only a few dared to attempt, and most deemed to be unrealistic.

As mentioned, smoking was prohibited on trains by this time; there was usually pressure from passengers to allow them to smoke, however, so some conductors would oblige them by taking them to a secluded place on the train to indulge in nicotine fits, usually in the baggage car. This soon became common knowledge to the crews and passengers, so at the beginning of every tour of duty the crew would quickly decide on where the unofficial *smoking car* was going to be.

Some conductors, like "Killer Bob" and "N.P. Bob," would use the lower-level handicap seating as an office and allowed some passengers to smoke in the baggage car under supervision. Other conductors, such as "The Greek" and myself, liked to block the rear eight seats of the rear car for a not-so-private office. Once in a while, we would escort passengers to the bag car to smoke. Sometimes, if the train was really light, we would use the whole rear coach for a private smoking car and office, complete with a sign on the door before entry that read, *appointment only.* During one trip, another conductor known as "The Pirate" and I seated twenty-two ladies in a bachelor party group with us. For years after that, we would fondly joke that we held the record for the private car.

For a while, we had a 1949 Santa Fe lounge car in our train. My conductor, "Skipper the Clipper," made the lower level of that car his private office and smoking area, complete with his portable cassette stereo with plug-in speakers strung out behind him playing Canned Heat's "On the Road Again." All the while, he and his special guests would smoke up a storm. One conductor handled the attrition of coworkers that took away all of the extra help by turning the baggage car into his private office for short stints, as he was now required to hump the baggage anyway.

In my career, stories circulated that one would dismiss as pure gossip and were thought of as being entertaining stories with little or no truth, just folklore. One of those stories that I heard in the '90s was that there was a pin-up calendar of girls posing for the different months in passenger train baggage cars. A copy of this calendar was rumored to be on the inside door of a conductor 's locker in the Portland, Oregon conductor and engineer's locker room. The owner of that locker was looked up to by many of us as a father figure. He rarely wore his conductor's hat, and was known as a safe conductor gifted in the art of multi-tasking the various duties relating to his job. But pin-up girls in the bag car? Really? Nobody had balls that big.

In 1994, after seventeen years railroading, mostly on the extra board or a switch engine and regretting none of it, I was awarded my first regular assigned passenger job as an assistant conductor working between Seattle and Portland. I would spend three nights a week in the company-provided hotel in Portland and I was assigned a locker in the Portland engineer and conductor's locker room. One evening, I arrived to the locker room to find the locker in question open with the fatherly figure conductor sitting on the bench in front of it. His train was late—normally, we did not cross paths. On the inside of his locker door was the mythical calendar, showing a pretty brunette pin-up girl in a baggage car wearing not much more than a conductor's hat.

I gazed in disbelief.

He smiled and asked, "How do you like her, my son?"

I gave him a nod of approval, suddenly realizing why he seldom wore his hat.

I could tell you a hundred stories of a similar nature, such as the lady passenger who rode every Tuesday, that day becoming known as B.J. Tuesday. Yes, I could tell you stories concerning locomotive engineers, sleeping car porters, bartenders, and other employees including train masters with their mistresses, but believe me—you are just reading the most decent ones I can divulge. Most of the other stories would be considered by most as immoral, at best, and are better left untold.

The practice of or any resemblance to a private office, private car, or smoking area on the northwest passenger trains was pretty much brought to a halt in the late-'90s after the state became more and more involved in the funding and micromanaging of the trains. As with any of the other sweeping changes that the railroad faced, some employees did not conform and were fired on *he said, she said* charges, while the rest of us managed to slip through the cracks.

After experiencing all of these situations, I can say with certainty that centuries before airplanes and the mile-high club, there were trains with tails on the rails. I am absolutely positive that somewhere those traditions still carry on today, initiated equally by both genders—or should I say in this day and age, *all* genders.

# Driving Homeless Men

*From about 1997 until 2012*, I did some volunteer work for our Lutheran church driving homeless men around. What our church did, and still does, is send a van from Des Moines, Washington to the big homeless shelter in downtown Seattle and pick up about ten homeless men in the winter months. I think the people that ran the larger shelter tried to give us the more stable and clean men if they could. There was a large showering area that was available to them and they were encouraged to clean up in order to go with us, if need be. I do not recall many men who went with us that reeked and made one's eyes water.

After picking them up, we would drive to our church about twelve miles and let our guests out into the sanctuary next to the kitchen where volunteers had been cooking them up a hot dinner. After eating, they were then given cots to sleep in overnight along with blankets and a pillow. When they woke up early the next morning, there was a deluxe breakfast being prepared by a different volunteer group from the church. After breakfast, they climbed back into the van and were taken back downtown and dropped off near the shelter to continue their homeless life.

I am not a saint, nor were any of these homeless men. Being around them always reminded me of the old proverb: "if not for the grace of God, there go I." Having said that, I got to know a couple of these homeless men and some of them made me look like an angel. One would tell me stories as if I were a priest at confession. The most interesting fact about him was that he had money, but enjoyed working the angle of being homeless and getting things free. One evening, I was driving the van and a man in the back started bitching about the food he was soon to be receiving. He wanted to see the food handling permits of the kitchen volunteers before eating anything, and if they did not have permits he was going to call the police.

"You know what I think?" I interjected. "I think we should do background checks on everyone before we let them in our van."

He was silent after that and ate like a pig once we got to the church.

Driving homeless men was a trip. One night in late 1998, while driving my homeless passengers around, I was in deep trouble in my life—in danger of losing my job for being a sober horse thief at work on the train. I do not know why, but I confided in a homeless man my situation and he asked me a few questions about what I had done.

"Are you sorry?" he asked me.

"Yes, I am."

He looked at me and said, "My name is John, and when John prays for somebody, they are forgiven. You need not worry, because I am praying for you."

That was one of the few truly spiritual experiences of my life, as I knew from that moment on that I was going to keep my job—and the sober horse thief began a significant behavioral change. I would never seriously jeopardize losing my job again. There is no other explanation: John was an angel.

# Beaver River Crossing Sign

*In 1999, I started selling* on eBay. At that time, just about anything you put on auction sold for much more than one would imagine. I bought a three-by-five-foot sheet metal sign at a second-hand store while laying over in the "beaver state" of Oregon. The sign read, *Beaver River Crossing* in large letters, and across the bottom was printed, *Department of Public Works Canada*. I was going to sell it on eBay, but changed my mind. Instead, I bought some lag bolts and mounted it on a post in the parking lot of the Seattle passenger coach yard during the transition period when most of Seattle passenger train employees were moved out of King Street Station into trailers on Holgate Street, while we waited for a new building to be erected as our headquarters.

The Beaver River Crossing sign was a favorite conversation piece of those with a sense of humor. The superintendent usually parked close to it. About a year later, one of our lady clerks, "The White Diamond," approached me and said in a concerned tone: *They're getting ready to tear everything down again and reconstruct the property. You'd better get your sign if you want it.* I unscrewed the lag bolts and took the sign home.

A short time later in 2001, right after 9/11, I took a job as a flagman in the coach yard that consisted of making sure construction workers and other contract workers did not get run over by trains while working. There were a couple of old metal sheds where I would position myself while looking out for the workers. One day, I brought the Beaver River sign to work and bolted it to one of the metal sheds that happened to be in front of a little footpath crossing for employees. Again, it became a favorite conversation piece, especially to those who remembered it from before.

Well, the yardmaster in charge of the passenger trains for Seattle switching operations did not share the same sense of humor that a lot of us did. To give you an idea what she was like, one day while walking by her office I stopped by for a second to say "Hi" and noticed that she had a new hairdo.

I can't believe what came out of my mouth, but I said, "Nice hair! You look just like David Bowie."

As soon as I said it, I was thinking, *Thirty days discipline, no pay, if I'm lucky.*

I could see her wheels turning, but to my surprise she seemed flattered. "You think so?"

I said, "Yes," and got the hell out of there.

Now, back to Beaver River Crossing.... The yardmaster would call the switch crew on the radio and ask where they were with the switch engine, and they would answer with their position relative to the Beaver River Crossing, such as: *we are just south (or north) of Beaver River Crossing.* A couple weeks later, I went to work one day, and my sign was there in the morning but gone in the afternoon. I asked one of the lady switchmen (nicknamed "The Blonde Bombshell") if she knew what happened with my sign. Well, we put two and two together and figured the yardmaster must have gotten rid of it.

I was going to let it go, but the Bombshell said, "You can't let her get away with that! You've got to get it back!"

So, after work, I went to the yardmaster's office and asked her if she knew what had happened to my sign.

She said, "No."

I started to leave. Then, she said, "What sign?"

"Look," I said, "if you tell me where it is, you won't ever have to look at it again."

"Third dumpster down on pit track 7."

So I dug my sign out of the dumpster and took it home.

A short while later, I was on a Seattle to Bellingham, Washington run. We would go up in the evening, discharge the passengers at the Fairhaven station in South Bellingham, and then take our empty train a mile or so north to milepost 96.2 (which is 269 backwards) and yard the train in the Pine Street Burlington Northern yard facility overnight. Near the main line at the Pine Street yard switch was a large old, dilapidated warehouse that had seen better days. It sat between the tracks and the saltwater waterway of Bellingham Bay and transients were known to inhabit the property.

I brought the Beaver River sign up and it was resurrected in all its glory on the outside wall of the warehouse, becoming a mainline fixture for the next several years. I was home one evening when a co-worker called with the news: the warehouse had burned down. The next night, when we put the train away at Pine Street, there in the smoldering rubble, the only thing to have survived, was that sign. Somehow, that wall must have been the last one to collapse. The sign was still intact, unblemished on top of the smoldering rubble.

The area was cyclone-fenced off and guarded by firemen. I saw two firemen walking in the rubble poking around.

I said excitedly, "Hey, that's my sign! Can you make sure I get it back? You can leave it up here by this switch," as I pointed to it, "and I will get it in the morning."

Well, they pretty much looked at me like I was crazy. It was gone the next morning and I never saw it again. I am almost positive that the Beaver River Crossing sign is mounted somewhere on some fireman's property.

# Union Man

*My father was a union man* thirty-three years as a laborer at the Bethlehem Steel Mill in Seattle, and myself, forty years on the railroad. If not for the union a few times, I would have never survived forty years; that is a well-known fact that I am not exactly proud of, although I am grateful.

After many years of the union saving my job and getting me set straight, it became time for me to give back, and that my friend can be a difficult, challenging job. I was encouraged by many co-workers and as a result held a union position the last fifteen years of my career, first by being voted in as the Northwest Safety Committee Chairman in 2002 for Northwest Passenger Trains, followed by an appointment as a state legislative representative for eighty passenger train conductors and a few locomotive engineers, then as a local griever for forty passenger train conductors, followed by president for about one hundred passenger train conductors and seven locomotive engineers (one by the handle of "Land Cock").

My tenure as the griever was the most challenging, representing members at investigation hearings charged for derailments, rules infractions, and sexual harassment. I feel obligated to keep most of the details of those investigation hearings from being told; however, I will gladly tell you about them over a cup of coffee. Here is the deal: whenever someone would start to bad-mouth the conductor's union, I would first tell them the short version of the career-saves involving me, then go on to tell them that as far as I know, union conductors made far more in wages and benefits than non-union conductors in the U.S.A. Then I would remind them that on nearly all the railroads outside the U.S.A., there is no such thing as a train conductor; they do have employees with different titles, such as *train manager* or *train coordinator,* who are required to do all the work that American conductors do, plus a lot more—and are compensated a lot less.

# El Dicko

*Religious and fraternal* organizations, as well as other societies, are mostly respected—but all have some bad apples. Railroad unions are no exception. Some of those apples are rotten to the core, being very despicable, such as a low-life pedophiles; much more common, however, are the thieves.

Over the course of my career, I heard of many crooked union officials that scammed and embezzled union member funds. We had a union boss in the '90s whom I met at a union meeting once in the Seattle King Street Station. I saw his picture in union newsletters many times. He appeared to indulge too much in fine foods, drove fancy cars, and owned a plush home. He was eventually caught accepting bribes from crooked lawyers in exchange for access to injured workers on the job. I suspect that was only the tip of the iceberg. He ended up being disgraced and serving time in jail with other weasels.

A couple decades later, I was president of our local chapter of the conductors union when our bank account became negative. It turned out that our low-life secretary treasurer with a wandering eye, "El Dicko," was the culprit. He was sucking our bank account dry. I felt some responsibility, as did other local union officers, for allowing the theft to get that far; we should have been keeping better watch on it. There may have been a different outcome had it not been for conductors Toby, Pat, and a couple others who were instrumental in getting an investigation going. It seemed the big shot union heads just wanted El Dicko to say he was sorry, pay back the money, and be forbidden to ever hold a union position again. Toby and Pat wanted him fired, the money paid back, and for him to go to jail.

He was reported to the Portland, Oregon Police, who directed us to county officials, then to Washington and Oregon State authorities. Then we waited. I got a call from a federal government agent in the fraud division, a lady who wanted to meet with me and our new secretary treasurer, "The Percolator." We met up a couple days later at a restaurant near Gig Harbor, Washington. After introductions, the investigator put me on the hot seat, asking why I had not reported this to the federal government. I informed her that we had reported it to city, county, and state agencies, but had no idea it was a federal matter. She studied me a moment and accepted my answer. We then got busy with paperwork, records, and details.

She conducted a great investigation, verifying what we had suspected and uncovering much more. El Dicko was charged with breaking laws pertaining to lying and stealing; after the lawyers, prosecutors, witnesses, and the trial, the judge ordered him to pay back all the money and do community service. He did not lose his job and go to jail like many hoped, but was disgraced and, depending on one's perspective, he left town or was run out of town.

# Hobo Don

*I worked with a passenger train* bistro car attendant out of Seattle on and off for about twelve years, and I gave him the nickname "Hobo Don." Don was bitten on his face by hobo spiders while sleeping in a crew car en-route to Chicago. The attack left him very ill and after recovery left him with quite a few scars on his face. I used to make an announcement while passing the Burlington Northern hump yard in Seattle that went something like this:

"Ladies and gentlemen, boys and girls, coming into view in a minute we will be looking at the Burlington Northern Railroad Balmer hump yard where I hired out in 1977. I did a lot of humping there when I was a young man. You can see the hump tower, hump switch shack, hump switch engine, hump lead, the hump that the hump switch engine humps cars over, and the hump tracks down below with a retarder on each of the hump tracks controlled by the hump switch foreman in the hump switch shack. There she is folks: the Balmer Yard car humping switching facility."

Hobo Don got a kick out of that announcement and always reminded me to make it. I, however, had a feeling that I was going to be called into the office one day, putting an end to any further humping announcements.

We were nearing the hump yard one day, and Don was egging me on. "It's a hump yard, you can talk about it."

I made the announcement, like I had a hundred times before, and all the while I could hear Don next to me counting each time I said, "hump, humping, or humped."

"...17, 18, 19, 20..."

"Enjoy that hump yard folks! In a couple of minutes, we're going to be looking at the Puget Sound waterway." I said, and hung up the microphone.

"That was the 21-hump salute!" Hobo Don said, chuckling.

For the remainder of my career, I only mentioned that the hump yard is where I hired out in 1977, managing to dodge the office on that issue.

Hobo Don had bought a mountainous chunk of property in Eastern Washington that he lived on, which was pretty much the truth, as people who have visited him told me. In order to get the property paid off, he worked a few years longer than he had planned. He turned 69 during one of our trips, so I had a banner made. Upon entering the diner car that he was working, he was greeted with, *Happy Birthday Hobo Don #69* painted across a large banner suspended on the wall.

# Dynasty Steve

*I gave coworkers* a lot of nicknames over the years. I worked with another bistro car attendant by the name of Steve who happened to be old-school Chinese. When upset, he would slightly mispronounce the English language. The bistro car was having problems with the refrigeration and Steve was calling on the P.A. for a Talgo Technician, Mike, who was the onboard person assigned on Talgo trains to fix things. We mostly referred to them as "Talgo Techs." Mike was not responding, and after ten minutes Steve became irritated and got on the P.A. In his haste, he stumbled over the word "Talgo" and called for "Taco Mike." Of course, "Mike" became "Taco Mike." He liked his nickname enough to change his email address.

Several months later, the train was having some refrigeration issues again. Taco Mike and Steve were not seeing eye-to-eye on the matter, and Taco Mike was telling me his side of the problem. Mike was hot, talking faster than he could think, and in his haste when meaning to say, "that f--king Diner Steve," it came out "That f--king dina Steee...."

"Dynasty Steve?" I said, and Steve had a new name. They gave each other nicknames in a roundabout way.

Dynasty Steve loved his nickname I would always announce: "Today our bistro car attendant is the number one in seniority, Dynasty Steve."

Steve is the only other person I presented the 69 banner to. A group of us employees surprised him in the King Street Station one evening with a cake and a *Happy Birthday Dynasty Steve #69* banner. I never saw him happier.

# Wheelchair Dick

*My nephew Dick* is pretty much confined to a wheelchair as a result of being born with cerebral palsy. His middle name is Richard, so when having a little fun, I would call him "Wheelchair Dick." One Christmas, he drew a little picture of himself in a wheelchair and signed it, "'Wheelchair Dick".

His first name is Curtis. After his father passed away from a drug overdose and his mother, my sister, had a nervous breakdown, at the age of fourteen he was placed in foster care for a couple years. But when his foster mother began having personal problems, the State approached my wife and I, asking if we would take him in, while being compensated a little for it. We agreed, while my wife did 90 percent of the care and my kids and I the rest. Yes, he lived with us ten years as we watched and assisted him through confirmation at our church, on to high school graduation, then graduating from junior college. He is now a productive member of society, volunteering at the senior citizen center helping the seniors figure out how to do things on the computer and Internet; in fact, he was the one who got me going on the computer back in 1999.

He also was an inspiration at the beginning of writing this book, helping me organize stories and formatting them for a couple months until the schooling I learned fifty years earlier came back to me. Curtis and his mother have been close to each other for several years now and the three of us have been having lunch together once a month during all that time.

# Denied Entry to Canada

*In the '90s*, and through today, when going north with our passenger train from Seattle to Vancouver, British Columbia, Canada, we did not stop at the U.S.–Canadian border.

We would cross from Blaine, Washington into White Rock, British Columbia and travel thirty more miles to the Vancouver V.I.A. station. Sometimes we would experience several unscheduled stops for freight train delays, weather delays, marine traffic delays, and a host of other unusual delays. Thirty miles we traveled into Canada before the Canadian officials would inspect our passenger's documents; I never understood that, and think it is not in the best interest of safety, as a devious train employee or passenger could think of many ways to smuggle people or drugs into Canada, passing them off in the thirty miles during one of the unscheduled stops or a planned one with some sort of ruse to stop the train, such as a misaligned track or a stalled vehicle on a street crossing. My concerns fell on deaf ears and I suspect that the before-mentioned activities may have occurred.

Before arrival, all crew and passengers were given a customs form to fill out to be presented to Canadian Immigration officers after detaining at the station in Vancouver. After waiting in line, the officers would look over their customs form and ask anywhere from no questions to several, as they punched the person's name into a computer.

The computer could sometimes tell them if the person had ever been convicted of a crime and if they had, they would be escorted to a back room to be interviewed further; sometimes they would be allowed entry after sweating out the interview, or they were placed back on the train and given a free ride back to the U.S. later in the day or early the next morning.

This was not an uncommon occurrence. What I find amazing was the fact that people were deep in Canada for hours before being rejected. Now, some of them may have deserved being turned back; however, there were reformed people who may have had a DUI. In Canada, a DUI is a federal criminal offense, so foreigners convicted of a DUI are not usually admitted to the country. Some were convicted as many as ten years prior, and I felt bad for them as I watched them cry their eyeballs out.

After the officers had seen us crew members a few times, they mostly would take our customs form and let us pass, skipping the computer and questioning routine. One day in 1996, however, when I was going through customs, a pony-tailed officer asked me if I had ever been arrested.

"Not since 1980," I said proudly. I was being honest.

He did not appreciate my happy attitude, however, and got on the computer.

"What happened in 1980?"

I mellowed my attitude. "Illegal fishing."

"What happened in 1979?"

I had to think.... "Resisting arrest?" I had quit drinking and drugging in 1980.

He was not impressed. "What happened in 1970?"

My mind raced for a split-second. "Car prowling?"

Ponytail said, "I am refusing you entry. You will have to stay on the train all day; you are to go back tonight and you can't come back unless you get some sort of permit from the Canadian Council."

I was devastated. I started to whine. "C'mon, you can see I've been staying out of trouble for sixteen years."

He then got a couple inches from me, and to this day I believe if I had so much as said another word—or god forbid, touched him—I was going to jail.

I was the assistant conductor that trip and sat on the train all day with the conductor and the bartender, who were also refused entry on account of recent DUIs. We went back to Seattle that evening and the next day The Little General and his wife and I drove up to the border to see the Canadian Council.

A very smart, pretty little lady at a desk asked me the nature of my visit. I told her about the events at the border from the previous day and asked if I could please get a work permit or whatever it took to get back into Canada.

She got on her computer and asked a few questions about 1980. Then she said, "I don't see anything on the computer. What other trouble were you in?"

I told her about my juvenile delinquent history of run-ins with the law on up and through my early adulthood. "I am a changed person," I added.

After a few more minutes on the computer, she said, "There are no records of anything here."

"Was ponytail making this stuff up?"

She did not confirm that, but her silence did.

"Well, I'm telling the truth," I said. "What happened to the records?"

"When a person like you—the exception to the rule—gets straight and stops getting in trouble for ten or so years, they microfilm your records and put them in the basement. I am going to clear you to be allowed back into Canada.

I wanted to give her a hug, however I shook her hand, thanked her, and left. The Little General wasn't as lucky; he had to pay for a work permit. And the bartender, "Don B," took a different job that did not go near Canada.

I worked the train to Canada the following day. Ponytail was not there, but the interviewing officer held me up while he called somebody. I am not positive who he called—I am thinking Mr. Ponytail—but after the call, he reluctantly let me in.

Ponytail called my superiors soon after and told them I had to have lied at the Canadian Council interview and wanted me banned from going into Canada. This prompted me being called into the office and telling the story again to one of my supervisors.

I was not banned; however, I was interviewed about once a month when arriving in Canada for the next 15 years— sometimes for a minute or two longer if it was a new officer. After a while, they would scan my passport and the computer would send them some sort of signal; they would start to say something, but before they could, I would simply tell them I was a juvenile delinquent and a drunk at one time—and most of the time they would wave me by.

Then one day after fifteen or so years a young officer said, "I am going to see if I can get this taken off."

I think he must have been successful, because the last four or five years I never had a problem. Thank you, sir!

# Penetrating Tunnels

*One day when working* from Seattle to Portland, while the train was still in Seattle's King Street Station, we were instructed by "Technical Tim," the train dispatcher, to back out of the station into the King Street tunnel on signal indication north into the tunnel, and once in the tunnel to head south on signal indication. The reason we had to back out was due to a minor derailment earlier in the day at the south end of the station track we were on, and they were still doing inspections on the rail. We got the passengers all loaded and I climbed up and into the rear non-controlling locomotive on the rear of the train, with the engineer in the lead controlling locomotive on the front of the train.

"All right, let's do this," I said. "Let's change radio channels and go to the yard channel."

I ascertained that we were all on the yard channel and told the hogger on the point, "We have an approach signal okay to back up thirty cars." We started backing up toward the signal. We passed the signal and a couple car lengths from the tunnel, as we began to enter, I confirmed, "We are penetrating the tunnel. Good for twenty more."

We made our trip to Portland, and before I get home later that day, a union brother tipped me off that I had been turned in to the diversity department for saying "penetrating the tunnel." When I got home, I had a message on my answering machine requesting that I call the diversity department; they were conducting an investigation and they had a matter which they wanted to discuss with me. The recording said she *wanted* to discuss a matter with me; however, it was not an *order* and she did not say *please*, so I did not see a reason to call her back.

Meanwhile, a little bird told me that there were two managers who were standing by a newly hired on board person, and that when I said, "We are penetrating the tunnel," the new hire overheard me on one of the manager's portable radios and said that was inappropriate of me. This made the two managers nervous, so to cover their butts, one of them called the diversity department as required by rules to report anything said that might remotely resemble being inappropriate.

Everyone on the railroad was giving me a...hard time. Their trains were all penetrating and mine was not for the time being. I was in the crew base a short time later when one of the managers who turned me in entered the room.

"Hi, how are you doing?" they asked.

"Pretty good. No calls from diversity lately."

The manager got quiet and quickly left.

A week or so later, I was up north in Bellingham, Washington on my layover when I called my wife to see how things were, like I always did.

"Everything is good," she said. "Oh, you got some mail from work."

"Well, open it up and read it to me."

She opened the letter. "Sounds like you are in trouble!" she said, sounding very concerned.

"What does it say?"

"Dear Mr. D. We have concluded our investigation. You are advised to refrain from your inappropriate radio transmissions. Signed: someone from diversity headquarters."

I assured my wife that I was in the clear; I just couldn't say "penetrate" anymore at work. I had already deleted "penetrate" from my vocabulary, however all my coworkers had not. When I was in earshot, they were *penetrating* stations, tunnels, tracks, and yards—really rubbing it in.

About five years later, we got a new company president. The company newsletter published his story, railroad history, and expectations that he would try to meet as president. He said that he was big on a safe work environment and that he

would be "penetrating the ranks with safety." I became ecstatic!
I started jumping up and down because if he could penetrate
the ranks with safety, than trains could penetrate the mouths
of tunnels.

# Fur Coat Frank

*Somewhere around the turn* of the century, I was working a regular assignment between Seattle and Portland when I was assigned an assistant conductor. His name was Frank, and other than being on his cell phone a little too much, he was a great help. I am pretty observant and began to suspect him of being gay. Fine by me, it just meant that all the women were mine! However, I could also tell that Frank did not want me or any of his coworkers to know that he was gay. He was "in the closet," as they say.

Well, one day Frank had his boyfriend on the train as a passenger and made great efforts in keeping him incognito, buried in the back of the train among the passengers. However, he stuck out like a sore thumb because of the fur coat that he was wearing, and Frank could not stay away from him.

I was still in my chalking days, and after that trip I started chalking up the property with *Fur Coat Frank* for a couple of weeks. One day, he had enough, and he strongly suspected that I was the chalker. So, Frank confronted me on the platform at King Street Station in Seattle while we were getting ready to depart, complaining about all the chalking on the property.

"Now people are calling *me* Fur Coat Frank! I don't even own a fur coat!"

"That's correct," I said, pointing at him, "but your boyfriend does."

# Heavy B and Secret Agent

*I used to work* with two black conductors in passenger service on and off for about fifteen years who were brothers. A trainmaster who we worked under nicknamed one of them of "Heavy B," as in *brother*. I took it upon myself to nickname the other one "Secret Agent," as he was highly secretive about some of his activities. They were from the south and had been policemen at one time; they had also been in a musical group when they were younger. I heard the both of them at one time or another belt out parts of tunes, and they sounded pretty good. Secret Agent went back down south and became a locomotive engineer on a freight line, and Heavy B stuck around until he retired on disability.

B was trying to get under my skin one day while we were working a trip from Seattle to Vancouver, B.C. He kept telling me about all his escapades with white girls. He was going on and on, bragging it up you might say.

"You know boss," he said, "once they go black, they don't go back!"

"That's right, motherf---er," I shot back. "If they ain't white, they ain't right!"

He got quiet after that.

# B.M.F. and W.M.F.

*I worked with a black engineer* who was my assistant conductor at one time. Back then, I called him "The Prowler," as he was known to have a few girlfriends at a time. In later years, he became a locomotive engineer and was on a regular assignment with me for a few short stints. He was a nice man when he wanted to be. We got along okay, but we were both the type that always had to be right. During our crew briefings, his demeanor was that I was inferior...and vice versa.

One of the jobs for a conductor is to remind the engineer a few miles in advance of any restrictions in the path of the train that need to be adhered to, such as speed restrictions or workers occupying the tracks. The Prowler's real initials were M.F., and one day at a crew briefing I told him I was going to call him "B.M.F." for "Black Mo-Fo" and asked if he had a problem with that. He said that he didn't, but he was sure someone else would.

I would have to call him on the radio to remind him of restrictions.

"Portable calling B.M.F., over."

"Yeah, I know 25 mph slow order at milepost such and such...."

Well, I admit I was a little nervous about someone calling the diversity department and causing me grief, so I got to thinking. There was a white conductor in our crew base whose initials were also M.F., so I started calling him "W.M.F." for "White Mo-Fo." Now I was covered. Should anyone call me a racist or bigot, I could say: *Wait a minute, I treat everyone equal!*

# Poop on Paper

*There were so many reasons* not to speed, however there were a few locomotive engineers who could not or would not stop speeding. Some learned that there was a way to recover the air brakes after the over-speed went off, only reducing the train's speed for a short time before recovering the air and soon be back up over the maximum authorized speed. I worked with one locomotive engineer who would do this two or three times every trip. I would hear the air go, the train slowed down for about thirty seconds, then go right back up to the more-than-authorized speed.

This particular locomotive engineer had another quirk—one of a kind (at least I hope so)—in how he decided to bend the rules. Besides being on the speedy side, he was also rumored to poop on the floor of the locomotive.

I would have thought that he could do that at a station stop like other locomotive engineers. After stopping and applying the air brakes at the station, they would take the reverser handle out and go down a couple steps into the nose of the locomotive and poop like a normal human being: in the commode. But, for whatever reason, this guy chose not to.

When he had to go, he would perform that duty while on the locomotive—sometimes doing 79 mph or more on three or four-minute straightaways. He would spread newspaper out on the floor close to the back wall behind the engineer's seat. Staying close to the alerter, this man would squat down and poop on the paper, punching the alerter if it was cut in as needed, all the while keeping focused on the track and signals ahead. When he was finished, he would roll the poop up in the newspaper like a big cigar and toss it out the window. This was all hearsay, and when teased about it he would neither deny it or admit it.

One day, while heading north to Canada and out of Bellingham, Washington, the New West train dispatcher, "C.S.F.," called on the radio and needed us to copy a slow order. In those days, the conductor was allowed to use a telephone and handwrite a copy for himself and the assistant conductor to read and keep, plus copy one to carry up to the engineer. I listened to the train dispatcher over the phone while receiving and writing down the slow order restriction that was coming up in thirty or forty minutes and repeated it back, as he gave me the okay on the repeat, time copied, and his initials .The assistant conductor and I read it, then I took the engineer's copy through the train, up through the bag car, and into the back of the locomotive. Just past the roaring engines, I opened up the door behind the locomotive engineer and there he was, lining newspaper up on the floor.

I handed him the order and said, "10 mile per hour slow order at Brownsville," and left as quickly as I could. I didn't want to stick around to see the proof in the pudding.

# The Rocket

*Many times, I worked* with a prior rights locomotive engineer from Montana off the old Burlington Northern Railroad they called "The Rocket." I'm not sure who gave him that name (it might have been me), but it was fitting, as he shaved two or three minutes off all of his running times and made good station stops without knocking down his passengers. Once, while he was handling a train southbound from Seattle, about two miles before arriving at his final destination of Portland, his train struck a vehicle at a crossing. There were no injuries; however, when that kind of incident happens, there is usually at least an hour delay waiting for the police, tow truck, and the local trainmaster or track foreman to all give their blessings before the train is allowed to continue its journey. They all came immediately, an exception to the rule, and gave their blessings. Despite the delay, The Rocket blew into the City of Roses, Portland on time, showing everyone exactly why he was given his nickname.

I worked with The Rocket on and off for fifteen years, but my fondest memory is of a trip north from Seattle to Vancouver, British Columbia in about 1997. We were just north of the border going through White Rock, B.C., avoiding harmonic rocking per special instructions, when The Rocket summoned me on the radio, asking for a cup of coffee.

I said, "Sure. See you in a few minutes," and headed to the bistro.

After grabbing a cup, I walked through the baggage car into the back of the locomotive, walking past the greasy noisy engine and up into the locomotive cab. I gave him the coffee and sat down across from him in the fireman's seat. We got out of White Rock, and The Rocket throttled the train up to the 50 mph track speed for the next two or three miles.

"Come over here and sit while I eat my lunch," he said, trading seats with me and pulling out a brown paper bag.

A minute or so into his meal, he said, "You have to be at 30 mph up here at Crescent Beach and have her down to 15 before coming on bridge 69."

"I can do that!" I said. "Hi-yah!"

# The Comet

*I worked with a prior rights* Burlington Northern Railroad locomotive engineer out of Seattle called "The Comet." The man had a few quirks, such as putting a clothes pin on his finger several miles before he had to reduce the train's speed for slow orders or workers on the tracks. When the circulation became cut off, and his finger started to hurt, that was his signal that it was time to slow down or call the foreman in charge of the workers. I was working with him on a southbound train from Seattle to Portland one evening and we had just left Centralia, Washington proceeding up and over Napavine hill past M.P. 69, on through downtown Winlock, then through downtown Vader past Vader's Little Crane Cafe. Now that stretch between Vader and the next station stop of Kelso, Washington had plenty of speed changes, as all routes do with several curves. We started banging around the curves enough to cause me concern, so I called The Comet on my portable radio.

"How fast are we going?" I asked.

"I'm not sure," he replied. "This speedometer went bad order on me. I can't get it to go over 60 and it sticks some of the time."

A few minutes later, we passed through the Ostrander Junction and the train dispatcher called us on the radio to ask us how we got there so fast. The Comet reiterated what he had told me earlier about the speedometer problems. I thought that the train dispatcher might have heard our previous communication and was messing with us, but in any case, The Comet holds the record for the fastest a train ever got from

Centralia to Kelso, shot there like a comet and earning himself a nickname.

Throughout the mid-90s, I worked a lot with The Comet and got to know him well. He was a church-going man; some called him a Jesus freak or *the preacher* and he was not shy about bringing it up. He loved Jesus then, and still does. Nice guy, and we got along well despite his refusal to engage in my language.

I was working regularly with him from Seattle to Portland three times a week. After arriving in Portland, we would take a cab to the hotel to get our rest and in the morning take a cab from the hotel to the Portland station to prepare for our trip back to Seattle. That is six times a week riding with him in a cab for four months. I noticed that when we would have a lady cab driver, he would jump in the front seat with her and start yapping, but whenever the driver was a man he would ride in the back with the assistant conductor and the conductor would ride up front. So, one day I decided to mess with him a little and try to make him feel guilty.

"Hey, Comet," I said. "I'm gonna start telling everyone that every time we get a lady cab driver, you jump in the front seat with her!"

He was not known for a sharp wit, but that day he shot back, "What are you going to tell them? That I'm a heterosexual?"

# Managing and Coaching Baseball

*From 1998 through 2003*, I managed the baseball teams my son played on. The last three years, I became the league scheduler in order to schedule the games around my three out-of-town work conflicts.

My first year as manager for my son's team, when he was nine, was my best year ever managing, as we took first place. What I remember best about the championship game is that my son played third base and made the last out of the game—snagging a difficult one hopper line drive and tagging third base for the force out to end the game.

For six seasons, I was involved in all sorts of ways, including umpiring about twenty-five games; umpiring, I would tell people, was like taking your turn in the pickle barrel—somebody had to do it. There were huge differences from when I played baseball as a youth in the early '60s versus the late-'90s and turn of the century, the biggest being that any child who showed up in the '90s for a tryout was placed on a team; in the '60s, children were not guaranteed placement on a team and were subject to being cut, leaving some of them kids and parents heartbroken. The other side of the coin was that in the '90s kids were dragged to the baseball tryouts; some had no desire to play, although their parents did. The rules required for the kids to play a minimum of two innings per game, batting at least once whether they wanted to or not.

Yes, I managed, coached, umpired, and served on the league board for six years while only ruffling feathers a few times. Some would say I resembled a productive member of society. My son told me once that all the kids were scared of me—but really liked me.

# Driver's License Bureau
## Investigation

*After 9/11, most people* will remember that security in America was tripled—and then some. About a year after the attack, I was called into the driver's license bureau for an interview...for what, they would not say on the phone.

I made arrangements to meet the next day on my way home from work and after arriving was taken to an office and questioned. The gentleman explained that the social security application I submitted in 1968 had my date of birth listed as 4-5-53 yet my driver's license application from 1971 had my date of birth listed as 4-5-54.

"Can you tell me why that is?"

I thought for a minute, and I remembered why. "I lied about my age on the social security card application, making myself a year older at fifteen instead of fourteen because you had to be fifteen to get a f---ing job."

Short interview.

# FBI Investigation

*Around 2008, the FBI* called me on my cell phone and wanted to interview me, as my nephew's wife had used me as a reference. She worked for the IRS and was applying for a promotion; she needed a security clearance since the job entailed making many decisions pertaining to very large sums of money.

I agreed to meet the FBI representative the next day at a local fast-food restaurant for coffee and the interview. After the formalities, he queried me about the young lady, asking me questions in reference to her integrity and honesty.

I told him she was good. However, she did deceive me a little bit once when I was chatting with my nephew on the old format of the Internet chat room; they were popular for a minute until the telephones got real fancy with the Internet.

I was chatting with my nephew, but I knew she was doing the typing, and rewording his conversation a little because of the content and the speed at which the interaction was taking place. There was no way he was alone, although ultimately I was not concerned by the manner the conversation was taking place.

I told the FBI guy that I understood what happened, but thought that it was a little bit deceiving, but no harm intended.

We finished our coffee and shook hands.

"You know," I said, "I was in the FBI when I was young."

"Really?"

I had him hook, line, and sinker. "Yes. FBI: female body inspector."

He paused for a moment, recovering from my antics. "And now?"

"Not so much now, anymore," I said.

She got the promotion.

# Monovision

*I had better than perfect eyesight* most my life, then it became perfect in my forties, and by around fifty I was having trouble reading. I went to the optometrist and it was determined that I needed reading glasses; I was losing some of my long vision, as well. He prescribed bifocal glasses, meaning lenses that would adjust when reading and then readjust when looking away at a distance, and vise versa. I wore them for less than a year, and then mostly for reading. I strongly disliked the peripheral distraction the glasses caused. It was like someone constantly messing with my head.

I went back to have an eye exam the next year and afterward told the doctor that I didn't like the distraction that the glasses had on my peripheral vision.

"There are three options," the doctor said. "You could just get reading glasses and use them when you read. Or, you get long-vision contacts and carry reading glasses and put them on when you read."

I had never considered wearing contacts; the thought of sticking something in my eyes was too weird. Nevertheless, I said, "That sounds good."

"There is a third option of wearing monovision contacts, doing away with glasses completely."

*WTF is he talking about?*

But the doctor started explaining right away. "We put a long-vision contact in your strongest eye and a short-vision contact in your weaker eye. For example, when you look at a bird sitting high in a tree your eyes will take a moment to adjust and you will have 95 percent of your long-vision sight.

Then if you look down to read something, it takes a moment for the eyes to adjust and then you will have 95 percent short-vision sight. Lots of people can't handle monovision contacts, though, especially if one is impaired mentally in anyway—and even those that are not. The constant vision going back and forth and blending just does not fair well with many people, yet there are those that it works great for."

I'm sitting there evaluating my options, when he continued. "There can, at times, be a problem with depth perception. as well. Say for instance that you are driving down the road and a car speeds past and cuts in front of you; for half a second you might think the car is going to hit yours."

I say, "So if I bend my wife over real quick, for a split second I might have a depth perception problem?"

He wasn't amused. "Something like that."

# Red Over Brown Signal

*One day in the early-'90s*, I was on the passenger #565 switch engine chatting with Jack the Hoghead. Jack was quizzing me on the various signal indications and what they meant when he caught me off guard. He asked, "What do you do when the signal is red over brown?"

"What?"

He said, "You stop and take it in hand throw kid."

To me, that was funny, but not so much to others. After Jack had retired, I deemed it my responsibility to pass that information on. Over the years I would pose that question to conductors and engineers, having a little fun. As you can imagine, there was not one of them who answered it correctly.

I should explain to those readers not qualified on railroad rules that there is no such signal as a red over brown. There are signals that are multicolored that mean different things relating to the speed limit of the train presently and in the very near future ahead, green meaning to go...all is well, red meaning to stop, while there are other signals requiring the train to slow down and be prepared to cross over from one track to the other. The colors are green, yellow, red, or lunar; they can be flashing, or arranged on the signal masts from top to bottom in different order. They are very important to understand—not understanding could be fatal.

The term *hand throw* derives from the term *hand line*. In situations where the train dispatcher was having control issues with tracks and signals governing train movements, they would instruct the train crew to stop their train, take the switches off power, then hand line (or, hand throw) the switch or switches for the intended route and give them authority to pass the red or dark signal. I will give an example related to the joke I would play: a red over green signal was called a *diverging clear*, meaning the train would be crossing over from the track they were on to the next one over and to reduce speed while preparing to cross over at a speed of 35 mph. The other thing the reader not of a dirty mind needs to know is that there is no such railroad signal as a brown one—so in relation to love making, if a person happens on a red over brown, they might want to put it in hand throw, or wait for a different day.

I was sitting in a crew change point in Spokane, Washington one night waiting for #7, the Empire Builder train from Chicago. The train was late and needed to be *dog caught*, railroad slang for when the crew needed to be relieved under the hours of service law. Due to the delay, the twelve hours that they were allowed to work was coming to a close. In this particular situation, the engineer did not need to be caught as their crew change points differed. The passenger trainmaster set the dog catch up, but since I was not qualified on the territory east of Spokane, I needed a *pilot*; which in this case refers to someone who is qualified to perform the duty that I was assigned. They would oversee me as I worked, ensuring that I didn't overlook any important safety factors. Our trainmaster set it up with the Burlington Northern Santa Fe Howitzer Yard trainmaster to get a locomotive engineer from his facility who would be my pilot when we caught the train at Sandpoint, Idaho.

We all piled into a van, and an operations supervisor drove us ten miles down the road to Howitzer Yard. We picked up the locomotive engineer/conductor pilot and headed for Sandpoint, Idaho. Along the way, we made some small talk.

About twenty minutes from Sandpoint, I turned to the pilot and told him, "Since you are going to be my qualified pilot, I need to ascertain for myself the extent of your qualifications. After all, I don't want to get fired."

I asked him where and when he hired on, and for a few minutes, he told me all about his twelve years of railroading.

When he was done, I asked him his experience on the route between Sandpoint and Spokane. From what he told me, he was more than qualified.

Then I hit him with the big question. "What do you do if you find a red over brown signal?"

The pilot squirmed a little and said, "I have never seen that signal...not even in any rule book!"

"You don't know what to do if you get a red over brown?" I asked again, as he continued to squirm. "You stop and put it in hand throw, kid!"

"Knock it off, Larry!" the operations supervisor shouted at me.

After the joke sunk in a little, the pilot started to laugh. We dog caught, and all went well.

One day a short time later, I was sitting at my desk in the downstairs section of the crew car on the Empire Builder train #7 somewhere between Spokane and Seattle early in the morning. A young black man from one of the bedrooms upstairs came into my office and uninvited sat down and opened his mind about old trains and rails, particularly the Norfolk Southern Line. In a matter of a couple minutes, I had him figured out as a foamer. He was a locomotive engineer on the Norfolk Southern Railroad, a freight line in the southern part of the U.S., and he was on vacation.

I chatted with him for a little while and then hit him with the big question. "What do you do if you find a red over brown signal?"

"I've never heard of that..." he said, trying to think if he had ever seen one.

"You stop and put it in hand throw, kid!"

He became quiet, then disappeared upstairs. I was a little worried that I may have offended him; if he turned me in, it could mean trouble. He eventually showed back up in my office.

"I called some of my railroad friends on the Norfolk Southern," he said, "and none of them have ever heard of a red over brown signal."

I decided to change the subject. I am sure that someone eventually spelled it out to him.

After I retired, I took a trip on my pass to Albuquerque, New Mexico to visit an old friend. I walked down from my room above where the Albuquerque conductors were sitting to ask them about Internet service and arrival time for my destination. I could hear the young conductor schooling the even younger assistant conductor on the restricted speed signal. When I entered the room, the conductor stopped and asked if he could help me. I asked my questions, to which he supplied answers, and then I let him have it.

"What do you do if you find a red over brown signal?"

He looked confused for half a second before saying, "I would stop—"

Then I hit him with, "After you stop, you put it in hand throw, kid!" And I headed back upstairs.

Near the top, I realized that the kid's answer was the best I had ever received, so I yelled down the stairs, "Good answer, kid!"

A couple years later, I took another trip on the train to see my godmother in Long Beach, California. On the way back, I was talking with a new conductor; I believe he was an Alaskan and I was thinking of messing with him a little, however decided not to. After a few interactions with him and the other conductor, I got the impression that he knew and understood my language.

So I hit him with, "What do you do if you get a red over brown signal?"

"*What?*"

"You stop and put it in hand throw kid!

"That wouldn't stop me!" he said.

# The Gladiator

*I was working in and out* of Seattle's King Street Station when we got a new baggage man by the name of Marcus. He was a real hard worker. After I got to know him, I started to call him "Marcus the Gladiator." Eventually, this morphed into "Marcus glad he ate her." Like everything borne from my twisted sense of humor, it was funny to some, but not so much to others. Most importantly, it did not seem to bother him.

A year or so later, we got another new baggage man by the name of Julius, and he was also a good worker. As I got to know him, I figured out he was gay, with a reserved personality, so I did not do what I wanted to do for several months—but I got to know him better and waited for the right time to strike. Finally, the perfect opportunity showed up when both Marcus and Julius were working behind the ticket counter with four others.

"Hey!" I said, pointing to Marcus. "It's Marcus glad he ate her." Then, pointing to Julius, "And Julius glad he didn't!"

Those present found the comment funny and we all shared in a good laugh—and I didn't get called in the office for once.

# Red Block Barb

***Barb is a smart doll-face lady*** who back in the '80s and '90s worked in station services in Seattle and Tacoma, as well as a few stints in other local stations. She was a hard worker and had good customer skills. Barb was also one of my lady coworkers who understood my language well; she would mostly smile after I made a remark, seldom would she comment on such remarks, though occasionally when she did, I got the clear impression she fully understood, but chose to be professional.

I was known as a safe conductor, although I did make errors now and then. One day at the Tacoma station stop, after I looked the train platform over before departure, I did not notice Barb had gone into the bag car for a second time as I hollered *all aboard* and gave the engineer the okay to highball on my portable radio. After we departed, the train dispatcher called us on the radio a few minutes later and said he had a report that our bag car door was open...so I went back and closed it.

After arriving in Seattle, our final destination, I was called into the office by Trainmaster Ed and reprimanded; it turned out that Barb had to jump off the train while it was rolling out of the station. *Sorry, Barb!*

Unbeknownst to Barb, a few other coworkers and I referred to her as "Red Block Barb." Barb was heavily involved with a company and union-sponsored program discouraging the abuse of drugs and alcohol by railroad employees called *Red Block*. The one agreed-upon rule of many that was always being challenged was when someone reported to work and was obviously impaired, a coworker could ask the impaired person to mark off Red Block, which meant in part if they were smart and coherent enough to agree, they were allowed to mark off Red Block and be assisted home under the authority of a manager. The impaired person would at least get some counseling and allowed to come back to work; some situations such as repeated mark offs, however, called for in-patient treatment before being allowed back to work.

There were a few success stories of recovery, but there were many that did not end well. All in all, the intent of Red Block was good; however, as most will agree, when it comes to the recovery of drug addicts and alcoholics, unless there is a deep desire from within the addicted person, the chance for recovery will be slim to none. Eventually, Red Block was dismantled in favor of more strict policies—such as being fired if one should report to work impaired and ask questions later.

I think the biggest reason Red Block went away was the money factor to keep it going. Just after the turn of the century, Barb became the head employment person involved with all the hiring of passenger train employees in the Pacific Northwest— she was the top dog. I always teased her that she didn't need to hire so many coach cleaners...that when the company was short cleaners, they could just call a conductor in on their day off and pay them a conductor's wage at the overtime rate. *I have Friday and Saturdays off, call me.*

For many years, before leaving company property at old trailer town, I would visit various employees at their offices for a minute or two. The last office I visited by the back door where I exited before going home was Barb's. There was a small waiting area outside her office where potential employees waited to be interviewed. I would always stop by and chat with Barb if she wasn't busy. One day, as I was about to exit, there was a bearded middle-aged man wearing clean denim coveralls sitting in the waiting area; Barb's door was closed while she was conducting an interview. I was feeling more quirky than usual that day and I asked the gentleman waiting what he was up to?

He conveyed in a couple sentences that he was waiting to be interviewed for an electrician job.

"The sure way to get that job," I said, "is to lick your eyebrows a couple times during the interview."

He gave me a confused look. "*What?*"

By this time, there were other people across the hall trying to listen in to the conversation, so I leaned in a little closer to the man and said a little softer, "Lick your eyebrows during the interview if you want that job."

I went out the door, got into my car, and started driving home, laughing to myself for about fifteen minutes. Then it turned into fear for a few minutes as I realized that should he make mention of my comment, I could be getting a call from the diversity department. But as I thought about it, the fear subsided...as far as I knew, there was no rule or law against one licking their eyebrows, let alone verbalizing it.

A couple weeks later, I saw the man in some not-so-clean denim coveralls in between locomotives grappling electrical cables.

# 2010 Liz

*I was working the Empire Builder* train #8 one trip shortly before I retired and there was a new young lady working in the diner on one of her first trips—cute, small, with a big smile. I introduced myself as her conductor as she touched my arm the first time we met, saying *glad to meet you.*

A few weeks later, I worked with her to Canada and we met for lunch on our layover. She bought me a cheeseburger; she smiled and made me happy. She was a lot of fun and super witty—I really enjoyed working with her.

For those that can remember, there was an old hit song in 1968 by Gary Puckett and the Union Gap called "Young Girl." One of the verses, in short, was: *you better run girl, you're much too young girl.* She was working the bar on the train one trip when I belted out that verse and she quickly replied that I better run!

A short time later, on a different trip, I asked her, "If I was twenty years younger?"

Without missing a beat, she replied, "And I was ten years older."

2010 Liz, I miss her.

# HI-DE-HO

I was working in and out of Bellingham, Washington around 2007 when a new station agent named Heidi hired on who was smart and serious enough at her work. She was a bit of a distraction, however, as she drew men like flies on honey. Many of my coworkers thought she resembled Marilyn Monroe and other pretty movie stars; however, my perception was slightly different, as she reminded me at times of Goldie Hawn in both appearance and mannerisms resembling Goldie's skits in the '60s comedy television show, *Laugh-In*—in short, a pretty blonde who appeared to be in la la land, although not exactly true, as she always came out smelling like a rose while she smiled and giggled.

One of my first interactions with Heidi was while she was being trained by "Scary Mary," the head station agent. One day after I gave Mary her custom back crack and hug, Heidi, who had observed, asked, "Do I get a hug?"

I really wanted to engage in a hug, however we were still adjusting to the ever-changing politically correct era; to give ladies hugs while on company property was deemed politically incorrect by certain people. Some men found that out by almost losing their jobs, while a few did.

So, since I barely knew her, I responded, "After you get your 120 days in, I will be glad to give you a hug."

What I meant by that was after 120 days she would join the union and the hugging would begin—the implication being that we would be bonded enough by then and could trust one another to do some hugging. I could hardly wait for the time to elapse.

Eventually we engaged in hugs while becoming good friends, and the bonus to the relationship was that I found out she understood my language and even spoke it periodically as she smiled and giggled. She turned out to be a pleasant station agent with good customer skills. I was involved in a company and union-sponsored safety program with Heidi for a couple years, spending many hours in the classroom with her. There was never a dull moment when she was around.

One day Heidi asked me what her nickname was.

"Hi De Ho," popped out of my mouth.

"Hi De Ho? Why Hi De Ho?"

"You know..." I said. "I just gave you a new last name—Heidi Ho! *Hi Yah!*"

# Some of the Time Deb

*While working as a passenger train* conductor in the late-'90s through the turn of the century, I became friends with a cute little lady who ran the bistro car. Her name was Deb and she was lots of fun. Deb would always give me a hug whenever she saw me, and would grin as I spewed my typical off-color jokes. After a few years of working with her, she told me one day that she was getting married soon and gave me one last hug. I was disappointed, but I understood.

Deb got married and soon transferred crafts to station services so that she could be home every day. She and her husband banged out three children over the next few years. I saw her frequently at the station throwing bags on and off the trains, almost always with a smile on her face.

One day, she gave me a hug. The drought was over! It was not exactly as it was before, however. If certain people were around she would refrain. Often, she would make up for it by seeking me out a few minutes later when the coast was clear to give me a hug. I soon figured out that some of our colleagues did not approve of public displays of affection, and in their presence there would be no embrace. As a result of our on-and-off again relationship, I started calling her "Some of the Time Deb." I miss her.

# Brown Sugar

*In 1988, when working* at King Street Station, I met a smiling black baggage lady named Kelsi who I immediately connected with, as she understood my language and I am sure had spoken it fluently in her younger days before she matured—unlike me. Her upbringing led her to the job corps and eventually to passenger services; her travels in life were similar to mine, however very tame in comparison. Having said all that, she was a kick in the pants and we eventually became good friends, exchanging hugs while engaging in off-color jokes—me more so than her. She would tell me when I had crossed a line, although I never felt as if our friendship was threatened.

She eventually transferred to a clerk job in the mechanical department and had a lot of dealings with the switch crew; I got to know her even better there, as I worked the switch job almost exclusively for three years. One day, I called her "Brown Sugar" and it stuck, leading to many people raising their eyebrows when I would call her that.

In 1999, Kelsi had a brain aneurysm and luckily her boyfriend found her before she died. She became legally blind, however, and as you can imagine her life became much different. I felt compelled to visit her while she was in the hospital recovering and did so until she was released and after she returned home for a while. I would take her out for lunch three or four times a year while she began navigating through her new life as a disabled person.

One day while we were out to lunch, the waiter asked how I would like my coffee. "Hot and black! Just like my women."

The waiter was shocked, and Kelsi said in a mildly disgusting tone, "Only you, Larry."

Brown Sugar went on to become very involved with organizations that specialized in disabilities like hers, making new friends, and our friendship became a little distant; we were still friendly on the phone and through the mail. After I retired, I got a retirement lunch started and now have picked Kelsi up several times and brought her along. She is still a kick in the pants.

# Switches, Bitches, and Bags

*After twenty-five years* on the railroad and an established passenger train conductor, I had pretty much done it all. I was at the pinnacle of my career with fifteen years until retirement, working a day run with weekends off. When I would get a new assistant conductor, they would always ask me what I wanted them to do, and I would answer, *I will do the switches, bitches, and bags. You do everything else.* Mostly what I meant by that was I was going to hand line any switches associated with our train movement, take care of the bags on and off at the station stops, and any passenger situation that my assistant conductor could not handle, I would take care of.

I maintained this mantra for the rest of my career, and one Sunday in 2008 while working the Empire Builder train I was given a newer assistant conductor named Trudy.

"What would you like me to do?" she asked.

I did not hesitate. "I will do the switches, bitches, and bags, you do everything else."

Trudy was very quiet, gave me a nod, and got to work. We left Seattle, skirting the Puget Sound waterway eastbound and made our station stops at Edmonds and Everett before turning inland.

I was sitting at my desk downstairs in the crew car when Trudy came in with a very worried look. "There is a lady in the rear coach car that wants to talk to you."

"About what?" I asked.

"I am not sure..." Trudy said, but I sensed she had a pretty good idea.

I made my way back to the fully packed rear coach and a well-dressed, attractive lady about my age approached me. "Your helper lady needs some lessons in being nicer to passengers. She is running us around like a drill sergeant!"

"So sorry, ma'am. She is pretty new and was probably overwhelmed. I will speak to her about being nicer."

She thanked me, and I reached out to give her a handshake with one hand and a very light hand on the shoulder hug with the other as we parted.

When I returned to the crew car, Trudy was sitting at the desk looking very worried.

"I just took care of one of those bitches for you."

# Uncle Paul and Uncle Tom

*Between 1998 and 2000*, I had an assistant conductor name Paul. He was sixteen years older than me, but didn't have much seniority within the company as he had hired on late in life—*did not get off the farm soon enough*, as they sometimes refer to people who hired on later in life. I nicknamed him "Uncle Paul," and he was pretty much family while we worked together. He would bring in day-old cookies for everyone and loved to tell old-school jokes. Later in his career, Paul had some medical problems and had difficulty walking, causing him to kind of walk sideways. I called him "Sideways Paul" a few times, but he asked, *Whatever happened to Uncle Paul?*, so I decided to call him "Uncle Sideways Paul." He was a great guy.

Eventually, a new conductor came to the Seattle crew base and bumped Uncle Paul due to having greater seniority (he got off the farm early in life) and became my assistant conductor. His name was Tom, and he was from the east coast. I asked him if he had any nephews or nieces, to which he answered *yes*. Therefore, I started having a little fun by calling him "Uncle Tom"—until I was warned that it may be a derogatory term and I had better think twice about using it. I decided to skip a looming office visit by eliminating that nickname. Besides, I was eight years his senior, and it's weird to call anyone younger than you "Uncle" anything.

Now, Tom had to be one of the most conscientious assistant conductors in passenger service—in multiple aspects of our job—that I ever worked with; he knew more about operating a locomotive than some locomotive engineers and no conductor I ever worked with even came close to his patience and tolerance with passengers. Getting to know him was an experience of a lifetime.

In the first few weeks I started working with him, I suspected he was gay—which I had no problem with. It was time to have a little fun as we were sitting in the bistro lounge at our tables at an idle moment.

"Tom, you have any kids?"

"No Larry, I've never been married."

"Tom, that is not what I asked you. I said, do you have any kids?"

He became quiet for a moment. "I'm sorry about that answer. You know, Larry, when I come to a new community and crew base it takes me a while to be comfortable with—"

I cut him off as he was getting ready to tell me he was gay. "Tom, I'm just sitting here waiting to hear some good girly stories."

"Larry," he said, "there won't be any girly stories."

He became one of the best friends I ever made in my railroad career. We worked a lot together and I nicknamed him "The Perkolator." I would make an announcement: "Ladies and gentlemen, boys and girls, Tom The Perkolator will be coming throughout the train with enthusiasm. If you have any questions about anything, like *where are we at?* or *when are we going to get there?* just ask Tom."

I used to tell Tom, "I will ruffle the passengers' feathers and you can smooth them out."

"That's right, Larry," he would say, "that's right."

# Shoulder Cannibal

*I spent nearly every Tuesday* from 2000 to 2010 in Vancouver, British Columbia from noon until five p.m. on a layover. I never lay around much in the hotel room, and spent most of my time on the move walking, riding the bus, in boats, and aboard the sky train, seeing what I could see. I would go hunting for bargains at the various secondhand stores to see what I could flip on eBay for a profit. I attended a few meetings and visited a sobriety hall or two. I liked walking Chinatown, Gas Town, and the slums, venturing down dark alleys, into the ritzy neighborhoods and everything in-between. I'd find myself anywhere from Stanley Park, Grandville Island, to adult entertainment businesses. I even went to a nude beach twice and once had a pretty little Asian lady perform acupuncture on me. I conversed with fortune tellers, drug dealers, pimps, hookers, con artists, transients, people of all religions, creeds, and a wide variety of people from the working class. I even made a few friends along the way.

It was while on one of those treks a couple miles from downtown Vancouver when I happened upon a building with signs that read, *Ripley's Believe it or Not Fame Here.* It was a large shop, and the sign on the door indicated that it was rarely open, but on that day it was. I entered and gawked at one hard-to-believe object after another: shrunken heads, spears accompanied by pictures of the tribesmen who carried them (all looking very serious), and pictures of crossbred animals that made me feel upset at nature.

In the back was the owner: a man with one foot in the grave. Sitting on a high stool, he had an oxygen mask handy, which he used after each sentence or phrase he spoke, and an oxygen tube that ran thirty feet behind him to a curtained room where I suspect his wife was.

We talked for a while and he told me that when he married his wife some fifty or so years back, he asked her, "Do you want to have children or see the world?"

She chose the latter and his shop was the proof. Near him was a picture of him with a tribe of cannibals. I asked him if the cannibals or any other tribes had ever offered up their women, as that is what I had read of some of the early explorer accounts from both reliable books and pulp magazines. He looked over his shoulder toward the room where the oxygen tube went to, then looked back at me and changed the subject.

I went back several times, but the shop was always closed.

# Killer Van

*In 2001, I owned a 1985* brown Ford utility van. It had two seats in the front and open space in the back. Came in handy for lots of things, including packing my son and all the baseball gear for the team I was managing and my son was playing on.

The big news at the time was that they finally arrested the Green River Killer after many years of investigations. He eventually confessed to killing 49 women; speculation is there were many more—and we lived in the community where this happened in. My van broke down at work one day, so I got a ride home, leaving it at work a couple days until I had enough time to fix it and bring it home. I got it home and the next day I was taking my son, twelve years old at the time, to baseball practice and he asked where the van had been those couple days it was gone.

"The police had it impounded," I told him, "as I guess it was the Green River Killer's van back in the day, so they had to remove crucial microscopic evidence that came off the bodies of the women he had killed and transported in here."

I let him stay in shock for five minutes until we got to the practice field, when I told him it was just a joke. He wasn't exactly happy with me.

# ORE-HEY

*There was an electrician* at the passenger coach yard who worked nights by the name of Jorge (pronounced "ore-hey"). He would always break a few safety rules during his eight-hour shift in order to get his work done quickly enough to fit in an on-the-clock nap. In the old days on the graveyard shift, if you got all the work done the bosses would look the other way while you got some sleep, but breaking safety rules to get the work done was absolutely not allowed, and for good reason—a lot of those safety rules were written in blood.

The main rules he was breaking were not putting up blue flags and derails, protecting himself and others working with him while they were in-between the cars of the train disconnecting electrical cables. The blue flags were used to alert other workers that somebody was in harm's way and the equipment was not to be moved. The derails were in place in case equipment were to roll toward the workers it would skip off the track before it could roll into equipment a worker might be working on, thus avoid injuring or killing someone.

Jorge was warned numerous times to quit violating the safety rules, but whenever he was confronted he would say he *no understand* the safety procedures given, *Sorry!* He was warned repeatedly, but still kept on violating safety protocol. Well, the mechanical foremen found out that Jorge ran a food service business in the daytime and needed all the sleep he could get to run it, plus he needed the medical insurance provided by the company. I was chairman of the monthly Northwest Safety Committee meetings and the matter was presented to me at one meeting. After that meeting, I would see him in the locker room at six in the morning when I was just arriving to work and he was clocking out. During this time, I got to know him a little. It was odd that he managed to pass several tough rules examinations to get the job, but now that he was employed he could not understand or comply with them. It was obvious to most of us what he was doing, but I figured that if he was having trouble understanding the English language, then it only made sense that I might get a little confused with the pronunciation of his name, so I started calling him "Heyhor" in front of all of our coworkers. I was having a little fun with him right up until he inevitably got fired for sleeping on the job.

One of my coworkers who was present during Jorge's investigation told me that when asked why he was caught sleeping on the job, he said, *The foreman told me to go lay low!* Finding this answer to be unsatisfactory, the railroad decided to terminate Jorge.

# Crack 'Em and Leave 'Em

*Some stories are hard* to swallow, and this is one of those stories. I was the conductor on a passenger train from Seattle north through Bellingham to Vancouver, British Columbia and back again three times a week. That is a total of six times a week that I interacted with Bellingham station agents. On top of that, for several of those years we originated and terminated our train in Bellingham twice a week, granting me even more time with them. One of those Bellingham agents was named Mary, or "Scary Mary," as some referred to her. She spoke my language fluently and then some. She is one of only a few ladies to make me blush more than once.

One day in the station while killing a little time, Mary started complaining about how she wished our insurance would pay more than it did to have our backs adjusted.

"Do you think you can do it?" she asked me. "You're tall enough."

"I don't know," I said. "I will give it a try if you show me what to do."

She turned around and crossed her arms across her chest. "You reach around, grab under my elbows, and pull me up off the ground, holding me against your body as I stay relaxed," she instructed. "When everything is right, you jerk me."

I did as she said, lifting her up, and got her into position.

"Okay...jerk me!"

I yanked her upward, heard a pop, and set her back on her feet.

"You're hired!" she said.

This went on for years, saving her lots of money. I actually enjoyed doing it except for the few times that I couldn't get it to pop, even after multiple jerks.

One time while lifting her into position her hair smelled freshly shampooed. "Hmm...your hair smells good," I told her.

"There is plenty more where that came from," she said.

In later years, neither Mary or I cared who was witnessing this event. I recall popping her in the station while passengers were watching and in the back of my mind, I figured one of those passengers was going to be offended and turn us into our boss, causing us some grief by sending us to a safety or a diversity class. Thankfully, nobody ever got overly offended.

One day on the station platform, I hollered *all aboard*, cracked her back, told the engineer on my portable radio to high-ball Bellingham, stepped on the train, and rolled out of town. *Crack'em and leave'em!* Two years after I retired, I made a trip to Canada and along the way I stopped in at Bellingham to visit Mary; I cracked her back and talked the good ole days. While visiting, a train came into the station so while on the station platform I visited with the assistant conductor and chief while Mary chatted with the conductor. When it was time to depart, the conductor came by to say a quick hi and shook my hand, smiling.

"Mary told me she knew you were coming to visit her today," he said, "so she put on her chastity belt."

# Tunnels: Canadian Girl and Guy

*Knowing the train routes* one works on is important—and learning them when new is a challenge. There is the timetable and special instructions to study, and you find yourself directing questions to the older crew members. Whereabouts can be confusing during storms, late hours, and many other situations.

Back in the day, I was working freight as a brakeman on the head end from Seattle to Wenatchee, Washington. There were several tunnels on that route and in my earlier years the names of them all could become confusing. There was the Everett tunnel, Cascade tunnel, Gainer tunnel, Winton tunnel, Swede tunnel, and Chumstick tunnel. The Everett and Cascade tunnels were not the problem—the Everett tunnel was at sea level and eighty miles later we went through the eight-mile Cascade tunnel.

This particular trip while coming out of the Cascade tunnel we were 4,000 feet above sea level descending down the eastern slopes of the Cascade Mountain Range. The next four tunnels were in a relatively short succession, and like I said, many had a hard time keeping the names straight, myself included.

The hoghead sensed this. "Kid, you want to know how to keep them straight?"

"Sure do."

"Every Canadian Girl Will Suck Cock."

As I was thinking, *WTF?* he said, "The first tunnel is Everett, so *Every*; the second is Cascade, *Canadian*; Gainer, *Girl*; Winton, *Will*; Swede, *Suck*; Chumstick, *Cock*.

Thirty years later while working passenger service I had a

lady locomotive engineer, Miss Judy, who spoke my language and then some. During a crew briefing in Seattle prior to an eastbound Empire Builder trip, we were informed about several slow orders indicated by mile post locations through the area of the last four tunnels mentioned.

"Good thing we got the mile posts," she said. "I hate trying to remember those tunnel names."

So I gave her the tunnel spiel. She raised her eyebrows, then giggled.

A few hours later, while passing through one of the four tunnels, Judy spoke up over the radio.

"You by any passengers?"

"No."

Then over the radio airwaves she transmits, "Every Canadian guy will suck crevice."

Miss that lady!

# Beaver Dam

*Coming south from Canada* toward Ferndale, Washington one evening, we got a red signal and the train dispatcher called on the radio to let us know that we would be stopped for a bit while a track section foreman checked out a possible flooding situation near the tracks a little south of Ferndale. About an hour went by before I called the train dispatcher on the telephone to see what was happening. He said that a track section foreman had been sent out along the tracks to check out a beaver dam; it had been known to cause flooding after heavy rains, which would soften up the earth near the mainline track and possibly making it unsafe for trains to pass on.

The track section foreman had not yet reported clear, so a second man was sent out to find him—but the foreman was nowhere to be found at the beaver dam. The second man was now being sent to the first man's house to see what was happening. Nobody had reported that the track was good to pass on yet, so we were not allowed to move ahead.

A few minutes later, the dispatcher called on the radio and said, *you will be getting a signal to proceed any minute, okay to take it, everything is good.* Curious, I made contact again with the dispatcher on the phone, only to find out that the foreman had gone home and forgotten to call in the "all clear." On the delay report, I showed delay code "DMW" (workers on the tracks), and listed a 69-minute delay on account of *man looking at beaver dam.*

# Mother-in-Law Picture

*I have always been fascinated* with antiques, collectibles, or *old stuff*, as some people refer to items no longer needed—while many just call it junk. Our home is filled with old stuff, as my wife relishes feminine collectibles and antiques, while I relish different calipers of junk. My main addiction is the pursuit of old vintage cigarette lighters.

I attended an antique and collectibles show at the Puyallup, Washington Fairgrounds in about 2010, where there were about a hundred venders selling just about anything you can think of. I came across a vendor with nude photos of ladies from the 1950s that he had purchased from an estate sale; he explained that the estate belonged to a photographer and that the photos were of lady models trying to hit the big time, like Marilyn Monroe. Many of them were just as pretty. The photos were not obscene in my view, just smiling ladies with no clothes on—like the pictures you would see in *Playboy* from the '50s or '60s.

I bought a photo, took it to work, and kept it in my conductor's briefcase. I think it's still there. I would wait for the right moment when working and at an idle time when there were no safety concerns, I would tell (usually) a young man that after my father-in-law passed away in 1999, a short time later my mother-in-law came to live with us—which is totally true (still with us today at 97 years old!). And then I would have a little fun and say I inherited a few items of his, such as a shoebox of old photos and mismatched broken jewelry, and when I was going through the box, I found this picture of my mother–in-law, as I pulled out the nude photo from the antique show.

Then I would say, *she looks much different now.*

# Focus in the Fog

*During the last ten years* or so of my career, the new "focus" rule came into effect. Under the new rule, we were required to adjust our radio communication when conducting passenger trains through certain areas on the railroad called "focus zones."

For example, the locomotive engineer would call out over the radio to the conductor in the body of a passenger train, "Approach signal in advance of bridge 4 Ballard." *Approach signal* meant that the next signal could be red and should be presumed that way. Should the train go by that red signal, there was a chance that the derail might fail to derail the train and prevent it from going off the end of the open bridge and dropping into the Salmon Bay waterway—resulting in people losing their lives. Another more common result of a train getting past a red signal is the train crashing into another train, which unfortunately still happens.

In the example above, after the Conductor heard the less-than-favorable signal communication from the locomotive engineer, the new rule required us to respond with approach signal "focus." The idea was that the hoghead would hear that "focus" and focus more than they were already focusing. There was lots of debate about whether this was overkill or not, and some argued that adding it to the already congested radio traffic could lead to dangerous miscommunications in certain situations.

I, for one, did not have a negative opinion on the matter. If they wanted me to say "focus," I could, and I did. I had already been saying responses of a similar nature years before, especially when I suspected the locomotive engineer was not even-keeled that trip for whatever reason. Before the focus rule came along, I would say something such as, "the next one could be red," or "don't forget to stop if the next signal is red." So the new rule was nothing new for me.

Some rails didn't agree. They believed that calling out "focus" was not needed, and made fun of us when they heard us calling it out. One day after I called out "focus," a crew member on a nearby freight train said sarcastically, "What does focus mean?"

I said, "Spell it backwards. That's what it means."

For all the minor grief that the focus rule caused me, I am still grateful for the one time that it saved my ass and also my perceived legacy of never serving time on the ground suspended with no pay for a safety matter concerning a train operation rules violation, which only a very few locomotive engineers or train conductors with long careers can say. I had a few character defects while railroading; however, most will agree being unsafe was not one of them.

I was the conductor on a passenger train that originated in Portland, Oregon. My assistant conductor was "G.H. Suzanne" and we had finished reading our orders and conducted a crew briefing without a key crew member—our locomotive engineer. He was late. I checked the paperwork on the rear unit as G.H.S. loaded the passengers onto the train. Finally, fifteen minutes before departure, our hoghead showed up.

"I was here on time, but couldn't find my wallet!" he explained. "I took a cab back to the hotel and still didn't find it, so I took another cab back to work, and I just found my wallet.... It was in my bag the whole time! Here I am, sorry."

I handed him his orders as we walked in the light fog along the train toward the lead locomotive, giving an informal crew briefing along the way. When we reached the lead locomotive, he mounted up and I walked back to the rear, closing doors along the way. G.H. Suzanne came out of the depot with the last passengers and climbed onto the business class car, giving me the *all is well* wave.

The red lens rear end marker on the rear unit was illuminated in the light fog. I told the hogger to set the air brakes and I watched the brake shoes on the rear unit hug the wheels.

"Good set. Okay to release when ready," I told him.

As the brake shoes released their hug, I added, "Good class 2 air test. Do we have lots of fuel?" I knew we did, but I always asked.

He assured me that we did as I made my way onto the business class car.

Looking and thinking everything over, I gave the okay to depart. As the train rolled out, the automatic door closed, and I looked at my 1978 railroad approved Seiko watch. *Wow, we were on time!*

As I heard and felt the brakes slow the train during the running air brake test, I said over the radio, "Hissing and squealing on the rear."

"Okay," the hoghead said, releasing the brakes.

As I felt the brakes release I said, "She is all done hissing and squealing."

"Good runner."

As an afterthought, I said, "Focus in the fog," and away we went.

Two hours later. up on the Puget Sound waterway near Nisqually, Washington, the train dispatcher told us to stop and inspect our train. We questioned the dispatcher about what we were inspecting for, but all we got was, "Trainmaster's orders."

G.H.S. and I walked around in the ballast in dark foggy conditions with flashlights looking at the wheels of the train and undercarriage. Discovering no abnormalities, we got back onto the train and reported our findings to the dispatcher, who then gave us permission to proceed.

When we arrived in Seattle, we were notified not to go home, but to report to the trainmaster's office for a urine test. As it turns out, when we departed from Portland our train went through a switch that was lined the wrong way, breaking it. A later train crew came along, found it, and reported it. For those of you unaware, a broken switch is dangerous enough to cause a derailment. They had us stop at Nisqually and inspect our train when they figured out we had broken the switch in the name of safety.

As a result, we were now being pee tested and pulled out of service pending an investigation. I tried to talk the trainmaster out of pulling G.H.S. and I out, but it fell on deaf ears, and refusing to pee in the bottle was grounds for immediate termination.

After the pee test results came back a couple of days later indicating that we were all clean, the higher-ups were still considering giving me and G.H.S. time on the ground. The only thing that saved us was that when they pulled the radio audio tapes, mixed in with all my mumbo-jumbo was me clearly saying, "Focus in the fog." G.H.S. and I were vindicated with back pay and returned to service while our locomotive engineer received a couple weeks of unpaid vacation.

# Diversity Disappointment

*People are amazed* (as am I) that I never talked to a person assigned to the diversity department—that I know of. I was informed many times that I was being watched, however. I was told many times by trainmasters and other supervisors that diversity had contacted them about my behavior, prompting them to reprimand me for something I had said on the P.A. of a train or something I said on my portable radio. I probably did talk to a few undercover diversity people on the train over the years, as many times I wondered how the trainmaster reprimanding me knew so much!

Day-long diversity classes started about 1999. For a couple years before that, it was an hour or two class, while preceding those years there was no such thing...that I recall. If you pinched someone's ass they either liked it or told you to knock it off and that is the way it was for me until the day I retired. That said, the times were a-changing, so I would feel a lady out sometimes months before pinching her ass and when in doubt take the safe course by not pinching her. In the beginning, the day-long diversity classes were very educational and informative for the most part, mostly enjoyable, and we were paid to attend, which was a plus. After ten or so years, I think they were having a hard time—*whoops*, I did not mean to use hard—I mean they were having a difficult time finding subject matter for the classes.

One year, around 2009, after the diversity class the next class held that day was on customer appreciation. They showed a movie about a supposed successful company; their motto was, *give the customer the pickle.* This is not a *B.S.* story. After that class, I told coworkers that I would do better than that by giving the customer the cucumber.

Yes the classes had in part become lame, especially the last three years that I worked. They kept adding new rules pertaining to certain behaviors. In a class in 2014, for example, they told us that we could no longer lick our lips around coworkers; of course, the lady sitting next to me and I immediately started licking our lips. In 2015, they added a new rule that we could no longer wink at coworkers and call them affectionate names such as *dear, honey, sugar,* or *sweet pea*. After some thought, I became a little bit upset that they were constantly trying to change who we were and dic...tate what we said.

As I thought about this, my mind racing, I came up with a new idea: I started to ask my lady coworkers, *do you want to see my summer trick?* Most would say OK, then I would hold up my right arm with my bicep partially showing, peel my short sleeve back a little and say, *If I can't lick my lips around you and I can't wink and call you sugar pie? Then I will give you this...*as I flexed my bicep three or four times while grinning.

A few days later, I walked into the assistant superintendent's office, a lady I knew fairly well.

"I am going to give you what I have been giving all the other ladies around here," I said. "I don't want you to feel left out." I lifted up my right arm and gave her a flex show.

I could tell she was a little concerned and was thinking, *I hope he doesn't carry this too far.*

"You been working out a little bit, huh?" she said calm as could be.

I offered a quick, "Yes..." and I got the hell out of there.

Here is my disappointment: I gave flex shows for two years, hoping sooner or later that I would get it in the rule book before I retired. But "No flexing while on company property" never made it in there. So disappointing. I figured some person would observe one of the flex shows and become so offended that they would demand that I refrain from doing it and when they figured out there was no rule against it? Form a week-long committee at diversity headquarters and implement one. It never happened.

So, as far as I know, you can still smile while giving coworkers a flex job...you just can't wink, lick your lips, or call them sweet names while doing it.

# Hug History

*My born-in-America* German Grandfather Earl hugged just about everyone and rarely missed a woman. His daughter—my mother—showed her affection in the same way. All said, that side of the family hugged people; that is what we did...it was our culture.

When growing up in the '60s and '70s, for a lot of us it was all about brotherly love and hugging was what we did. In 1980, I went from the brotherly love life into the halls of sobriety life, which entailed the theme, *hugs not drugs*. As you can see, I had been hugging and receiving hugs all my life.

In the late-80s, hugging started to become unpopular, and by the '90s the handshake had taken its place in most every scenario due to some of society deeming hugging as a sign of sexual aggression. And it *was* for a few, but for the majority it was not—it was a gesture of kindness and nothing more.

I eventually started refraining from giving hugs to certain men, as many perceived men hugging men as being queer; yes, homophobia was and still is present today. I still hug men if I think we are both okay with it. I don't think I ever stopped hugging women, and receiving hugs from them, but there were many exceptions to that rule.

In the late-'90s and the turn of the century, it became even a touchier matter; in almost all circles of American society, once again many people started associating a hug with sexual aggression. I said, *screw this* (*whoops*, did not mean to say *screw;* let me rephrase that). I said, *the hell with this, I am a hugger and it is my human right to hug people if the recipient is okay with it*. On the passenger railroad, I hugged every female coworker who appreciated it, and only a few of those hugs went sideways. I usually knew after a hug if there would be a second one and respected that; upon our next encounter, it was a handshake—although those handshakes led many times to friendly hugs.

One week around the turn of the century, the conductor union bosses came from the east coast and for a few days had meetings with train crew members before we commenced our workday on the train. They told us while on company property that unless the woman was your wife, it would wise to refrain from hugging them, as they were swamped with harassment investigations—and some of those men were losing their jobs. They said that recently a woman hotel van driver was offended when receiving a hug from a train conductor in the hotel parking lot after he tipped her for the ride and assisting him with his work bag. He lost his job and they were not sure if they could win it back with union grieving, even though he was not on railroad property or being paid on the clock. Regardless, at that moment he was representing the railroad. It seemed to make sense to most.

I had been silent for the whole meeting and decided to have some fun with it. I became a little loud, though I kept my composure.

"Let me get this straight," I said. "First, you said we can't hug the lady passengers on the train, then later you come with we can't hug our lady coworkers, now you're telling us we can't hug the van drivers. What the *f--k* is this world coming to?"

That was pretty much the end of the meeting. What I noticed during that week is that one of the union men leading those meetings was busy sniffing all the lady coworkers in the Seattle crew base while getting a hug here and there.

One day, a station employee by the name of Shea asked me, "How the hell do you get away with hugging all the lady coworkers? Anyone else would be fired by now.

"This is how it is done—I hug them all and should one of them become offended and call diversity, leading to an investigation trying to get me fired, here is what we do—the union griever and I, we have a *get out of jail free card*—we call in all the ladies on the property that I hug as witnesses and they testify on my behalf that the offended lady should not be offended because he hugs all the ladies."

Shea thought for a minute. "You don't hug *all* the ladies."

"Yes I do."

"You don't hug Samantha."

"You mean six-foot-three, three hundred-pound Sam who got a sex change into a woman who people call *a boy named Sue*?"

"Yes! Samantha is a lady and if you are a man of your word, you would hug her too."

I mulled it over as I passed by her the next couple weeks while in the station and then one day I gave him a hug—I mean her. It was all okay, but knowing him before and her after took a little getting used to. After I started giving Samantha hugs, it never again crossed my mind again that I would get into trouble for hugging a lady coworker. Samantha was the greatest *get out of jail free card* one would ever hope to have. There was also another person who worked as a bartender/snack bar staff on our trains the same gender as Samantha who never seemed to like me. For months, I tried to figure out what it was that brought her displeasure of me; then it came to me—I suspected she saw me hug all the women, but not her, and was a little hurt. I came behind the counter one day (*whoops*, did I really say I came behind the counter?).... I mean, I went in back of the counter one day to make an announcement and afterward I gave her a hug. She smiled as big a smile that I had ever seen. That day she fed me her allotted company dinner and gave me all her out-of-date commissary items to feed my three black dogs.

One day, Rob, one of the supervisors of food service, asked me how I was doing.

"I am doing so well that I have to create all my problems," I replied.

"What kind of problems might that be?"

"I hug all the women and sometimes that can be a problem, because every once in a while there is a woman who after I hug her wants to screw me right there. That can be a problem. And then there is the lady who wants to call my wife and diversity after a hug, and that could be a problem."

Rob said, "And those two ladies would be the one and same."

"Hi yah!"

I never saw or heard of a person being fired for a kind-spirited hug, however there were many men who I knew of who were fired—or would suddenly retire before being fired—for grabbing boobs, goosing crotches, and doing the pelvic grind during a hug. I worked with a nice lady at King Street Station for many years who I nicknamed, "Hourglass Lady"; she was a pretty and witty lady, always smiling, with an hourglass figure. After one of those men would get fired, she would say, *Apparently he thought he was Legendary Larry.*

# Safety Committee Chairman

*About 2003, the safety chairman* position within the company opened up, and it was agreed it would be filled by a union passenger train conductor. Three conductors were nominated, and I was one of them. I successfully won that election, taking 68.9 percent of the vote. I was given a secretary for notes and paperwork and chaired two meetings each month until my retirement in 2017. Each month, I would chair the main meeting where a representative from all departments was present and another meeting for the T&E Operating Crafts (trainmen and engineers).

Besides chairing the meetings, I was expected to delegate tasks and assignments to people concerning safety concerns. For example; locomotive engineers would often present a list at the T&E meeting of obstructions blocking or partially blocking their sight when trying to ascertain the color of signals governing the route of the track or tracks. My work was usually simple, as a trainmaster would normally step up and volunteer to contact the host railroad and have the situation taken care of by having trees removed or bushes trimmed.

Should there fail to be a person at the meeting to step up, then the secretary and I would present the issue at the main meeting and, at the appropriate time, voice our concerns about the view-blocking safety hazard. I would ask for a volunteer and, should there still be no volunteer, the superintendent present at the meeting would delegate the issue to a train master.

When other safety hazards were presented from the different departments, we would all listen, offer each other solutions, and volunteer to remedy the situation. I would often be left with a task to handle before the next meeting. As an example, many times I had to have talks with employees that drove company or their personal vehicles too fast while on the property.

I chaired the meetings with an even-keeled demeanor the best I could. I have a fair share of character defects, but being unsafe isn't one of them. I did have a little fun chairing those meetings, but mostly kept it serious and made many observations over the years. One is that whenever the superintendent was present, people who usually never said a word would have to come up with something to say. The meetings usually lasted well over an hour, but when the superintendent was absent, the meetings ran barely forty-five minutes.

In a good safety culture, the people remind each other of unsafe practices and encourage each other to take the safe course. As time went on, I was recognized by many of my peers as a leader to whom they could voice their concerns regarding safety, and I would do what was necessary to try and help solve the problem. As new safety programs came and went, I was expected to do safety walkabouts and observe my peers to praise them for all the great things they were doing and to gently point out to them the at-risk things they might be doing.

Eventually, I started having fun with it. I would ask women if they knew what the safety rule of the day was. When they said that they didn't, I would sometimes say, "Don't get your boobs caught in the ringer!" With men, it was a little different. I told them the safety rule of the day was, "Don't trip on your dick." This mostly drew looks of disbelief and silence.

However, one day after telling a Bellingham station agent the rule, without missing a beat, he reached down and tugged upward on one of his pant leg cuffs.

"Well, I guess I'll just have to tuck it in my sock!"

When in mixed company, the safety rule of the day was always, "Don't f--- up!"

# Serenity Prayer, Long Version

*I had attended A.A. meetings* for about ten years when our family joined our local Lutheran church, which also had a 12-step meeting for sinners. A.A. meetings are usually opened with the *serenity prayer*, although most members do not know it is the short version that they are reciting.

I didn't know for ten years. One of our members, "Jim," at a church meeting introduced us to the long version, which our group liked and recited. The short version made no mention of Jesus, as it ended before mentioning him. Here is the short version:

God, grant me the serenity to accept the things I cannot change, the courage to change the things I can, and the wisdom to know the difference.

Now the long version:
God, grant me the serenity to accept the things I cannot change, the courage to change the things I can, and the wisdom to know the difference, living one day at a time, enjoying one moment at a time, accepting hardship as a pathway to peace, taking as Jesus did this sinful world as it is not as I would have it, trusting that he will make all things right if I surrender to his will that I may be reasonably happy in this life without him and supremely happy with him forever in the next.

I pray the long version most every morning at the end of my morning prayer and medication time, and when I don't, I know that I will be praying at least the shorter version later in the day when I start to become angry for some lame reason, netting me a bit of serenity. Most commonly, when I simply start the prayer the situation upsetting me goes away; however, depending on the seriousness of the matter it might take the long version.

To me, the key to the prayer is acceptance, meaning that I do not have to like the matter which is disturbing me, however until I accept it my serenity will be little, if any. The long version is, in part, about accepting hardship as a pathway to peace. I could go on and on with my insight pertaining to the serenity prayer; I am forever grateful for having learned it because it has extended my earthly life of mostly being a kind productive member of society. Before the serenity prayer, my response to anything in life I didn't like was to get drunk or stoned, many times leading me to the gates of insanity but somehow managing to dodge death. For those of us clean and sober in the program (whether we like it or not), it is my belief that Jesus has been instrumental in our sobriety, as the short version serenity prayer is all about what Jesus stood for: acceptance, courage, and wisdom.

When Jim introduced the long version, I pondered and thought about it for months while trying my best to practice it. As I reminisced about my early days in the halls of sobriety, I kept asking myself, *why the short version and not the long version?* I recalled that some members had the mentality that the church and Jesus never helped them to get sober and that A.A was based on an individual's perspective of a power greater than themselves or a god of one's understanding. Yes, more than once in my early sobriety did I hear the mention of Jesus before, during, or after a meeting only to be turned off— as were other members. Since that time, I've had a spiritual awaking and I realize it was the devil—cunning, baffling, and powerful—that was turning me away by portraying Jesus as a weakling in a girly robe, when in fact Jesus was constantly directing me to Lady Wisdom in order to keep me sober by praying the serenity prayer. *Thank you, Jesus.*

# Inspector General
# and Company Investigations

*I am going to share* a few short stories about people being fired. I say *a few* because I could tell you hundreds.

The Inspector General, (or I.G.) is a government official assigned to catch government employees milking the system, fudging paperwork, or leaving company property early while still being paid—basically catching government workers stealing. Since the passenger rail corporation was greatly subsidized by U.S. taxpayers, it came under the government's jurisdiction.

Around 2001 or so, an I.G. investigation led to several locomotive engineers being fired in a Pacific Northwest crew base for stealing time. When their train would pull into their away-from-home terminal, most of them were fudging the arrival time. According to their contract, the crew went off duty thirty minutes after arrival. Twelve hours after that, the crew while resting in a hotel would receive "held away from home pay. Employees received up to eight hours of pay waiting to take a train back to their home crew base. The sooner you went off duty, the sooner you started getting paid. Now, you might be wondering what was the hurry to go off duty since you were being paid already? The answer is, this job and many like it were less than eight-hour runs and according to contract, employees received eight hours pay regardless of whether you worked four, five, six, or eight hours; the earlier one went off duty, the sooner you started getting paid again. There were also times a job was on overtime and getting off as early as possible would work out to making less money.

The fudging of arrival times had gone on forever on the railroads, and officials tended to look the other way. The long-standing practice was that when the train's head end went by the sign indicating they were in the limits of the city, they were going off duty in; thirty minutes later they would go off duty and twelve hours later be paid their "held away" pay. The arrival time should have been when the crew stopped the train at their final terminal, not when the train arrived at the city limits. Just about everyone and their mother did it. This practice only netted crews an extra ten or fifteen minutes pay in most scenarios.

One day, the I.G. for whatever reason went through that particular crew base and fired five locomotive engineers for stealing time, as they were using the city limits sign for the arrival time. One engineer was terminated for less than a hundred dollars! This was very disheartening to these engineers and their families, so much so that one engineer even died from the stress associated with being fired. I, as did most everyone, thought that if they had just given them the standard thirty days suspension without pay, the practice would have ended. Terminating those competent locomotive engineers cost the company over a million dollars, training new ones for a year to replace those they fired. They were trying to send a message by throwing the book at these guys. Not the wisest choice; the end result was that it cost the taxpayers more money to fire them, when a standard thirty days with no pay suspension and the shame associated with that would have more than sufficed.

A few years after those locomotive engineers lost their jobs, the I.G. launched a nationwide investigation into the Alaska Airline Miles program. Alaska Airlines and Amtrak had an agreement program where Amtrak passengers could turn in an Alaska Airlines card after each time they traveled and be awarded airline points for future travel on the airline. The idea was that after earning so many points they could redeem them for an airline ticket, saving people lots of money. I was a conductor at this time and recall every tour of duty receiving cards to put in my ticket pouch. I turned them into the station agents who turned them into revenue, which they sent to Alaska Airlines. Some of our conductors and locomotive engineers thought that if they were on the clock working from point A to point B and got a free ticket on their pass at the same time they were working that they were entitled to turn in cards and earn points. There were many other employees of different crafts who used their free pass to travel on Amtrak while turning in Alaska cards for bonus points. Yes, for most of us employees, the thought of turning in these cards never crossed our minds; eventually, almost every employee who turned in a card while riding free on their pass was caught and fired. Some of these employees lives were suspected of ending in suicide. There were a few who after being fired won their jobs back through union arbitration; however, the vast majority did not. Of course, there were the weasels who for no rhyme or reason were never caught. I knew of a few who appeared to be caught, but knew the right people and survived. I also know of one who survived, the reason being the old saying, *it is not who you know, but who you blow.*

I crossed paths with and worked side by side with several passenger train conductors who were fired after forgetting to remit the money they collected for ticket sales; one conductor forgot to do it for eight years. I worked with several bistro car attendants who were fired for shortchanging customers, cooking the books of their sales, and selling their own products such as booze and water bottles. I could go on and on about bistro car attendants stealing, but the craziest being an attendant who was selling company emergency first aid kits for a dollar; after he sold one to an I.G. spotter, however, he retired before they could fire him.

Many station employees were walked off the property and fired after the money they were handling disappeared. I knew two of them. There were many commissary employees fired as well, a few in the Northwest, one that liked to trade the commissary products for drugs. In Chicago after an I.G.

sweep, many employees were fired and some court-ordered to pay restitution. Yes, many onboard cooks figured out ways to substitute company products with their own and sell or trade the company's food for drugs. One cook was caught condemning food and selling or trading it off for drugs.

There was no department immune from employees stealing in some sort of way. At one time, every department had individuals who stole time—and the most common way this was done was by leaving company property and going home while still being paid.

# Shortchange Artists

*There were many of my coworkers* who worked the food service cars in different capacities who were shortchange artists. Many were caught and fired, however some were caught, reprimanded, and returned to service; a few learned their lesson, while others who didn't eventually got fired or suddenly resigned or retired after being caught again.

Then there were those who made it all the way to retirement. Yes, all the way to retirement shortchanging customers. I witnessed them being caught by the customers many times. After receiving their change from a purchase, the customer would say something like, *Hey, I think you owe me ten dollars more*. Then the employee would go into *I am sorry about that* mode and hand them the ten dollars, apologizing again. We all wondered why these coworkers owned homes all over the world and wore custom-made, expensive jewelry. I figured it out eventually.

# Tales of Messing
# with Black Coworkers

*I've already introduced you* to a coworker of mine named Tom, whom I nicknamed "Uncle Tom." I worked with him a lot and we always had some fun ruffling each other's feathers. I also worked with another guy named Tom, a locomotive engineer, between Spokane and Wenatchee, Washington for a few years. He was about fifteen years my senior, a white man whom I occasionally called "Uncle Tom" on the portable radio: for instance, *number 8's portable to Uncle Tom, over* and he went along with the fun, *Uncle Tom on 8's power answering, over; slow order on the Columbia River drawbridge 10 mph, over* and, *I got that 10 on the bridge, Uncle Tom out.* Now, whenever I was working with Tom and there were any black coworkers near, I made sure they heard me do the Uncle Tom thing; I got a few stares and raised eyebrows, but was never called into the office on that one.

*

I had three black dogs at home—*I really did*. When I felt like having a little fun with a black person at work, I would tell them, *I have three black dogs.* Sometimes they seemed interested and took the bait, asking me what breed, how old, or how big they were. I would tell them all about the dogs for a couple minutes and then launch in.

"I do therapy with them three or four days a week."

"*What?*" would be the typical response.

"They jump into the back of my pickup truck; the whole time they are excited as hell, while I am calling them *black motherf---ers*, and they are just smiling and loving the ride. When I get to the swamp, I let them out and say, *you black motherf---ers go have some fun in the swamp.* I let them run twenty minutes as I walk with them. They love it. Then I have them jump back into my truck and drive home, all the time calling them black motherf---ers, and they just smile."

Now, when telling this story it usually would be interrupted and ended way before I could get through the whole spiel, as my coworker would tell me to quit talking nonsense, or just *shut the f--k up.* There was the time I was working with a new black cook on the Empire Builder. I was downstairs in the kitchen with him and the assistant cook and I started in on the therapy story. He listened, not saying a word, while flipping pancakes; his eyes were bugged out with a look of deep concern as I spewed. Out of all the times telling this story, I only made it to the punchline one time, and that was with him, when I hit him with it: "I take my three black dogs to the swamp and call them black motherf---ers for a while—that's the therapy I need, because I get it all out of my system before I come to work."

He told me a couple of years later that at the time he was freaking out a little and asked a few people about me, but they told him that I was just messing with him.

*

Centralia, Washington is a city founded in 1875 by a black man, the son of a slave. His name was George Washington— though not *the* George Washington, our first president. When I heard that fact, I read up on it.

His story is very educational and fascinating. One of the not-so-great things that happened to George Washington was that he was taxed out of the ownership of Centralia. While reading up on Centralia, I came along a lot of other interesting facts—one being that a white man was lynched on Armistice Day, November 11th, 1919. Depending on what you believe, he may or may not have deserved it; however, it is mostly agreed that had he not belonged to the very unpopular woodworker's union, "The Wobblies," he most likely would not have been hanged.

I worked the passenger train in and out of Centralia hundreds of times, detraining and boarding passengers as need be. Many a time when a black person was destined for Centralia I would strike up a conversation with them, asking if they lived in Centralia. Most the time, they did not; however, a few did, although they did not know much of Centralia history other than a couple facts about the founder. Most did not have a clue that the founder was black. Here is what I would say to the ones not educated in Centralia history:

"Did you know that Centralia was founded by a black man?"

Stunned, the passengers would always respond with something like, "No. Wow!"

"Centralia has a lot of history," I would continue. "I'm a union man and I read where the people of Centralia hanged a man from the Wobblies union."

The passengers would become disheartened, at times even emotional.

"Do you know how they got rid of the founder, George Washington?"

Now they were feeling sick, and feared hearing the worse.

"They taxed him out of his township, but his grandkids got the last laugh because he owned almost all the land in the county and they ended up with it."

As the passenger was processing everything I said, "I would say Centralia is a much friendlier place now."

*

When I was a kid, many a time I (or another kid) would get caught putting a coin in my mouth, or getting ready to, when an adult would yell, *don't put that in your mouth! A colored person might have touched that!*

While working many decades later with coworkers who were black and mostly younger, when they were handling money on the train as bartenders, diner staff, and various others, I would holler, *hey, don't put that in your mouth! White people might have touched it!*

\*

Many a time my train would be waiting in a siding or a junction point for an oil train or coal train to pass. These trains were almost always a mile long, or longer, and were mostly black and carried black crude oil or black coal. I knew almost exactly when they would pass by us, as we were standing still waiting, and what side to look out to see the train.

A minute before they would come into view I would announce, "Ladies and gentlemen, boys and girls, apparently the train dispatcher forgot there was a passenger train today. We are stopped here at Colebrook to meet a coal train. Yes siree, Bob, if you look out to the right momentarily you will be able to see it." As it came into view and started rolling by, I would add, "There it is folks, a...long...black...coal train."

\*

One day, just after the turn of the century, I was working the northbound passenger train from Seattle up to Canada with a nice black man named Clark. They called him "Sitting Bull." He was the chief, I the conductor, and my assistant conductor was "Smokie." He smoked a lot, no relation to the pretty chief lady with the smoky complexion—her name ending with a *Y*.

Our train arrived in Canada and the first duty is to offload baggage. After we finished, Smokie got on the P.A. and said, "Clark, set your people free!"

What was customarily said was something like, *Clark, you can let your passengers off,* meaning to let the business passengers off to the platform and continue through Canadian customs.

It was the politically correct era. *Still is.* What a person could say or not say was constantly being revised. For a white person to say that to a black person, "set your people free," concerned me a little.

I told Smokie, "You can't say, 'set your people free' to a black man, and besides, we have black passengers who heard you. I hope nobody turns you in."

"They say that all the time in the Chicago station," Smokie answered.

"I hope it doesn't go bad this time."

Our crew in this era took a five or six-hour rest period and would come back on duty in the late afternoon for the return trip to Seattle. That evening I was sitting in the station with Sitting Bull before departure.

"I gave Smokie a bad time about the 'set your people free' announcement."

Clark chuckled. "Let's have some fun with him."

When Smokie showed up, Clark spoke up right away. "That 'set your people free' announcement didn't bother me cause I know you, but you got to be careful man, someone could take that personal."

Smokie readily agreed and we commenced to do our work loading passengers and preparing for departure.

We had a black couple on the train that went up to Vancouver with us, now on the return trip as well. A little while after we departed, I told Smokie that the couple asked me the names of the crew members from the morning trip up, but would not divulge why they wanted the names. Smokie got visibly nervous and started talking to himself. *I didn't do anything wrong.* Clark a little while later informed Smokie that he got an email message from the boss lady manager requesting that Smokie come to talk to her before going home that night.

Now Smokie was really freaking, and it was time to announce the upcoming Mt. Vernon station stop. I said I would get it. "Ladies and gentlemen, boys and girls, we will be arriving Mount Vernon in a couple of minutes. If you're getting off at Mount Vernon, don't forget to get off the train. Clark, set your people free!"

I barely had hung up the microphone when Smokie was in my face, yelling.

"Now we're screwed! We're both going to get fired!"

At that point, I told him it was all a joke because he appeared to be having a heart attack.

After he calmed down he said, "Glad you told me when you did because I was just about ready to approach the black couple to make amends."

I always enjoyed working with Clark. He was of my coworkers who encouraged me to play my harmonica in the bistro lounge as he would grin and slap his knees when I blew the harp and sang some off-color blues.

# Me Too

*I was told by many* of my retired coworkers and friends still working that I retired off the passenger railroad just in time because shortly thereafter the *Me Too* movement was in full...swing. Over my lifetime, the times have constantly changed; however, one thing for sure is that the reporting of sexual harassment is made almost always by a female offended by a male.

Before I convey my views any further on this matter, let me explain my view of sexual harassment...(*her ass met?*). On a serious note, my definition, or view, of sexual harassment pertaining to children and disabled, senile, or otherwise impaired adults is that it is despicable; there is to be no tolerating of that behavior and violators should go to jail. My view of adult sexual harassment is much different. Should someone offend you in any way, for instance, say something of a sexual nature intended as a joke, and you do not appreciate it, or should a person creep you out by touching or hugging you—basically, if a person makes you feel uncomfortable in any way—you, the offended person, must tell that person that you do not appreciate their behavior. And should the person not stop their behavior that offends you? Then it becomes sexual harassment, and it must be dealt with accordingly. Now there are a few exceptions when a person would not be warned and reported ASAP to authorities, and we all know what those would be.

Having said all that, in my lifetime I have had many interactions with ladies, girls, and homosexual men that resulted in me feeling uncomfortable; I think many people would deem these interactions sexual harassment, although when the behavior was not repeated a second time I did not feel harassed. There were many times I would have to dodge a person a few times before they got the message that I was not interested.

Between the ages of twelve and seventeen, while in the public school system and the reform school system, I received many hugs from lady teachers and staff workers that many times left me wondering if they had wanted more than a hug. I was fourteen years old, looking at donuts through the window at a doughnut shop in the Pike Place Market in Seattle, when an elderly woman approached me and said, *You like looking at them holes? ...In those donuts? Hee hee.* When I was in treatment my first time for substance abuse, a nurse would come into my room at night and give me back rubs. When I was in treatment the second time at a different facility, a different nurse inferred more with her remarks than I cared to hear. One time when being treated at the hospital after a train wreck that I was in, the lady doctor felt me up twice each time for about twenty or thirty seconds...*looking for injuries,* she said. Many times while having routine examinations lady practitioners said off-color things to me.

In my lifetime—nearly half of it on the Passenger Railroad—I was no angel in regard to my behavior; however, there were women who were my equal, and then some. I have no animosity toward them, as most were just returning what I dished out, while some of those ladies made me look like an angel. The intent of this story is to convey my perspective that women have fought for years to attain equal rights and social justice and are still not there...and in a some very small, isolated cases, neither are men.

# Bad Girls

*I worked two stints* with an assistant conductor—the first for a year, the second for six months—who was a young lady that not only understood my language, she spoke it fluently. On the railroad, we have crew briefings before doing any work on the train before every tour of duty. We receive train orders pertaining to the route, or routes, we would be taking and the whole crew would sit at a desk and talk over the new restrictions; if there was anything new on the train bulletin boards, we would read and go over them as well. We would have a safety rule or two to read and discuss and we were all required to sign a register indicating we had met all the obligations of a crew briefing.

One day, my young lady assistant conductor showed up and set down a huge banana in front of me, as she grinned from ear to ear.

I said, "I am not even going to pretend I resemble that," and before anything more transpired, we got to the business of our crew briefing.

The next time we had a crew briefing a couple days later, she showed up and laid the smallest banana I had ever seen in front of me, again grinning from ear to ear.

"I am so disappointed in you. I don't even come close to resembling that, either."

For the remainder of my time working with her, she would almost always bring a banana somewhere in the happy medium of the first two. I noticed that the signage on her locker read, *banana girl*.

*

I worked with a lady engineer and I remember the day when she hired out as a coach cleaner, went to on-board services, on to passenger train conductor, and then locomotive engineer. She was sweet as they come one minute and raunchy to the core the next. I called her "Bare Ass" and she called me "Hairy tongue." She is a pretty good locomotive engineer.

One day, the train was late coming out of Canada and the crew was going to have to be relieved on account of the hours of service law; we can only work twelve hours. They needed a conductor and engineer to meet them somewhere to relieve them. The phone rang on my day off—*ka ching, ka ching*. I accepted the call and agreed to meet the locomotive engineer who accepted her call, Bare Ass, at King Street Station in Seattle then take a cab north to dog catch the expiring crew. We got a cab and proceeded north. Bare Ass was spewing x-rated material all the way to Bellingham for about two hours as I enjoyed it; however, I am not sure what the male driver was thinking as he listened.

The train was already stopped at Bellingham waiting for us when we arrived. We got on the train and had a crew briefing with the crew we were relieving, going over the orders and all the particulars of the passenger count. All this was done at a table in the bistro. Then, according to rule, the conductor or engineer had to call the train dispatcher and touch base with them before taking over officially.

So I picked up the phone and make the call, telling the dispatcher our on-duty times, engine number, number on our train orders, and the relieving engineer and conductors names.

I barely got all that information out and Bare Ass said loudly, so as all could hear, "That's Engineer Bare Ass and Conductor Hairy Tongue, and the hair on his tongue came off of my ass."

\*

I worked with a *pretty-when-she-wanted-to-be* lady clerk who resembled the actress Farrah Fawcett from the hit TV show in the '70s called *Charlie's Angels*, the plot being three lady detectives working for their boss Charlie on special assignments. For the first few years, our working relationship was hot and cold, and as time went on, it became mostly warm as we engaged in hugs and jokes. I nicknamed her "Tear Ass Terry," meaning that if you ruffled her feathers in any way she would make it her goal to tear you a new ass.

It took me many years and until just recently to halfway figure her out; however, it all makes sense now. She had her share of character defects, such as talking my language and then some; however, tolerating anything or anybody remotely connected to pedophilia was not one of them. For good reason, it was her mission to rid our company of such perverts. She would seek them out, and was instrumental in several of them being fired or suddenly retiring. As I look back on our early relationship being hot and cold, I now realize she was conducting an investigation just like a Charlie's Angel by throwing a little verbal bait out here and there and when none of my reactions indicated anything sympathetic to pedophilia, our friendship grew.

# Nutcase Moments

*I made thousands* of announcements, legendary to some and not to others. I always said 51 percent of the public liked me, 48 percent turned their heads the other way, while 1 percent hated my guts. For example, many times, coworkers made claim that I made an announcement about navy ships near the port of Everett, Washington—that they were full of "seaman." I never did, or at least I don't think I did.

That said, I planned an announcement for my last trip up there, though I retired before I could deliver it. The announcement:

"On the waterway, folks, you are now observing the Navy Ship U.S.S. Dwight D. Eisenhower CVN #69, currently full of seamen, with a few ladies mixed in there. Yes siree Bob, there she is now."

*

There were the slip-of-the-tongue, one-time-only announcements, and announcements that I was called into the office for and told to delete...or else. I will also mention some I deleted before I got called into the office.

I had two locomotive engineers, both named Richard, and both went by Dick. One was the regular engineer and the other was familiarizing himself on the route to stay qualified. "Ladies and gentlemen, boys and girls, today we have two Dicks on the head end operating the locomotive, Dick Matson and Dick Tolbert, yes siree Bob!"

\*

Many times our train would need to back into a siding or a station for various reasons and usually I would get on the rear of the train and direct the back up movement with my portable radio. On one trip, I had a newer assistant conductor and we needed to back up, so I suggested that they shadow me to see how this was done. First, I made an announcement so the passengers knew what is going on.

"Ladies and gentlemen, boys and girls, there is a lot of congestion today and we have been instructed by the train dispatcher to back our train into the north end of the English siding here on top of a freight train that is just in the clear enough for us to do so. We will wait until our southbound sister passenger train passes and then the route will be clear to our next station stop of Stanwood. This should only be a ten or fifteen-minute delay and we will keep you updated. Okay folks, both conductors will double mount the rear...of the train...and watch...the shove...into the siding. Do not be alarmed; you're in safe hands.

\*

Not exactly an announcement, but when approaching the Nelson Bennett tunnel near Tacoma going north, when the engineer would call out the clear signal for the tunnel I would respond with, "Okay to penetrate the black hole."

One day, a lady in the back of the bistro with excellent hearing said loudly, while grinning and looking my way, "You better wear some protection."

My wife told me one day, "I know you're handsome and the ladies are attracted to you, but I don't worry about you because as soon as you open your mouth, they should disappear."

# Nicknames

*When I hired on the railroad* in 1977, the rails with nicknames were mostly of an infamous nature, some more than others. At Stacy Street yard in Seattle, there was "Dirty Ernie," a switchman who was said to sleep with any lady he could, including his mother-in-law. At Auburn yard, there was "Crash Arnold," whom I've mentioned, a locomotive engineer who was in more than his fair share of train wrecks. There was also another locomotive engineer from Auburn, nicknamed "Society Sam"; however, he was pretty much the opposite of a Society Sam.

I worked eleven-plus years in freight in and around the Seattle area and heard stories told about numerous employees on the railroad; only a few I recall had included people with nicknames. After being on the railroad fifteen or twenty years, I started giving people nicknames and many stuck (though many that did not). Many times, people did not like their nicknames and asked that I refrain...which mostly I did.

When I started writing this book, many of my former coworkers from mostly my passenger years would ask me if they were in the book. Most the time, I said they were not. Many seemed dismayed, so then I would take out my pen and paper and say, *I can put you in the nickname chapter*, to which they would grin. What I have decided is that if any of my colleagues are not in a story in the book, I will try to remember to include them in this chapter.

I would guess that about half of the nicknames in this chapter I am responsible for. I will start with the King Street yard, employees from the late-'80s and early-'90s, and then everyone I can think of who worked in and out of Seattle through my retirement in 2017:

There was "Blonde Bombshell," a lady switch bitch who if you crossed her would go off like a bomb...I say that fondly. "Hey Paula," a lady switch man all the men wanted to get in the hay. "Tall Colonel," switch man that was tall in height and mellower than "The Little General." "The Pirate," switch man missing most of two fingers. "N.P. Kim," locomotive engineer who pounded spikes in '69 on the old Northern Pacific Railroad. "The Grinch," switch man who was a Grinch until you got to know him. "Russian Girl," a blonde coach cleaner I was fond of. "Homer," locomotive engineer. "Hand Throw Jack," locomotive engineer. "Cantaloupe Girl," a black lady coach cleaner...boobs like cantaloupes. "Curly," a gifted bald car toad. "Nicotine Bob," car toad who chain-smoked. "Mr. Green Jeans," electrician who wore green coverall jeans. "40-40 Tom," engineer 40 minutes late to work one night, said he was at a stoplight when a crazy lady jumped into his car and she would not get out until he gave her 40 dollars. "Catfish Hunter," G.N. trainman who did some cat fishing for ladies. "Virge the Scourge," conductor who forgot to remit his ticket sales. "1/2 and 1/2 Pamela," conductor I was fond of. "Hooterville Doug," engineer who ate at Hooters. "Unga Bunga Dave," locomotive engineer who liked unga bunga. "Doc Holiday," locomotive engineer...real name Steve. "The Menace," locomotive engineer named Dennis, a nice man who left us way too early. "Flying Hawaiian," smiley man locomotive engineer of Hawaiian descent. "Ride 'em high Debra," blonde station agent I am fond of who rides horses. "No Flack Roberta," black lady station agent who took no flack. "The Black Gentleman," a nice black station agent.

# The Window Lady

*After I retired*, I began to write stories—mostly about my railroad career. About once a week, I started taking scenic drives from my home in Roy, Washington along the back roads to the Centerville passenger train station thirty-eight miles away. I would usually visit some antique malls along the way, then catch a train from the Centerville station to somewhere like Keltucky using my rail pass, spend some time at a museum or antique store, and sometimes just walked around town. Then I would catch a train back to Centerville and drive home. While riding the train, I would promote my upcoming book with former coworkers, sometimes passing out a copy or two of stories I had written.

The station agent at the Centerville station was a cute, smart little fifty-something blonde lady that smiled a lot. I remembered her working the ticket counter in the Portland station before I retired when I was bringing trains in and out of that terminal. I always had pleasant interactions with her.

One day while standing and visiting with her at the ticket window, waiting to catch a train that was tardy, she said, "Do you want to come into my office? We can visit while you wait. I can let you do that. After all, you worked here forever."

She let me in the side door for the first of many times, and I took a seat at her desk as she stood at her window and sold tickets and answered questions with the public.

I soon realized that I was not the only man fond of her, overhearing men as they put the charm on at the window. Having said that, she had one of the best demeanors I had ever witnessed when she was dealing with customers. She was especially gifted with nutcase customers, as one after the other would challenge her in all sorts of ways—from being just plain belligerent, asinine people to others who could not help being mentally ill. Foreigners, the elderly, and stressed-out people; she handled them all very well.

I noticed that there were some lonely, challenged people who might travel once in a blue moon who showed up randomly at her window just to talk. People who used to be what were called "outcasts of society." She was very kind to them, going above and beyond the call of duty. She counseled them and gave many of them advice, but most importantly she listened.

The window lady and I would talk about the book I was writing, and she seemed genuinely interested in it, so I started giving her rough copies of stories to read. She would read and give me her opinion on my stories, encouraging me to continue. I am really grateful for her support and inspiration during the trials and tribulations of writing this book.

As people came and went at the window, I started encouraging her to get a journal and start keeping notes—as she should write a book of her own when she retires called "The Window." As time went on, I realized that I was the nutcase that made it past the window.

# Nicknames: Honorable Mention

*My thoughts for this section* of the book originally were if a railroad coworker I liked during my career was not mentioned in the main railroading content, including the nickname section, I would try to remember to mention them in this section, especially those who hinted that it would be appreciated. I have included nicknames and short explanations of how some of them came about.

There are also some random off-the-rails thoughts scribbled here and there that seem to go nowhere at this point, but they're seeds for stories not yet written. After I retired, I crossed paths with people in my daily life that knew very little about railroading. When learning I was busy writing a book, a few became "off-the-rails" friends and some of them now have nicknames and will also receive an honorable mention.

Here we go...first with my railroad career.

Freight days: "Cheap Thrill Rodger," 1969 Great Northern Railroad locomotive engineer that took great pleasure scaring the head donk "Brakeman." My first trip with him, he sped the train toward the open drawbridge number four spanning the Salmon Bay waterway, charging right up to the red signal and coming to a smooth stop just ten feet short.

G.N.R.R. 1-4-66 Switchman Gibby. N.P.R.R. Trainman B.N. Hogger "Pitbull John." We're the best, you know the rest. C.N.R.R. Boomer Rob. Conductor from Canada "Disco Don," rumored to disco the women from the disco club to the bedroom back in the day. Smoky Cab Jerry. Stacy Trainmaster booze story. The Polish Prince is of Polish descent, a nice man, but not exactly a prince, hired out in 1969 as a King Street switchman and became a locomotive engineer many years later. Mitch. Buck. High Rail Vern. High Thor. Hi Rye. Orton on the shove. Bill Stevens. Bob Klein. Jump up and down Yosemite Howard. B.N. Conductor Claude The Barber or Skipper the Clipper, nice man that left us way too early. Blackie Moser. Bob Lewis. Chima. Hand signals for Buffalo and Annie tracks at Auburn. Harry and Lester Balls. First day on railroad, my army fatigue jacket was stolen. What a Rip-off Robin. Budd H. Frosty. Train Dispatcher Earl. Technical Tim. Toutle River Girl, train dispatcher that grew up near the Toutle River. M.P. 27 wreck. Snohomish missing rail wreck. South Seattle wreck. Ruptured gas car tank at Ridgefield tragedy. Marysville wreck. Oregon Slough disaster. West Seattle drop tragedy. Off Color Roy, Spokane conductor. Seattle G.N. Brakeman Matson. G.N. hoghead Full Uniform Mac or "The Sheriff." G.N. Empire Builder hoghead Diamond Jim and his Fireman Ron. Union man Eman. Dirty Ernie. Conductor's Bergy, Tiger Davis, Illchuck, Handlebar Shipley and Raleigh. G.N. Brakeman Not So Bitter Ron. My Wishram beanery buddies Kenny and Clarence. Seattle G.N.R.R. Conductor Camano Island Ron. N.P.R.R. hoghead George Hapala. N.P.R.R. hoghead Dick Fiddler. N.P. King Street Clerk Mary Jo. King Street hoghead Ken. N.P. Conductors at Auburn the Fish brothers and the Jaeger boys. Hockey Nut Reggie. Wenatchee Conductor Tim. Close Clearance Clarence. M.P. #4 Cassidy. Light at the end of the tunnel came fast Feb 10, 1980, when B.N. had runaway locomotives at the west end of the Cascade tunnel; I have an inside perspective. In 1990, a transient stole three locomotives from a Seattle yard. Alerts came on the radio. I then watched as the locomotives sped by King Street Station. At Longview Junction, a tragic head-on collision occurred November 11th, 1993, resulting in five crew-member deaths. I had worked with three of them. After three days of shutting down the tracks while cleaning up the wreckage and investigating, our train was the first to pass through the collision area at restricted speed. I played taps on my harmonica over the radio airwaves.

Locomotive engineers Mad Dog and Speedy Elmer. Car Toad John. Stacy yard switchmen Big Red Tim. Pasco Mitch. Left-Handed Pat. Hide something in train orders hoping to fire someone. Black engineer at Stacy Yard whose vision went bad, had to retire to a different occupation. Milwaukee Rails Mike N., Lawless Dave, Dog Brown, Yardmaster Ed, Rob, Edgewood Bob, Craig, Dale, Mean Gene. Zook. B.C. Smith. G. brothers. ZIG. Starkovich.

Amtrak Seattle: Lori the Talgo Queen, pretty little L.S.A. Peter Peter Pumpkin Eater, Asian station agent. The Talgo Bitch, pretty little L.S.A. Agent Bill Lee. John H. Dunhop Vicky. New Orleans Laura. Barry McGuire's bastard son. North Carolina Linda, very nice lady clerk. Miss 86, a very nice lady clerk that hired out in 1986. Michael, a Seattle clerk with a nice mom. Bo, Tana, Aaron, Calvin, Eric, All-Star Randy Hedington.

"Happy Trails," pretty little prior rights B.N. freight clerk lady in Bellingham, Washington who gave me hugs while passing through, always telling me *happy trails!* In Vancouver, Canada, while on a layover, a pretty little lady that owned a high-end thrift shop also gave me hugs. When she said *happy trails*, it was time to disappear, as either there was a customer with money in the shop or her husband was expected soon. Pittsburg Potato, Louisiana La La. 21 beaters.

"Wonder Woman," a pretty little lady yard conductor that came to work dressed as Wonder Woman that we all wondered about. Thai Pie Mike. Viking Woman. Hop Along Bud. Mr. & Mrs. Larry Ridgeway. The Pirate or 3 finga sniffa. 4 finga sniffa. Tall sniffa. Crazy ass sniffa and the king sniffa. One-time-only Miguel, Talgo technician from Spain; after explaining 69 to him he said, *me try one time only.* Lars, smart A-1 Talgo Tech. Big Richard Talgo Tech. Shit Face Eddy. Filthy Phil. Rapping Raphael. Reset Dick. Uncle Fester. Hot Rod Larry. Guam Tom. Magnetic Anton. Handsome Rick. Monty. One sniff over the line Charles. Not half bad Chad. Ricardo 69, a Talgo supervisor. Hoghead Sailboat Tom. Trench Coat Sam, wore a trench coat to cover up his bulge. Premature Keith. Insane Lane. Johnny

Bale Off. The 8-year-old. French Taco 'F.T.' Midnight Goat, Decipher my switch list Dave. Seattle Car Toad Dave S.

The Gentile. Boring is good Derek. No needs McNeil. Minnie Mouse. Longview crossing crew van wreck. Commissary Keith. Rickshaw Helen. Commissary Esther. Commissary Paulette. Commissary Lloyd. Broad Street Pete was a coworker friend that lost track of time while assisting the food service car at Seattle's King Street Station one morning, and the train departed with him still aboard. After we got through the mile-long King Street Tunnel, I stopped the train at the Broad Street crossing, and he hopped off. "Tabitha," a very nice pretty little lady clerk that resembled Debby Boone, lighting a few lives up; she left us way too early.

"Smokey," a pretty little coworker lady, had somewhat of a darker complexion. I really thought she resembled Smokey Robinson, the singer, and was hesitant to tell her "as a joke" she should have her DNA checked because she might be his daughter. Eventually, I told her that, and she came to like her nickname. Walla Walla Craig. Matt O., friend of Bill W. Work, work, work and take big, long breaks. "Goddamn it!" You kiss the trainmaster's rear, then you have to kiss his wanger, too. You give them the silver dildo! Then they want the gold one, too. Chicken Soup Sue, a lady that made me look like an angel. Hostler Helper Jeff. Skinner Leonard. "*Linder*," whose name was Linda, however in diversity class one day, the black southern man teaching kept calling her Linder. "Ah-So Linda," a nice pretty little lady clerk, when visiting with her and she needed to get on with her work, she would say, "Time to stop hovering, Larry."

Fur Coat Frank. Flattop Frank wore a flattop haircut in an era when few did. He also did very good vocal impersonations of coworkers, mostly on the radio airwaves. Monica of the west coast. Canadian Red Cap Greg. Broken Legs Louie. Three Buns. Orange Juice Bill. Canadian Red Cap Pepe Le Pew. Pocahontas was a pretty little lady conductor that moved from Seattle to California. Jail Bait Girl was a pretty little lady conductor that moved from California to Seattle. Figurehead Larry. Down Low Lois. Low Down Barlow. The Prowler. Andy & Gail. Bubba Lite. Miller Lite. Widow Lover. Die Hard Sears. Walt Disney's bastard son, a station agent "Walt." "Skykomish Girl" in the town of Skykomish, Washington, near the tracks lived a lady that liked to wiggle her bare skinny little butt from her porch as the passenger train rolled by, thank you. "Fill her up Phil," conductor that loved his handle awarded him after it went no bid from the older Phil's on the district seniority rosters. Banned on the Canadian National Railroad. Black in the back at the crack. Liquor and wine or whine. Testicle's stitched up more then once. Broken trampoline. Whining to the restroom. Larry the lady killer. Jordan spreader of the west. Luscious Larry. Far East Cab. Far East Laborer.

Foot Job. Shoeshine Parlor Car. Shoe Shine Stand King Street Station back in the day. Big Guy, a good guy now in the sky. King Street Two-Timing Ted. Red Head Chris. 1969 G.N. Paula. Tom & rest in peace Fran. JFK's bastard son. JFK's bastard grandson. See any gray hair, "Anna." Rad Dan. Wong Way. "The Dirt Sniffer" Material control. Festus Travis. Read Wilson. Idaho Tracy. Des Moines Pamela. If not for guys like you? There would not be guys like me. Okay to have fun but not too much. How's the hole?......family. As a joke I always asked for a room with two beds; if I got lucky I did not want to be rude and ask them to leave so I would offer them the other bed. Red-faced old men sitting with young Asian ladies. Alphabet system spotting train at Ephrata A-B-C-D-E-F and the G spot. Hotel room furniture work out. When young I was addicted to crack, just about any lady with a crack. Dear Abby story. I was a dinosaur. Did a lot of predicting when young. Observe the pistons ejaculate on the rear during air test. Transvestite had a seat problem. One-armed man. Dong Eater. Passenger Bee Hein. Fuck family from Germany, real name and spelling. Shove her deep. They found her face down in Rickie Lake. Anytime there is someone in a hole I will be watching. Must be a record. They used to dump the crappers on the tracks or in the pit track. They got him for stealing garbage. Sperling, Willingdon bridge 69. 1948 Santa Fe lounge car. Big Deal Joe. Detective 69. Two cops miss their station stop while sniffing ladies. Mafia guy, not the end of the world comment. Cop eyeball screwing ladies at King Street station. W.M.F. Helped me in 1998 and I helped him years later. Close call reporting. Poop on desk in Bellingham mystery. Swapping grain cars in Snohomish investigation. Nutcase black passenger often stated *I hate white people*. Russian lady stowaway on locomotives, I was amazed. Maltese tavern. Lady boards train dodges ticket collecting while changing into men's clothes, finally put stop to it. Lady with pet rat. Lady with cat in cage the lady with two...I scooped out broken overflowing handicap toilet with a paper cup on Builder. Three privates on the rear record. Drooling Ron. Smiling Canadian Lady agents pointed at me and the Little General's bags. Dating game with seats. Butterfly bush on my desk. Harry Seamen, party of three. Common Whore confused with commodore restaurant. Caught a guy masturbating. Favorite port in every girl.

Coach Cleaner Jill was mega fun. Coach Yard bosses Green, Bruiser, Big Dipper, and Rags. Electricians George, Ron, Harry, J.C. And off the grid Bob. The Gun Fighter. The Animal, great Seattle electrician. Blonde Bombshell & U.P. 69 Jack. Mo Fo Senior & Junior. "Hope," nice lady coach cleaner that left us way too soon. The Shadow. Coach Cleaner Ray, or not so blind Ray. Tarlene. Just a man Chris. Honeymoon totaled car. PTA or Ponytail Al. Emery. Always smiling Mo Fo. Slingshot Tom, a good man, left us way too early. Long Sleeve Tom. Mike Snow nice man left us to early. Toe truck. Coach cleaner what rhymes with Chuck & O.B.S. Mom. We don't report sexual harassment here, we grade it. Pink Helmet Debbie. Howie. Pockets Sam. Des Moines Peggy. Georgia Peach 21. Removed stowaway passenger at Ephrata, he then commits suicide. Coach Yard employee Straighten up Andy. Wally. Ed. Don. Lady Coach Cleaner show me who Marcella. Wacky Jackie. Nicole. Ruth the clerk. Crazy Tammy. Nila. Tom, Barbara, and Daughter

Donna. Anna Williams. LaDonna. Seoul Man, a good man, left us too early.

James Brown's bastard son. Cab ran a red light. Redder than you know what on a you know what. Rosey Grier's bastard son. If I was doing any better I would be sick or in jail. That will stunt your growth. Lord take me. Chiefs on trains. Shipwreck Shipley, Carter. Chopsticks Louie. Grease Lady. Spindly Sniffa. Mr. Nelson. Smokey-Die hard. Leephus. Glad Dan. Alex, very nice man that left us way too early. J.C. made me look like an angel. Good Golly Miss Molly. McAllister Creek. Conductor Psycho Sam. Black in the back at the crack. Fake Leg by tracks. Bare ass Barron. Tom Casket. Story of my response after people would question me after I turned sixty, *why haven't you retired?* Never slept on the job because I wanted to be awake for it if I got fired. Toilet paper rolls to block the doors. Died on hours of service one potential violation. Male M & M's. White spot on the radio antenna. White spot black air hose King Street Station. Castration conversation with lady politician on the train. Hid oral, anal medicine in bakery basket on bistro. Do not want to hear about Uncle Jack's divorce or Grandma Edna's colon operation. Black squirrel.

Amtrak hogger and conductor that looked like a cavemen. "Peaches," nice King Street well-preserved lady that left us too soon. Jim Greiter, best boss ever, left us way too early; accepted many of my *get out of jail free* cards. Pale Face. White Diamond. Brake Shoe Bob. Brent the Bullet, nice man that left us too early. Bag Lady, got two special bags for her. Pear Tree Dave. "Adam Ant." "Chad F." "The Free Man." Senor Balls. "The Kid" retrained me in the yard. "Rocky," bastard son of James Gardner. Seattle conductor, Captain America. Halo Jay lo Jason, Seattle conductor, good man that left us way too early. Pot Belly pilot. Fired pilot. Rhymer & Reamer. WMF Junior. Sugar Sue. Make out Bob. Quadruple Dipping in Spokane. 2-door Peter. Arnie's Little Brother. Seattle operations at times was a Nut Ward. Dieringer Scotty. Hang Down your head, Dooley. Klondike Karl. Conductor Tony Teras, a good man, left us way too soon.

The Creecher, a good man, left us too soon. G.N.R.R. Conductor Mike F. My dear friend, the "Hourglass Lady." "Windy City LaToya," funny little ticket maker. Brittany, nice ticket maker. Houston. Riverside Susan, nice ticket maker. Pasadena Dena. Tim H. Mister Bates. Paul Clementine. "The Energetic Conductor" from the East Coast. "DT," or Deep Throttle, a nice lady engineer. L.B.J. Tone the Bone of the North, a van driver in Seattle. Tone the Bone of the South, a supervisor in Portland. Poon Jab, a friend of Father Brown. Emerald City OBS Boss John K. Uncle Paul. Smoky, a conductor that smoked a lot. Doug Orr. Eugene & Myla. Martin & Christine. Snidely only when he had to be Dick, nice man. Sir Thomas of Centralia. Gina Face. Tacoma Station. Tall Dark Don. Brad. Not dim Kim . Auggy doggy. Drop a dime Jim. Lace-em up, Don. Reverse Hug Debby. Claude Akins' bastard son Chris. Coast Guard Matt. Not A Mason Mason. Long Haul Johnson.

Flash Gordon. Bob Cobb. N.P. Bob. Jeff Wellgreen. The Cobra, name was Jake; however, there were too many Jake the Snakes. Billy Sorebutt. Bangkok Dave. Rose City Kerinne. Sacajawea. Barbi Doll, a very nice and sweet diner server who left us way too early. Anna Banana. Don the LSA, a very funny bad, bad boy but a good man that left us too early. Church Lady, but not a lady. Diner Queen Jean. G.N. Paul. Pornal Paul. No more Moore. Janet rhymes with planet + Phil. "480 Joe." "449 Karlinsky." Ed Quicksall, a great boss who got me out of a couple huge pickles, left us too early. Paul the Prince. G.N. Snohomish Ray. King George, who showed me mercy once or twice, keeping me out of the dungeon. Psycho Mylo. Jonsing Jones. Pretty Mama Fran. Montana Josh. Bellingham Katie. Snohomish Vick. Sumo John.

Stub Track Russ. King Street Russ. Susan. Marlene. Red Cap Lisa. Red Cap George. Red Cap Louis. Juanita. Anita. Straighten up Mike. Watermelon Jugs. White Betty. Black box Gregory. Gobbler Angel. Throat salve. Six Times John *hi yah!* Suzanne & Jeff. Safe2Safer Corrie. Alligator Chris. G. Spot Ban. No heal her up Robert. Cow Lick Eddy. No second fiddle. Cockroach is a left-handed compliment; hard to kill, live forever, get around in all the cracks. Republican Sniffer. See Jane, See Dick, See Spot, see spot dick Jane. C.C. Rider or See See & ride her. Seattle electrician C. Box. See blood dripping from hidden overhead meat in pantry. See Thomas get well. Amtrak Kojak. Amtrak Motha Stewart. Gig Line. Allen L. Edmonds station agents "Hard Licker" and "Journaling Jim." Precision Dick or Picky Dick, a locomotive engineer of high operation standards."Sandi," very nice OBS lady that left us way too early. Larry the Chicken Man, nice man left us to early. Arnie Z. 'Z' for zealous, a great boss instrumental in me surviving the Mo Fo investigation. Louisiana Joe. Motown Betty, a very nice lady station agent who became a conductor; she grew up in Detroit, but left us too early. Betty, I don't have that problem anymore. OBS Ralph and Romell. No feed-em Mike; eventually that changed, nice man. Old Man Rivers, also known as Sitting Bull, a good man, left us way too early. Lynda with a Y, a nice pretty little bistro car lady. Rowing machine. Lumpy and the Beav. Annie Fanny. Train Dispatcher Arlene. "Wabash Van," only person I ever knew that worked on the Wabash Railroad.

Tukwila Laurie, nice Bellingham station agent. Slightly Insane Elaine, a nice Bellingham station agent. Baggage Bob. Cheryl. Short-term John. E.T.A. Or E.A.T. Crazy Mary was a train dispatcher that spoke and understood my language. Sorboni, a conductor that was sore a lot when younger. Serious Sniffa, a trainmaster that appeared serious when sniffing. Builder Queen Joyce, funny lady even on her deathbed; I was really fond of her, she left us way too early. Funny pretty little Builder cook, Downtown Debbie Brown. Mary and Tom. Mr. Clean. The Bird Man was a diner car steward fond of birds and chicks. Pretty Karen. Boss man Gary. Sisters Diane and Georgia on my mind. Spokane Cheri, a very nice lady that left us way too soon. Wenatchee Patty. Young Gary. She said, *I like the way he tucks his shirt in.* Breastfeeding on the train. Down South Tracy Girl. Box lunch at the Y. Humptulips. Lincoln gun story. Paper bag on rock. Manhole cover. Three

W's. Mailbox Ass. Cooking up a storm Pete and Ziro below. Angel Down Low in the Diner. Night Ghoul. Gordana. Shot Glass Erica. Super Hooper lady. Jayma, nice little lady that left us way to soon. Noelani. Des Moines Girl. Burien Girl. Bothell Girl. Pretty little diner server, enjoy your meal "Camille." Glad Hand Suzanne. Public Market Ray. Pac Man. Tall Redhead, a nice lady sleeping car porter with a good figure and wit. Long Leg, hard-working Empire Builder OBS lady with long legs. "Little Joe" "The Gentile Joe" "Off-color Isaac" worked sleeper on the Empire Builder, nice man that left us early. The Prince. Stan the Man. Drawbar Terry & Chris. Diner Top Kevin. Big long breaks "Twee" Olive Oil Dorothy, a nice sleeper car lady on the Builder. Codependent Cody. Everett Jena, Chicago Miss Donna, Edgewood Gary, Des Moines Laura. Bonney Lake Brad, Pinay Anita. Nice little smiling"Jocelyn," left us way to early. Clam Chowder Ric. Thai Guy Johnathan. Betty, nice funny L.S.A. that left us way to early. Tom Sandie Vietnam Veteran and L.S.A. that left us to early. Spread 'em a little. The Fuzz, a former cop turned conductor. The Demon. Dreadlock Jose, wore hair in dreadlocks, mostly liked, but dreaded by some. Oly 4 dot .... 530 dead lift.

The Commie was a conductor with communist affiliations. Big Cox was a Sounder engineer and Coast Guard man. Sounder and Lilac city hoghead Chris.

Redondo Neal, freight and passenger conductor. Willy Sounder. Nancy, Jim & Jeanie. What rhymes with Rich? Todd Sounder. Yakima Jim. Nephew Tommy. Marshall Brown, left us too early. Clint Walker's bastard son.

Sookie Su, an engineer who is a cousin to conductor Long Dong. Snatchee Jim was a locomotive engineer from Wenatchee. Ankie, or AS, and CSF were train dispatchers in Canada. Saint Taint. Foamy Brown.

Hot Tub Dave. Agent Orange. Queen Sniffa. Made Marion. You're old when you have to take the blue pill to tork the pork. Assigned locker Number 69. My retirement lunch was June 9th. Ebony Woody. Lawson, a trainmaster, a good man that left us way too early. Cascade Cindy. Lemon Drop Erick. One toke over the line, Dave. Hi De Ho, + Sig. Rosa Parks Vashon Island. Smoke stack reminds me of when I was young. To succeed some suck seed.

Portland Rails: Conductor Jim Walsh, a good man, left us way too soon. English Charlie, a good man, left us way too soon. Spanky and the gang. Conductor Chris. Adds up to 69 Lisa. Cockeyed Neal. Portland V.C. Tom.

Montana Josie Coles, Portland hoghead, and friend. I would have a little fun and announce on the train's PA that today our locomotive engineer is the great-granddaughter of Casey Jones. Josie Jones, a nice lady, she left us way too early. Smiling Pat Everhart, Portland hoghead, a nice lady that left us way too early. Portland locomotive engineer that looked like Sammy Davis Jr. Portland hoghead S.P. Dave. Hoghead S.P. Craig. Portland G.N.R.R. hoghead "North Dakota Jim"; hired in '69, still working with fifty plus years of service. Portland hoghead Leo Landers. Portland hoghead Titlow Doug, my friend, and a good man, left us way too soon. Portland Lady hoghead Slim Kim. Portland hogheads Free Wheelon Dave the "Caboose Killer." Larry H. Larry S. Larry M. Omar, Mick, Lloyd, Ed, George, Pat, East Coast Tim, and Mark. Switch hitter Kevin. Tomahawk Bob was a Portland locomotive engineer of American Indian descent. J Clark. Bill W. Tim the rules examiner.

Portland N.P. conductor Redhead Kelly. Conductor "S.P. & S Roy." Portland SP&S conductor John L. U.P. Cal.

Portland S.P. conductor Coping John. Portland S.P. conductor Roach. "The Puffer," S.P. conductor that would puff out his chest whenever a pretty lady was near, a good man who left us way too early.

Portland U.P. conductor Pow Wow Art. Portland U.P. conductor Make a case, Gary.

Portland Oregon Electric Railroad conductor Bob Fahey, AKA "The Coach."

B.N. Portland conductor Satch. B.N. Portland conductor

Maria. Portland conductor Trudy. Conductor North Dakota Ray. Kenny Jackson, conductor/musician. Portland conductor Sherry. Canned Heat's bastard son, or conductor "Isaac." Portland conductor U.P. Ray. G.N. Portland conductor Steve, an ex-cop. Not So Straight Dave Straight. Gleeful Gleason. Matt Turner or Taylor. Pot Belly Chris. Facade Arod. Conductor Oatmeal Craig. "Rocky Mountain Dirk" or Dirk the Quirk, a conductor and union boss from the Rocky Mountain region, helped me get to retirement. Portland S.P. & S conductor, Stun Gun Horsey. Banjo Dan. Portland conductor Alaska Gene. Portland conductor Hello Kitty. Rocket Rider Calina. Portland conductor, Moan and Groan Jeff. Thunder Club Archie. California Kitty. Help help me Rhonda. Steve. Rob. Portland conductors Big Tim, Big Dave, Big Nick, Big Big Toby, and the big boss conductor "Fred," nice man, local union boss, left us way too early. Portland mechanical foreman Chris, a good man who fought a brave battle with cancer, left us way too early. Tom the "Home Wrecker" left us to early. Portland conductors Harry Zeal, known to balk Ken and The Cry Baby. Portland car toad/conductor/hoghead Hot Rod Rod. Sold my Viagra to Judy. The Sarge, a pretty little coach cleaner girl who gave me hugs; she became a conductor griever. Hum Job. Innsbruck. Tom Buick. Ladder butt. Marysville 105-year-old-man. Cliff rescues dog. Crushed cab of logging truck. Lady on Bellingham hill strike. South Seattle near-miss gas truck strike. No air at the Y. Mud slide on tracks next to waterway. Red signals coming into Reservation, M.P. 18 and Cashmere. Heinlich Maneuver. Engineer threw orders in trash. Pot breaks. Almost scraped off side at Lander street industry track. Knocking brakes off at Covington near disaster. Fusees in bathroom. Torpedoes under foot board. Flat car rolls over derail at Renton. Dragged while boarding caboose at Orillia and Skykomish. Southwell saved the day at Auburn. Hid two injuries. Smoking pot with O.D. on the caboose. Killer Bob. eight hours O.T. to flip switch. Stall locomotives on purpose. Faint voice on purpose. Paid until caboose arrives. Extra pay to add locomotives, copy train orders change from road to yard work or visa versa. Four days pay to work one night in Kent. Three and and a quarter days pay to drive to Sumas, get lucky, and drive home. Tacoma waterfront strike blew his shoulder out. Willamette River drawbridge. Broadway Cab Company and Molly Mcguire's Saloon. She gave him the nod. My favorite train station is Portland Union Station; it was built in 1896, which is 69 8 1 backwards. 7-Eleven Sheri. Nice old school ticket maker lady "Nancy" left us way to early. Pretty little lady Portland station agent "I know you, Lori Lee." Portland station agent Cycling Scott. Mr. Smith. Jerry. Blue Socks Greg. Blooming Dave. Frank. Sarah. Upstairs T & E Mary. Take a letter Maria, nice pretty Portland ticket clerk. Portland Packard. Karla. Little Dan. Portland Red Caps Craig, Chris, Triple P. and the Jolly Red Giant. Portland baggage lady that left us to early, Lynn. Foxy Portland baggage lady Sue. Mike. Cozy Peter. North Dakota Dan. Coffee Tea or Me Steve. Baggage man, Woodpecker Larry. Griever Mark. Ken Ticker. No Meth Linda. Ken Black Smoke. Vancouver station agent Lucky Kevin 17. Vancouver station agent Byron. Vancouver station agent Debby, nice sweet lady who left us way too early. Vancouver station agent Jerry. Libby of the North, a station lady in Seattle. Libby of the South, a pretty little station agent in Portland. B.N offspring Darin. Centralia station agent Ken, nice man that left us too early. Centralia station agent Joan, nice sweet lady who left us way too early. Date nails. Klamath Falls blues. Salem toilet paper scandal. Dirk, Oregon ticket maker. Randy, Oregon ticket maker. 3-hole Fred, a laborer that was an avid bowler. 3-point contact Sylvia. Sweet Triple E. Ken. Paul. Missy. Three Times a Lady Lori, pretty little Oregon ticket maker and Centralia station agent.

Spokane hogheads: Rest in peace, David Grimmer. Shafted Steve. Kodiac Bill and Lying Bill. G spot Kevin. Will He Les. Should have known better Brent. Spokane Trainmasters/Road Foremen Pat, 40/40 Tom, East Coast Steve and Winslow Neal. Spokane Operations supervisor Irwin and Jacob. Downtown

Marlin. Spokane G.N. hoghead Cornwall. Spokane Hoghead don't call me Dick, Richard. Spokane Mechanical Argonaut Jason. Allen. Black Cloud Aaron, a nice man, left us way too early. Spokane Station Agent's Matt, Terry, and Vickie. Conductor T.J. Cassandra. Young Matt. Uncle Tom, hoghead from Spokane, a good man, left us too early.

Amtrak Montana: Great Northern Bax, very safe G.N.R.R. Spokane switchman that became Shelby Amtrak trainman; had an unmistakable high-pitch tone at times to his voice. "Fur Collar Coat Dave," BN switchman, brakeman, conductor, engineer, Amtrak assistant conductor; wore a fur collar coat as an Amtrak assistant transportation manager and van driver, became an Amtrak road foreman and Amtrak engineer; took his work calls from the bar back in his B.N. days. Shelby conductor Big Will. Shelby locomotive engineer, Crazy Chester; rough life, left us for the spirit in the sky. "Renegade Loren," Shelby hoghead Section 8 G.I. Dump in the suitcase "Belton Bob." Grizzly Bear McMillan. Jack Shit Joe. Foamer Bruce. Montana G.N. passenger train conductor "Blue Balls." Witty, semi-pretty Shelby clerk "Sue" and her hoghead brother. Whitefish Suzanne. B.N. Shelby passenger train conductors "Wayno Wayno" and Jordan spreader of the east. Gentleman passenger train conductor in Shelby, Montana "Micky." Montana baggage man "Havre Dave." Shelby conductor Keith. Philly Brown. Mustang Salley. Sharp-dressed man. Buff Job Tom. Shannon. Squiggy. Bob and cousins. Bipolar Express. Conductor on the tee Dee. Whitefish Scandal.

U.P. engineer Pioneer Joe and U.P. conductor Ziggy, worked the Pioneer train back in the day. B.N. Jim Cox was conductor that worked the Pioneer train back in the day; a good man who left us way too early. S.P. Steve Bazz, good man left us too soon. Women are good for three things Pioneer "Big Ed." Add an hour Pendleton crew. Engineer's short fart and Fitz.

Some of my favorite passengers. The She-Wolf. Sumas Helen. Toaster Head Susan. Kelso Catherine. Bellingham Tanya. Mount Vernon Sue. Susan the head doctor. Celebrities on railroad property: I met Slick Watts. Dan Akroyd. Wynton Marsalis. Tony Ventrella. Slade Gorton. Cougar bounded tracks. F.N.G. Bellingham priest. Charlie Manson trailer. Sen Sen. Slanted tracks. Chunk of rail gone. Cherries at the border. Buttermilk oyster marriage. Math test. Clusterf---=O.T. Wet Sheep. Platonic to putonic. Brown Cherry. 6-pound Pot Roast. Bouncer, male hooker. One Sunday a month to the cat house. Pepsi, Snodle, Curly, Beaver, Bear, Bruin, Reddy, and Baily. Frosty Shadow. They should leave when I open my mouth. Heard Spanish fly and she died on gear knob story fifty times. Switch broom P.A. Junction. Vashon Island Rosa Parks bus. When I can't throw the switches. The Stomping Ground. Trident fork. Big Pen. Meat lugger pick pocket. Hotel 18. Have to forgive to be happy. Rapid City 1971. Indians in Wolfpoint, Montana Bar. Detector test stories. Hormone or whore moan. Green Parrot and Embassy movie theaters. Brace for the big unit. Pink cloud. Tradition 3. 6x9 = 54 I was born in 54. In 1969 I turned 15, 6+9=15. Dad passed when he was 69. Never saw a sunset until sobriety. Gravel pit. Dupont dock. Seasaw switch move. Big Bob. Stan in wheelchair. The swallow. Kalispell mosquitoes. Haircut at dentist. Pubic hairs in wallet. Passed blue pill to Judy.

No nickname Tom Spees. Carpet burns. Double-breasted sap sucker. Ruffled spouse. New Hope Gigolo. Boob Reduction. Coach yard brothers, Tom & Paul. Sunny Cher.

Off the Rails Honorable Mention: Sweet Packwood Librarian Ladies. Packwood Rocking Barbara. Postal Liz; she never went postal on me, however, during our first few interactions it might have crossed her mind. After retirement, while mailing my eBay packages at the post office, I developed a friendly relationship with "Postal Liz." Eventually, I told her I was writing a book. She became interested in it, and when there were no other customers around, I would tell her a story. I soon figured out that she understood my language. However, I never heard her speak it. One day while smiling, she implied that I was a naughty old man. I said that reminds me of a lady railroad coworker, "Naughty Nancy." When I was a young man, she told me I would be the world's worst naughty old man; I will have to put that in my book's honorable mention section. Postal Liz says, *you might as well add me to your book*, and I said, *will do*. Then there is Joyce "N.P.G.," or Northern Pacific Girl, as I address her. I met her at several antique shows that she worked at as a vendor. I found out she was the daughter of a Tacoma Northern Pacific Railroad trainman whom I had crossed paths with in the late '70s. As we got to know each other, I figured out some of her father's old-school rail mentality had rubbed off on her. She was *funny*. She addresses me as HTL, partly for Happy Thoughts Larry. Another honorable person to mention is my insurance lady and friend, "Doll Face Laurie." She is a source of great inspiration as she battles with Parkinson's while still keeping her sense of humor. I would email her stories from my book, and she would respond with a smiley face and, "I can read between the lines."

Hilltop friends Black Out Bob, Happy Medium Scott, The Black Pirate, My Two Sons Kara, Shawna, Terry, Tim, Opretta, Battery Charger Brenda, My Three Sons Kristine, Detroit Cordell, Dawn, Angie, Vanessa, Tabi, Sophie, Melody, Julie, Sarah, Darrin, Amy, Cedar Street Dana, Catch and Release Alison—and all their children.

My loving grandparents, Augusta and Earl. Darling Aunt Darlene. Caring Aunt Karen. Sweet Aunt Norma. Kind Aunt Sally. Wild Blue Yonder Uncle Ernie. Second Mother Bernice. Jerold and Laurie.

Coming in the next edition...my Top Ten Lists: Top 10 Derogatory Statements Made by Minorities about Minorities. Top 10 Degrading Statements Made by Women about Women. When young, many ladies would dodge me when they saw me coming. Many years later, I am now dodging the ones who used to dodge me.

Manning The Caboose, 1984.

Top: Cupola Shot. Bottom: Union Station and King Street Station, Seattle.

King Street Station clock tower.

# PART THREE

# Announcement History

*I was on a passenger train* working as an assistant conductor with a former Northern Pacific Railroad Conductor, "N.P. Bob," on the Seattle to Portland run in 1994. We were sitting in the lower-level handicap area of a passenger double deck "Superliner" coach that we often used for our private office. I was wearing my nice dry-cleaned assistant conductor uniform with my polished Sears Diehard shoes. On this particular day, the train was pretty full of passengers, so we had to share the private office, which was also the lower-level seating for our passengers who could not manage stairs very well, or at all.

I was engaged in a conversation with a passenger, traveling on business, in our office about matters of the world when he asked me about the duties of my job. I could tell that he was a bit annoyed with the transmissions and static coming over my portable radio as he was trying to concentrate on his work. He specifically asked me, somewhat sarcastically, *what is it exactly that you do?* After taking a minute to explain to him in a serious tone the requirements and duties that my job entailed, I could tell from his negative response that he was not impressed, deflating my ego for the moment.

This interaction caused me to dwell on the aspects of my job. At that juncture in my life I had seventeen years railroading, fourteen of it sober. I knew the territory and rules better than most, and I was among the top of my peers when it came to the safe operations of trains. In customer service, I was well above the status quo. But with the sarcastic jolt given to me by the businessman, I felt that I had to give more and do more than just sitting around during breaks. Brooding in our private office, I was more than a bit hurt by the businessman's comments, but then I had a spiritual awakening of a different kind.

I suddenly felt compelled to pick up the microphone and speak to the passengers on the public address system about landmarks and points of interest that the train was passing, scheduled station stops, general public information, and some not so general public information. Some of that not so general information would come back to haunt me over the next twenty-three years. I say that I had a, "spiritual awakening of a different kind" because as soon as I began to make those announcements, I could hardly believe what came out of my mouth! Whether I liked it or not, I had a way with words. The more I tried to refrain the better I became (or the worse, depending on a person's perspective).

Some would call me a creative genius, while others would disparage me as an evil degenerate. It was a Catch 22. For the remainder of my career, I was called into the office religiously and reprimanded for announcements that I had made that offended someone. Most often, these were trivial remarks intended to lighten the atmosphere. I was even banned for life at one point from making announcements, except for in cases of emergency. The life sentence was reduced through union grieving to six months and, with good behavior, I was let off with only one month served.

The announcement that led to me being banned, the trainmaster had told me, was an example of dry humor in poor taste regarding a creature that need not be mentioned, as it did not even inhabit the route that I delivered my announcement on.

In short, here is the announcement in question: "Ladies and gentlemen, boys and girls, the Puget Sound waterway we are looking at is the home of killer whales and gray whales. However, there are no sperm whales."

I agreed in the end that the mention of a sperm whale that did not inhabit our train route was unnecessary. I could somewhat understand where they were coming from. For years after, whenever I was tempted to repeat that announcement, I would fight off the urge by remembering the life ban and the words of the Trainmaster: *The mention of a non-indigenous sperm whale was dry humor of poor taste.*

Soon after, I developed a territorial bird announcement that my superiors challenged me on. This time, I had to explain to critics that these birds actually did exist along the train route and were listed by the Pacific Northwest Audubon Society as inhabitants of the Puget Sound waterway.

That announcement, in part, went something like this: "Ladies and gentlemen, boys and girls, the waterway you are observing is home to 267 known species of birds, including the bald eagle, golden eagle, red tailed hawk, and the rare and elusive gray seagull. there is also the pileated woodpecker, the flickertail woodpecker, and yes, the hairy woodpecker.

On nearly every trip, a passenger or two would seek me out and thank me for my entertaining or educational announcements. As a coworker, "Wonder Woman," once told me years later, I had *developed a following.* There were also the passengers who found me either annoying or offensive. Some of these people went so far as to write letters or call passenger services or the Washington Department of Transportation to complain about my announcements. One example of a complaint that I received stemmed from me referring to the passengers as "transients." I would often begin my announcements with "Ladies and gentlemen, boys and girls, and transients..." before delivering the rest of my announcement.

Throughout my career, when called into the office to face complaints about announcements, my best defenses were the dictionary, history books, geographical maps, theology books, and even our railroad rule books. I will remain forever thankful for those books. The pressure was never off me by certain superiors to relieve me of my public address system privileges. Did they not know that persistence caused resistance?

I had a reprieve for a while when they came out with the customer service comment cards that were stocked in the literature racks on the train. The idea was that passengers could fill them out and write about their experience pertaining to their train trip—postage paid. For about two years, we had the comment card project and two or three times a week a passenger would thank me for informative or humorous announcements I had made. When that happened, I took the opportunity to present them with a customer comment card and suggested that maybe they would like to help me out, because I was getting reprimanded for making those very same announcements that they enjoyed. I even offered to mail it for them; after all, that would be an extension of good customer service. The comment cards actually earned me bonus points with some of the upper management, but not all. Eventually, the card system went away, and passengers were back to writing letters and making phone calls relating their train ride experience.

My announcements became more refined over the years, as I would provide the riders who were unfamiliar with the territory education and brief history of the sights they were looking at, with a little bit of my patented dry humor mixed in. The dry humor was perceived by some officials as *non-positive*, although accurate.

Near Tacoma, Washington, I made an announcement that was deemed non-positive and there is a little bit of history with this one. At the south end of Tacoma, in the community of Ruston, for many years there was the Asarco Copper and Aluminum smelting plant situated between the train tracks and the waterway. It looked like something out of a science fiction movie, with several cement stacks spewing gases and smoke. It was determined that the toxic gases and spillage of chemicals from the plant were poisoning everything in the waterway, and the plant was closed down.

I watched along with the public and my fellow employees as the plant was dismantled through the years, and read accounts of medical havoc and lawsuits connected to the plant. Eventually, it became history. The announcement that I made concerning that property a couple of years before I retired was deemed non-positive, and it went like this: "Ladies and gentlemen, boys and girls, on the right in a minute you are going to see the Asarco copper aluminum smelting plant in all its glory, spewing out toxic and poisoning gases. Oh darn, wait a minute, I need to retire folks. I forgot they tore that place down and covered it all up and built condos on top of it." At that point, we would be going by the new condos with huge *for sale* signs on them, and I would say, "There they are folks, Coppertone condos, get 'em while they're hot!"

Well, that announcement and a few others I made that day—along with an interaction I had with two state officials on the train—resulted in formal charges being brought against me via Federal Express to my house on Christmas Eve. That was the worst Christmas for me since 1966 when I spent it in reform school. My union boss, "xxx F," got the charges dropped contingent on me not repeating similar behavior.

I made a trip to Spokane and back without making a single announcement while I contemplated my situation. After that, I became active making announcements again, taking great care in my wording and making sure I did not say "Octopus" and "Hairy Woodpecker" in the same sentence, or make a reference to trains "penetrating" tunnels more than once per tour of duty.

I became a changed person, and things went along fine for eight months, when I got another charge letter. I will have to explain a little. One day in 1995, I was on a layover in Portland in the company hotel lobby when I recognized Oregon Senator Bob Packwood. He was also the head of the department of Oregon Transportation, and a friend to passenger trains. I took out a green seat check card and asked him for his autograph. After signing the card, we shook hands and went our separate ways. After that fateful day, whenever my train would cross the Columbia River from Vancouver, Washington into the state of Oregon I would make an announcement: "Ladies and gentlemen, boys and girls, we are now crossing the Columbia River and entering the great Beaver state of Oregon. Home state of Senator Bob Packwood. Yes siree Bob! Seventeen minutes to Portland, folks."

I made that announcement with slight variations for twenty-one years, and one day a passenger who did not like Bob Packwood or me wrote a letter stating that I was belligerent, and that Packwood once had lady problems. *What man never had lady problems?* That letter was enough to get me a charge letter via Federal Express to my home citing me with insubordination, among other things.

There was an investigation scheduled to determine whether or not I was guilty of anything. This investigation would require the person who wrote the letter to attend, which I had no problem with, as I did not say anything that warranted punishment. I was only "belligerent" from the passenger's point of view because he did not like Bob Packwood. Again, my union boss, "xxx F," and I discussed the investigation, and we knew we could win, but the writing was on the wall; somebody wanted me off of the public address system. Period. We could win the investigation, but there would be more charges. Of that, we had no doubt. "xxx F" agreed that I could negotiate my discipline. The company offer was five days off work without pay and, if ever charged again with similar offenses, termination from employment was a possibility.

I brought copies of five 'atta boy letters written by passengers on my behalf and recognized by the company prior to ever being charged. I presented those to the charging officer, along with an explanation letter detailing my meeting with Bob Packwood in 1995. The best I could do was to negotiate my sentence down to three days without pay with the termination possibility hanging over my head. I reluctantly accepted, and it was agreed as part of my punishment, I would miss a two-day trip to Canada that paid close to three days' wage with the overtime.

318

Now, as most non-railroaders do not know, there is an insurance policy one can purchase from the union fondly called "bonehead insurance," officially named "job protection insurance." I carried the maximum coverage. As an example of how this protection applies, say the train I was in charge of derailed, causing millions in damage and lawsuits. If it could be proven that there was any negligence on my part, I could be fired. In that case, I would be eligible to collect job insurance and unemployment payout for a year, equaling about what I would have made working and still have a good chance for the union to win my job back.

I had bonehead and had never used it. I stood to lose three days' pay. My discipline was three days off, so after serving three days suspension I applied for three days of bonehead pay, not really thinking that I would get it, as I always thought it was only good for operation rule violations. I was surprised and happy to get a check for $600, ($200 per day missed). The kicker was that the union took no taxes. When I penciled it all out, I lost about $69. Had I known the insurance was going to pay, I would have taken the five days discipline first offered. I went back to work and was extremely careful from then on out when talking on the P.A.

# However

*I had never been reprimanded* in writing about the use of my mouth organ, so for the last six months of my career, during the last minute or so before arriving into my final station, I would play my harmonica over the P.A.. In honor of the Civil Rights Movement still ongoing today, for all the anti-war activists including disabled veterans, I would let loose of my rendition of "Blowin' in the Wind." I was waiting and anticipating being called into the office and reprimanded for playing non-positive music on the P.A.; when that happened, I was going to ask them, *what is wrong with you people? That's the most honorable song ever written questioning humanity.*

I was never called in, leading me to wonder why?. One might say, "the answer my friend is blowin' in the wind, the answer is blowin' in the wind...."

After retiring, and in the course of writing this book, I took a few cross-country trips on the train to visit relatives and friends. Great time to pull out my laptop and continue writing about my career; it had a good feel to it. I would be in the flow when the P.A. would crackle with some nutcase going on and on about dinner reservations while cracking jokes. Karma.

# Dike Access Road

*Between Kalama and* Woodland, Washington there are a few sights to see from the train. For instance, in Kalama the tallest totem pole in the world carved out of a single piece of wood at 140 feet tall is situated in a small park along the Columbia River. Just before passing it, I would tell the passengers a little history about the totem pole and add at the moment we were passing by, "That is some tall wood!"

A few minutes later, when headed southbound, we would be traveling 79 mph down the middle of the I-5 freeway as the railroad mainline tracks run parallel between the northbound lanes and southbound lanes of the freeway. At that point, if all operations were in order and there were no passenger issues, I would make an announcement:

"We are currently doing our maximum authorized speed of 79 miles per hour down the middle of the freeway, folks, and in a minute or so if you look to the right, you can see the Dike Road Access freeway exit sign." Then again a minute later, as we were passing by, "Yes siree Bob! There she is, the Dike Road Access exit."

As you can imagine, that announcement could be taken a lot of ways. I am really surprised that I was never called into the office concerning what I had said. One day around 1996, out of Seattle we had a group of about seventy-five lady passengers who reminded me of men in a lot of ways. The ladies were on their way to some sort of women's convention in Portland. They seemed to enjoy my announcements, but I was getting ready to ruffle some feathers.

Our bistro car attendant was the "Talgo Queen," a cute little lady known for providing good service with smart wit.

She said to me, "I bet you won't make that dyke announcement today. I dare you."

Well, after making the announcement I continued my duties and from what I could tell, most the convention ladies took it well, although I did get the evil eye from one or two.

# Conductor Big Boy

*In the '90s*, during a layover in Portland, I was hanging out with the rest of my crew in the lobby of the hotel we were staying in. The conversation became a little raunchy when the prior rights Burlington Northern Railroad hoghead from Montana whom I was working with stated that one day when he went to pick up a conductor coworker to play basketball, he answered the door in a towel and in the commotion of being in a hurry, the towel came off. The hoghead could hardly believe his eyes, as his conductor friend's resemblance to a horse was uncanny. We all laughed at the story, but I quickly put the image out of my mind and moved on.

A year or so later I was working with an old head prior rights Great Northern Railroad brakeman when he told me a story of when he and the conductor in question, while on a Portland layover, went to a topless club for some adult entertainment. While there, they met a couple ladies of the night and got into a cab. On their way to the hotel, the lady with the gifted conductor got a little ahead of herself, and she was heard to exclaim, "Hello, big boy!"

I started calling that conductor "Big Boy," and he would always grin.

Now this was all hearsay, and I sometimes wondered if they were…pulling my leg, until I got the chance to find out for myself. I was downstairs in the old King Street Station in Seattle relieving myself at the urinal when Big Boy stepped up to the urinal to my right to relieve himself. I looked straight ahead and then I prayed. *God, please forgive me but I'm going to look!* I peeked and he had it in hand while looking at me to make sure I saw it. I was definitely taller than him; however, I was also definitely shorter .

As the years rolled by, I would tell this story to coworkers I knew well and of course they passed it along to others. Eventually, it was no secret. However, nobody ever heard it from the...horse's mouth. I was telling a fellow coworker lady, Lois, the story, and when I finished, she told me, "I had a boyfriend like that once. It's such a shame; so much goes to waste."

After telling another lady coworker about what I had seen, she said, "I don't want to touch it or anything, but I wonder if he would just let me look at it."

I had a little fun with it on the P.A. for years after that with the local announcements. When going north through Everett, Washington, we would pass over the Snohomish River at 10 mph alongside a large log yard and I would announce, "On the left is the Big Boy logging facility where some of the largest logs in the world exist."

A few miles south of Tacoma, Washington, near Dupont, is a giant gravel chute that extends off the hill on the east side of the tracks. At the top of the hill is a gravel producing facility and they shoot the gravel through a giant chute off the side of the hill high above two mainline railroad tracks into barges moored in the waterway. Approaching from the north along a sweeping inland left curve, you can see the chute clearly from two miles away and I would make an announcement, "You can see the giant Big Boy gravel chute on the right in the distance extending over both mainline tracks above a barge folks. When we get closer, we will be able to tell if they are in operation today." As we would draw closer and about to go under the chute, I would say, "Let's take a closer look now.... Oh yes, I can see it shooting into the barge, folks! Yes, siree Bob!"

Conductor Big Boy provided a lot of entertainment for me and to the unsuspecting public over the years.

# Passengers with Disabilities

*In the mid-'90s*, I worked a train between Seattle and Portland. At our station stop at Kelso, Washington, many times we tried to assist a man boarding and traveling to Portland with no legs, I never heard how he lost them, however he refused any help from us, both getting on or off the train, while being adamant that we not so much as touch the wheelchair ramp. He would wheel himself up next to the train, slide himself to the ground, and lift his chair onto the train, then pull himself up into the train and into the wheelchair, and wheel himself into the lower-level seating.

As I think back about it after all these years, it was one of the most amazing feats I ever witnessed—highly inspirational, while bordering on being a miracle. I am still struggling with empathy and hoping to grow in that respect. Same kind of story with the lady with a wooden leg and bicycle who was pretty much insistent on getting on and off without help, including the job of hanging her bike up on the bike rack in the bag car; she had a very pleasant demeanor.

Before the power wheelchair lift on trains, there was the manual wheelchair ramp; that said, still to this day there are manual ramps on many trains. The manual ramps can be handled by one person, although it is much easier if there are two people. 99 percent of the time, passengers requesting the service of a ramp are warranted. I can tell you several stories about times that I suspected it may have not been needed, however I am going to give most of those passengers the benefit of the doubt, with possibly one exception. I was the conductor on a passenger train from Bellingham, Washington to Seattle and we had a power wheelchair lift. We pulled into Edmonds,

Washington with a nearly full train, expecting to fill the last vacant seats. On the station platform, there was a small family of three, one being a man in a motorized heavy duty wheelchair. They had bought tickets at the last minute, destined south of Seattle; the situation required some quick thinking, as there was only one wheelchair spot left on the train in car number 3 with no other seats available for the two other family members—we were oversold.

The Talgo train technician got the power wheelchair lift started on car number 3 while I got the man in his heavy-duty power wheelchair in position. In a matter of five minutes, we had him and his family on board and we were rolling west out of Edmonds, thirty minutes to Seattle. The car we boarded was full, except for the wheelchair space. I told the chief to situate the man's wife and daughter in the bistro for now and we would get them all together after we arrived in Seattle, as there would be plenty of room; most of the passengers in car number 3 were leaving us at Seattle. It was a tight spot in a corner where the power wheelchair was positioned and the wheelchair being so large, it stuck out, blocking half the aisle and door entry to the bistro. The disabled man was trying to maneuver it with the controls tightly into the corner with little success.

I had to leave for a couple minutes to attend to important duties, but returned to one of the most shocking things I have ever witnessed concerning handicap situations. The disabled man, around sixty years old, about 5 foot 7, and a 140 pounds, was out of the chair and he and a frail 80-year-old man were manhandling the 500-pound power wheelchair by lifting and attempting to push it tightly into the corner. I told the 80-year-old man to please get back in his seat as the disabled man sat back into his wheelchair. I then finished the job they were trying to do. I wanted to say something, however something told me I had better not., I am just going to have to accept there must have been a reason he needed that power wheelchair.

Yes, there were passengers with documented disabilities and those with un-documented disabilities, and I think I handled them as well or better than most my coworkers. One time, I helped an elderly man to the restroom and unzipped his fly and after he finished, zipped it back up for him; I think something medically came on after he boarded the train and after arriving Seattle I made sure his relatives were told what happened and that he could no longer ride without an escort.

One trip east on the Empire Builder train at Spokane we were instructed to get all the passengers off the train at the Spokane station on account of a freight train derailment in Montana. Buses had been ordered and our passengers were going to have to transfer and ride a bus to their final destination. I realized an elderly man traveling with us was very confused about who he was, where he was, and where he was going. Rather than gamble that the bus driver was going to babysit him, one of our managers and I made arrangements for me to babysit him in Spokane where I was getting off, as it was my home-away-from-home terminal. We got him a hotel room down the hall from me as I kept an eye on him until one of his relatives came and got him.

One trip going from Portland to Seattle just north of Olympia, a man was having an epileptic seizure—at least that is what I and some other people observing figured it was. I do not recall whether I put my wallet in his mouth, or if it was someone else, to keep him from biting off his tongue. I had the locomotive engineer call the train dispatcher and make arrangements for an ambulance to meet us at the Steilacoom ferry dock crossing (this was before everyone had cell phones). Ten or fifteen minutes later, we were stopped and the paramedics took him away unconscious. The next day, I was working and the man who had the seizure was on my train going back the other direction. Instead of thanking me, he bitched me out for having the medics take him off the train, saying I should have known he was going to snap out of it and be okay.

Yes, regardless of my many character defects, one of my never-ending fail-safes was that when in doubt? ...Take the safe course.

# Dumping Family

*Many times I have heard stories* from my onboard service coworkers who worked the Empire Builder train cross-country between Seattle and Chicago of family members putting so-called *loved ones* on the train—usually elderly family members. What these less-than-responsible relatives—mostly adult children—would do is convince the elderly relative with Alzheimer's, dementia, or some other mental disorder, that taking a train trip across country to visit or live with another relative a thousand or more miles away was going to work out, knowing full well that there would be problems shortly after the train left town—such as memory problems, paranoia, and controlling bodily functions.

I heard these stories often, but fortunately I never had to deal with them for more than a short period. I remember one time an elderly man was escorted by the Seattle red cap on to our lower-level seating area of the Empire Builder train #8 and a few minutes before departure a fellow passenger reported to us that the man was mumbling and acting weird—and it smelled like he had pooped his pants. Sometimes we had onboard chiefs on these trains, and I was glad to have one that day, as he did the deed of escorting him off the train into the hands of the station employees, who in turn handed him to the caretaker hired by relatives to come get him. Yes, some families have different ideas of what family is.

# Devil Said I Could Drink

*In the big book* of Alcoholic's Anonymous, there is the story of the man who quits drinking at age 30 and has 25 years sobriety at 55 years old; he retires to his robe and slippers while figuring he can now drink with no consequences—that the disease must indeed be gone. He starts drinking and within a few months he is in poor condition, and dead in four years. I have seen this many times in my sobriety, although not after a person had 25 years of sobriety. I've seen it with one, two, five, even several years of sobriety, however.

Alcohol is the same as the devil to me: cunning, baffling, powerful, and relentless. He has tried several times to persuade me to take that first drink, while never coming very close. He did get me thinking about it for a couple weeks after my thirty-third year of sobriety. He got in my head. He said, *you got more sobriety than the guy with twenty-five in the big book who drank himself to death, you got sober four years younger than him, and have eight more years than he had when he went back out. You can drink like a gentleman, have a drink with your adult kids.*

I listened and imagined myself having wine at dinner on Sundays and a beer once in a while to quench my thirst, maybe a nightcap as seen in old picture shows. My friend at work, Steve, who was about ten years sober, I told him what I was thinking. He listened and interjected with his concerns, warning me that it could be fatal should I partake. His concern did not phase me; I was nearly convinced that I could control my drinking. I was going to be the exception to the rule, the one that could control his drinking—I was absolutely sure.

A couple days later, I ran into Steve again and we talked.

"You know, I been talking with a couple brothers in the program and I been thinking," he said. "I think that you might be able to do controlled drinking, it is a possibility, but it would be so disheartening to us who look up to you as an example of sobriety." And he left.

Not what I expected to hear, and I began some soul searching. I had a spiritual awakening: should I drink again, someone who looked to me as an example of sobriety might take up the practice again, pursing it to the gates of insanity or death. That, my friend, I want no part of; the devil never gives up.

# Pink Seat Check

*For a few weeks* in the '90s, I had some fun with our gay passengers with the pink seat check. When taking passengers tickets onboard the train, we would punch their ticket twice, once for the ticket portion we kept for our records and once for the receipt stub portion the passenger kept for their records. We would then take a colored cardboard seat check and mark their destination and number of riders on it in abbreviation such as "Sea 1," meaning one passenger for Seattle, Washington, another example being "Bel 3," meaning three passengers for Bellingham, Washington. After marking the seat check we placed it overhead of their seat or seats in a little slot on the luggage rack in plain view—the idea being the seat or seats were taken, and more importantly, to get them off at their station stop. I always told the sleepy ones, *if you're sleeping with the seat check overhead, don't worry, I will get you off.*

There were several different colors of seat checks: white, blue, green, orange, yellow, and pink. If I thought a passenger or passengers were gay? I would give them the pink seat check while giving the other passengers riding in the car the other colored seat checks. Most all of those with pink seat checks figured it out, as did some of the other passengers; some were amused and others were not.

One day, when going up north to Canada early in the morning, I gave a couple of men the pink seat check, and the one was not happy—more like paranoid—as he looked at the other seat checks in the car and back at the pink one overhead. I think they were on drugs, as I have a pretty good sense for that—their jittery behavior and dilated eyes being two of several clues.

We made our train trip up to Vancouver, British Columbia, arriving about noon, off-loaded all our passengers, and went to the hotel for our five-hour layover, going back on duty later for a return trip to Seattle departing at 6 p.m. The two gentlemen to whom I gave the pink seat check to were on the train for the return trip; however, I gave them a blue seat check, while giving somebody else the pink one. These two gentlemen were high on something more than grass, that I am sure of.

I was the assistant conductor and Big Boy was the conductor. Shortly after departing Vancouver, the paranoid man went into a panic attack. Or a heart attack? Drug overdose? Not sure what it was, but his partner was holding his trembling body and trying to comfort him. He requested that we have them removed and taken to the hospital.

Big Boy had the locomotive engineer call the train dispatcher on the radio, as this was way before we all had cell phones, so the dispatcher arranged for an ambulance to meet us at the Elevator Road crossing just south of the Brownsville Seaman's Center in Brownsville, British Columbia.

# Passenger Train Bingo

*In the mid-'90s,* Conductor "Killer Bob" and I played bingo with the passengers. Killer would tell me the seat number and car number of a pretty lady on board. I would then make an announcement over the public address that went like this:

"The winner of tonight's passenger train bingo draw is seat 6 of car number 9. You can claim your prize from the conductors at the bistro."

Most the time, the lady would show up, while knowing we were just having fun, and would go along with it, as we would give her a soda or coffee and a bag of male M&M's. Had a lot of fun with bingo, except one time when a lady did not think it was funny. She had a fit when we tried to give her a beverage and peanut M&M's as the prize, saying she thought she had won a free trip somewhere. She was not happy and I smelled trouble.

I said, "Ma'am, sorry to have disappointed you. Tell you what—lunch is on us today, anything on the menu."

She mellowed out, looking the menu over and picking out the most expensive sandwich, pastry, and a beer. It hurt me in my wallet a little bit, but it was better than a trip to the office.

After that, we changed up the game a little by announcing the winner being in a seat in car number 10; there was no car number 10.

# Lost and Found

*On one trip* in the mid-'90s, I found a nice ladies' turquoise bracelet on the floor of the train. I made an announcement on the P.A. that if anyone lost any jewelry, please see the conductor in the lower-level lounge to claim it. I had two different men show up and I asked them what they had lost; neither described anything that resembled a bracelet.

Then a lady showed up and said she had lost a bracelet.

"What kind?"

"Turquoise," she quickly replied.

I was just about to give it to her, however intuition told me to ask her one more question.

"How many stones are there?"

"Three."

There were seven, however. So I said *sorry*, and she returned to her seat.

I think they may have been a little crooked, so I turned the bracelet into the lost and found at King Street Station in Seattle.

Shortly thereafter, I came up with an idea for some fun. I bought a plastic toy ring out of a little machine at the grocery store. Yes, the machines used to be common and were next to the bubble gum machines and other candy machines at various places, mostly near the exit doors or lobbies of stores. There are still a few around here and there. Back then, you would slip a quarter into the machine and out would come a little plastic round container with a toy ring in it that you could open and close as needed. The ring resembled the real thing, sort of, at least it did to a child; adults called them *kid's rings* or *fake rings*.

I would have a little fun on the train by making an announcement that we found a ring and if you lost one, please come claim it. There were always two or three people who would come to claim it. When I presented them the ring still in the plastic container from the quarter machine, however, they became embarrassed and usually left as fast as they came. I had a lot of fun with that until I was warned that I better knock it off.

The bracelet I turned in became mine after thirty days when nobody claimed it, so I gave it to my oldest daughter who was about sixteen at the time.

# Close Calls
# with Canadian Officials

*Passengers were always asking* if we could let them ride on the locomotive. Almost every trip there was one of those requests, and there were many times that I made great efforts to make it happen.

I took my wife and all my children up at one time or another and an aunt or two. Also my mother-in-law when she was 75, conductor "Tall Colonel"'s mother at age 70, my dentist and her spouse, state officials, newscasters, and friends of friends from the good ol' days.

This had always been against the rules, punishable with a slap on the wrist, until later years after one too many deadly wrecks caused by distracted locomotive engineers. In 2008, there was a head-on train crash between a passenger train and a freight train in Chatsworth, California, killing twenty-five people. That crash ended most of the use of personal cell phones of train operation employees. It was determined that the passenger locomotive engineer was distracted while being on his personal phone, texting shortly before the crash and somehow managing to miss a stop signal. There was a widespread investigation and the public soon found out what we on the railroads already knew: many locomotive engineers, train conductors, brakeman, and switchmen had been using their personal cell phones during train operations for years, when the rules against using them were not enforced nor infractions viewed very seriously. During the investigation of the wreck, investigators determined that the unauthorized use of personal phones was rampant, resulting in immediate new stiff rules.

Different railroads had slightly different variations of the new rules, however basically while on duty at work your personal phone was to be turned off and stowed in your work bag, only to be used in the event of an emergency. I have read many accounts of locomotive engineers and trainmen being fired for the use of personal cell phones, and as a union griever, represented a conductor that was charged with a personal cell phone violation; somehow we managed to dodge him being fired with a sixty-day suspension.

Coinciding with the new personal cell phone rules came cameras inside the locomotives, observing the operator and anyone else present. At that time, using a personal cell phone during operations or having an unauthorized rider in the locomotive during operations—both rules infractions that officials used to turn their heads at—became grounds for employees involved to be fired—no more wrist slapping.

As rare as it is, there are still the ones that have sex on trains, report fake injuries, use drugs, and support Jim Crow laws. Likewise, I am positive the weasels have figured out how to use personal cell phones while working and whenever there is not a camera inside the locomotive, or the camera is defective, there is a possibility that an unauthorized head end rider might be present.

*

Back to good ol' days, on the way south from Canada one day, while working as an assistant conductor for conductor "Killer Bob," two lady friends of Bob's requested a head end trip on the locomotive. Bob agreed and was going to take the girls up to the locomotive before departure at Bellingham, Washington, letting them ride for thirty minutes to the Mount Vernon station stop with the locomotive engineer—that day being Dare Devil Dave.

At that time, we would stop at Blaine, Washington and board US Customs officers with K-9 dogs. Then we would travel the next thirty minutes en route to Bellingham, Washington while the officers passed from car to car interviewing passengers and reading their customs form, while the dogs sniffed for drugs. While the officers were riding the train, another officer was heading south in a van to pick them up upon arrival at the next station stop of Bellingham and take them back to Blaine.

This trip, the sniffer dogs sniffed out a pair of passengers, and the one gentlemen said it was medical marijuana for his ailment—*everything was legal*, he said. The officers challenged him. It was a cluster and the laws were new, or about to become new. Killer Bob was in the middle of it, as he was the conductor, and we had an onboard service chief, "Clementine," as well; the commotion in that car was nuts.

Then, Killer asks me, "Can I get the girls a ride at Bellingham?" I said I would try.

The train stopped at Bellingham, and the van was there to pick up the officers. The conductor, chief, and officers were all huddling on the platform talking over the pot situation. I closed up the doors of the train, except the one at the commotion, and took the girls through the business class cars, through the power car, into the back of the locomotive past the greasy noisy engine, and into the locomotive cab with Triple D.

Killer Bob called on the radio, *okay to depart*, and off we went, delayed in the block southbound. About the time we got through the Bellingham tunnel five minutes later or so, the train dispatcher called us.

"North Branch Dispatcher to passenger train #517, over."

"Yeah, what ya want?" DDD answered.

"You left your chief at Bellingham, plus you still have one of the officers on your train who failed to get off. The customs van is heading for Mount Vernon with your chief to pick up the officer and hand you your chief."

*You can't make this stuff up*, is what I was thinking. That was a nervous twenty-five minutes to Mount Vernon because these girls were detraining from the coaches at Mount Vernon and Customs was still on the train.

DDD says, "What do you want to do?"

I thought a little—there is the Skagit River bridge a few minutes before Mount Vernon that the train slows down for when crossing the river.

I ask DDD, "Can you slow way down at the Skagit today while we go back to the rear? I will holler on the radio when we're in the clear."

DDD says, "No problem."

As we approached the Skagit River, the girls and I went to the rear of the locomotive, and when DDD pinched her down, we passed from the engine room over the draw bar and electrical cables to the power car, closed everything up behind us, then I transmitted on my portable radio, *all is good*.

Now we had about three minutes to get in position on the coaches to discharge them. As we came out of the power car into the business car, there was the customs officer sitting face-forward as I passed with the two girls heading for the coaches. The officer looked a little bewildered.

I got the girls back to Bob and headed back to the business cars, just in time to open doors for the station stop. The van arrived, and we traded the officer for our chief. The pothead was still on the train.

I held my breath for a week and heard nothing pertaining to the unauthorized head end riders.

*

I let a friend's daughter and boyfriend ride free up to Canada in the days when a conductor was really in charge of trains. They were to come back with us on the evening train and as I was doing the train's air brake test that evening as is required before departure, a Customs officer approaches me.

"Why doesn't this couple in the station have tickets? They said it was okay with you."

I said the only thing I could say. "The girl's father is a friend of mine. You know, like if you were my friend, I would let your daughter ride free."

When I survived that, I never let anyone ride free to Canada again.

*

I took my son to Canada one day while working shortly after 9/11. He was about twelve years old. We had a lot of fun in Vancouver, going to Chinatown, Gas Town, rode the Sky Train—a really enjoyable day.

On the way back that evening, we had a really light load of passengers, so my son and I had a whole car to ourselves. Now, I would have to leave my son for a few minutes here and there, so at the beginning of the trip I put my alligator briefcase in a closet at the other end of the car so my son would not be looking in it. You could only get into those closets with a special key given to employees. At Blaine, the train stopped and we let the Customs officers and a sniffer dog on for the ride to Bellingham; as usual, they took the customs forms from passengers and interviewed them along the way, as the dog sniffed for drugs.

Two officers came into our car and went directly to the other end. I heard the older officer say to the younger, newer officer that these closets could be hiding spots. Before I knew it, he had it open and was looking very concerned when he found my alligator briefcase.

I hurried up to them. "That is mine, sorry about that."

Not good enough for the senior officer, who was possibly thinking the worst, like a bomb or drugs. "Why do you have this briefcase locked in this closet while we're doing an inspection?"

He was not gonna believe a BS story, so I told him the truth. "There are things in that briefcase I don't want my son to see."

"Like what?"

"You know, pictures and jokes."

He studied me real close. "What kind of pictures?"

I was talking quietly as I could. "You know, ladies in bathing suits." That wasn't the exactly true, but the last thing I wanted to tell him about was the nude photo I kept in there to set up my *mother-in-law* joke.

"Uh huh," he said, not amused.

I was thinking my career was in trouble.

He looked at me like I was crazy and said, "Don't do it again."

And believe me, I didn't.

*

While in junior college in 1979, I came to class tardy one morning and the teacher wanted to make a point of it.

As he looked my way, he said, "Early to bed, early to rise."

Before he could finish, I said, "Your girl goes out with other guys."

I don't know where that came from, however, I put the two lines together and for the next thirty-plus years would apply that in certain situations: "Early to bed, early to rise, your girl goes out with other guys."

Late in my career, I was passing through Customs early one morning up in Canada in full conductor uniform; I handed my customs form to the Customs officer. He looked it over and stamped it.

"Did you have a good stay?" he asked.

I pointed to him as I said, "Early to bed, early to rise, your girl goes out with other guys."

I gave him a moment to take that in and then I said, "I used to be one of those guys." I don't know where that came from.

*

I worked many years with a locomotive engineer who hired out on the old Northern Pacific Railroad as a trainman, "Brake Shoe Bob." I even worked freight with him and in fact gave him his handle of Brake Shoe Bob.

He liked to use the train brakes, and they would get a little warm; you could smell them on the train, smelled a little bit like an electrical fire. I would make an announcement on the

PA: "Ladies and gentlemen, boys and girls, that peculiar smell you smell is the smell of warm brake shoes. Do not be alarmed; that means the brakes are working."

Bob had a couple health problems late in his career and could have retired on disability, but chose to stick it out even though his hearing in one ear was impaired. Damn good engineer; one of the few I knew to work their whole career and not get time on the ground.

At the Vancouver Station before departure, the conductor was cleared with Customs like everyone else and got a form to be taken to the American border called the *gen dec*, short for *General Declaration*, to be given to American officers at the border.

Well, I got in the habit of calling it the *gin dic* and most people never caught that little pun; if they did, it was usually people who understood my language. In fact, I had a lady assistant conductor, "Banana Girl," who loved saying it.

One day, Brake Shoe Bob and I were clearing the Customs together, and I asked for the *gin dic*.

The Customs officer came unglued. "What did you say?"

I don't know what I was going to say, because before I could say anything Bob came right back at him.

"He asked you for the gen dec! I'm hard of hearing, and even I could hear that!"

*Thank you, Bob!*

# Tunga Bunga Beach

*Just north of Samish, Washington* and just south of Larrabee State Park on the waterway, there is beach that can be seen from the train that often had nude sunbathers in the warmer summer months—mostly out of shape elderly people all waving and smiling. I would make an announcement a minute or so before we passed there that we were approaching "Tunga Bunga Beach" between the Samish tunnel #18 and Dogfish Point, or vice versa depending on our direction. There were almost always a few gasps and some laughter as we went past.

One day, I had a pretty little lady who worked as a journalist from a local newspaper traveling on the train. She enjoyed her trip so much that she wrote an article in the newspaper all about "Legendary Larry and crew," her wonderful trip, and how she especially liked, "Larry's tongue-in-cheek announcements." This article earned me a rare commendation letter from my superiors.

A few months later, a different lady passenger with a different point of view wanted me fired for the same announcements. The train master, "Double Track Kojack," called me into his office and said I was done with announcements or there would be serious consequences.

I went home, took out the commendation letter and a "get out of jail free" Monopoly card and scanned the two together. The next morning at 6:30 a.m., I walked into the train master's office and placed the photocopy on his desk in front of him. He was silent, looking unamused as he studied the document.

I avoided serious consequences thanks to the lady

343

journalist, however "Tunga Bunga Beach" became "Sea Lion Beach." So then when we passed by, I would hear people cry out, *Hey, those aren't sea lions!*

# Merry Christmas

*As soon as Thanksgiving* had come and gone and Christmas was approaching, I would take a couple minutes before pulling into Seattle or Portland to make my *Merry Christmas* announcement over the intercom; just short and sweet:

"Ladies and gentlemen, boys and girls, I would like to wish you a Merry Christmas."

Wishing people a *Merry Christmas*, however, had become politically incorrect, and company policy had changed to reflect that. As a result, I could no longer wish you a *Merry Christmas*; instead, I would say in a disappointed tone, "Happy holidays everyone." Following that, I would play a short rendition of "We Wish You a Merry Christmas" on my harmonica. On the platform after arrival, two or three people would always stop by and thank me, and many others would give me a nod and a smile before continuing on their way. Occasionally, an offended person would make their feelings known, to which I would just smile.

During the last decade of my career, I would work the *snow train* once or twice each year. One year, I was able to get in there three times. The snow train was organized by a local travel agency using our older railroad equipment, our locomotive engineers, conductors, and a few of our onboard employees to run two bistros. The travel agency had somewhere around forty part-time employees that were accommodating the sometimes seven or eight hundred passengers spread across sixteen cars, with an additional private car or two on the rear for the passengers that could afford to pay more and receive special amenities.

The train was heavily decorated for the Christmas season, complete with Santa Claus. There were several musical talents entertaining on the train. They would travel from car to car, performing various holiday songs. Some were vocal groups, some had instruments, and all were made up of a variety of genders, ages, and races. They were all pretty talented. There was even a magician or two. A lot of them were dressed in the traditional Christmas spirit of Bavaria, and coincidentally the train was heading for Leavenworth, Washington—a town that strongly resembles Bavaria to attract tourists.

I would take that job on a Saturday (my day off) for overtime and wear a Santa hat on top of my conductor hat during the shift. *It was a blast!* The train would climb up the Western slope of the Cascade Mountain Range with plenty of beautiful snow for the passengers to admire, head through the eight-mile Cascade Tunnel, and descend down the eastern slope of the Cascades, through Winton and into Leavenworth, Washington.

At Leavenworth, we would offload the passengers and direct them to the buses that would take them into town and leave them to their own devices for a few hours. In the meantime, we would take the train thirty miles down the line to Wenatchee, where the mess of eight hundred people was cleaned up by half of the forty part-time employees. We would switch the locomotives to the other end of the train for the trip back, have some lunch, kill an hour, and head back to Leavenworth to pick up our guests. Once loaded, we would head for Seattle.

What did I love about the snow train? Their motto was about the same as Las Vegas: *what happens on the snow train, stays on the snow train.* The lady who owned the agency, and the five working girls who wore the mistletoe hats, were a hoot.

# American Orient Express Train

*With the help* of the Tacoma Railroad, I had the pleasure of working this train twice, once from Eatonville, Washington to Tacoma, Washington and another time from Chehalis, Washington to Tacoma. The American Orient Express was *vintage*, some might say, a passenger train of antique equipment owned by a private entity that paid the freight railroads for operating on their lines, while contracting locomotive engineers and train conductors from Amtrak to physically work and coordinate the movements of the train. On some routes, Amtrak engineers and conductors were not qualified on the territory, so conductors and engineers from the host freight railroad would be provided as pilots—the idea that we would all work together as a crew, making it much more safe. There were several employees inside the train, catering to the mostly rich and not so famous; however, I did meet Dan Aykroyd once.

I said to him, "Didn't I see you on TV in '69?"

He thought a moment and said, "'71."

The train equipment was small and tight—built in an era when people were shorter and thinner—so a taller person had to do some ducking here and there, while out of shape people had to constantly suck in their guts. It was very clean and well-maintained, however, and the staff were mostly middle-aged and older, which had the flavor of royal butlers and maids; this fit with the *snubbing tendencies* some of the passengers had.

Both times I worked these trains, I made a walk-through and met everyone who was awake and got an official head count from the person in charge. I then crew-briefed with the pilot crew members from the Tacoma Railroad, a locomotive engineer and a conductor, along with my engineer and assistant conductor, if I had one. In this situation, I did the brake test, inspecting each and every brake shoe. There was no way I would move a train if I was not 100 percent sure that it was safe to do so.

The trip I recall the most was the Eatonville to Tacoma run. My engineer, "Coalition Sniffa," and I were on duty at 2 a.m. in Seattle and transported in a cab for some ninety minutes to Eatonville, Washington, where, after going in circles a couple of times, we found the Tacoma Railroad locomotives cut away from rest of the train a short distance away. We wished the cabby farewell and climbed up into the locomotive. I was in full passenger train uniform, hat and tie, and an old black engineer in railroad coveralls stood up from his seat.

As we shook hands, I said, "Glad to meet you. I am Legendary Larry."

He smiled. "'Harry Tung Larry!' My name is Robert."

Yeah...guess we had a mutual friend; Amtrak conductor "Flat Top Frank" called him up and told him a story or two.

My Amtrak engineer and I had never been on the territory so we relied on Robert and the Tacoma Rail conductor pilot to supervise the train movement from Eatonville down to Tacoma—and I say *down* because there were a few steep downhill grades. After formalities, the crew briefing, and air test, we departed as I rode in the lead locomotive with Robert and Coalition Sniffer rode in the second unit. The track was very old and rickety, so the speed limit was mostly 10 mph. There were no gates or lights to protect road crossings on the route, just the old cross buck signs. The pilot conductor drove his car ahead and protected them as needed, usually with his truck on one side with flashing lights and him on the other side with a stop paddle. He would call us on the radio with the *all is clear.*

# Rocky Mountain Train

*The Rocky Mountain Train* is an excursion train owned by a Canadian company, mostly running in Canada. It has vintage deluxe equipment and many employees catering to the rich and not so famous. When running between Vancouver, B.C. Canada and Seattle, Washington, it was required that a qualified operating crew from Amtrak be in charge of the train movements, working with and alongside their operating crew. I was the conductor several times and always had a great experience; I had not one bad interaction with any of the employees—in fact, many fully understood my language, the younger enjoying it and the older ones displaying dropped jaws. When communicating with everyone, including train dispatchers, I raised a few eyebrows when I referred to the train as the *Rocky Mountain Oyster*.

"Rocky Mountain Oyster portable to the Oyster head end crew, over."

The train had some very customized vintage equipment and had the overall feel of one stepping back in time. There were some very elderly passengers who seemed to have never left. Halfway into my first trip, I had it pretty much figured out that they wanted me to be the operations boss—period; they did not want me ruffling feathers of their money-bag passengers, as it could result in fewer tips. They would feed me all I wanted and I could sit anywhere I desired, but I was not to concern myself with passenger issues—just keep an eye on the safe operations of the train.

I sat mostly in the front portion of the upper deck sightseeing lounge car, located in the middle of the train, that was slightly higher than the locomotives; with a 360-degree panoramic view, I could almost see as much of the forward motion as the engine crew. I could see the track side signals ahead. I could look out one side and see the Olympic Mountains and the Cascades on the other. Turn myself around and see the track we just passed over. As I reminisce, it was equally as enjoyable to some of my early caboose journeys on freight trains back in the day—maybe even more so if you take in to account all the rich pretty ladies prancing around.

# Puyallup Indian
# Tribal Headquarters

*When the train* was traveling southbound from Seattle toward Tacoma, about a mile before the Tacoma Station there is the Puyallup Indian Tribal Headquarters to the east, close to the tracks on the left; it's a large compound with buildings as well as their old cemetery. The main building that used to be a hospital, and later, an institution for juvenile delinquents, has been gone for a while now. When the old building was still standing, I would make an announcement as we passed by that some would consider to be pushing the envelope:

"Ladies and gentlemen, boys and girls, we will be in a coma shortly. Yes siree Bob, Tacoma: city of destiny in just a few minutes. On the left, momentarily we are going to get a look at the Puyallup Tribal Indian Headquarters. Yes siree Bob, coming into view now that large old building there was once a hospital built for Indians who had contracted white man diseases such as tuberculosis and alcoholism. It was later turned into a state institution for juvenile delinquents. I was incarcerated there three times. However, it has now been turned back over to the Puyallup Indians as their headquarters. You can come up here and buy cheap cigarettes and booze."

One day after making that announcement, I hung up the microphone and turned around, only to be face-to-face with an Indian lady who looked mad as hell. My heart sank and I was thinking that I could be fired.

She said loudly and firmly, "Sir, I will have you know it's not cheap cigarettes and booze; it's *inexpensive* cigarettes and booze!"

"Yes, ma'am!" I said. "From now on, it's 'inexpensive cigarettes and booze.'"

The irony to this story is that twenty years later, after I retired, while driving in Puyallup on River Road, within the Puyallup Indian Reservation, I saw a sign that said, *cheap cigarettes and booze here.* Just to make sure I was not mistaken or dreaming, I turned around, drove back, and turned into the drive-up window, where there was a young Indian lady who greeted me as a potential customer.

When I started telling her what happened twenty years earlier, she looked at me like I was crazy—so I relented, told her to have a good day, and drove away. Yes siree, Bob! Cheap cigarettes and booze!

# Chief Leschi

*I am interested* a little bit more than the average Joe in local history, especially when the train I was working on passed through interesting places. I wanted to know where we were and what we were looking at. There was always at least one passenger with questions about everything of note that they saw out of their window. I would point out the Chief Leschi Education Center along the tracks near Puyallup, Washington as we passed by and passengers were always asking me about it; however, I didn't really know very much about the place.

I read up about the history of Chief Leschi and I was very disheartened to learn how the white people treated him and his people. In the end, Chief Leschi was hanged by the U.S. Calvary. I wanted to make an announcement about the facility, however I had been reprimanded so many times about controversial announcements that I had made that I was more than a little hesitant to say anything. I decided that I had better do some diligence. I did not want to offend the Puyallup Indians or get fired, so I called the Chief Leschi Education Center. I told them who I was and explained my desire to make an announcement from the train as we passed by. I asked to speak with an elder tribe member on this matter and was patched through to a lady.

"Are you an elder Puyallup Tribal Indian?" I asked, hesitant to let her know about my intention.

I was surprised as she volunteered her name and some facts about herself that made me believe her to be an elder. I told her who I was and what I wanted to do, and she agreed to hear me out.

"How about I tell you the announcement I want to make and you tell me what you think?" I asked.

"Let's hear it," she said.

"Ladies and Gentlemen, boys and girls, on the right coming into view is the Chief Leschi Education Center built for young native Americans who want to get an education. For those of you unfamiliar with Pacific Northwest history, Chief Leschi was hung...by the U.S. Calvary shortly after the Indian wars of the late 1800s. Over one hundred years later, the U.S. Government said, 'You know what? We shouldn't have hung him.' So they built an education center in his honor."

I thought the lady would have a not-so-positive comment or two.

She surprised me when she said, "Pretty correct. Sounds good to me!"

I thanked her and wrote down her name in case I needed a get out of jail free card.

My coworker at the time, "The Percolator," after hearing the announcement a few times, said to me, "Larry, you know that 'hung' is not the proper terminology for that despicable event. It's 'hanged' not 'hung.'"

I said "Well, Tom, I guess he was hung and hanged."

# Hammer Man

*I was at King Street Station* in Seattle on the station platform with the Empire Builder Train #8 preparing to board passengers, when the pretty little black lady working as the station agent approached me. She said that she had a passenger destined for Spokane, Washington that did not smell very good and asked if I would be comfortable taking him aboard. I said that I would have a talk with him and sort it out, and we went inside the station.

He was a tall man, slightly taller than I, about thirty-five years old, with a strong build and long hair. He seemed pleasant enough, but did have a very pungent, foul smell of body odor. After asking him a few questions, which he answered respectfully and politely, I told him that I had an extra shirt and that if he agreed to wear it, I would let him aboard. He agreed, and I told him to follow me. I took him into the crew car and gave him my extra shirt. The man turned his back to me, pulled off his soiled shirt, and let it drop to the floor. It seemed as if he did not want me to see his front and he struggled five or ten seconds to tuck the front of his shirt in. This seemed a little strange at the time, but I figured that he must have been embarrassed.

I scanned his ticket and directed him to the coaches and we departed Seattle, heading east and penetrating the mile-long King Street tunnel under downtown Seattle. After emerging out the other end, on the left there were piers 71, 70, and 69, and on the right we were looking at the world-famous Space Needle erected in 1962 for the World's Fair, once the tallest man-made structure west of the Mississippi River...and then we continued eastbound.

The trip was uneventful until just after we left our stop in Everett, Washington, when one of the dining crew summoned me on the train's PA.

"Conductor report to the diner."

If the matter is not urgent, the crew will say "report at your leisure" or "at your convenience." It was clear that I was needed immediately. I hurried toward the diner and was met by a coworker along the way. He informed me in a worried tone that a man was walking around the train brandishing a hammer, and was currently in the diner.

As I entered the diner, there sat the semi-stinky passenger, in my shirt, at a table with a claw hammer in his hand. It occurred to me that his turning his back to me and the awkward struggling of tucking his shirt was to conceal the claw hammer in his waistband.

"Sir?" I said. "Would you please give me that hammer?"

"No!" he returned. "It's mine!"

"Well, would you please follow me to my office? We can't have you wandering around the train with a hammer."

"The Hammer Man" followed me through two sleeper cars, into the crew car, and downstairs to my desk. I offered him a seat, took mine across the table from him that was also my desk, and we had a long conversation. The unhinged man told me about his drug addiction, his personal struggles, and many unnerving things that made me fear that I could be attacked at any moment. I did my best to hide my nervousness, and kept him occupied as we headed toward Spokane.

Now, I have been in a few situations over the course of my long career that required me to have someone removed, and having the police meet us at a station stop is almost always the best option. Trying to coordinate a removal at a street crossing with a police unit takes a lot of communication, and if things don't go according to plan, such as the police taking too long to arrive, it complicates things even more. This has happened many times and it is not fun. The best way to handle this, in my experience, is to keep the problematic passenger occupied while another crewman arranges for the police to meet us at the next station. In the '70s and '80s, you just stopped the train at a street crossing and kicked the unruly passenger off, but over the years, to avoid being sued, we were gradually forced to coddle disruptive passengers and babysit them until we could hand them over to family or authorities.

I kept the Hammer Man busy by letting him ramble, doing my best to psychoanalyze him, all the while planning to get the police to meet us about two hours later at Leavenworth, Washington. My assistant conductor stopped by intermittently to make sure that I was okay and to quietly observe for a while, eventually leaving the car to continue his patrol of the train. Hammer Man needed to use the restroom, taking his hammer with him. While he was in the restroom I wrote a note for my assistant conductor, nicknamed "The Kid," to call the Leavenworth Police and give them this guy's name, inform them of his nutcase condition and habit of skulking around with a claw hammer, as well as our arrival time in about ninety minutes, so that we could coordinate a removal. After using the restroom, Hammer Man wanted to explore the train. I told him that he could, but only if he surrendered his hammer. He refused, and sat back down, complaining that he was hungry.

I fed Hammer Man as many emergency food snack packs as he could eat, and when my assistant conductor came back around on his patrol, I slipped him the note, sending him along to discretely to call the police.

The Kid reappeared quickly and motioned for me to speak with him at the top of the stairs. He informed me that we had no way to reach anyone at this time, as we were deep into the Cascade Mountains and had no reception. We would have to wait.

I told The Kid that he was going to have to babysit Hammer Man downstairs while I tried to call the police. I sat in a sleeper room at the top of the stairs, staying as close to the situation as I could, attempting to call the police. Ten minutes before reaching Leavenworth, I was finally able to reach the police dispatcher and explain the situation.

"Well, did he break a law?" the dispatcher asked.

"No, I guess not, but he's wandering around a train full of passengers, clearly unstable, appears on drugs, and brandishing a claw hammer!"

"Well, unless he is breaking a law, we're not sending an officer."

We pulled into Leavenworth and I kicked him off the old-fashioned way, with my hand near the emergency crowbar in the vestibule in case he decided to swing his hammer at me. Hammer Man gleefully disembarked and I kept my eye on him as we pulled out of the station to make sure he did not hammer a window or attempt anything else. I then redialed the police dispatcher.

"You now have a nutcase walking around your city with a claw hammer."

There was a long pause at the other end and I rephrased what I had just said. "The man traveling on the train under the influence of drugs with the claw hammer that you did not want to send a police officer for? I left him at the Leavenworth train station."

"...I will send an officer out to check on him."

I hung up the phone, filled out the customary report pertaining to the incident, and turned it in at the end of my tour of duty at Spokane.

The next day, the company detective from Seattle gave me a call and asked a few questions. That was the last I ever heard of the incident. I hope that Hammer Man got some help.

# Scary Passenger

*I was working a train* from Portland destined for Seattle one evening when we stopped at Kelso, Washington for our station work. One of the people to board was a taller and much younger man than me going to Tacoma; he was without a ticket, however he said that he'd paid for it on the phone and lost the confirmation number.

In cases like this, we look at the person's ID., then call the reservation desk and get confirmation that a ticket for travel was purchased. Just so happens, he lost his wallet, also. My assistant conductor took his name and called reservations; there was no such purchase, so we asked the passenger to call and straighten this out because we were told that there was no record of his purchase.

He reluctantly agreed, insisting, however, that he had already paid. Then he claimed he could not make contact with reservations.

I smelled a rat and told my assistant conductor, "Tom, we need to call the police and have him removed at Centralia in twenty minutes."

But Tom being the nice person he is insisted that we give him the benefit of the doubt. Well, Tom did most of the work with passenger issues and I appreciated that, so I let him make this call, to let the guy ride.

I continued to lean on the passenger, however, reminding him to keep trying to call for a ticket, even though I knew he was full of it and was faking the calls. At one point, he stood next to me, almost chest-to-chest, giving me looks to kill, as I gave him looks pretty similar—but my look was, *you may be able to kick my ass, but it won't be easy and I will see you go to jail.*

A few minutes before Tacoma, I saw him in the bistro car having a good time interacting with the new pretty black lady bistro car attendant. After we departed Tacoma, I asked her who the man was. All she said was *just some guy on the train.* Two weeks later, she was fired for adding large tips onto people's credit card purchases.

# Worst Trip Ever

*I was working the Empire Builder* passenger train #8 conductor only, no assistant conductor on account of a manpower shortage. The consolation was that I had a chief this trip with over thirty years service; that would soon prove to be more valuable than most assistant conductors would ever hope to be.

We departed Edmonds, Washington eastbound and a couple minutes later the train went into emergency braking and came to a stop as the engineer was on the radio shouting *emergency, emergency, emergency, we have struck a person at M.P. 19.2.* I was near the front of the train and I made an announcement on the PA:

"We have a medical emergency. Any passengers who are medical professionals who could assist, please make themselves known to a train employee."

I hit the ground and rushed back to the scene, arriving in less then three minutes after the strike. The train chief and a diner waiter were already there; they were on the rear of the train when the incident happened and could see the person we had struck. We had struck a lady and her boyfriend was holding her badly mangled, deceased body crying his eyes out. I could hear the engineer telling the train dispatcher where we were, the mile post location, however the dispatcher needed some sort of street address for the medical emergency people to find us. I told the waiter from the diner to go up to one of the houses above the tracks and get someone to call 911 and use a house address to get the emergency people down to the scene of the accident.

After a bit, the medical people showed up, along with the police, the BNSF trainmaster, and eventually, the coroner. My chief was all over the place doing his chief work—comforting passengers and making phone calls to all who were required to be informed, and a few who were not. When the coroner showed up, it was the first time I had ever met a woman coroner, *a pretty little lady*, and also the first time I had ever seen a chief so ready to assist with one. I figured that since he had gone above and beyond the call of duty he could assist in the coroner briefing and formalities.

They asked me if I wanted to be relieved from duty and replaced by a fresh conductor, which I politely declined; however, the locomotive engineer accepted relief. After a couple hours, we were given permission by all in charge to proceed east, continuing our trip. We did our Everett station stop, turned inland through the foothills of the western Cascade Mountain Range, and so forth.

Three hours later, when leaving Wenatchee, Washington, the bad trip I was having turned into my worst trip ever when a lady confided in me that another woman sitting near her said she had been raped on the train and appeared too ashamed or scared to report it—so she felt compelled to report it to me. The man accused of the alleged rape had gotten off at Leavenworth, Washington, forty minutes earlier.

We ended up in the empty diner, talking: the chief, myself, the lady who informed me of the alleged rape, and the young lady who alleged that she had been raped. I was in mild shock as to what we were discussing and as we delved into interviewing the young lady on the particulars of the incident, I was clearly not the best person present to ask the delicate, sensitive questions, so the chief did the deed. The police, along with the young woman's father, met us in the Spokane, Washington station and again the chief did most of the formalities, handling the situation above and beyond the call of duty.

# Passenger Carry Bys
# and Head Counts

*I was a stickler* for the passenger head count, telling coworkers if the train goes in the ditch and emergency crews arrive and ask for the head count, I want it to be right or close; if we are one or two off we might retain our jobs, but should we be way off we're going to get fired. Before fancy devices and tickets on the phone, there were paper tickets that we would punch with a conductor's ticket punch, once for the portion of the ticket we kept and once for the passenger's ticket receipt; then we put a seat check card above their seat marked with their destination. We also sold tickets by cash and for a short while we had credit card devices. I kept the tickets in a stack in station order, with a green seat check card on the top of the stack listing the number to get off at each station with the total passenger head count and revising the list after each station stop by subtracting the ones that got off and adding the new ones who got on. It was important to me.

Keeping the head count for safety was the most important reason; another was that carrying passengers past their station stops was never fun and it could almost always be blamed on the train crew. I only recall a few carry bys on the trains that I worked, and should we only be a minute or two out of the station, many times I had the engineer stop and back the train into the station. Or, if the carry by person was able, willing, and conditions safe, instead of backing up I would leave them off at a street crossing to walk back.

I would go to great lengths to avert carry bys. There was the time that my assistant conductor was keeping track of the coach passengers on the Empire Builder #8 eastbound, while I kept track of the sleeper passengers. We had a coach carry by in Ephrata, Washington and we didn't realize it until we had been out of town six or seven minutes. The lady was not happy; however, I had her call her ride at the Ephrata station and tell him to head for Odessa, Washington and we would meet there and get her off. I remember we had to talk with the driver a few times, explaining where to meet us, as there was no train station in Odessa. We had to sit a few minutes in Odessa until her ride showed up in an uncomfortable atmosphere; we carefully helped her step down to the step box off the train to the street. She looked at the assistant conductor and said, *you will be hearing about this* as she squeezed my hand and gave me a wink, hi yah!

Yes, I did not have very many carry bys and when I did I tried to take care of them, even threw cab fare on two occasions. My most memorable carry by and back-up-the-train story happened in 1997 at Vancouver, Washington. We had two minor kids in the lower-level handicap coach section, a brother and sister getting off at Vancouver, plus several other passengers. My assistant conductor was to take care of the coach work, including handing the minors to their parents, and I would take care of the baggage car. We made our station stop at Vancouver, Washington and departed south over the Columbia River into Oregon and then over the Oregon slough waterway when the assistant conductor hollers on his portable radio in an excited tone, *I forgot to get the minors off the train!*

I was in my prime and lucky that I had a good engineer, Brent. I was thinking on my feet. "Brent, tell the dispatcher we want to back up from North Portland Junction back to Vancouver signal indication. We have minor carry bys."

Just so happens that the train dispatcher was listening to us. "I got that," he said. "Pull through North Portland Junction and when you get the signal, okay to back up to Vancouver."

I made my way into the rear coach up high at the back door and stopped us over the North Portland Junction control point and waited for the signal. When I got the signal I gave the *clear signal okay* to back up fifty cars, and I am not kidding you my hoghead never doubted any of my instructions as I called out signals for the next two miles as we backed up crossing over the Oregon slough waterway, the Columbia River, and into the Vancouver station. As we were shoving in to the station, I could see the total disbelief of the parents. After we stopped, I hit the ground and we passed the kids to them—nothing but joy and appreciation as I told them we were sorry. We then went on to Portland, arriving pretty close to on-time...and never heard a thing about it.

# The Penny

*I lived on the edge* with just about every interaction I had while railroading, whether it be remarks I made while speaking on the public address system to the public on the train I was working or radio transmissions I made with my portable radio concerning train operations or passenger situations. My verbal interactions with coworkers and passengers were mostly of a pleasant, intelligent nature, although many times I ruffled someone's feathers.

I will state again: I never knew what would be coming out of my mouth. The superintendent told his trainmaster to tell me, *you can think those things, just can't say them.* Two different supervisors said I was my own worst enemy. I usually knew when I had offended somebody and would make amends right away, but many a time the amends did not go so well and I would worry for days, sometimes a week, hoping there would be no phone call to come to the boss's office, or worse yet, a call from diversity or a charge letter in the mail.

I would be sick with worry when I would happen upon a penny in a parking lot somewhere and that would be the sign from above that all was well. I would then be good sometimes a week or more, until I made a smart-ass remark or an off-color joke that was not well received...or displayed some other bad-boy behavior. When I retired, I thought that searching and hoping to find the penny was going to be history; however, having five grown kids, there is always one in some sort of crisis and now when I happen upon a penny it is a sign from above that the child whom I have been worrying about will be okay for today. One day at a time.

# Aqua Velva
# and Other Announcements

*I was the assistant conductor* in the early '90s on a northbound train from Portland to Seattle during that era when there were still two locomotive engineers on all passenger trains. One was the engineer, the other the assistant engineer; on this trip, both their first names were Dick.

I made an announcement: "Ladies and gentlemen, boys and girls, we have two dicks on the locomotive today, Dick T. and Dick M."

We had a locomotive engineer named Bates and as you can imagine we all liked to call him "Master." Whenever I had him for our locomotive engineer, I would make an announcement: "Ladies and gentlemen, boys and girls, today our locomotive engineer is Mister Bates."

When I said *mister*, I would say it as fast as I could and it almost sounded like *master*. Those that understood my language got a laugh out of it, of course, and there were the ones who didn't.

One day, I made a Freudian slip when making that announcement and I instantly started to worry as I hung up the microphone. I walked into the bistro lounge; in the lounge, the passengers were all smirking, but I knew somewhere on that train there was a passenger who did not think my slip was funny and might turn me in. I had only one defense—if I got called in the office I would plead insanity.

I made an announcement for ten years or more when our train passed through Mukilteo, Washington, which is about twenty-five miles north of Seattle and five miles south of the city of Everett, Washington, part of it on the Puget Sound waterway. There is the turn–of-the-century 1906 Mukilteo lighthouse and just after it northbound (or just before it southbound) was a mom and pop grocery store that also sold fishing supplies. The store was called *Woody's Market*; big sign, hard to miss. I would announce: "Coming into view is the turn-of-the-century 1906 Mukilteo lighthouse..." and then I would add, "...we are now passing Woody's Market; that is where the conductor buys all his M.D. ('Mad Dog') 20/20."

It was a joke because M.D. 20/20 was an inexpensive wine I drank in the '70s and anyone who knew me well, knew I gave all that up. After ten years of making that announcement, one day the trainmaster called me into his office. He handed me an email from his boss that had been around half the company. A lady called the hotline from the train on her cell phone and said the conductor was drinking Mad Dog 20/20 while working on the train. I told the trainmaster I would delete that announcement and he said, *I wish you would.*

I did, however, replace it with something a little different. I would tell passengers about the lighthouse and then: "There is Woody's Market where the conductor buys all his Aqua Velva..." and then add, "...there's nothing like an Aqua Velva man."

My assistant conductor at the time was Banana Girl. She kept saying to me that you should say, *that's where the conductor buys all his Aqua Velva and slaps it on his cheeks...there's nothing like an Aqua Velva man.* I refrained, but she persisted and after a while it was a dare—so then I had to start making the announcement: "Coming into view, folks, is Woody's Market, where the conductor buys all his Aqua Velva and slaps it on his cheeks...there's nothing like an Aqua Velva man."

This was a short-lived announcement, only said it a few times, when one day about forty-five minutes after making the announcement while assisting passengers on the platform at Seattle, Washington, our last station stop, an elderly crusty old guy came up behind me and whispered in my ear, *on your cheeks, huh?*

I liked to make announcements, especially when we were along the Puget Sound waterway. A lot of people appreciated it, but over the years there was always a critic somewhere that despised me for whatever reason. I was constantly changing and refining announcements, trying to appease my superiors who had to handle the formal and informal complaints made by passengers that wanted me off the PA, period. When officials would challenge me, I would tell them that 51 percent of passengers liked my announcements, 48 percent did not have an opinion, and there are the 1 percent who hate me and make the phone calls and write the letters.

My last three years working, my announcements were so refined that the only way some of my superiors could demean me was by saying my announcements were *not positive*; they did not like the truth in the subject matter in some of my announcements. For instance, just south of Tacoma along the waterway is—or was—the McNeil Island State Penitentiary, which had been a federal prison at one time and changed back to a Washington state prison. During my last years working, it became a minimum security prison for convicted male pedophiles.

I would make the announcement: Ladies and gentlemen, boys and girls, you can see the McNeil Island State Penitentiary across the waterway now. If you look close, you can see the machine gun towers. The men incarcerated in that prison you would not want to babysit your children.

# Main Line Dave

*I liked to ride* in the locomotive now and then and actually was required to do so periodically to stay qualified on the routes I was subject to work on. Occasionally between station stops, just for the adventure of it, I would climb into the locomotive during a trip and chit chat with the locomotive engineer when safe to do so. One day while riding southbound between Bellingham and Mount Vernon, Washington, I witnessed what had to be one of the greatest multitasking performances ever when the engineer while holding a syringe and needle in his mouth, he used his hands to manipulate the throttle, air brake valve handle, whistle and punched the alerter button as needed—and when the time was right, while doing 79 mph, he took the needle and syringe out of his mouth and shot himself up.

Yes, he mainlined himself on the mainline! From what I understand, in order for some people to avoid high blood sugar, shooting themselves up is a requirement to staying alive. *Ah, ha, ha, ha, stayin' alive, stayin' alive. Ah, ha, ha, ha, stayin' alive....*

# Lady Judge

*One of our regular passengers* was a judge. She always spent her trips poring over her case notes. How she ever put up with me is a testament of true tolerance. One of the first times I conversed with her, I said that she looked like a lady in the news who was in jail for dating a minor.

"I don't look anything at all like her," is all she said.

"The Judge" was witty, smart, pretty when she wanted to be, and well-dressed, wearing a cute hat every now and then. She spoke with wisdom and always chose her words carefully. She would not engage in my language, but I could tell from the twinkle in her eye that she understood it well, and on special occasions she would give me hug. Again, she was a true saint of tolerance.

On just about every trip, she would ask me about the particulars of an announcement I had made or query me on a railroad rule. We became friends and even exchanged books once to further our relationship. Her senses were keen, as she could always tell the days when I wasn't even-keeled, and I confided to her some of my concerns with life.

She brought her husband along one time.

"Glad to meet you!" he said. "I have heard nothing but good things about you."

I still wonder if she held back a thing or two.

She was poring over her appeal cases one day at her seat during the final days of the Clinton presidency.

I got her attention for a moment and said, "You know, I think there is a Bill Clinton in every family."

She looked up at me from her paperwork and said, "You're lucky if that's all you've got in your family."

I retired and was on the train a year ago for a short trip and there she was, so I sat with her awhile and talked about the book I was writing. I informed her that I was including a story about her.

Then I said, "Most the women in my stories are referred to as 'pretty little ladies.'"

She smiled real big and said, "Instead of 'Legendary Larry,' we're going to have to start calling you 'Literary Larry.'"

# Mouth Organ

*During my three years* in the army, I bought a harmonica in West Germany and learned to play a few tunes during the tail end of 1975. I picked it back up again while working for the Burlington Northern Railroad in Wishram, Washington around 1982. I spent a lot of time sitting in hotels with "Rosie Palm," or in the sidings on trains, so the harmonica was a good pastime. It was something constructive to spend my time on, rather than what I used to do.

Over the years, I was able to put together about fifty fairly decent renditions of well-known songs and quite a few others that did not sound nearly as good. I got plenty of practice, but I was never good enough to play along with other musicians. I just don't have the ear for it. Some say I march to the beat of a different drum.

However, I did learn my instrument well enough to come up with little blues licks, and to toss in some lyrics to come up with my own simple tunes like the "Dare Devil Dave Blues." Speeding up the same basic tune and changing the words, I came up with "The Tunga Bunga Melody." I would occasionally play my harmonica over the train PA, usually when arriving into Seattle. Typically, I would play "Wabash Cannonball" or "I've Been Working on the Railroad," nothing that could get me fired.

While I never thought myself to be particularly talented, one day in Seattle's historic King Street Station, an elderly woman sought me out after leaving the train. She came up to me with a big smile on her face and said, "Nice mouth organ, kid!"

# Hot and Cold Ladies

***Yes, one minute the lady*** is hot and the next minute they are cold. With my background and the mentality that I developed, I did not fare so well sometimes with certain coworkers—almost all being of the female variety. Often, I would be working with a pretty little lady making jokes and having fun—things went well; then the next time while working with her things were the opposite. Most these situations ended up becoming the start of pleasant relationships, however.

I learned that finding one's feelings and boundaries can be a bit touchy. I can tell lots of stories pertaining to hot and cold ladies, however I will narrow it down a bit. I worked with several ladies that liked to talk about kinky sex and things of that nature; should I, or any other male coworker, expand on the subject, however, we became the bad guy. I learned to listen and enjoy the very off-color remarks these ladies made, while only further indulging in the conversation when prompted to—and even then I knew to be careful and choose my words wisely.

# Richard Tung

*I was working as a conductor* one evening, heading north from Portland to Seattle. We had a full train, including a whole girl scout troop and their leaders. I noticed a man who had gotten on with a lady, and they appeared to be a couple. However, as we made our way north, I saw him sitting in at least two different cars talking with two different ladies. He kind of reminded me of some of our conductors.

About halfway to Seattle, one of the girl scout troop leaders approached me and wanted to have a little talk. She was not happy. Apparently, the gentleman that I have just mentioned told one of her young girls that she was cute, and the troop leader felt that he needed to go to jail. Now, I was thinking, *jail for telling a girl she's cute?*, but I wasn't going to say that to the troop leader. I do think that he should not have said that, however. I wanted to avoid causing a scene, so I told the lady that I would keep an eye on him and have him removed in about an hour once we had reached Tacoma.

I called the Tacoma Police, told the dispatcher about our situation, when to expect us at the Tacoma station stop, and to let them know that I needed this guy removed. When we arrived, he was sitting with the lady he got on with initially, having a good time. He didn't seem at all out of the ordinary. I stepped onto the platform and was greeted by four police officers. I told one of them what had happened, how the troop leader felt about it, and that I needed him to be removed.

"Well, take me to him," said the officer.

Which I did, sort of.

I stood in the vestibule of the train and pointed to the guy, and the officer went up to him quietly. After a few words, the guy looked a little worried as the officer escorted him past me off the train. I needed his name for my report, as the paper tickets we were using at the time were mainly used for a head count, so I stepped off the train. The four officers had him surrounded in the parking lot, having a talk. As I approached, one of the officers intercepted me well before I could make it to the huddle.

"I need the guy's name for my report."

"You wouldn't believe it…" said the officer, smiling.

"…What?"

"Richard Tung!"

"Dick Tung?"

Now, I thought for sure that I would be getting a call from somebody on this matter, but I never did. That makes me believe that they let Mr. Tung slide.

# Shove 'Em Down Harry

*I was on the King Street Station* platform in Seattle loading and assisting passengers prior to a southbound departure one day when I observed the station agent, Harry, having a quarrel on the platform with a man and lady. He was focusing his attention on the man, as the lady stood by occasionally interjecting with her own grievances. They were complaining about a bus trip the company had given them because of flooding conditions on the tracks. The man got right in Harry's face, and Harry put up his hand, gently touching his shoulder. The angry customer fell back into his wife as if he had been pushed and gently flopped over onto the ground, lying there as if he had been hurt.

I had never seen a fake fall before, but I had seen several real ones, and this was obviously the biggest fake job you could ever hope to see. I approached the situation, and the customer slowly picked himself up from his pratfall, moaning and groaning that he was going to sue us.

Now, Harry should not have touched him, so he was now in a predicament. It was time to depart, and the passenger could either stay and fill out the accident report with Harry, or ride with me. He rode with us. I got through filling out the passenger injury report of his claims, had him sign it, and gave him a copy. He was only going to Olympia, about a ninety-minute trip.

After he detrained, I solicited statements from three different passengers that had been sitting near him. He and his wife had been drinking and were too loud talking about what had transpired, leading the witnesses to confirm my suspicions that the gentleman we had taken aboard was, in fact, faking it.

I gave those three statements, along with my own, to the company detective, who passed them along to the Seattle Police. A Seattle Police detective called me once a week for the next three weeks, asking me to repeat what I saw. Through all of this, Harry had not smiled in weeks. On the third call, the detective told me that they were not going to be any charges.

The next time I saw Harry, he was smiling again. For the next ten years, when I would see Harry working near the passengers, I would yell: "Hey, Shove 'em Down Harry! How you doing?"

# Ray and Monty

*For many of my early years* in sobriety, I was a speaker at jails and institutions. I was also involved in trying to carry the message to men in their homes, while listening to one-on-one confessions of their heinous crimes as part of the conditions for sobriety—at least for some of us.

After about ten years of sobriety, I became open for something new and I was convinced by my wife to join the Lutheran Church and get us and our children some new friends. On a mostly good and productive path, our five children were baptized and confirmed there. Plus, the one we went to had a weekly Sunday morning meeting similar to the ones I was accustomed to—12 steps for sinners. I still attend occasionally.

When all the children had grown, I was again looking for something different in my life. I thought that possibly I could use my little bit of talent playing the harmonica for small groups in nursing homes or just one-on-one to people in homebound situations. I heard of an organization called Friend to Friend, sponsored by many charity organizations, including the Lutheran Church that coordinated people to visit people who could use some company now and then, people who were isolated.

I emailed the organization and told them my thoughts and idea about playing my harmonica to those that might appreciate it. After what I believe was a three or four-week background check on me, they said I was good to go. Because of my background, they had designated a special individual for me to visit, should I agree. They explained that this man had done serious prison time and was now in poor health as a result of substance abuse and approaching the end of his life. I agreed to meet Monty, who lived with his cat in a small garage that had been converted to living quarters that his sister and brother-in-law had been kind enough to make happen.

I called Monty up and invited him out to lunch to Denny's for the one and only time I took him out in public, as he was dependent on oxygen with a severe case of COPD. The tank and his poor health made the task of getting in and out of my car and into the restaurant a giant challenge at the least.

I may have continued taking him out, had it not been for his remarks and storytelling while in public, as he told story after story of sexual conquests back in his hippy days—some that even made me blush. When we made it back to his living quarters, I played him some tunes on my harmonica and we told each other stories. The next fifty visits or so after the first, I would call him and ask him what he wanted for lunch and usually pick us something up from a fast-food place and bring it by. As we dined we would visit, him telling crazy stories of back in the day, such as once meeting Charlie Manson. I told mostly stories about my railroad career. I let Monty know that the visits were as helpful to me as him because his position in life very well could have been mine had I not found sobriety. About the last fifteen minutes, I would play the harmonica while he played on the computer. Then I would give him a hug and sometimes we told each other *I love yous*.

During this time, my youngest daughter had run off with a man while doing drugs and would not listen to anyone. It broke her mother's heart, and mine. I confided in Monty, and what he told me was better than the professional counseling I had received.

"It is not your fault," he said. You gave her all the love possible and everything she needs, except for one thing."

"What is that?" I asked.

"A man pleasing her."

As a result of that conversation, I was better able to accept the situation. Monty eventually required being in a nursing home 24/7 and several emergency visits to the hospital, where I would continue to visit him each time in a pleasant manner and he always telling a story that was usually of the cheap-thrill variety. One day, his sister texted me and said the end was near, so I went up for our last visit. He had already slipped away, his organs starting to shut down. With some of his family present, I said a few words of prayer and played a Jesus song on my harmonica. Then said good-bye. He passed the next day. Peace.

Friend to Friend soon called me again and told me they had a blind man nobody would visit for more than once or twice, usually once. Upon further conversation, I was told he was rude, crude, and of bad hygiene on top of living in a foul-smelling house full of belongings that mostly belonged in the dump; he was a hoarder like no other. I think they sweet-talked me a little to get me to agree to meet with him once a week, inferring that if there was a person that could manage this? I was that person. I told a few of my family and friends I was the pinch hitter, which is not exactly humility.

After this warning, I went to his house to meet him. He looked like a seventy-five-year-old dwarf (though he was sixty-five) and his home was as they indicated—stacked to the hilt with junk of no monetary value, at least of what I could see. That first visit I thought I would get the upper hand on him and try one of the crudest jokes I knew on him.

"What did the blind man say when he walked past the fish market?"

"What?"

"Hello, girls!"

I am not sure if he got the joke, as he did not seem offended, and he told me later several times he had never been with a woman—and once told me that ten-year-old girls were appealing to him. He also told me a few stories that suggested he may have had sex with a dog in his youth.

The first several visits he always had his zipper undone, fiddle-f---ing with it for whatever reason. He would brush by me in the house too close for comfort, and once scared me when he felt my right pectoral muscle up for a couple seconds, as I bristled, not saying a word.

I did not maim him, nor did I give up on him. I was there, I kept telling myself, as redemption for my bully days when I used to make fun of anyone I deemed inferior to me—and had even hurt some of them physically, as well as scaring a lady or two. After the first several visits, he quit playing with his zipper and never tried anything funny with me again. He knew that if he did, I would not be visiting anymore.

He smoked a tobacco pipe and talked about getting out for a beer—and would I take him to a ball game, restaurant, or anywhere? I kept quiet and he got the picture that I would visit him one hour per week, and that was all. He shed tears, whined, pissed and moaned, and I refused to take him anywhere. He even wanted to come to my house for the holidays; it was not going to happen. I did not trust him, nor did he smell good sometimes wearing the same outer clothes for weeks—not sure about the others, or if he ever bathed.

He did not care for the harmonica and preferred talking... and when in disagreement, was the most asinine person I ever dealt with, sitting in his recliner chair bitching about all the blind charity organizations that had black-listed him for his attitude and behavior. Then one day, I had a spiritual revelation of a different kind, going against all my beliefs, when I brought him a 16-oz. beer for our one-hour visit. He was grateful and became easier to tolerate, and eventually that 16-oz. beer became a 32-oz. beer—and a mostly pleasant visits, talking about the good old days of the late '50s and '60s, since we had a lot in common with music and TV shows from back in the day. We would always test each other's knowledge on them.

After eighteen months of visits, he asked that I bring him something to eat with the beer, so then I got the beer and two cheeseburgers at the AM/PM store for the visit; I paid for the beer and he reimbursed me for the burgers. The virus came along, but only changed our visits a little; now I hold my breath while handing him the goods at his front gate, step back a few feet, and visit a few minutes.

One time, he locked himself out of the house. Long story short, I called 911 and said, *this is not an emergency, but very urgent.* Twenty minutes later, the fire department showed up with tools and cracked the front door lock.

Ray told me interesting stories of his loving parents and stories of people in society not so loving. He was born premature in 1950; back then they put premature infants in oxygen tents to keep them alive, since their lungs were not fully developed. Many of these children survived, but became blind. It took a couple of years for the medical profession to figure out that the oxygen was causing havoc to the retina of these babies eyes, resulting in them becoming blind. As I understand it, oxygen tents are still used today, but they have procedures that vastly reduce the risk of blindness.

# The Window Washer Man

*We had a man* who would regularly board our trains carrying a bucket and a six-foot wood-handled squeegee for window cleaning. He was a very big man, standing at six and a half feet tall and weighing nearly three hundred pounds—with a booming voice. He would usually have a reservation in place of an actual ticket, hoping we would be too lazy to write him a ticket; I suspect that happened once in a while. Most of the other conductors and I would write him a ticket the old-school way. He was always looking to strike a deal, though, which we were able to do once in a while.

He went from city to city and asked people if they needed the windows washed at their house. One of our lady bistro attendants had him wash the windows at her house; she said that with all the turmoil and drama he brought with him, she would have been better off just giving him the money and leaving the windows dirty.

When the window washer was on our trains, it was a known fact that when he passed through the bistro car half of the condiments would disappear. There was something not quite right about him, but I grew to like him. When he was on the train, I would start my announcements with: "Ladies and gentlemen, boys and girls and window washers...."

He would look at me as I passed by him later as if I was crazy.

Eventually, the window washer started to develop bad hygiene. We would place him as far away as possible from the other passengers—until one day I had enough. We had just arrived in Seattle, and I knew he had a ticket to return back north later in the day, so as he was leaving I walked with him a short way toward the station.

I told him, "I think you should change your clothes tonight before you get back on the train."

"Why?" he said, real loud and slowly with his deep voice.

"The clothes you have on don't smell too good."

"I will see what my lawyer has to say about that!" he boomed back, clearly offended.

"You might want to let your lawyer smell your clothes."

# The Clown

*There was a man who rode* our trains in the Northwest that would sit in the bistro lounge blowing up balloons and twisting them into puppy dog shapes and other figures. He didn't paint his face, but he did dress as a clown with a big floppy hat. And he was very overweight. He covered up his bad hygiene with some sort of fragrance I couldn't recognize. If you were within five feet of him, you could smell his stink. Not good, but we let him ride as long as he sat in the corner of the bistro lounge.

I had a couple of problems with him. I had a woman assistant conductor who he made a pass at, so I had to tell him to quit flaring his nostrils at her or else he would not be allowed to ride on our trains anymore. He would leave all his balloons on the table when he got off at his station, and people (mostly kids) were welcome to them; they were in shapes of animals, actually pretty well done.

But one day I noticed about ten minutes before his station stop that all the balloons looked like penises. I gave him his last and final warning, threw them in the trash can, and covered them with garbage. I never had a problem with him after that, but we had a bistro car lady nicknamed "The Talgo Queen" that would come out of the bistro with a can of air freshener and glide around like a fairy, spraying it all around where the balloon man was sitting (unbeknownst to him) whenever he was on our train.

As the years rolled by, we became friends sort of, as he would grin and make positive comments about my announcements and was wise enough not to elaborate on them. He knew I collected, bought, and sold vintage cigarette lighters and one day he brought me a few; we struck a good deal for the both of us.

Sadly, the "Window Lady" just recently told me he had passed on. I am not sure whether I will see him again, as one never knows.

# My Uncle Duane

*Duane was born in 1941.* He was maybe about six months old when he contracted double pneumonia. His father went to fetch a doctor, who made a house call. He had a high fever and later that night it spiked while he had a convulsion as his sister (my mother) held him. In the morning, his mom and dad took him to Springfield Hospital and they were able to get the fever down; however, the damage was already done. Had the doctor admitted him the previous day, things would have been different.

After he recovered, the medical profession said he would not live to see his teenage years—that he would be what they deemed *mentally retarded*, along with other ailments, including epileptic seizures being the biggest concern. He is seventy-eight years old today; so much for that not living to be a teenager prediction.

When I was young, my Seattle family would visit my Minnesota family—my mother being originally from Minnesota—and I did a lot of running around with my mother's dad, Grandpa Earl, and his son, my Uncle Duane. Grandpa would tell people we came across that were always wondering about Duane that, *this here is my retarded son, Duane.* Some of the time, if the conversation warranted, he would tell Duane's history, adding that he could have a seizure at any time. I was around numerous times when the seizures took place, as I actually lived with him and my grandparents three months at one time, plus they lived across the street from us for a couple years.

After my grandpa passed, grandma eventually went to a nursing home. Duane was sent to a group home. I would make arrangements with his sister, my Aunt Eileen, to have Duane fly out from Minnesota and stay a week with me and my family in Seattle. I would take him to work with me on the passenger train and believe it or not; I have a video of him driving a train (under very close supervision). Many times while working passenger trains I had him assist people with bags. Eventually, I would just have him sit in the conductor's area as he became older and unstable.

As he got older, he needed more care, making flying out to Seattle no longer feasible. So, a couple times I took the train from Seattle to Minnesota, got him, and we came back to Seattle for a few day's visiting; then we got back on the train and returned to Minnesota. He loved being on trains.

It was while on one of these cross-country train trips when eating in the diner I became a little angry with a couple arrogant pricks—they were *more arrogant than me.* The diners were always full, with four seats per table and you were almost always seated with other passengers, placed very closely to each other. Most of these meals were cordial and polite as we made conversation with our fellow passengers. Two different times while dining, a man at our table was giving Duane rude looks and appeared very irritated with Duane, making me angry.

I looked across at them, reached deep into my bad-boy mentality, and put on my meanest demeanor. "This here is my Uncle Duane. He used to be a brilliant brain surgeon, but something went wrong; you never know what he's going to do now."

Both men quickly adjusted their attitude.

Duane is still in a group home in Minnesota. Every year I go back and see all my aunts and uncles who have one foot in the grave, and then the ones who don't. If I have time, I might visit a cousin or two. I always tell people that I am going to break my Uncle Duane out of the nuthouse for a while—yes, two nuts on the loose. Actually, I lodge at my Aunt Eileen's place and she makes arrangements for me to get him for day trips, taking him out to eat at restaurants and exploring secondhand stores. Love that man!

Many years back, my godmother, who is also my Aunt Marilyn, sister of Duane, asked me why it was that I felt so close to him. At the time, I did not answer her because I wasn't sure she would understand why, nor did I entirely. It was (and still is) a condition of my sobriety going back to what Indian Ed had told me concerning making amends to all whom I had harmed; it would be nearly impossible to find all those people, but you owe it to society to never drink or drug again and the way you are going to make amends is by not drinking and drugging and going to meetings and when you run across someone you owe amends? Make those amends, unless to do so would cause more harm. Eventually, I figured out I had been a thief, liar, and a womanizing alcoholic drug addict. For some time, I had been active making those amends pertaining to those character defects; however, I had overlooked the fact that I had been a bully—or I should rephrase that—I had buried those shameful bully things I did out of guilt. By having a relationship with my Uncle Duane, I was in some way making amends to all whom I had bullied, some of it very despicable.

I had never physically bullied Duane, however there were many times prior to sobriety that I was not very kind to him, either by ignoring him or talking down to him in a condescending manner. Nearly all that is nonexistent today. As the years rolled by, I would be with Duane on an adventure somewhere and at times for five or ten minutes it seemed as if he wasn't retarded. As my Aunt Eileen would say, he is *special*.

Being with him could present a truly spiritual experience. When we talked, I would admit to god, myself, and Duane the exact nature of my wrongs.

Duane would say, "Why you do that Larry?"

"I don't know, Duane."

"You know you're not supposed to do that, you better not do that again, Larry."

"Okay, Duane."

# Funny to Me!

*In my later years* while working passenger trains, quite often a concerned passenger would ask me about a noise they were hearing from beneath the floorboards of the train, usually where the cars were coupled together—various kinds of creaking noises. I would listen and if the noise sounded a little out of the ordinary, I would say: "Sounds like it needs a little grease down there. You know, if we followed all the rules? The train would never move." I would quickly follow that with, "Don't worry sir/ma'am, I personally know we have good brakes, and if we didn't, I would not be on this train. I will report the issue to mechanical."

I would always stay with the passenger until they felt safe again, and more importantly, report the issue. Yes, safety rules are important to comply with; however, I suspect that in almost every industry there is some creaking and whining that needs lubricating.

One morning as the train was leaving Bellingham, Washington, a young man on his laptop computer asked me if we sold earplugs. I told him *no*, but let him know that I could find him a couple of filtered cigarette butts that would work just as good. Not very amused, he declined my offer.

A little while later when, I had a minute, I dug a pair out of my grip. I kept them for myself for situations like helping the hoghead in the engine room. There were also many times that I had to ride solo in a second unit or the rear humping/ pushing locomotives that were having wheel slip issues. In these situations, we were governed by rules buried in the special instructions.

The ear plugs were still in the wrapper, and I offered them to the young man, telling him they were free to enjoy. He accepted and unwrapped them, putting them in his ears. I don't think he wore them for more than a few minutes, as they are not the most pleasant things to wear. I was reprimanded more than once for not wearing mine, right behind safety glasses.

When we got to Seattle, where my tour of duty ended, a young man who had been sitting in the same coach of the earplug conversations said to me, "Filtered cigarette butts for earplugs? One of the funniest things I've ever heard!"

\*

The train used to originate out of Bellingham every morning headed south, terminating in Eugene, Oregon. Now Eugene is known for people who still enjoy certain aspects of the hippy era during the 1960s and '70s, one of those being women who did not shave their legs or armpits. One of my favorite cousins was that way for a while—and she lives in Eugene.

In the summer, while pulling tickets out of Bellingham, on almost every trip there would be a lady or two with obviously unshaven legs or armpits. Before they handed me their ticket I would say, *I bet you're going to Eugene.*

Most of them thought it was funny, however there were one or two who gave me some very sour looks.

\*

Back in the early to mid-'90s, I worked between Seattle and Portland quite a bit. When I saw an attractive mother and daughter pair, I would ask if they were the Palmolive sisters. I never ruffled anyone's feathers with that comment, and twenty years later I was approached by a pair of ladies that remembered me telling them that and were fond of that comment.

*

I would often be busy assisting passengers with pets, senior citizens with ailments, handicap people, minor children, and almost always a couple of nutcases, all with baggage on the station platform trying to get on the train. For the last ten years of my career, I would tap into my army experience and go into drill sergeant mode on the platform. I would not let anyone on the train until I had all their attention. I would then put any obviously disabled people on first and assist as needed, followed by elderly people, then I would ask if there were any groups, and if so they would go next. Then, I would ask for couples, and lastly, I would tell the singles to *go fill the cracks*. After we got the train out of town and everything got settled, I'd make an announcement: "I'm sorry about running you around like a drill sergeant back there. If you have any complaints, you can write the U.S.A. Department of Defense, because they are the ones that trained me this way."

*

I had a habit of referring to people obviously older than me as *grandma* or *grandpa*. I never had any repercussions from it, until one day while loading the train on the platform at Bellingham. I told the waiting passengers to, "Let me help this grandma first."

Well, *grandma* got really mad about that comment and started having a hissy fit about how she was no grandma, and that I shouldn't be calling people I didn't know "grandma." All this while, I assisted her onto the train. After we got rolling, I approached her at her seat and apologized for calling her "grandma."

"She went again. "Those damn kids of mine never did make me a grandma!"

All I could do was apologize and move on.

\*

When it would rain a few days, or the snow was melting in the mountains, the rivers would run high and I would make announcements that we were going to cross the *bulging* or the *swollen* so-and-so river. There was the Nooksack River we crossed over in Ferndale, Washington, and one day it was flowing high from the rains. I made an announcement that we were getting ready to cross the *swollen* Nooksack River and a minute later we slowed down to the 50 mph speed limit on the curve on the Nooksack bridge spanning the river.

"There she is folks, the swollen Nooksack River."

A couple minutes later, as I was passing through the business class car, a grinning elderly lady got my attention.

"Sir, did you say swollen nut sack?"

I smiled and said, "Nooksack. I gotta go."

# Railroad-Approved Queer Watch Band

*I am proud* of my railroad-approved Seiko watch that I bought using *payroll deduction* in 1978 off of a Burlington Northern train conductor. I was working for Burlington Northern at the time, deadheading on a passenger train between Portland and Seattle. Also onboard was an off-duty conductor traveling on personal time who sold jewelry and watches on the side. He pulled out a briefcase full of goods and sold me the watch; he arranged for Burlington Northern to do a payroll deduction of $50 for three paydays, for a total of $150. Seiko's were expensive when they first came out; however, engineers and trainmen were required to have a bona fide, railroad-approved watch.

I hocked that watch twice in my early years, once at a restaurant when they would not take a check, so I gave them the watch as collateral and got it back the next day. Another time, I filled my gas tank and said that I had left my wallet at home; I asked them to take the watch as collateral. I got it back a day or two later.

Twenty-two years later, I inherited a beautiful turquoise and red coral stone gold and sterling-laced watchband from my father-in-law, a World War II veteran complete with the strong mentality that went with that era. I put my watch on that band and started wearing it around the turn of the century. I received many a compliment on my watch, particularly the band, and I would thank people for the compliment. However, as I became older, my mentality was becoming similar to my father-in-law's.

Some nice, unsuspecting passenger would compliment me on my watch, usually a lady, and I would say, "You mean the band?"

"Yes, the band. It's so beautiful!" she'd say.

"Thank you. Would you like to hear the story of how I got it?"

"Yes, please."

"I inherited it from my father–in-law, who received it from a fraternal organization that helped crippled kids, honoring him for his service as their president. But, you know, he would not wear it."

"He wouldn't wear it? Why not?"

"Because he said it was too queer for him. But it isn't too queer for me!"

# Smoke Detector Lady

*There was a lady passenger* who resembled the Wicked Witch of the West from the original *Wizard of Oz* movie that we, unbeknownst to her, called "the Smoke Detector." Every time she rode, she would find the conductor, give a report of who she suspected of smoking in the bathrooms, and wait for us to at least make an announcement reiterating the no-smoking policy. Sometimes, we would indeed have to talk to certain individuals, or threaten to remove them. On one occasion, we even had a passenger removed; he was, of course, intoxicated with a vulgar mouth, and those were the main reasons, but the Smoke Detector Lady's keen sense of smell lead us to him.

I left the job on the south end for ten years and went up north. When I came back, the Smoke Detector Lady was in line as we were doing seat assignments. When it came time to scan her ticket and give her a seat, I said, "It's the Smoke Detector Lady."

"What?"

"You didn't know that we call you 'the smoke detector'?"

I thought it was funny; however, she did not.

# Lickety-Split

*I was working as a conductor* one day, having a not-so-pleasant conversation on the train with a lady who was complaining about us running late. She had me cornered in the bistro lounge, venting loudly asking me why, in front of several passengers, we were late. I kept telling her the facts, keeping my composure. She wanted to know what I was doing to keep the train on-time, and I told her I was making the station stops quickly and safely.

Irritated, she said, "Well you need to do it lickety-split!"

"Lickety-split? Wow, not sure if I can do that in this situation."

She turned red and left.

When coming into Wenatchee, I would make a PA announcement: "Those who want to can indulge in a nicotine fit, as Wenatchee is a smoking break stop. They took the spittoons out in 1946, but it is against Wenatchee city law to spit in public and against Amtrak policy to spit on the platforms. You can smoke, but you can't spit."

Well, during the station stop I would have to do a few duties on the platform, including a crew briefing with a new locomotive engineer, and people would joke with me, some pretending to be hacking up a big loogie and spitting.

One day, a funny lady came up to me and said, "Are you sure you don't want me to spit?"

I said, "I hate it when they spit!" Hi-yah!

# Three White Balls

*At the Mount Vernon*, Washington Amtrak station stop, about one hundred feet south of the station doors, there are three large white steel balls. Each one is about five feet tall with a white steel connection laced between them. Unless you were a seaman during the 1940s, or are a student of antique underwater explosives, you are going to wonder just what the hell these things are when you see them, like everyone else. There is a plaque at the site explaining that the spheres are deactivated American underwater mines from World War II. Apparently, some Americans thought they represented an important part of our history and had them erected for all to see.

I was known for my "borderline" announcements from the train's PA and was careful when touching on this subject matter. I had most of my fun during the two or three minutes we were stopped at the platform. There were always a few people congregating near the structure, sitting or standing around, smoking and drinking from brown paper bags. Both ladies and men were what people used to call outcasts of society: *There but for the grace of God go I.*

I would walk over near them and point at the mines, asking "What are those things?" as if I didn't know. Someone, usually a man, would always pop off an answer with a smile, speaking my language. I was especially thrilled the time a lady grinned and said, "Big white balls!"

# Black Cadillac Headed South

*Around 2001 or so*, I was working a train from Portland, heading north to Seattle. We had a group of people from a radio station and we gave them the two rear cars of the train. They had paid for one car, but it was a light load so I gave them a break and let them spread into a second car. It was the Christmas season, after all. The group had a small band in one car that was entertaining everyone and from what I could tell, they were purchasing all their booze from our bistro instead of trying to smuggle in their own—and not causing any problems like so many parties tend to do.

The leader, a gentleman from the radio station, wanted us to let them get off at station stops to let them smoke, and I kept telling him "Sorry, no can do." He was nice, but persistent with the smoking request. About ten minutes from Tacoma, Washington, he approached me again, this time with his pretty little wife. Together, they made the smoking request and I said, "I tell you what; you stay near the train and listen for the *all aboard* and be sure to take something to butt your cigarettes into, because the Tacoma station agents will cause me grief if you smash them out on the platform. Especially that John guy."

We pulled into Tacoma, a busy station stop. It takes at least three minutes to get in and out of there and for me and my assistant conductor (on this run, "The Percolator") to off-load and assist passengers, and attend to a few other duties. While we were busy with this, a few of the radio group had their nicotine fits on the platform. It was time to get everyone back on, so we hollered, *All aboard!* When everyone was back on, we locked down the doors and high-balled the train.

I was sitting at my desk in the bistro lounge about five minutes out of the Tacoma station when the smoking gentleman from the radio station slid into the chair in front of me. He was hollering that he couldn't find his wife on the train anywhere and we must have left her back at Tacoma. He was insisting that we had to back up and get her. I told him to simmer down and let me call Tacoma station. I called the station and a station agent picked up right away.

"Did we leave a lady back there?" I asked.

"Yeah, we put her on the bus. She will be in Seattle about the same time as you."

"Okay, thanks." I responded, and said good-bye....

The worried man says, "Well?"

"It's all right," I said. "She got into a black Cadillac and headed south."

The man was frozen in shock, his mind racing, before I said, "Just kidding, she is on the bus and will be in Seattle about the same time as us."

He steamed off before I could apologize.

# My Top Seven Funny Ladies

*My last ten years working*, my first announcement of the trip started this way: "Ladies and gentlemen, boys and girls, today your conductor is Legendary Larry, legendary because I still have a job and a wife." Then I would introduce the crew, say for example: "Today my bistro car attendant is "Down Low Lois," number 69 on the seniority roster," and then introduce the rest of the crew.

I liked to make scenic announcements, as well, and one of my favorites: "We will be skirting the Puget Sound waterway today, home of killer whales, gray whales, octopus, oysters, clams, seaweed, sea lions, sea cucumbers, and geoducks. There are also 267 known species of birds along the waterway: the bald eagle, golden eagle, red-tailed hawk, and the rare and elusive gray seagull; there is also the pileated woodpecker, flickertail woodpecker, and the hairy woodpecker. The mountains you will be enjoying are the Olympic Mountains; the one with the tallest peak being Mount Olym..pus. Enjoy the view, folks."

I had the pleasure of meeting interesting people and almost every trip a lady would come into the bistro lounge, sit at a table near mine, and observe the Legendary nutcase who had a way with words. Most of these ladies observed me a little while, some asking a few questions to ascertain for themselves that I was indeed a safe, qualified conductor who was just having a little fun. What follows is my list of the seven funniest ladies whom I have ever dealt with; another way of putting it would be the seven times that I met my match. Number 7 is my wife and there are six from my railroad work.

A couple years into our marriage I had developed a fairly muscle-toned body from working out in the gym. In the bedroom after pleasures with my wife one evening, I was admiring myself in the mirror when my wife said, "I don't think I like that muscle-bound look anymore."

"Why honey?" I said, with a concerned tone.

'It makes your dick look small!"

# No. 6

I was working the Empire Builder train #7 and had been up since midnight. The train departed Spokane, Washington at 2:15 a.m. headed westbound for the final terminal of Seattle, an all-nighter. After leaving Edmonds at 9:30 a.m., it is about thirty minutes to Seattle. In that thirty minutes, I had a lot of operational things that day to think about, as there were crews reconfiguring the tracks at Seattle's King Street station; crews were working near the station and in the station. There were tracks and signals out of service, so this arrival was going to take my full attention. I had to remind the locomotive engineer of all the situations ahead and listen carefully to our orders as they came in. To violate one aspect of the instructions received by anyone in charge of a piece of track, or the train dispatcher, carried serious consequences—such as being fired.

The sleeping car attendant, a nice lady, stopped me as I walked by. "There are two ladies in my sleeper who want to ask you a question," she said. "They like your announcements."

"Not today," I said. "I've got to focus on the situation ahead."

"Ah, c'mon. It will only take a minute. Please, they are good customers, been with me since Chicago."

I agreed and asked where the ladies were, quickly heading the one car over to where they were staying. Inside the room were two young, twenty-something-year-old ladies, both sitting, ankles crossed, in their seats. I looked at them, trying to keep at eye level.

"The attendant says you have a question for me," I said.

"Those ships back there..." one began to ask.

My mind racing, I tried to think back about what I may have said about any ships we passed. I had mentioned the old 1920s shipwreck at Mukilteo, and I had also mentioned the U.S. Naval Seaport at Everett with all its many ships.

"What ship?"

"You know," she clarified. "The one with all the seaman in it!"

I was stunned for a split-second and we all shared a laugh. I shook the girl's hand whom I had conversed with and said, "That's funny! I gotta go."

# No. 5

Going from Seattle to Bellingham, Washington on Sunday nights was pretty much always a full train. A lot of the passengers were students returning to Western Washington University after a long weekend in the Seattle and Portland areas. I would make several announcements about the scenery and wildlife along the way. One of those announcements was the one about the Puget Sound waterway: "...home to the killer whale, grey whale, octopus, oysters, clams, seaweed, sea lions, sea cucumbers, and geoducks. The waterway is also home of 267 known species of birds, including the bald eagle, red-tailed hawk, the pileated woodpecker, the hairy woodpecker, and the rare and elusive grey seagull."

I was sitting at my desk in the bistro lounge after making that announcement when two young girls sat down at the table in front of me grinning.

"Can I help you?" I asked.

"We want to see the hairy woodpecker," one said.

I pointed out the window and said, "They are out there."

She pointed toward me, under my table, and said, "No, we want to see *the* hairy woodpecker."

I squirmed for a minute, and they ran off giggling.

# No. 4

I was at my desk in the bistro lounge on the way to Vancouver, B.C. on train #510 one day, when a fifty-five to sixty-year-old, attractive, tall, thin lady wearing what they call *yoga pants* approached me and asked if there were any seats available. There were several tables, some with four seats and some with two, but each table had at least one person sitting at it.

"There are plenty of open seats, you just have to share a table with someone," I told her.

She looked around and opted not to sit down. Instead, she decided to turn around and stand two feet in front of me, with her rear end at my eye level. I was tempted to have her sit in the other seat at my desk, but wisdom prevailed.

After a while, she started doing some yoga-type moves, then she would stop and play with her smartphone a bit before going back to the yoga moves. When the train hit rough track, she would brace her pelvis up against the bulkhead of the seat in front of me to steady herself before continuing with her yoga moves, every now and then reaching around to adjust her underwear. I got up some three different times to make PA announcements and when I returned she was still positioned in the same spot doing yoga. After about fifteen minutes, she took a seat with a slightly younger man. I later saw them sitting together in the coaches.

I am not making this up! I had two witnesses sitting across the aisle from me when this happened: my assistant conductor (who enjoyed the show) and a fairly new lady chief of onboard services.

I told the chief, "You have to put that in your report. I was enticed for fifteen minutes and did not succumb!"

After reviewing this story, I am seeing a strong resemblance to the girl contortionist from reform school. *Hmm.*

# No. 3

Train #508 had just arrived in Seattle one evening around 9:45 and we were helping passengers with baggage, escorting minor children, and doing our duties on the station platform when a young lady, about thirty years old, nice enough looking approached me.

"Sir, do you know where Wood City is?"

I thought for a second. "Do you mean Woodinville?"

She poked me on the arm and winked. "No. Wood City!"

"That's funny." I said. "I gotta go."

# No. 2

I was sitting at my desk on train #501 just after loading the passengers and leaving Tacoma, headed southbound. We were barely out of the station when a petite, attractive fifty-something lady kneels on one knee at my desk and starts in. "The bartender is rude! He says that I can't get off the train to smoke or else you will leave me."

I said "Ma'am, that is the rule. If you got off to smoke, you could be left."

"Sir, I'm really having a bad day," she pleaded. "Can I get off to smoke, please?"

"Well, if you figure it out, there is really not too much I can do about it".

At the next station stop in Olympia, I did not see her and we high-balled on toward the next station stop in Centralia. When we pulled in there, I was working the business class car, and she was the first to pop off. She had a cigarette lit by the time she hit the ground and stood out of the way of the work, indulging in a nicotine fit. She watched us do the station work as she smoked, and about thirty seconds before I yelled *all aboard*, she butted her cigarette and hopped back onto the train and into the business car. After we departed, I saw her seated with her dad, or someone old enough to be her dad. Possibly a sugar daddy.

Forty minutes later, we stopped in Kelso, and she popped off to repeat her Centralia performance. Again, she re-boarded before the *all aboard* call.

As the door closed and we started to roll, she asked me, "How long have you been on the railroad?"

"Thirty-seven years," I said, proudly.

"Thirty-seven years! How old are you?"

"Sixty."

"Sixty!" she said. "Sixty! Wow, you look really good for sixty."

I couldn't help myself. I raised up my right arm and flexed my bicep three or four times.

"You know, I can do that too!" she boasted.

"Oh yeah?"

"Yeah," she said. "With my butt cheeks!"

We both had a laugh and that was it. She got off the train with her *dad* (or whomever he was) in Vancouver, WA, and I never saw her again.

# No. 1

We were southbound on train #501 from Seattle to Portland on a series-8 train set. Everything was in order, and I was standing across the bar from Down Low Lois, our lady bistro attendant, having a conversation. She was not busy at the moment.

In the corner, a lady in her early twenties was fishing things out of the condiment trays for the purchase she had just made. She was short and dressed like a nightclub dancer—lots of skin showing, tattoos, and piercings.

As she came my direction to go around me back to her coach seat, I saw a well-done tattoo of two birds on her chest, and as I pointed, I asked, "Are those doves?"

As she walked past, she looked me in the eyes and all she said was, "Swallows."

# Not So Funny Ladies

*I told you the top* six stories of ladies on the train when I met my match. There were many ladies, however, who wanted more than to be funny. I was able to charm my way out of most of those situations without ruffling feathers or hurting one's feelings too badly. There were two times I needed some help, however, once from a trainmaster and once from a coworker.

We had a young lady eighteen or nineteen years old who heard me say during an announcement that the train was going to, "penetrate the tunnel" and it was all I could do to dodge her as she suggested we should hook up as she touched herself. Of course, there was something not quite right about her, as she was after all the men working on the train. I feared that one of my men coworkers or I could end up getting fired, so I called the trainmaster and asked for some help. He had a lady supervisor meet our train on arrival into Seattle, where the young lady was destined, and give her a first and last warning.

The other not so funny lady who caused me the greatest concern...I will have to take at least half the blame. Some would say *all the blame*, and others somewhere in-between. I was working the Empire Builder #8 train from Seattle to Spokane, Washington. I made my customary announcements about being *legendary* and introduced my crew, plus mentioned the sights along the waterway, including the hairy woodpecker. We made our Edmonds and Everett station stops then turning inland away from the Puget Sound waterway, eastbound through Monroe, Washington at Milepost 1769 on through Gold Bar.

Leaving Gold Bar, I would make several announcements, one being: "We are now in the foothills of the western slopes of the Cascade Mountain Range with lots of beautiful scenery to enjoy, including 69 varieties of moss and lots of wildlife. If you look out into the bush, you might see a bear...beaver or a wolverine. There are also weasels and cougars, although it is highly unlikely you will see a weasel or cougar looking out from the train; it is more likely that you will see one walking around inside our train."

As we passed through the town of Index, I would mention the historic Bush House Hotel that had been around since 1899, and fifteen minutes later while passing through the town of Skykomish, I would mention: "On the right you can see the oldest Y 'railroad wye' in the territory with the Jordan Spreader snowplow on the west leg of that Y. Yes siree Bob, there she is now, the Jordan Spreader."

We would then start climbing up the 2.2 mountain grade as I would explain that the 2.2 grade meant that for every 100 feet we traveled, we would be gaining 2.2 feet in elevation. I would then add that in about twenty-five minutes, we would be entering the eight-mile Cascade Tunnel, and a minute before we were there, I would announce: "We are going to enter at the mouth of the western portal of the eight-mile Cascade Tunnel momentarily and we will still be climbing up hill these eight miles; we will climax at our highest elevation at the mouth of the eastern portal as we discharge out the other end. Folks, we are now penetrating. It takes about fifteen minutes to pass through to the other side; please do not try to hold your breath through this tunnel."

This trip, we did not have our customary dormitory transition car for crew members, but I will explain a little the best I can remember. The top of the car normally had ten crew sleeper compartments for mostly the crew and sometimes for pass riders. Upstairs also had a one-bathroom combination shower and a room with one more bathroom. Downstairs there were two tables with cushion seats for the conductor and assistant conductor, used as an office open work area, along with a handicap room with a toilet/shower combination. There were four more restrooms, two of them with showers. This car was meant for employees; however, we didn't get one this trip. Instead, we got a regular sleeper that was designed differently. The biggest difference was the downstairs; it had no office work area for the conductors, and at one end there was a handicap room with a toilet and two other rooms, while on the other end was a family room and two other rooms.

That day, they put us conductors in the family room and gave the other employees the other rooms—some were in deluxe sleeper compartments. Having added this car at the last minute in Seattle made the whole situation a cluster, to say the least, as there were a lot of things overlooked—the biggest being signage before entering the crew car (that it was for *employees only*) signage at the top of the stairs, as well as at the other end of the car (again, stating *employees only*).

I was the only person downstairs sitting in the family room office when a lady appeared and sat down next to me. I might add she was slim, very pretty, about 40, wearing a cute jogging suit.

"Are you the one making the announcements?"

"Yes."

"69 species of moss...are you sure it is 69?"

I was in a predicament now. It was a potential he-said-she-said situation.

"Did you see the *employees only* signs?"

"There weren't any. We need to hook up," she said, as she rolled up one pant leg and spread lotion just above her knee.

Now, I wanted to leave, but it would still be a potential he-said-she-said situation. Then a thought came to me: *Intuitively know how to handle situations which used to baffle me.* So I asked her where she was going and made small talk as she continued to behave seductively. I was in a situation like this in 1998 that I mishandled and was nearly fired.

She continued to insist that we hook up. We were now a few minutes out from our next station stop of Wenatchee and I politely encouraged her to return to her sleeper, that I had to do some work shortly. Finally, she made her way upstairs back to her sleeper, just before arriving Wenatchee.

At Wenatchee, we did our engineer crew change while loading and unloading passengers and departed. As soon as we did, I went and talked with the lady sleeper car attendant in charge of the sleeper car where the lotion lady was riding. I told her most of what I told you and asked her to please ask the lady to stay out of the crew car. I quickly made some *keep out, employee only* signs and duct-taped them up.

A little while later at Ephrata, Washington, I was passing through lotion lady's sleeper car and she got my attention; she apologized, saying she didn't mean to offend me; she was very apologetic, almost in tears.

"No worries, everything is good," I said. "Enjoy your trip." And then I kept moving.

After I retired from the railroad, I was riding the train and the lady employee who helped me out was working. I thanked her for helping me out with *the lotion lady* and she didn't even remember doing so.

I know of several men who were fired while working sleeper cars on he-said-she-said situations. One time, a black lady invited me into the handicap bathroom to help her brush her teeth. Another lady, while taking her sleeper ticket, asked, *can I expect anyone to be joining me later?* There were many times ladies had too much to drink who made comments that were off-color, some bordering on obscene, and I would have to remind them that they were on public transportation.

Almost every trip, a lady would wink at me; after many years, my definition of a wink was that the lady thought I was attractive and not much more, just acknowledgment. I had many ladies tell me exactly where they would be having a drink and at what time. I used to tell people, *right behind the fascination of policemen in uniform was a conductor in uniform.*

# The Gay Hoghead

*One day, at one* of our station stops, my locomotive engineer stepped off of the train to check the air hoses on the front of the engine. One of them was dangling and getting banged up every time we went over a street crossing, so he needed to hook it back up. A lady who liked to watch trains was at the depot that day, and she approached my engineer to make some pleasant conversation. She must have taken a real liking to the guy, because after that, she started showing up at the station every time this particular engineer was working to bring him flowers or candy. She had a big-time crush on him.

This guy was a real sweetheart. He would climb down the ladder and receive the items, thanking her and making conversation. She wasn't aware that the engineer was friendly with absolutely everyone, and thought that his attitude toward her was more than cordial. She was incessant with her visits, and over time became a little bit of a nuisance to him and our operations.

Somebody called our trainmaster, and he came down to talk with her one day before she could get close to the engine, telling her that it was really against the rules for the engineer to engage with people while working. He politely informed her that she would have to stay a safe distance away and just wave at him.

Still, she did not get the hint that the engineer was not interested in women in the manner she was hoping. The engineer in question was at his wit's end and asked me if I could have a word with her. At the time, I wondered why the engineer did not inform her himself, but now I realize that he was just too nice of a guy and didn't want to break this poor woman's heart. He knew me well enough and was sure that I wouldn't...pussyfoot around, and would have no problem putting an end to the issue.

We came into the station stop, and I walked over to where she was standing, waving at the engineer.

"Hi, how're you doing?" I asked.

She smiled at me.

"You know, he's a good-looking guy...."

"Yes," she said. "He is!"

"...But he's as queer as a 3-dollar bill."

That broke the poor woman's heart, but they remained friends. She continued to show up at the stop, and they kept on waving at each other every time we rolled in.

A few weeks later, she wasn't there anymore. I guess that she found a new love.

# Marriage Counseling

*I once heard* that when a woman marries a man she is thinking she can change him, while the man is thinking she will never change; that's pretty much the way mine has been. Marriages on the railroad are difficult, and a marriage that lasts *until death do they part* is rare when one spouse or the other is on the road as a locomotive engineer, trainman, or onboard service employee spending half their life away from home.

After thirty years railroading, I was starting to age and had survived twenty-five years (now thirty-seven) of a mostly pleasant marriage when I developed a desire to become a counselor—after I retired—for disgruntled married men. Often the men whom I worked with were having difficulty with their marriages, and I would listen to them whine and piss and moan about how their wives would not make love to them 24/7.

While they would spew and prattle on, I would interject with pertinent questions like "How does that make you feel?" Or, "What do you think you should do about it?"

When they had finished venting, I would usually say, "Here is what I think you should do; go home, get in the shower, and take care of business, because it ain't ever going to get any better."

That advice got a lot of reactions, mostly laughs, and some of the men appreciated it, while others did not.

We had a lady passenger who rode the train almost every week with us for three years. I came to find out that she was a professional psychiatrist and would listen to my announcements. In the vestibule for two or three minutes before her station stop, she would quiz and analyze me about the things I said over the intercom.

One day she asked, "Tunga Bunga Beach? What's that?"

"Oh you know, *ooga booga tunga bunga.*"

"Yeah, uh huh...."

Believe it or not we became friends. We would talk a little when I was passing through on the train doing my duties— about our marriages and kids. Nice pretty little lady.

One day I told her my *disgruntled-married-man marriage counselor* ambition, and the advice I would be giving them.

When I was done, I was surprised to hear her say, "You would be good. Sounds about right to me."

I told her that the only problem was that I didn't have a counseling degree.

"You don't need one." she said.

"What?"

"All you need is to be able to pass a background check, pay for the license, put a few things on your office wall for credentials like your honorable army discharge certificate and your marriage certificate and you're in business."

"Wow, thank you!"

A couple of years later, I told my daughter's girlfriend, who happens to be a social worker for the state, about my ambition. She said my advice would be as good as any counseling she had ever heard of for that situation.

About a year before I retired, I was working the Empire Builder passenger train between Seattle and Spokane, Washington. I was in Spokane, which is a locomotive engineer and conductor crew change point. The trains were late, it was four in the morning, and I was sitting in the crew room with six crew members from two different trains, including a trainmaster and an operations supervisor. Four of the crew members were ladies, three whom I knew well and one the jury was still out on at the time. I was old-heading everyone with stories when I told them about my *marriage counselor for disgruntled-married-men* idea.

When I hit them with, "Go home, get in the shower and take care of business, because it ain't ever going to get any better," the room became silent.

Then Trudy, one of the conductor ladies, said, "I think you better get your money up front first!"

# The Asian Connection

*When coming into Seattle* on a train that came from the north, such as Bellingham, Mount Vernon, Everett, or Edmonds, I would make an announcement just before arrival: "On the left is the world-famous Seattle Space Needle, erected in 1962 for the Seattle World's Fair. My grandpa drove out from Minnesota that summer and took us grand kids to the World's Fair one day. What I remember the most about that day was that about every thirty minutes my grandpa would have a conniption fit, saying, among other things, 'I can't believe I paid a dollar to park!'"

A minute later, I would make another announcement: "On the right, you can see some of Seattle's waterfront establishments, including pier 70 and pier 69 and we will momentarily be penetrating the mile-long King Street tunnel... we are now in the King Street tunnel folks, a couple of minutes from the King Street station. For you folks continuing on past Seattle, the train will be dwelling in the station for about twenty minutes. That is not enough time to go to skid row or up to Chinatown, so if you do get off to indulge in a nicotine fit or to stretch your legs? Please stay close to the train and listen for the *all aboard*. Seattle is our next scheduled stop in a minute or two." I would then play my harmonica for the last minute before arriving, usually "I've Been Working on the Railroad" or "Wabash Cannonball."

On one trip, I had barely hung up the microphone when a man (who I am guessing was Chinese) got in my face about calling the International District "Chinatown." I listened and apologized, however I do admit I was forced to cut him short, as the train was landing. There were doors to open, seniors to help, and minor children to escort. I would have been willing to talk with the offended man some more, but he had vanished by the time I had finished my duties.

A few days later, I was called into the office and was told to refrain from the mentioning of Chinatown, or refer to it as "the International District." I chose to not mention it. Several months later, I was in uniform walking from the crew base to the station to meet my train when three young Chinese ladies approached me. They asked me, *Sir, could you please tell us where Chinatown is?* I gave them directions and put "Chinatown" back in my announcement.

\*

In 2001, Seattle Mariners right fielder, Ichiro Suzuki, born in Japan, won Rookie of the Year and Most Valuable Player awards in the American league. The greatest Mariner ever. He was number 51 and I wondered why he would choose number 51? After some pondering, I had a theory of why he chose the number. If you flip the number 51 you get 15, and 6+9 =15. Hi-yah!

"Hi-yah" became my positive ending to PA announcements and radio transmissions. It caught on with some of my coworkers and my family, but up to this point very few were aware of my numerology theory. I corresponded with a train dispatcher up north who was good enough at his job; however, I had never met him in person because they were located in Texas. I had no idea what this guy looked like. I was called into the office again one day, and the train master, "Double Track Kojack," said "You know the dispatcher up north made mention of your 'hi-yah' transmissions. He is some sort of Asian. I think you had better cool it with those statements."

I took his advice and refrained from "hi-yah" when communicating with him on the radio.

A few days before Christmas, we were headed southbound nearing Mount Vernon, Washington. There was a cluster ahead.

I could hear the dispatcher over the radio talking to trains thirty miles south of us in the Everett area about restricting signals, this train meeting that one over there, and the passenger train was coming. I very seldom called a dispatcher by cell phone, but the situation warranted it, so I called in. He was very polite, much more so than usual. The dispatcher I was worried about offending was calling me Mr. Drawdy, and giving me a lot of "yes sir" and "no sir" answers. As we talked over the upcoming situation, I felt as if he was feeling a little guilty about calling attention to my "hi-yahs." After we had finished ironing out the cluster ahead of us, it was time to say good-bye.

"Well thanks again," I said. "Have yourself a Merry Christmas."

"Merry Christmas to you too, Mr. Drawdy."

"Hi-yah!" I shouted and quickly hung up.

*

For many years, on the run between Seattle and Portland there was a B.N.S.F. train conductor named Long who worked down there on freight trains. He was from Cambodia, I think. I later learned that he had walked out of that country, nearly getting killed several times in the process. Long had broken but very understandable pronunciation of the English language and I would hear his train coming for many miles, as he did most of the radio work on his trains. I would have a little fun every time his train would pass. I would try to imitate him a little: "Ahhhh...Conductor Long!" to which he would never reply.

This went on for about two years until one day as he was passing I said, "Ahhhh...Conductor Long Dong!"

Immediately, Long responded. "Ahhhh...you got that right!"

A couple years later, I was working up north between Seattle and Vancouver, B.C. We picked up several B.N.S.F. deadheaders at Everett, one of them choosing to sit in the back of the bistro car. As I walked near him, he was smiling from ear to ear.

He put out his hand and as we shook he said, "Glad to meet you! I am Conductor Long."

*

Somewhere around the turn of the century, we hired a South Korean gentlemen to work in the stations. New employees start in baggage and most eventually become station agents. I would occasionally see him at the north stations: Edmonds, Everett, and Bellingham. He would never talk to me. Not a word! He looked mean as hell and seemed to avoid me.

One day, he started to approach me. All this time, I'm thinking *he is going to karate chop me*, but instead he said, "Hi-yah!" and walked away. I nicknamed him "Kato's bastard son," with a nod to *The Green Hornet*.

There was a carman down at King Street coach yard from South Korea. He was a real pleasant guy, born near Seoul, South Korea. Naturally, I nicknamed him "Soul Man."

*

The Talgo train sets from Spain that Amtrak and the state of Washington purchased together to run passenger service all have onboard technicians (OBT). They do everything from fixing electrical problems to air brakes. This is an essential part of operations for those train sets. We had two technicians who were brothers born in Saigon, of South Vietnamese descent. The older one I nicknamed "Rat City Paul," as that was the slang name of the community he lived in (White Center), but the other brother I did not nickname right away.

Rat City Paul also helped his brother-in-law get a job as an OBT. His name was spelled something like "Huaang," and when most Americans tried to pronounce it, it came out as "hung." He was so efficient at his trade that he became "Dr. Hung." There was another brother-in-law OBT by the name of "Fuuk." He was one of the few who did not need a nickname.

When he would be selling headsets for the movie on the train, I would announce: "Ladies and gentlemen, boys and girls, Talgo Technician Fuuk will be coming throughout the train selling headsets for the movie."

The brother with no nickname eventually got a job as an electrician with us and went on to become a passenger train conductor. One day, he caught a job with me as my assistant conductor to go to Portland. En route, he asked me why he was one of only a few people whom I worked with who didn't have a nickname.

"You just got here," I said.

"C'mon!" he said. "I was an OBT, an electrician, and now I'm in train service. I have been here for five years!"

We made it down to Portland and had a bit of work to do. Over the radio, I told the hoghead to have the *tunnel rat* cut him off and run the locomotive around the train, and that I would meet him at the joint. Afterward, we met in the crew shack. I was alone with the tunnel rat and he was not happy.

"What is this tunnel rat shit!" he asked, looking me square in the eyes with a pissed-off glare. I envisioned thirty days on the ground from diversity and humiliation from my peers, but still I took my right index finger and cupped my left hand in a fist. I inserted my finger into my fist.

"Tunnel rat."

He looked back up from my hands, no longer pissed off and said firmly, "Okay. Tunnel Rat. But make sure that whenever you say it, that you use that gesture."

Tunnel Rat is now an operations supervisor. He married a nice lady and have since tunneled out two beautiful children.

# The Bipolar Express

*In 2004, an animated movie* came out called *The Polar Express* starring Tom Hanks. It was based on the 1985 children's book of the same name, about a boy on his way to meet Santa Claus at the North Pole aboard the Polar Express train. The movie is pretty much a must-see for younger rail fans and after it ran in theaters, a few of my coworkers said that I resembled the conductor from the film. My family rented the movie that summer and I saw why some of my coworkers made the comparison.

For the next twelve years, I had a little fun with the kids who loved the film. Every so often, mostly during Christmas time, there would be a family with children on my train, and when pulling their tickets someone would start up with, *Look! It's the Polar Express Conductor.* In the movie, punching tickets was a form of art and the conductor would spell the passenger's name when punching holes on their ticket. I wasn't that talented, so instead I would ask the kid how old they were, punch that many holes into a cardboard seat check, and hand it to them, letting them know that it would make a great bookmark. Sometimes, a parent or grandparent would want one too, so I would punch as many holes as I could fit onto the seat check card and hand it to them. Then, I would ask the kids if they wanted to be conductors when they grew up. There was usually at least one who did, so I would tell them to finish the eighth grade and get their GED. Then they could become a conductor just like me.

Before leaving, I would bend down close to mom or grandma's ear and say softly, "This is the Bipolar Express."

I always made an effort to give kids aboard the train a little special attention year-round whenever possible. I often stopped my walk through the train to talk with kids obviously excited about the train ride. I'd do the whole seat check punch thing and give them the education spiel, (which, by the way, is pretty close to the truth). I really enjoyed my work for the most part. Many a time, while entertaining a mother and her children, I would tell the kids to tell their dad later when they got home that the conductor kept coming by to talk to mom— he will think that is funny.

I extended myself at the various station stops and final terminal stations where there were rail fans of all ages. They especially liked to hear the *all aboard* call, and if there were just adults present, I would mutter softly, "Come, on you guys. Get your butts on the train!" Then I would let out the official *all aboard* that resembled the ones in old movies.

I had a tendency to break one of the golden rules by leaving a door or window open as the train rolled out of the station to toss safety pens to people whom I had seen a few times, or condiments from my hotel stay such as hand lotion and shampoo. Sometimes, I'd even blow a kiss to a pretty, doll-faced grandma.

# Alligator Brim and Doctor Bag

*Around the turn of the century*, I bought a faux-alligator doctor's bag and briefcase off of eBay. Both were in near mint condition and made in the '50s by the Upjohn Pharmaceutical company. They were given as gifts to doctors offices that purchased their drugs. I had them professionally embossed, "Conductor L.E. Drawdy Seattle, Wash." To complement the bags, I bought some faux-alligator material and had the brim of my conductor's hat tailored by a cobbler. I still have the doctor's bag and briefcase and even use them on occasion— the hat I will get to later.

As you can imagine, just about everyone would take second looks at the *gators* and me. Many would smile, grin, or laugh. They were perfect for day trips and short overnight runs, but the 17-hour layovers in Canada and 24-hour layovers in Spokane that I chose to endure later in my career made me resort to one large roller bag. Still, I wore my prized alligator-brim hat.

In about 2007, a new trainmaster came to town. This trainmaster was ruffling feathers with just about anyone he deemed out of line. Some of his perceived offenses were very trivial. He approached me one day with another trainmaster (for a witness) as he ordered me to get rid of my alligator-brim, or else. I'll admit it; I was not happy but, after thinking about it, I went to the clerks and got a new hat.

As word got around of my ordeal, I was getting a little angry.

When one of my wiser coworkers said, "You're lucky that's all he got you for," I simmered down.

So, I put my gator-brim hat on eBay with a little explanation of the history to it. Someone from Japan won the auction for $200.

When the trainmaster retired, I had a new gator-brim hat a few days later. There were about ten years that I used the alligator material exclusively. You could always see them displayed on my desk in the bistro lounge. The bags were quite the conversation pieces. Many times, passengers would smile and comment while passing by. There was even one lady who actually stopped by for a moment, caressed the doctor's bag, and asked if I was ready to "play doctor."

*Devil with the blue suit, blue suit, blue suit, Devil with the blue suit on, Devil with the blue suit, blue suit, blue suit, Devil with the blue suit on, Fee, fee, fi, fi, fo-fo, fum Look out ladies, here he comes, carrying alligator bags with an alligator brim, not too fat and not too thin.*

# Horse Semen

*My favorite delay report* of all time was around 1999, while working a Talgo passenger train built in Spain that was still nice and new. We were coming north out of Portland headed for Seattle and we pulled into Centralia station. On the platform, I watched as the station agent lady, Joan, was working and searching the baggage car with another woman. After a couple of minutes of searching the bag car, they approached me.

"What's going on?" I asked.

"This lady is missing some express baggage; we can't find it," the baggage agent said.

"What is it?"

"Horse semen on dry ice."

I wanted to have some fun, but not knowing the one lady, I refrained. I told them that I would hold the train while they contacted the baggage department in Portland. This was before everyone had cell phones, so they went into the depot and called on the landline. The Portland station let them know that it was on the bottom rack of car three, right next to the bistro car; they said that someone was supposed to have informed us of its location before departing Portland. We then found her cardboard box full of horse semen on dry ice. We matched the woman's baggage ticket with the other stub and sent her on her way.

It seemed odd that such an expensive and important piece of luggage was left in such an unsecured location. On the delay report, I listed the incident under delay code *BAG* for baggage, and in the remarks section listed it as an eight-minute delay on account of a lady looking...*for horse semen.*

# Body Bag

*One evening after leaving* Bellingham, Washington southbound, we were somewhere in the vicinity of Larrabee State Park along the salt water when the train dispatcher called and asked us for a favor. He said that near Dogfish Point, around mile post 85, the police needed our help in transferring a deceased person. My hoghead, "Doc," and I both agreed that we could handle the situation.

A few minutes later, Doc stopped the train for us to speak with a policeman standing with a couple medics with a person in a body bag. The officer explained that a car went off the road up the hill from where we were standing and pointed to the steep hillside. The car rolled down about three hundred feet through the brush, nearly to the bottom, killing the driver. He said that rather than carry the deceased back up that steep hill through the brush, it would be much easier for us to transport the deceased person down the tracks a few miles to the crossing at Bow, where they could get him into an ambulance. Doc got back into the locomotive and he pulled the train down six hundred feet until the baggage car was nearest to the body bag. We opened the doors and put him in the bag car with all the baggage.

We headed down the tracks a few miles to Bow, stopped, and unloaded the corpse into the care of the waiting ambulance crew; we shook some hands and went on our way. I think the whole delay lasted about twenty minutes at the most because, as I recall, we arrived into Seattle on time. Come to think of it, I never understood how we could be twenty minutes late everywhere while en route, but be on-time to our final terminal station. I suppose that's a question for the schedule gurus.

In any case, on the delay report I explained it all clearly. The delay between Bellingham and Mount Vernon was twenty minutes: fifteen minutes picking up the deceased at M.P. 85 per dispatcher's orders, and five minutes delay transferring deceased at Bow.

The coroner called one of my supervisors the next day wanting a little more information about what had transpired, of which she had no clue. I heard that she was a little upset with me and she approached me when I reported for work the next day. She demanded to know why I hadn't put the incident in an unusual incident report.

"I documented it all on the delay report," I said.

"Well, don't you think transporting a dead person in the baggage car is more than a little unusual?"

She had a point.

# Dead Man's Cove

*I guess that the area* where we stopped and received the deceased man has seen its share of bad accidents, because a short time later on an early morning southbound trip through the same area, I had several passengers become very upset when they saw a body floating in the water. I told the hoghead, "Brake Shoe Bob," that we needed to stop.

Bob started to bring it to a stop and asked me what was going on. He was a little miffed that we would be stopping because of what passengers said they saw. As we came to a stop, I hit the ground and hustled back about six hundred feet and spotted the body about a hundred feet off shore, floating face down.

It seemed to take forever to get ahold of the train dispatcher to convey what was going on, but after about five minutes she answered. I gave her some information about where we were, what the man was wearing, and that he was in fact very dead and not just going for a swim. After a few minutes, she gave us the okay to go, and said that the police and paramedics were on their way.

I followed up a couple of days later, and found out that like the man we had transferred in the bag car, he had also driven off the road up above and survived the crash, only to stumble into the water and drown. That little stretch there was between Tunga Bunga Beach and the Samish tunnel. From then on, whenever we went through that area, I would announce: "We are now passing through Dead Man's Cove...."

# X-Rated Bookmarks and Rulers

*Around 2002, I went to work* one morning and in the crew room with all our other forms and paperwork in relation to the operations of passenger trains, on the crew table was a stack of laminated cardboard rulers and bookmarks along with a stack of plastic bags with the image of a clown on it. The back of the rulers and bookmarks were white and blank, absent any wording, and on the front at the top was an image of a steam locomotive; the bookmarker and the ruler each had a photo of a locomotive slightly different than the other. The ruler ran 0 to 5 inches, with a couple blank inches at the top where the locomotive was. The headline was, "All Aboard Passengers!" Below that, the company website and 1-800 number was included along with the Amtrak logo. The bookmark was the same length and said, "All Aboard Kids! Take the Coast Starlight and play in the Patch-Kiddie Car! Hey Kids! Visit the food service car for sweets and treats!" This was followed with the Amtrak logo and contact information, as well.

The plastic bag with the happy clown image had an opening to where the rulers and bookmarks were to be inserted below the clown's waist. As I looked at these objects a minute and turned the ruler over, there was no mistake that the blank white side facing up resembled a fat white seven-inch penis. I looked at the bookmarker and it was the same.

Now I am going nuts, (whoops, did I say nuts, I mean I was going crazy) thinking *WTF!* And I slipped a bookmarker into the rear of the clown bag for the first and last time. We were supposed to give these to kids! I am thinking *no way* and our company had just wasted a lot of money.

I simmered down after a few minutes and took about a hundred of the two hundred rulers and bookmarks—but left the bags. Officials woke up that very day as calls went out all over the crew bases across America to find and destroy these items. I had one hundred of them! Too late, *ha ha hee hee.* It was now time to have some fun.

Now, in my defense, I never showed one to even a minor, much less a kid, which reminds me of what one grandma coworker, "M.M." said to another grandmother coworker, Down Low Lois, in reference to me: "He's really a nice man, I like him. He is sort of a pervert though, but he's one you can trust with your grandkids."

Yes, I had a lot of fun with those bookmarks and rulers for fifteen years, first by slipping them under office doors of managers and clerks of both genders. I had them in my alligator briefcase at all times, giving away a few to coworkers; many a time, someone needed a ruler and when handed one it was pure fun when they would realize what they were holding.

I decorated the bush with twenty of them during Christmas season up in Bellingham one year, right next to the Beaver River Crossing sign. The trainmaster called me in the office one day; he was usually a happy-go-lucky man, but not that day, as he made reference to the bookmarks and rulers. It was a short meeting, as I said *I'm done.*

I do, however, still have one of each. Hi Yah!

Top: Deadheading on the Empire Builder. Bottom: Josie Jones Coles in 1992, pioneer woman locomotive engineer from the '70s.

# Amtrak's Toys For Tots
# Santa Express

# Happy Holidays
### 12/21/95

Skip, Santa, and Larry.

Legendary Larry watercolor painted by an Amtrak passenger.

# PART FOUR

# Foamers

*Trains are impressive* pieces of machinery with a rich history rooted in the very heart of the American story. Kids love trains, and sometimes those kids keep on loving trains into adulthood. You will often see people standing at railroad crossings with expensive cameras or riding trains just for the fun of it. Some of these people are *really* into trains, bordering on obsessive. We call these people *foamers*. Foamers, in many cases, know more about railroading than the people who work on the railroad. We call them "foamers" because they are so excited when discussing trains that you would expect them to start foaming at the mouth at any second.

As a passenger train conductor, I had hundreds of mostly pleasant encounters with rail fans. Sometimes, I would mess with their heads for a bit for fun. On occasion during my announcements, especially while traveling southbound when approaching the B.N.S.F. delta yard in Everett, Washington, I would tell the passengers on the PA: "We will be looking at the delta freight yard system for the next two miles on the right and the Snohomish river on the left. On the right, you can see freight locomotives, roundhouse facilities, boxcars, and various yard tracks. You might even see a carman putting hot box powder on the journal of a hot box. We ask that you rail fans, you foamers, please do not foam on our curtains."

When collecting tickets or passing through the train, often rail fans would start asking questions. When I figured out that they were foamers, I would tell them, "You're a foamer. You only get three more questions."

Depending on the situation, they would have the questions handy, while others would have to think about it for a bit while

I was busy with other duties—and they would ask me later. Some had very articulate questions that would take more than a quick answer. Some of their questions I did not know the answer to, but I would take it upon myself to ask other crew members and almost always came up with an answer to their questions. There were, however, some foamers who were irritating. I always managed to keep a cool demeanor, except for one time....

Going north out of Seattle, I was sitting in the bistro lounge where we had a crew table. There was a man in railroad-type coveralls seated at the desk in front of me: a foamer. He looked like a big time wrestler, standing at about 6'5" and 300 pounds, a muscular build that dwarfed mine, and a full mane of long hair. Between Seattle and Edmonds, for a solid twenty minutes he bombarded me with questions about passenger trains and I pleasantly answered them. After Edmonds, I sat down at my desk and again he started asking questions.

After about ten minutes, I had had enough. *I have to get away from him!* I thought, and got up to head toward the bistro to make an announcement. The foamer stood up and blocked my path, forcing me to slide up against a table to get around him.

As I was going around him, he was still foaming and said, "Ever since the inception of The New Passenger Railroad in 1971, the employees have been so nice to me."

I can hardly believe what came out of my mouth next. "That's because you're so f---ing big!"

He stood frozen in disbelief as to what I had just said. I was thinking if I survived this encounter with just thirty days on the ground, I would be lucky. But then the big man grinned at me, and I knew that everything would be all right.

# 1888 Safety Culture

*The culture is a changing.* I hired out April of 1977 as a "Gandy Dancer," slang name for a section worker. In December of that year, I became a Switchman. Both of these are extremely dangerous jobs with a history of some very disheartening injuries and deaths. I switched out boxcars alongside cohorts who were later maimed or killed in railroad accidents. I have visited them in hospitals, gone to their memorials and tried to console their family members. I met a locomotive engineer with a plate in his head, two trainmen missing legs, and met a switchman missing three limbs. These unfortunate railroaders and their families received compensation, but it wasn't always that way. Tragedies on the railroad have curtailed, but are still ongoing.

A century before my career started, workers and their families were not entitled to compensation if injured or killed on the job. Finally, the "Federal Employers Liability Act" (FELA) of 1908 was enacted. This act, spearheaded by union activism, ensures that railroad workers who are injured or killed while working will be compensated (or their family). This act made the less compassionate railroad owners more safety conscious in a roundabout way. If they were going to have to make settlements, it would be less expensive to keep workers safe.

The FELA Act was not just for switchmen who had fallen in between boxcars or Gandy Dancers covered by tunnel cave-ins, it was an important protection for every railroad worker. The dark side of this great act was that over time certain individuals started taking advantage of the system. Almost every railroad employee knew or knows of a railroader who took advantage of FELA by putting in a suspect injury report and collecting a settlement, or by putting in an injury claim after a serious or not so serious accident and milking it, usually with the help of a lawyer. They'd call this "hitting the lotto" or, should it lead to a disability retirement, "the golden parachute." It was and still is a common practice. Some shysters even make careers out of it.

Most railroaders have had thoughts and opportunities of milking the system, but only workers with a certain mentality can rationalize this behavior enough to take action. I have been tempted more than once myself, early in my career.

I was the conductor in the caboose on the rear of a freight train. As the three-quarter-mile-long train was coming to a stop, it felt like I was cold-cocked as five thousand tons of slack hit the caboose so hard that my forehead banged into the wood frame of the cupola window; it nearly knocked me out. I had a bloody, knotted forehead and a concussion, while taking several stitches at the hospital. I was out of commission for a week. Some say I was never the same after that accident! It could have been the lotto or even a golden parachute opportunity. I settled with a claim agent for double my lost wages.

I worked with many *rails* and watched them limp their way to early disability retirements. Some, it seemed, were winking and grinning all the way. I am not making this stuff up, ask any old head and they will tell you similar stories with slightly different perspectives. To some it was rogue behavior, others call it entitlement, and to many it is somewhere in between. What is sad is that I have seen too many limping and hobbling off the railroad who were so crippled up that no amount of compensation could make it right.

Prior to the 1980s, railroad owners for the most part did not hesitate to pay claims. It was considered part of doing business. Most the time, fighting the claims was only a break-even proposition at best if the owner won.

Then the culture changed. After years and years of certain lawyers refining the art of pulling huge settlements out of suspect injury claims, railroad owners started fighting back.

In the early-'80s, they began new safety programs that felt like intimidation and harassment to most employees. These safety programs focused on employees that broke safety rules and employees that put in injury reports. We all became targets for harassment. Safety guidelines and rules were increased, while managers hid in the weeds (we'd call them "weed weasels") and spied on us working. They'd jump at any opportunity to write us up, failing us for any perceived violations.

Employees were called into the office and demeaned for breaking minor safety rules. I was in there myself more than once. When you broke enough rules, discipline in several different forms was administered. The most common punishment was unpaid time off, but could be as severe as job termination. For a while, safety violations and injuries were kept track of and when a period went by, usually six months, without a lost time injury, an award was given along with a company luncheon; the idea of safety luncheons caught on, being a very positive way to promote safety. This hardly phased injury reporting, however, as the subculture of employees with suspect injuries continued to milk the system, only becoming more innovative. The luncheons eventually continued, with or without reported injuries, in the name of safety. What we had and still do was a small minority of employees angering owners who were court ordered to make erroneous claims, and the other employees were caught in the middle.

Through the '90s, the culture ramped up again in safety programs that emphasized tracking employees who were breaking safety rules. If injured one time on the job, termination from employment was a real possibility. I heard about many, and knew of one. Most of those terminated eventually the union won their jobs back, sometimes with compensation. Some weren't so fortunate. I know one. Some employees injured on the job hid their injuries, not reporting them for fear of retaliation. I hid two injuries myself; one still nags me to this day.

Finally, after the railroads lost one too many lawsuits of proven harassment against seriously injured railroad workers, the culture was put into shock. A lady on the railroad in Seattle injured her leg at work and was fired after being treated at the hospital and putting in an injury report. That incident was the straw that broke the camel's back, as she became the Rosa Parks of harassed injury reporting by railroaders. She was given her job back and a settlement with the help of legal assistance, leading to the passing of the Whistleblower Protection Enhancement Act of 2007. All of a sudden, harassment of railroad employees who filed injury reports was no longer tolerated. We hardly had time to comprehend that change before the Rail Safety Improvement Act of 2008 was passed, requiring employers to become proactive rather than reactive toward their approach to safety.

The culture started to change, with much less harassment. Railroaders who now had the unfortunate experience of an injury would have their ass kissed while being taken to the hospital or doctor's office, ass kissed while being treated, ass kissed while being released, and allowed to take paid time off or perform light duty with pay during recovery—with excessive ass kissing. They were not intimidated or harassed in any way, so it seemed, with the exception of excessive ass kissing; at least it was a little better than it used to be.

Now after someone reports an injury two or three years later when trying to get a promotion, for example, let's say from train conductor to locomotive engineer, for some lame reason they would not get that promotion. I know of one. I also heard of a laborer who had put in an injury report and two years later was awarded a long-awaited job with Saturdays and Sundays off; after working the job one week, the railroad changed the days off to weekdays.

Even with all the laws and rules put in place to protect workers who report injuries, there is still fake injury reporting going on. So, in conclusion, the laws protecting the injured worker from harassment of reporting real legitimate injuries is also protecting the workers who are reporting illegitimate, fake injuries.

# Crew Briefing History
# 1977–2017

*When I hired out in 1977*, most crews had four members, some five if there was a fireman. When reporting to work for road jobs, including passenger trains, the crews were required to read the bulletin boards in search of any new rule changes pertaining to safety and train operations. There were system general orders and Pacific Northwest general orders, both important to read. Then the crew would receive train orders pertaining to the route or routes they were to soon be working on and conduct a crew briefing. They were to discuss in detail the restrictions such as exactly where they were and how to be governed. Speed restrictions and workers on the tracks were always two of the main concerns, however there were many others.

The way it worked was while all crew members were present at a table, the conductor or engineer would report what they saw in the orders. For example, "We have workers at Mile Post 54 right at the Centralia station, then a 30 mph slow order at Mile Post 70 in downtown Winlock, and then clear sailing all the way to Portland. Anyone see anything else?"

Now, that was an example of a good crew briefing, of which I was only involved with a few times back then when all crew members were present and coherent. Most the other crew briefings had crew members absent or members present that may as well been absent, myself being a prime example during my first three years. Yes, for the whole crew to follow all the rules pertaining to crew briefings back in the day was rare. What was even rarer was a crew briefing on a yard switch job according to rules as many times there wasn't one, just a switch list and a note from a yard master for the crew to decipher.

During this era, after I got clean, I started paying close attention to rules. I did not want to get fired because that would piss off my wife. I made a trip from Seattle to Portland and back on the locomotives with a hoghead who taught me a way to keep track of everything that I never forgot. He read his orders and then made notes in geographical order on a pocket notepad of all restrictions pertaining to the trip, then he double-checked what he had with the conductor and revised if necessary. He put the pad in his shirt pocket, thus eliminating having to look on eight different pages, lots of times not in geographical order, to remind him of the restrictions ahead.

Years later on Amtrak, I read the orders and put the restrictions in geographical order on a green seat check card and put in my shirt pocket. Then I conducted the crew briefing from my card and made adjustments if necessary; really worked well running around a passenger train full of two hundred passengers. One day, the superintendent was riding the train and saw me referring to my green seat check card and then call the engineer and remind them of a restriction ahead.

He got my attention a while later and asked in a concerned tone, What if you screwed up when transcribing the orders to your green card?"

"I conducted the crew briefing with this card with all the members of the crew, to their satisfaction." *Hi Yah!*

Crew briefings are of the utmost importance and keeping vigilant and reminding each other of the potential dangers ahead are of paramount importance. As the years rolled by, and especially after the deadly 1987 train wreck, crew briefings were looked hard at and good changes were made pertaining to them. On passenger trains the half-hour sign up time was added on to the already half-hour sign up time, making it a one-hour sign up, thirty minutes parking your vehicle and getting changed in the locker room, thirty minutes allotted for a crew briefing. There were days when if things went well, fifteen or twenty minutes of that briefing was limbo time, spent mostly visiting.

Eventually, management started adding a safety rule to be read from a rule book and discussed; then it was two safety rules and a sign in sheet to acknowledge that one had attended the briefing. Yes, the longer briefing was a good idea, however I think later there was some overkill, especially when we were required to acknowledge proactive safety suggestions, such as: *If you can't be safe? Be careful.*

My favorite crew briefing story happened in 1997. We had a train that ran from Seattle to Portland that departed in the morning; about five hours on duty, which included the initial one-hour crew briefing. After arrival Portland, we then took an hour break, put new passengers on, and returned to Seattle in the early evening, about a four-hour run. That was a total of ten hours on duty, two of it at overtime. When we got to Seattle, we went off duty thirty minutes after arrival. We were still using the paper time slips back then, and we would sit in the crew room for another thirty minutes on overtime discussing safety concerns of the trip just made and report the extra time in the remarks section of the time slip: *Extra thirty minutes on account of crew debriefing.*

It was a couple weeks later that the trainmaster told us to knock it off.

# Animosity and Conductoritus and Rule 90

*When I hired out*, it was not an uncommon scenario to work on crews where there was animosity between the locomotive engineer and train conductor. Some of it was very childish and surprisingly booze was usually not the culprit, that award going to ego, arrogance, and *pride.*

Many a time I worked on crews where the engineer and conductor could not agree on much of anything and if there wasn't an even-keeled brakeman or fireman on the crew to mediate the situation? It could become unintentionally dangerous, as I and many others can attest to; many times while working on the locomotive, caboose, or the body of a passenger train, did I have to remind the animosity boys or girls of a dangerous situation ahead.

I can remember being the brakeman on a work train in Skykomish, Washington back in the day. We were having a crew briefing at the old Skykomish Depot with the roadmaster of that territory, and our locomotive engineer kept interjecting with legitimate questions.

The conductor mumbled loud enough for all to hear, "You're nothing but a glorified truck driver."

On a different day and crew in the same era, I was the head brakeman on a northbound freight train from Portland to Seattle ,riding in the locomotive. The conductor was barking legitimate orders out from the caboose radio a mile behind us.

The engineer looked over at me and said, "He ain't nothing but a glorified clerk."

That sort of mentality went on years before I hired out although it was greatly diminished when I retired, but not extinct. I was told that one of the reasons locomotive engineers were called *hogheads* was because their heads were swelled up with an ego as big as a hog's head.

Some engineers referred to their conductors as "cornductors," the implication being that they knew little of what was going on being situated on the rear of the train in a caboose—and may as well been in a cornfield.

Having said all that, in retrospect, neither one craft or the other was more notorious in their character defects than the other, and had you reversed their occupations it would have netted the same result. I learned fairly early that getting angry over the egocentric antics of a crew member could be a direct contrast to safety, so staying even-keeled during the operations of a train was paramount.

My last nineteen years working was mostly as the conductor on passenger trains and to say I harbored no animosity toward any crew members would be a lie; in spite of that, I learned to stay even-keeled at all times, my "never failing fail-safe." Kill them with kindness and pray they get what God thinks they deserve because what I think they deserve is an *ass whooping*.

"Conductoritus," is a disease afflicting most train conductors at various times of their careers. The disease of the obsession with controlling the movement of the train in all aspects, similar to the term "control freak" in the larger world. I had a severe case of it while working conductor on a passenger yard job in 1991 at King Street Station and coach yard.

I can remember hitting my bottom with that behavior when I barked out over my portable radio to my crew members: "I'm the conductor on this job, and you will do as I say!"

Now, there can be a fine line between a safety-conscientious conductor and one with conductoritus. As I will attempt to explain, there was an official rule called *Rule 90* which in part stated that the conductor was to remind the locomotive engineer of all restrictions (for example, slow orders, or workers on the track) not less than four miles in advance of said restriction. In my prime, I rarely missed calling them out and as retirement age came and passed, rarely became not so rare, an indication that one should consider retirement. But in my prime, I was on top of Rule 90 when many conductors were not, which is not exactly a humble statement, I know, but mostly true. I reminded the hoghead of all restrictions ahead and requirements pertaining to track authority, weather, and many items hidden in the special instructions or timetable, rules that if not adhered to could get us into a dangerous situation; should they be violated, even with no injuries or damage, the crew could be pulled out of service for a lengthy time frame without pay.

Some of these infractions were and still are subject to employment termination. Most hogheads accepted Rule 90, and some even appreciated it. And there were those that were resentful of being reminded of the dangers ahead.

One time a hoghead came by the cafe car before departure and reminded me to get the passengers off at the station stops. Needless to say, he was one of the hogheads we had to keep an extra eye on.

Another hoghead referred to me as *the voice from the rear*, a not-so-kind reference, while others called us conductors *backseat drivers*. There were the many who respected us, though.

I am about to say something not exactly humble about my career, not so much as to brag, but saying it is therapy for me, plus I believe it will better help the reader understand why I got away with the behavior that made me legendary to some and not so legendary to others. In my forty years, I was pulled out of service twice for immoral issues; I spent time on the ground, plus signed a few discipline waivers, and was reprimanded hundreds of times for what came out of my mouth. Railroaders will tell you only a few trainmen or engineers with long careers ever make it to retirement without ever spending time on the ground for a safety operation rules violation. With the combination of vigilance, lots of luck, and the grace of a higher power, I became one of the few.

# Toxic Era Switch and Road Jobs

*On December 19th of 1977*, I was assigned to a switch job at the Burlington Northern Railroad Balmer Yard in the Magnolia district of Seattle as a switchman. This was my first job as a trainman. I was called in to work as a switchman on an afternoon switch job. I can still see the locomotive engineer's face, but I couldn't tell you his name. I remember him handing me a flask of booze and having a taste, but the rest of the night is pretty hazy. A few days later, I was working a different switch engine job standing on the foot board, long nose forward. When the engineer would stop the locomotive, I would get off and hand line the switch for the route, get back on, and away we would go. We stopped at a switch and I paused, unsure if the switch needed to be lined up. The hoghead stuck his head out the fireman's cab window and yelled, "Look at the switch points you stupid fu--er!" Ten years later, I satisfyingly witnessed him receiving the same sort of treatment from a brakeman that he had given me.

Just before I hired on, they had recently passed new laws concerning safety. We were no longer allowed to climb on the tops of cars for any reason. Most were glad to adhere to the new laws, but a few refused, and I had the pleasure to work with one. One day, I witnessed an old black switchman named K.C. amaze us in the art of walking along the tops of moving boxcars, passing signals with a *fusee*. For those of you that don't know, a fusee is a ten-minute flare; a few had a spike in the end that would stick into railroad ties, while the others just lay flat. It was nice to hear that he lived until retirement age, even with all of the hopping between and on top of boxcars.

I was still toxic in my ways at this time, and it would be another three years or so before I would be toxic free. I may not have been the best trainman during this time, but I always maintained a strong emphasis on safety despite my more than periodic indulgences. I worked a short stint on the Balmer yard extra board governed by the former Great Northern Railroad rules before I was bumped to the Stacy Street board, governed by the former Northern Pacific Railroad rules. Stacy street yard was called by many "Spacy" Street yard, and for good reason. I am embarrassed and a bit ashamed to think of the toxic conditions that I and many others worked in during that era, but I believe that it is important that the truth be told.

The extra board was a true test of tolerance. About a quarter of the jobs I worked my first three years were road jobs, and the others were yard jobs, yard transfers, and short locals at Stacy yard some at Balmer yard a few at Auburn yard. These were mostly all-night shifts as they were given in seniority order, and you had to have some *whiskers* to work swing or days. Some night jobs were more desirable than others, depending on your perspective. An eight-hour tour of duty usually included a one-hour coffee break, another hour break for beans (lunch), and a one-hour *quit*. The quit was new to me, but it meant that if your crew completed all of the yardmaster's instructions, you got to leave the property after six or seven hours and be paid for the full eight. In the first couple weeks, I would listen to the crew I was working with complain about not getting an hour coffee, lunch, or quit and laughed to myself at how ungrateful they sounded; but soon enough, I was right alongside them singing the same tune.

# Second Avenue Job

*There were other shifts*, such as the second avenue job, that had a different type structure of work. Most the time we would leave out of the north end of Stacy yard taking a short train up Seattle's waterfront about a mile with twenty or thirty cars with a caboose on the rear and pull through the North Portal Junction just past the control tower sometimes operated by a pretty little black lady. Then we would get signal indication westbound, officially southbound, on the main track into the King Street tunnel in the dark, with one or two switchmen riding the rear caboose platform with at least one lantern, sometimes a caboose red rear-end marker, a spotlight if it worked, or a fusee. As we came out of the tunnel at the South Portal, we would usually get a favorable signal and shove past King Street Station and the Kingdome to Lander Street, stop and hand line ourselves off the main track into an industry lead, and work the industries in the area for about two hours with no coffee or lunch break. Instead, we took a sleeping break on the bunks in the caboose. There was at least one old hoghead who worked this particular job in order to get some sleep so that he would be rested to work his day job as a roofing contractor. Some of us would smoke a little reefer and have the Stacy roving yardmaster, "Tenny," give us a ride to Sambo's restaurant to eat before taking us back to the caboose with enough time to take an hour-long nap.

After sleeping, if all things were in order, we would enter the southbound main track at Lander Street, go south a short distance about a third of a mile, and hand line ourselves from the mainline at the Stacy Street Wye (a triangular junction), line back, report clear, and come around the wye veering right onto the Pacific Coast track three lead, or "PC3." If pushing the train, we would kick the caboose into the caboose track, switch the cars into the designated yard tracks, and then put the engine onto the engine track. If we were pulling our train, it was different. We usually pulled onto a clear track, cut the engine off, and ran the engine around the train to couple on the other end and pull the train over the switch onto the lead and then do some kicking, switching the cars onto the designated tracks, the caboose onto the caboose track, and put the engine onto the engine track. Once in a while, If the crew wasn't too high, and the drag not overly long, when pulling our train we would do *drops*.

Now, for those of you unfamiliar with the sometimes-dangerous art of dropping cars, I will explain as best I can. It involves the engine and the cars being separated on the fly with the engine between the cars and the switch and then the engine speeding into the clear so a person on the ground can throw the switch and allow the cars to roll into a yard or industry track. Once the cars clear the switch, the engine can come out and grab the cars if that is the purpose for the drop, or just leave them there. Got that? Dropping cars might also be briefly explained as when pulling a train and wanting to get the car or cars behind the locomotive on the other end of the locomotive, then you would make a drop.

Okay, sometimes we would drop the caboose onto the caboose track and on occasion drop the cars onto a track, then put the locomotive on the engine track and go home with a one or two-hour quit, actually working a total of four or five hours and getting paid for eight.

The most interesting thing to happen while working the second avenue job was the night the police took us aside and asked us questions about the Superior Fast Freight warehouse, wondering if we had noticed anything suspicious in the area. Eventually, they told us that someone was stealing color TVs and they suspected a switch crew or a warehouse employee. A few months later I saw on the news that they had found the thieves: it was the two officers who had questioned us.

# Six or Twelve-Hour Rule

*If it appeared a job* was not going to get long breaks and a quit, the rogue workers decided on a "six or twelve-hour rule." That meant that if we didn't get our customary breaks of coffee, lunch, and a quit that didn't add up to at least two hours while getting paid for eight, or if we had to actually work more than six hours while getting paid for eight, we were going to "screw the dog," meaning drag our feet, follow all of the rules, and work twelve hours, four of those hours at the overtime rate.

The problem with that rule is that sometimes they would send you home after eight hours and we gained nothing. But there were times when the job could be stretched into twelve hours. Another frequent problem was that there was almost always one member of the crew who had other obligations waiting for them at home, so screwing the dog did not always work. Now, there were jobs on which the entire crew was made up of the six or twelve mentality and we got twelve hours most everyday—another example of a trainmaster looking the other way. I am sure somewhere the six or twelve rule is still being practiced today.

# Seventh Avenue Job

*The Seventh Avenue job* crew worked nights and had some serious seniority on it. This was in 1978-80 and there were men who had 1940s seniority dates. With this much seniority, they could have been working a day shift job with weekends off. The attraction to this job was the amenities that went along with it. That job switched out the Rainier Brewery and it was well-known that a job well-done earned the crew some brew. That job also switched out several scrap industries with gondola cars that many a switchmen were scavenging through for copper, brass, and anything else of value. The only real downside that I can recall was the switching of livestock at one of the facilities. These cars smelled terrible, but mostly I felt sorry for the animals.

The job even got regular breaks and a good quit. What I remember most about that job was the foreman; he did all the field switchman work those few times I worked it as the field man had disappeared. The foreman was thirty years my senior, but in just as good of shape as I was. He was a prior rights Great Northern Railroad switchman who played a lot of tennis in his spare time. He would tell me to stand at the switch and calmly holler when to throw it. He was amazing, as he would have the engineer kick the car, get the pin himself, climb up the ladder to the handbrake, and tie it down at the exact spot of a building on one track. Then, he would walk up and throw an inside switch to a different building and tell me to pull the pin on the next one before giving the engineer the kick sign with his lantern. I would then get the pin and he would give the stop with his lantern and catch the car on its way by climbing up the ladder and tying it down at the spot of another building. He ran circles around everyone and was one of the few railroad employees in all of history without a foul mouth.

You might be wondering where the field man was during all this work. I am not sure, but he may very well have been in the brewery lunch room.

# Snoqualmie Museum Train

*Sometime between January 1978* and June of 1980, I was the head brakeman on a museum train, I believe from Balmer yard in Seattle, to Snoqualmie, Washington. I do not recall the starting point, somehow. I had to email a retired old head coworker to sort this out, and from what he tells me is we must have come up through the Old Black River Junction onto the old Pacific Coast Railroad Line from about Renton, Washington and on to the old Milwaukee Road line.

I don't remember that...what I remember is it was an early weekend morning and I was hungover. There were no track signals, an old rusty track, and trestles over rivers and ravines that were ancient and scary. We crawled along at about 10 mph, eventually coming upon the Weyerhaeuser lumber company at Cedar Falls, Washington; they had the main line blocked with cars which had to be moved out of our way so that we could get by. I can't remember if it was us or a Weyerhaeuser crew that moved them out of the way.

I do not recall the crew I worked with that day, but I do remember them as being older than dirt, like I am now. We were taking cars and materials to the Snoqualmie Railroad museum and the museum people were happy to see us.

I don't remember the trip back and if I told you anything more about that trip I would be making it up....

# Belly Full of Piss!

*I caught a train* out of Seattle in 1978 or 1979 for a trip to Portland and back. There are a few things I can remember about that trip, but not a whole lot, as I was still in my toxic phase. The conductor I was braking for that trip had survived a head-on collision of trains in South Seattle a couple years earlier on account of pure luck, as a fast-moving, 50 mph train collided with his standing-still train, as told to me. All crew members on both trains lived through it, but the engineer and head brakeman of the moving train suffered serious injuries; the brakeman ended up with a plate in his head and engineer with his jaw wired shut. They both came back to work eventually. I recall working with them: the engineer was known by all as, "Crash Arnold," and the brakeman became an engineer as part of the settlement. In later years, I made a casual comment about the plate in his head that he did not appreciate. The conductor who I was working for that trip did not elaborate on the accident, although there were at least three theories to why the accident occurred: one, blaming the moving train crew; two, blaming the standing train crew; and the one that the majority went with—the signal system was at fault.

Back to our trip...we were on our way home late at night or early morning nearing Seattle, riding in the cupola of the caboose across from each other, when I made mention that I would be glad to get home.

"Me too. I have a belly of warm piss and bad breath waiting for me."

# Clocking the Speed of the Train

*Over the course of my career,* I worked with a few locomotive engineers who were absolute speed demons—violating speed limits, ignoring rules, and cutting corners. In my early years as a train conductor or brakeman while working in the caboose on a freight train or while working the body of a passenger train, it would be very difficult at times to tell if the train was speeding; most of the time we trainmen did not worry about it, however there were exceptions to that theory in the name of safety.

I was taught early on to look for a milepost marker by looking out the window of a caboose cupola window, or by standing on the back of the caboose platform, or even just sitting at the conductor's desk and chair that faced the tracks we were passing over. Should I be on a passenger train, I could go to the vestibule and open up a window and look out. The milepost markers were usually double-sided and could usually be found on either side of the tracks.

When you see the milepost marker coming up, you look at your railroad-approved watch and the instant you pass the marker you note the time. Then you start looking for the next milepost marker and when you pass it, you note that time. You take the time it took to travel that mile and convert it to miles per hour. If it took 60 seconds, you were going 60 mph, and if it took more or less time than that, you could ballpark about how fast you were going. Just about every engineer and trainman carried a cheat sheet to refer to, and if not, there was always a chart in the timetable or special instructions.

There were a few T&E who had it all in their head. This method of figuring out how fast the train was going was used mostly when the locomotive's speedometer was suspected of reading incorrectly; however, in my early years there were old guys who were constantly clocking from both the locomotive and the caboose or the body of a passenger train. They had it drilled in their heads from their predecessors of the steam engine days, when all train routes with signals were but a dream and most all trains ran on telegraphed train orders from point A to point B, with no other trains allowed in those limits until the opposing train arrived or a specified time had been reached allowing opposing trains enough time to clear in a siding or off the main track. Should that not happen for any reason, that train was governed by torpedo and flagging rules.

Having said all that, back to the original intent of this story....

We had speed demons, and in certain situations, we would clock them with the milepost procedure. When we figured out that they were going a little too fast, we would ask them on the radio if their speedometer was good, tipping them off to the fact that we knew that they were speeding and that it might be wise to slow down.

I know of many engineers and two conductors who were fired for speeding. Most eventually got their jobs back through union grieving. One conductor was manning the caboose when the train he was in charge of ended up in a horrendous wreck, resulting in lives lost. The railroad officials figured that he had been around long enough to know the running times from A to B, B to C and so forth, and that he should have known to put the train into emergency braking miles before the accident. I also knew a passenger train conductor who was fired along with his locomotive engineer who had grossly exceeded speed limits between station stops. He was fired under the same reasoning—that with all of his experience, he should have known to stop the train. In that case, there was no train wreck. The locomotive engineer just managed to scare a lot of people, while the conductor turned his head the other way.

I could go on and on about a few engineers who only observed speed limits when someone was riding with them who could cause them grief, such as a train master. Even then, some of those train masters were known to look the other way. For many years on the locomotive, there was the *dead man pedal* connected to the train's air brake system that the locomotive engineer was supposed to keep their foot on; keeping a foot on it in the name of safety should one faint, have a heart attack, or die at the throttle, they would hopefully release their foot off the dead man pedal and the train brakes would apply emergency air braking, bringing the train to a stop before going through a red signal and crashing into another train, or from going around a 10 mph curve at 50 mph and derailing. The pedal was to divert catastrophes. As I said in another story, almost all the dead man pedals I ever saw had an air hose bent to keep the pedal applied, thus not having to keep one's foot on it.

In the '80s, a new system came out to replace the dead man pedal, the *alerter system* connected to the control panels of the locomotives. The idea was that if the operator did not perform a function on the locomotive for twenty seconds or so, then a flashing light would come on along with a beeping sound; the flashing would get brighter and the beeping louder and would continue until the operator pushed the button, blew the whistle, or performed some other locomotive function. Now, if the locomotive engineer keeled over dead twenty or so seconds later, the alerter system would start beeping and flashing first quietly and dim, then gradually louder and brighter, and when after a minute nobody pushed it, the train's air brakes would apply, bringing the train to a stop. It could just as well be called a dead man's *button*.

When this system came out, it was not that big of a deal to most operators pushing the button every now and then; however, I heard of a few hogheads who set up automobile windshield wiper delay devices on their control stand with wires and alligator clips connected to circuits behind the control panels. This little setup eliminated the need for them to push the alerter button as the windshield wiper delay would send a signal every twenty seconds or so. I saw this one time too many.

Along came another safety device to keep locomotive engineers from speeding, despite the alerter over-speed device. I was not a locomotive engineer; however, the first eleven of my years about half the time I was riding shotgun in a locomotive, and then my last twenty-nine years I was mostly in the bistro lounge of a passenger train. The way I understood the over-speed device was that it was set for 80, 81, or 82 mph. The maximum speed for our passenger train was 79 mph, so the idea was that when the train reached a speed over 79 mph, the over-speed would put the train into emergency braking and come to a stop. This was usually a ten-minute delay or more, depending on who, what, and why. We had operators who figured out how to bypass the over-speed system, jimmy rigging it some way, enabling them to operate the train at 85 to 90 mph. I know one locomotive engineer who was caught doing this, one of the many things he survived making it to retirement.

# King Street Switch Tender Shack

*There was a time* when all the train tracks in and out of the south end of Seattle's King Street Station were manual hand throw switches, and before my time they were hand throw at the north end as well. In the late-'70s and early-'80s and many years before, there was a little shack named the King Street Switch Tender Shack (some called it a *shanty*) near the south end of the depot tracks on the east side of the southbound and northbound main line tracks. The shack was situated near two hand throw double main line manual crossovers that led into the station tracks; the lower, or most southern, crossover led directly from the northbound main track to the southbound main track and into all the station tracks, while the upper or northern crossover only led directly to the southward main track into a couple tracks, although a reverse move could be done in a southerly direction on the southbound main track, allowing a train to get into the lower station tracks.

Also in the vicinity was a small building referred to as the *yard shack* owned by the Burlington Northern Railroad, and formerly owned by the King Street Terminal Company. The building had a yardmaster office with lockers and a restroom where switch crews reported to the yard master for work assignments and took their breaks, sometimes playing the popular card game *pitch*. Some drank coffee while others indulged in spirits. Behind the building was a stub track for the switch engine.

As best as I can recall, the switch tender shack, yardmaster building, and stub track were gone by around 1987; however, the two double main line manual cross overs remained at least fifteen more years, the switch tender's personal car replacing the shack—I parked there myself many a time. The King Street switch tender's job was to hand line passenger trains through the crossovers in and out of the King Street station tracks—a relatively easy job; a late train or two, however, would require some quick and safe thinking for things to go smoothly. I was called off the Stacy Street switchmen's extra board a few times to work the shack job and enjoyed it. I was told by a couple old guys, and more recently "The Polish Prince," that the union worked something out with the company that the switch tender job became designated for switchmen who came back to work after a serious injury. I believe this to be true, as I saw one guy hobbling around in and out the shack a few times. When there was not an injured person recovering to fill the job, they would call someone off the extra board. In today's world, injured workers and light duty are much different.

Yes, when people look at or visit the beautiful historic 1906 King Street Station few realize that its clock tower was once the tallest man-made structure west of the Mississippi River. Nor do they realize that back in the day there were many structures with connections to the station, just as beautiful, that are long gone.

*There was a crazy little shack beyond the tracks, and everyone called it the switch tender shack. One of these days I'm gonna head on back, in the direction of that switch tender shack. Whoa uh oh, O that switch tender shack.*

# Protecting a Back Up Movement

*Hogheads and trainmen* are required not be colorblind and to have excellent eyesight—anything less could be fatal. They need to be able to see the color of the signal governing the movement of the train they are handling or in charge of and know the indication requirement. Hogheads observe them much more than trainmen. When shoving or backing up a train, a qualified trainman would need to be watching and protecting the move from a position on the rear to see the signal and relay the indication verbally with their portable radio to the locomotive engineer—green meaning go and red meaning stop, yellow meaning to slow down and get ready to stop (just like a traffic light). Prior to the '70s hand-held portable radios were rare, meaning most of the time hand signals were the only option for back up train movements. Most the time the locomotive engineer could not see the signal aspect governing their train when backing up, but could see out the locomotive bay window a hand signal from a crew member; if the work was on the fireman's side (and there was a fireman working) the fireman would verbally convey to the engineer the signal that the crew member hanging off the side of a boxcar behind them had sent after receiving a hand signal from another crew member hanging off a boxcar closer to the rear; this was more practical than trying to receive a signal from someone actually on the rear of the train, which was sometimes a mile away. This was all done by hand with the help of fusees and lanterns at night, and there were many daylight weather conditions when fusees were practicable.

When I hired out in 1977, one portable radio was given to about a third of road crews and I do not recall having them on switch jobs until the mid-'80s when just about every crew had one; by the late-'80s, most trainmen carried one. Of course, there were those who refused and insisted with the old school mentality of passing hand signals, but when crew sizes started to be reduced in the '90s, they were left with no other option. As mentioned, prior to the portable radio, when making a back up movement it sometimes took three trainmen to pass signals to the locomotive engineer. One scenario I was involved with many times in the late-'70s and early-'80s was at the north end of the Burlington Northern Stacy yard in Seattle. When doubling sometimes tripling and even quadrupling tracks together to make an initial outbound train sometimes close to a mile long, we needed three trainmen to pass signals to the hoghead.

I will explain as best as I can remember a switch move we made at night at Stacy yard in the '70s, man job number 75. I was involved with this particular move some hundred times or abouts over forty years ago. On the north end of Stacy yard, we would put the engine on a track of twenty or so cars and pulled those twenty out and doubled to another track of twenty; that would take two trainmen passing lantern signals to the locomotive engineer to make that double over, one at the joint and one at the curve by the north end yard shack. When pulling the track out, the person at the end of the cars where the joint was to be made would pass a lantern stop signal to a person standing on the curve by the north end switch shack. That person would then pass a lantern stop signal to the locomotive engineer and the cars would come to a stop. The person at the end of the cars would hand line the train toward the next track with twenty cars on it usually about two hundred feet away and give back up lantern signals to the person at the shack, who passed them to the hoghead in the locomotive five hundred feet away, and while sending and passing lantern count down signals the cars would be shoved slowly to a joint on the intended track. At this juncture, we would be tied on to forty cars and sometimes doubling those forty over to another track of twenty or more; pulling those forty as in doubling over required three trainmen to pass lantern signals to the locomotive engineer, one at the end of the cars to send lantern signals to the person by the north end switch shack on the curve, who then passed lantern signals to a person five hundred feet away under pillars of the highway overpass on Seattle's waterfront, dodging transients, cars, debris and who knows what else, and that person would then pass lantern signals five hundred feet to the locomotive engineer who was craning their neck out the window trying to find and make out the lantern signal and not confuse it with any other lights along the waterfront, all the while keeping an eye on possible vehicle and or pedestrian obstructions in the path of the locomotive. Add rainy weather on a moonless night and it was the ultimate of switching—night moves. The passing of signals in this manner went on 24/7 all over the world until the portable radio arrived.

# West Seattle Record Drop

*Of all the switch jobs* that I worked in my toxic era, I worked the West Seattle Switch the most. I grew up in West Seattle, so that may have been the attraction—or possibly the rate at which we worked. The job was not for slow pokes, and people of that nature stayed away; it was for the adventurous, live fast and hope you don't die railroaders who coincidentally liked to partake in a variety of substances, mostly grass. My eyes get watery just thinking about it.

I worked that job on and off for two years and eventually moved up to the switch foreman position in mid-1979. The job did not have a caboose for the late-night sleep break, so we slept in the West Seattle Yard Office. Almost every time I worked that job, it was with one or two different switchmen, but almost always the same engineer, so he and I got to be in sync. Run, run, run, and sleep, then run, run, run, make the big drop and go to Stacy for the tie-up. Now I know that does not make sense to a lot of you, so I will do my best to explain....

We reported to the Stacy Street yard office in Seattle at 11 p.m. and sat through a 10-minute work briefing with the roving yardmaster, Tenny. We then would hop into an engine and get on a track, sometimes double one track to another, couple up air hoses between each and every car attached to the train so that we would have air brakes as required for moving over public crossings. We would then head south about a half mile or so before veering off right in a westward direction at the Buffalo Sanitary Wipers Company just before the Union Pacific Railroad Yard, proceeding west with Harbor Island to our right and Lone Star Cement on our left. We would then use the locomotive radio to call the bridge tender operator to lower the bridge in order to cross over the Duwamish River on the Burlington Northern drawbridge (formerly the Northern Pacific drawbridge).

Once across, we would go right a short distance to the West Seattle B.N. yard office and yard. A little way over the bridge there was a crossover and once the rear of your movement cleared, you could hand line the switch and reverse your movement in the opposite direction of the yard shack and bridge and go a southerly direction down West Marginal way to where most the work was done. Taking care of all of that work took about two hours and before we took our break we left a string of cars destined for Stacy yard just south of the cement plant with a couple hand brakes on them and go lite engine two-thirds of a mile or so up the track past the bridge crossover on to the West Seattle yard office where at about 2 a.m. we would take our beans and sleep if we felt like it.

After resting, we would go back to work about 4 a.m. and make our last industry move at the cement plant. We would gather up all the empties, double to the cars we left earlier, and pull them a mile or so into a West Seattle yard track. We would then cut our switch engine off from the cars and run the engine around them in a clear track while one or two switchmen coupled up the air hoses for the air brakes and another tied on the engine. Then we called the Duwamish River bridge tender on the radio before crossing over the Duwamish River through Harbor Island and into Stacy yard. After that, we just had to tie up before heading home around 5 or 6 a.m.

The engineer said one day, "Why don't we drop those cars we pull at the cement plant after doubling them to the ones we leave before our break, instead of taking all that time running around them?"

Good idea, and we soon started dropping them. I am pretty sure dropping cars is a serious rules violation nowadays, and might be grounds for termination. Now for those of you unfamiliar with the sometimes-dangerous art of dropping cars,

I will explain as best I can again: It involves the engine and the cars being separated on the fly with the engine between the cars and the switch and then the engine speeding into the clear so a person on the ground can throw the switch and allow the cars to roll into a yard or industry track. Once the cars clear the switch, the engine can come out and grab the cars, if that is the purpose for the drop, or just leave them there. In our case, we needed to grab them and head to Stacy. We started with dropping just a few and then it became twelve and fourteen, each time more exciting than the time before. The engineer and I would only drop cars if the other two switchmen were competent and not too loaded.

Then the night came when we had twenty-seven cars to take back to the yard. We had good help, and it was *no guts, no glory* time. There was a street crossing a couple hundred feet before the West Seattle yard that needed protecting, so we left the head man there with a fusee to stop any vehicular traffic that might impose a danger during the drop. We then took the engine down to the cement plant, pulled the empty cement hoppers out and doubled them over to the drag of cars we had left earlier and knocked the handbrakes off. I told the field snake to roll the *drag* by when we pulled and make sure that all the brakes were knocked off and nothing was hanging up, then he could catch the rear. When we made the drop, he would ride the rear, manning hand brakes as needed and making sure that he got her tied down when the rear was in the clear.

We pulled the twenty-seven cars down about an eighth of a mile. I was on the engine with the hogger and I could see the rear man catch the rear, giving a big *go ahead combination hi ball* kick sign with his lantern. I could also see the head man had the crossing protected with a fusee. I was on the locomotive back platform with the rear door open within earshot of the hoghead. We were long nose forward, and the hogger was on the opposite side of the work and could only see half of what I could, so he was relying on me to be his eyes. He was on the edge of his seat looking back and forth at what he could see.

Satisfied that we were all in position, he turned to me and asked, "Are we ready?"

"Let's do it," I replied, and he stretched her out a little more, then put the throttle in the 8 notch. I was on the platform and could hear the engine roaring and see the stack smoking. When he got it up to about 20 mph, he bunched the slack, I pulled the pin, and then he gunned her again up to about 25 mph. The crossing was clear and we went over it a few car lengths, then he slowed her down to about 15 mph. I dropped at the switch as he raced into the clear, and I threw the switch. A few seconds later, the twenty-seven-car drag was rolling by, and there was never a doubt that it would clear. As the last car cleared, the rear man was applying a handbrake. As far as I know, that is the most cars ever dropped in that yard.

Shortly after writing this story, I was on my way to West Seattle to visit family and decided to drive by and look at where that drop took place thirty-seven years earlier. There is now the West Seattle freeway high above the area with its on and off ramps, as well as the surrounding cement works underneath. I drove around for a few minutes before parking my car to study the area for a little while. Things have changed drastically over the years; there is no yard shack, but the track between the start of the drop at the bridge and over the street crossing to the yard is still there. Everything else was very different, but I was able to confirm that I did not dream up that drop. I emailed my old friend, the throttle manipulator on that drop, to have him review this story and confirm that I didn't miss or embellish anything. He said it was pretty accurate, but added that during the drop there was more smoke billowing out the windows of the cab than the stack.

# Double Pin Move

*I was working the Auburn yard* in 1981 and was involved with the rare double pin move a few times. At night when Jim W. was the switch job foreman in the main yard, we would pull a thirty or forty-car drag train north, veering to the right on the lead toward the south leg of the Auburn wye. We would typically just call it the "south leg." Jim W. would have a lantern attached to a fifteen-foot rope and in one quick motion he would wrist snap the lantern upward in a spinning motion high in the air with the slack rope for the kick sign; when the lantern ran out of slack rope, it stopped spinning and Jim would reel in the rope while catching the lantern before it could hit the ground. This was the kick signal for the pretty, well-preserved little lady engineer, "M. Slide Wheel," to give the engine everything she could, pushing the drag. The head man was high on the lead and would get the pin on the first cut, then Jim would give the wash out signal, or a stop signal, slinging the lantern with the rope from side to side for the locomotive engineer to stop the train. He would be running alongside the drag by the next cut and when the slack ran out, the first cut separated. Somehow, Jim managed to pull the pin on the second cut.

I was in the field watching for the first cut to clear the switch points and had about two seconds to flip the switch for the second cut to go by. If not successfully done, we would cause a derailment. There they would go, thirty feet apart, two strings of boxcars going the same direction down two separate tracks, all the while sparks and smoke were coming off the wheels and brake shoes of the switch engine, complete with squealing and sliding noises. The drag would be so long and heavy that it sometimes stopped below where I was. The wheels of the switch engine on that job ended up flat a few times and had to be replaced.

I worked the field a lot for Jim W. and had a lot of fun. Not too long ago, all the locomotives and cabooses had flares and torpedoes stored on them. For those of you unfamiliar with a railroad torpedo, they were little metal packets with gunpowder-like ingredients. The packets had little metal straps that allowed the torpedo to be attached to the ball of a rail. Torpedoes were left on the rail for emergency situations. For example, in the days when there were no radios or track-side lighted signals, a disabled train crew member could lay them out in either direction with red flags well in advance of where they were stopped. The idea was that any train approaching, after running over the torpedo, would hear a loud explosion or see the flag. The locomotive engineer would immediately reduce the speed of the train so as not to run into the disabled train; officially, it was called *restricted speed*. Workers on tracks also used torpedoes as well to warn trains that someone ahead was working on or near the tracks. I hired on in 1977, worked forty years, and the only torpedoes my crew ever ran over was during a test by "weed weasels" (as I fondly called trainmasters). Torpedoes were obsolete by 1977 on almost all routes that I worked on, and are now deleted from most rule books.

For a little fun at the Auburn yard, we would take torpedoes, pack six or seven of them tightly in a paper sack and stuff the bag in the open knuckle of a drawbar on a box car in a yard track that we knew we would be kicking a car into. We would then let a car or cars roll in to a joint. It made one heck of an explosion. It sounded like a stick of dynamite and sent a plume of black smoke up like a small atom bomb, waking up anyone within a mile. The fire department and police came down one evening after an episode of our little fun. We managed to escape any fines and possible arrest. After that incident, we decided to retire from that activity.

There were a lot of good times in Auburn yard and a great cast of characters, including an Asian hoghead who allowed switchmen to run his locomotive on a regular basis. I could go on and on about Auburn yard. After all the years of being an unproductive member of society, I was starting to resemble a productive one. In early-1982, a depression hit and the once thriving Auburn yard was reduced to almost nothing. About 90 percent of the workers were furloughed out of work and most of them exercised their seniority to transfer elsewhere. For me, this meant going two hundred miles south to Wishram, Washington.

# A Rule May Have Been Broken

*The train move* I am about to describe to you is almost unbelievable. Those of you who are not familiar with how trains are operated, understand that in this case the locomotive engineer performed the work of two men at the same time, and at one point the train was rolling with nobody aboard the locomotive. I think it's safe to say that a rule or two may have been violated.

I was on the head end of a westbound freight train running from Pasco, Washington to Wishram, Washington. We had a mile of train with a caboose containing the conductor and rear brakeman on the end.

The hoghead on this trip formerly worked with the Spokane, Portland and Seattle Railroad (The SP&S R.R.), just like his older brother. The old head conductor in charge from the caboose was known by yardmasters and train dispatchers as a guy who didn't screw the pooch and slow everybody down behind his train, thus we were getting high green signals. The engineer proposed an upcoming set-out move of some of our train several times before arriving at the set out destination. I say *proposed*, because he left me the option to chicken out if I so desired.

"The head ten cars of our train, the first ten behind our locomotives, set out on the industry track off the siding coming up," he explained. "We want to do this quickly and not bother with the train dispatcher or anyone else. Our money is made whether we get to Wishram in 10 hours or 4 hours. We get paid by the miles. We can save at least thirty minutes on this move I have in mind. I already talked it over with our conductor and the dispatcher knows he is one not to lollygag."

"Okay," I said, "I'm listening."

"The siding will be on the right and about thirty cars into that siding on the right is the industry track with a derail. The hand throw switch to the siding is well past the governing signal for that siding, and we will have full protection to make this move."

I nodded along. "Okay, keep talking."

"When we get close, I will slow the train down and get it steadily rolling at 6 or 7 mph. When we are about ten car lengths from the switch, we both bail off and I will run ahead, unlock and hand line the switch toward the siding and get back on the engine. You stop me at the cut, bottle the air, and make the cut. Make sure you leave two engine lengths of room for when we tie back on."

I thought it over for forty-five minutes or so, asking a few *what if* questions, like: "If you don't get the switch lined up for whatever reason...?"

All I ever got for an answer was, "Don't worry, this is going to work."

*No guts, no glory* time.

The hoghead slowed us down to 6 or 7 mph and stepped to the front foot board of the lead locomotive. I stepped onto the rear foot board, and about ten car lengths from the switch we both bailed. My partner ran ahead of the engine while I walked quickly, observing and getting ready for the cut. I think he may have done this sort of move once or twice before, because when he reached the switch it was unlocked and lined up lickety-split. The hoghead climbed back up the foot board of the lead locomotive and ten seconds later stuck his head out the bay window to look for my sign. Half a minute later, I gave him a wave to stop.

Once we stopped, I may have violated a rule by low-crawling under the train to reach the angle cock and turn it on the portion of the train we were to leave standing. Then I crawled back and closed the angle cock on the set out cars and pulled the cut lever and gave the *go-ahead* hand signal to separate the train while climbing up on the rear as we were pulling onto the siding, I could see the derail up ahead on the industry track on the right, and the hoghead was pointing to it out the bay window. I bailed off and ran ahead as he slowed the movement down to 2 or 3 mph. I got to the derail, unlocked it, and flipped it over into the non-derailing position. I ran over to the slowly moving set out to catch the rear and ride it up about five cars to the switch.

I bailed off the end of the cars and waved the movement down to a stop, unlocked, and hand lined the switch toward the industry track. I gave the hogger a big *back up* sign and climbed on the end as it began rolling. As we backed up, I was out of sight a few seconds, and I dropped back off just past the derail before shoving ten cars down a clear track with nobody on the point or watching the shove. That sort of shove might be a federal case today. When the locomotives reached me and stopped, I made the cut and gave the *go-ahead* sign; as the locomotives parted, I climbed up on a boxcar and tied a handbrake.

The hogger took the locomotives up over the industry track switch, stopped, got off and ran back to hand line us down the siding track back toward our train, and then ran back up to the lead locomotive and was getting seated and backing up as I finished lining the derail back into derailing position and locked it up before climbing on the foot board of the rear locomotive as it came by. We backed up through the siding onto the main to a joint on our train.

While I was in between connecting the air hoses cutting in the air, the hogger jumped off the locomotive, lined up our train for the mainline, and we both climbed back up on and in the lead locomotive as the caboose crew called, "All released on the rear, give her a little squeeze"

The hogger then applied the air brakes.

A couple minutes later, they said, "Good set, okay to release and go."

The hoghead released the air brakes while jerking on it easy until the caboose crew said "Moving!"

We then proceeded, prepared to stop at the next signal, but it was clear, so no stopping.

For those of you wondering what *bottling the air* means, the phrase refers to when you leave air in the train brakeline system by closing the angle cock, a type of valve. So, when we bottled the air before separating on our move, that kept the air in the train brake line so that when we returned from making our set out move and got coupled up again, it would only take a few minutes to get the system recharged—otherwise it would take much longer. Leaving a train with bottled air can be a dangerous situation, as trains have been known to roll away and cause some tremendous catastrophes. In this situation, should our train have rolled, the caboose crew would have plugged, dumped, or dynamited the air brakes, stopping the train.

# Distracted Hoghead

*I was working a train* from Wishram, Washington eastbound to Pasco, Washington with an engineer who was known to be a little fast and easily distracted. Upon arrival Pasco, we usually handed our train to another crew for what was called a main line change. This day, we were given a few trick-moves by the Pasco yardmaster upon our arrival, meaning that we had to yard our train on two different tracks in one yard and then take our locomotive power on a new-to-me route to the roundhouse to put the engines away.

My engineer was from Pasco originally, and said that he knew the way. We yarded our train and then went lite engine on the main line a ways and stopped to back into a track I had never been in before.

The hoghead assured me it was the correct one and said, "You get me lined in there, I will get us to the roundhouse."

We had two units and what I thought was going to happen was that I would stop the engines on the main line track just beyond what I thought to be the roundhouse switch, line it up, and back him up to clear the switch points, line back and lock the switch, then walk back to the rear of the consist, get in his view and give him lantern signals backing up to the roundhouse.

We stopped and I lined back. I started walking toward the rear unit to get on the foot board to protect the back up move, but he took off like a madman. I barely managed to climb onto the controlling unit. I made my way up the stairs, into the cab, and out the fireman's door to the left, hurrying as fast as I could to get to the point. I was about halfway up the side of the first locomotive when I saw our rear unit headlight shining on a boxcar. We hit it hard at about 20 mph, derailing our rear locomotive. Luckily, nobody was hurt.

The trainmaster came out to figure out what had happened, but never talked to us together. He talked with me on the ground while the engineer sat sulking in his seat. He asked me what had happened, and I told him the facts just like I have told you. It was weird, because he got me a ride to the hotel and I heard nothing more about it. To this day, I really don't know if we were on the right track. I think the trainmaster looked the other way.

I don't remember the trip back to Wishram, but thirty-eight years later while taking a trip on my pass to Spokane, Washington, a freight deadhead crew that got on at Pasco, Washington told me that the distracted engineer had a few more mishaps before finally getting straightened out with medication, becoming a much better engineer and making it to retirement.

# Red Signal at Bridge #4

*There has always been a rule* that a running air brake test be performed at the start of each trip as the train starts to roll and gets moving a little bit, as well as many other situations, such as when a train crew hands their train over to a new train crew at crew change points—the main idea being that the brakes work throughout the train.

I was called off the conductors extra board in 1989 to work the Empire Builder train from Seattle to Spokane. We loaded the passengers at King Street Station and left town eastbound, a minute later penetrating the King Street tunnel. In those days, the engine crew would say over the radio, *here comes the running air* and apply the brakes a little. Then the trainman on the rear would ascertain whether they were working on the rear by listening for the hissing of the air and the squealing of the brake shoes. A good trainman could feel from the movement whether they were working or not. The superliner coach cars have small lights on each side of the car that indicate blue when the brakes are released and red when applied; they are not 100 percent reliable, but close.

My brakeman (aka assistant conductor) said he would do the running air and went downstairs to watch the lights go from green to red and back to green during the test and off he went. I listened as the test was performed and the brakeman said over his portable radio, *good running air.* '

It did not feel exactly right to me, however. But when the brakeman came upstairs, he reiterated it was a good test and I did not argue, as he had ten more years experience than I. We discharged out the tunnel on Seattle's waterfront and as

I walked through the train collecting and punching tickets, something did not feel right. The train had a sloppy movement with what little slack we had, as it was running in and out. I muttered to myself, "The hoghead had better smooth this operation out or somebody is going to get seasick."

A few minutes later while traveling at about 20 mph, the train stopped abruptly, putting a scare in everyone, but luckily no injuries.

I listened as the bridge tender manning bridge #4 asked over the radio, "Did you guys get by that red signal?"

The airwaves went silent, then my brakeman said on his portable, "Bill, this is me, Jim. I'm on the Builder." I hit the ground and could see that the lead locomotive had gotten by the signal by about fifty feet or less. I met one of the engine crew at the rear of the rear locomotive.

"Someone turned the angle cock on my rear unit," he said. "There was no air in the train so I cut it back in."

After a few minutes, we backed up behind the signal, it turned green, and we went to Spokane. The angle cock being closed behind the locomotives I suspect was closed by the mechanical craft or the engine crew, as sometimes they would do that before departure in order to test the locomotives for various reasons. After they performed their tests, they forgot to cut the air back in. I do not believe there was any malicious or deviant intent involved.

The brakeman that said he was going downstairs to do the running air test. The locomotive engineer, the locomotive fireman, and myself all blew that test. The train stopped just past the red signal using the locomotive brakes, short of a derail in the derailing position.

A little way beyond the derail, the bridge was open to allow marine traffic to pass. The derail was there in the name of safety; should a train get past a red signal, the derail would derail the train off the tracks before it could run off the end of the tracks and fall into the waterway below. When the brakeman said, *Bill, this is Jim, I'm on the Builder,* he saved us from being turned in, because they were good buddies. When I met the engineman on the ground and he told me of the closed angle cock he found, I thought he was acting a little funny.

I was going to go to the grave with this story; however, most the people involved in the story are in the grave or have one foot in it.

# Setting Retainer Valves

*I caught a job off* the Seattle brakemen's extra board one Sunday night in about 1985 to deadhead by personal vehicle to a hotel on I-90 near Cle Elum, Washington. I spent the night getting my rest and reported to the Cle Elum B.N. yard a short distance away the next morning. I met another brakeman and a locomotive engineer named "Fred." Joining us was a section crew, their foreman, and several machine operators. There, we were to be governed by Conductor "Handlebar" Shipley, who was to be governed in turn by the Burlington Northern trainmaster, roadmaster, and the train dispatcher of that territory.

We were a work train crew, and our mission was to be putting flat car sections of a train we were building in position while the section crew pulled old rail up off a segment of the defunct, out-of-business Milwaukee Road Railroad. The section crew loaded it onto our flat cars, which we would store on vacant tracks until the last day, when we would double all the tracks together, making a rail train, and transport the old heavy rail down a steep mountain grade named "Stampede Pass," starting at an elevation of four thousand feet and going down to sea level in Auburn, Washington.

After two weeks of preparation, the day came when we doubled everything up to a bulkhead flat car as a safety buffer between the rail and the caboose. The idea was that should there be emergency braking or a derailment, the bulkhead flat could prevent the rail we were transporting from being thrust into the crew in the caboose. There was also a bulkhead flat between the back-to-back locomotives on the head end of the train, as well. If I had to guess, I'd say we were about 3,000 feet long and weighing in at 6,000 tons.

We made an initial terminal air test, which includes walking the train when the brakes are applied, eyeballing each and every car to make sure that the brake shoes gripped the wheels properly, and then walking the train again with the brakes released, making sure they no longer hugged the wheels. Everything looked good.

I was on the lead locomotive with Fred and Conductor Shipley; the rear brakeman was on the caboose. Normally, the conductor would not be on the locomotives, as they would be in the caboose, but on this trip Shipley was going to show me in the name of safety how to properly set retainer valves on the cars in a train. We departed Cle Elum headed west, twenty-five miles up the mountain to Stampede Pass, where we reached our predesignated stopping point. I had never been involved in setting a retainer valve, other than restoring them to normal position after finding them turned by kids or hobos, but I knew what they were for, as I had heard old heads tell stories from back in the day. In short, an air retainer valve on train cars can be set for direct release or a hold-type function where air brakes are held even when brakes are being re-charged. The device can be set on a certain number of cars to prevent a runaway train on long downhill grades. Conductor Shipley and I hit the ground and he supervised me as I set the retainer valves on five cars and I got back on the power as Shipley rolled the train by and caught the caboose.

Somewhere prior to Auburn, the conductor instructed us on the head end to stop anywhere along our way and have the head brakeman (me) restore the retainer valves to normal position. We did, and then proceeded into Auburn.

Later, Fred said to me, "I think I could have got her down the grade without you setting those retainers."

"Probably, but you can't argue with safety." I said, as he nodded in agreement.

I know this story is neither very exciting nor humorous. However, I just wanted to brag it up a little. After all, not every railroader can say that they set retainer valves before going down a steep mountain grade.

# Frigid Train

*We came to work* one morning in Bellingham, Washington in Whatcom County during deep freeze conditions. I say *deep freeze conditions* because the weather had been hovering around zero degrees for a few days. We reported to our Talgo train at the Burlington Northern Railroad Pine Street yard facility and had our crew briefing in the bistro lounge. Then the engineer got on the locomotive and I went to the rear of the train to prepare for the air brake test; that all went fine, as the air brake set was good on the rear and I walked the rest of the train about eight hundred feet and had the engineer release the air brakes as I walked and observed the release. We called the train dispatcher and got permission to open up the mainline switch and after waiting five minutes according to the rules, we were now prepared for movement a mile south to the Bellingham train station in the Fairhaven district in South Bellingham, our initial station, where we boarded our first passengers.

I said, "Pull on it 513," but nothing happened.

I repeated the call and the engineer said, "I am, it won't move."

We were frozen to the rails is what I came up with, so I went to the rear and asked him to back up. I could hear the motor loading, but the train only moved backward a few inches.

Once again, I asked the engineer to, "Pull on it 513," and it loaded going a few inches forward, and stopped.

I said to the engineer, "Barry," I think if you rock this thing back and forth for a while we can get out of here."

He started rocking her back and forth and each time it went a little farther.

"Pull her out on the main," I said, and as he did, the assistant conductor rolled her by, making sure all the wheels were rolling and nothing dragging, and we made our trip to Seattle.

I am not exactly sure why the train would not move in the beginning, but it was weather-related and some educated guesses are frozen axles, wheels frozen to the rail, frozen brake shoes to the wheels, but whatever it was, warming it up with the rocking movements did the trick. Yes, a frigid situation with a happy ending.

Now, for you rail enthusiasts, you know there are no brake shoes on Talgo trains, as there are in traditional equipment, so when I said that frozen brake shoes might have been the problem? You were probably getting ready to call me out. Relax, it was a test.

# Delay Reports

*In the day, all delay reports* were kept and filed by conductors on passenger trains, with only a few exceptions. Sometimes the locomotive fireman" (later renamed to assistant locomotive engineer) would keep the delay reports, but most the time it was the conductor. Until a few years ago, all reports were done on paper and then faxed to operations upon arrival at the conductor's final destination. Before the fax machine, they were telegraphed. Now days, they are logged into a fancy phone device.

As you can imagine, many conductors provided their own spin to delay reporting. I may be considered one of those people, but I believe that I was as good and factual as anyone else. I was called into the office a few times concerning my delay reports, which is understandable, but not always for my off-color sense of humor. I was reprimanded for mundane things as well, such as writing my reports in pencil, or listing "TBD" (To Be Determined) as the cause for a minute delay. The trainmaster wanted that determined by me, even if I had to make something up—that sort of attitude prompting many to call it the *delie report.*

I could write many stories when I (or others) was told by a trainmaster to change the reason for a delay, even though it was only partly true. I never understood exactly why, except it had something to do with on-time performances and one's bonus. Many times after having gone off duty and left the property did a Portland trainmaster call me to strongly suggest that I revise and re fax a delay report, indicating it in large lettering as *revised.* I would do so willingly; however, if ever called into a criminal investigation by the inspector general? I would tell the whole truth and nothing but the truth, my defense being I was ordered to revise the report by my superior. I am relatively sure I would have survived with thirty days suspension and no pay, while the trainmaster would be fired, or if lucky, demoted back to their previous job pulling on a throttle in New York.

# Battlestar Galactica

*I got called into the office* one time right after we got some new locomotives that some of us referred to as "Battlestar Galactica," as they were longer than the ones we had been using for years and the controls were much more modern than our older locomotives. They had not been tested in the Northwest on our curves, so we could only go freight train speed around curves. The engineers were taking a little time getting used to them and we were losing time here and there. Delays weren't too long, typically around twelve minutes total over a four hour run.

One evening while heading south from Canada to Seattle, we lost two or three minutes between each station stop and it was all because of having the new locomotive. On each section of the trip, I put the delay under the code, "ENG," for engine, and wrote in the remarks section: On account of the new locomotive, Battlestar Galactica Genesis #77."

The next afternoon, the trainmaster met me in the parking lot before work and showed me an email that was sent around the world from top management down to him. The company made it very clear that they did not think that I was very funny and to make sure I refrain from this sort of delay reporting.

While I was reprimanded for some fairly inoffensive actions, I somehow managed to avoid any sort of corrective action for what might be considered more offensive incidents.

# Flagging

*Work crews working* on or near train tracks require a rules-qualified train conductor certified in the job of protecting men and equipment working on or near the railroad tracks to perform work as a Flagger. In short, the flagman would watch the backs of usually contracted workers not accustomed to being around trains, keeping them safe.

Situations sometimes required portable derails to be put in place on the tracks to protect the workers. The idea was that if a train or part of a train rolled down the track toward where workmen were positioned, the derail would skip, or *derail*, the car off the tracks before reaching workers, averting any deaths, injuries, or damage. Some flagger jobs entailed putting up flags, derails, and having a bullhorn handy while watching as many as twenty-five workers, while other jobs might only require shadowing a surveyor who wanted to take a few measurements and pictures for the planning of future work. I think you get the idea that any non-employees of the railroad had to be properly protected and escorted while on the property.

Before the laborers could get to work, the flagger would meet with all of them and take part in a crew briefing, sometimes leading the meeting, supply a couple safety rules and some *dos* and *don'ts* like looking both ways before crossing any track. During my crew briefings, I would go on to elaborate a little. I would tell my crew that the safety rule of the day was, "When in doubt, take the safe course." Always, I would let them know that I have a few character defects, but being unsafe was not one of them, and I would ensure my workers that I would be watching their backs.

Then I would tell them that I did not want to see anyone get injured because I would get fired, and that would really piss my wife off. Each worker would sign a sheet acknowledging that they had attended and understood the briefing.

Should I work a few days with the same crew, I would have a little fun some time during the day after the morning safety meeting. I'd ask them if they knew the safety rule of the day and when they couldn't remember or gave me some other lame excuse, I would let them know that the rule was, "Don't trip on your dick," or "If it don't smell good, don't eat it." When in mixed company, the safety rule was simply, "Don't f--- up."

On one of my rest days, I was called in at overtime to flag one of the King Street Station platforms while a contractor pressure washed it. I showed up and met a congenial Latino man, and we had the customary crew briefing. There was not really a whole lot of danger, as the track was lined and locked away from him, so I would watch him from my car at the entrance to the track. Easy money.

After finishing the briefing, I started to settle into my car, in viewing position, when I saw a different man setting up the pressure washer. I hurried over to him and asked him who he was. He looked puzzled and said, "No comprende."

The man who was at the crew briefing was starting to drive off the property, so I ran and stopped him to confront him about this non-English-speaking employee who was absent from the briefing. He assured me that he was good and that he understood everything.

"He never signed the crew briefing form," I said. "You and I need to talk to him. I'm not sure if this is going to happen."

With both of the laborers in front of me, I pointed to several tracks next to the platform he was to work near and told the one who spoke English to tell the other "Those are train tracks, and a train could run over and kill you!"

He looked at me, confused.

"Tell him!"

He said something to the other man in Spanish, and the newcomer nodded as if he understood.

"Now," I added, "tell him if he gets killed, my wife is going to be pissed off."

My translator hesitated for a moment before saying something to him again in Spanish, to which he enthusiastically responded, as if he understood perfectly. Satisfied, I handed him the clipboard and had him sign the crew briefing form.

It worked out, but I think most flaggers would have handled it a little differently.

# Three in the Locomotive

*For many years*, there were usually three men in the locomotive of every train: the locomotive engineer, locomotive fireman, and a brakeman. With the addition of women on the railroad in the '70s, it became three "people." Twenty-five years before I hired on, during the steam engine days, there was the locomotive engineer and his fireman. The engineer ran the locomotive, and the fireman shoveled coal to keep the locomotive running and eventually learned how to operate the train. Most firemen were eventually promoted to engineer. The head brakeman had a few duties, the main one being the hand lining of any track switches associated with the train route. There was also a caboose on all freight trains manned by the conductor and rear brakeman. On passenger trains there was no caboose, so normally the rear brakeman and conductor could be found in the parlor car.

In the '50s, diesel locomotives began replacing steam locomotives and it looked as if the fireman position was history. From what I understand, as it was told to me, the railroad unions during that era had a lot of leverage and used it to sign agreements protecting the fireman workers who were being made obsolete by the transition away from steam power. There were many railroads with many seniority districts all over America during this era, and they made side-pocket agreements to keep a few local trains as two-enginemen jobs. To try to explain these arrangements would be out of my realm, as I was a conductor and could barely keep track of our own side-pocket agreements.

Job protection (also called *grandfather protection*) protected the jobs of all previous firemen on the condition that they were expected to go on to become locomotive engineers. However, should they not be able to work as or hold a locomotive engineer's position, they could work as a "fireman," assisting a locomotive engineer without having to shovel coal. From what I understand, it was in the name of safety that the agreements during that era were made, mandating that there were to be two qualified locomotive enginemen in the controlling locomotive of all passenger trains. In theory, I think that this is mostly a very good idea. Sometimes, however, there were exceptions to that rule. Pure animosity between any two individuals in the cab could be a problem, as were individuals sexually attracted to each other.

The job-protected, "grandfathered" enginemen retired and went away. Through the years, the two enginemen in the cab requirements saw some changes. In 1996, unions and Amtrak agreed that if a passenger run took less than six hours at the throttle, then only one person was needed. Any run longer than six hours still to this day requires two operators.

# What Color Is That Signal?

*As I've mentioned*, hogheads and conductors are required to not be colorblind and to have excellent eyesight—anything less could be fatal. They need to be able to see the color of the signal governing the movement of the train they are handling or in charge of and know the indication requirement.

In the mid-'80s, I was called off one of the Seattle B.N. extra boards to deadhead to Bellingham. I drove my car up to Bellingham, Washington, checked into a hotel for the night, and reported the next morning to the Bellingham yard to work the Townsend local. On that local, we took a train from Bellingham along a twenty-mile route north and crossed over from Blaine, Washington to White Rock, British Columbia in Canada before continuing on bridge 69 over the Nicomekl River through Colebrook and on to Townsend, where we went off the main line and did industry work on the Tilbury branch line. This was one of the locals that had a grandfathered engineman vest pocket agreement, thus we had two qualified throttle manipulators formerly from the Great Northern Railroad. One of these men was to be nicknamed "Handbrake Henry" many years later, Henry was the fireman on the protected job that week.

Henry did most of the running that day, and the four following days, the senior engine man mostly observing from the second unit like a parrot peeking over our shoulders, especially when approaching signals. Henry was serious and good at his job. For the next eleven or twelve years, I crossed paths with him, mostly after we both went to work on passenger trains up in Seattle. He was always on a job that had two engine men. In 1996, when the requirement for two enginemen on most passenger trains was changed to one, Henry transferred to a day shift switch engine job. I was called in on my day off for overtime on a few occasions to work the switch engine with "Handbrake."

Henry and I had to take trains out on the mainline now and then, and he was always squinting as our train approached signals asking me, "What color is that signal?" I thought he was messing with me, but I would always answer him.

There were times we would be going a short distance on the mainline to wye our train and turn it around. With other locomotive engineers, I would eventually drop back to the rear; however, Henry insisted that I stay on the locomotive with him, that he appreciated it.

Well, one day a few years later, the big news was that they had pulled old Henry out of service and he retired. After all those years, it turned out that old Handbrake Henry was colorblind. After writing this story and passing it on to a few retired coworkers, I was surprised when some volunteered stories of a similar nature of people memorizing eye exam tests, and doing so for decades, all the way to retirement.

One fellow told me that when he hired out, the practitioner examined his eyes with a flashlight and said, "They look good, all you need now is the vision test."

He said, Okay, but I really need to take a leak, can I do that first?"

"Okay," said the practitioner.

When in the bathroom, he slipped some contacts in and passed the exam a few minutes later.

# What Exactly Is It That You Do?

*Many times on the train* while sitting in public view at a table in the diner or the conductor's desk in the bistro lounge, decked out in full conductor uniform with spit-shined boots and a cup of coffee in front of me. a passenger would ask me, *what exactly is it that you do?* The implication being I did little or nothing.

I would usually answer with, *what would you like to know?* After answering their questions, most were satisfied that it was a good thing having me around. Every now and then, if I feared no repercussions, I would answer: *If my crew are at the top of their game? Not much. However, should one of them be having a bad day for whatever reason, especially the locomotive engineer, I will be studying their every move.*

Yes, when it came to safety I almost always knew exactly what to do.

Most people who knew me trusted me; however, I heard many say that I was my own worst enemy—meaning the things that came out of my mouth face-to-face, over the radio airwaves, or the public address speakers, would result in many a person *not* knowing me to wonder.

In 1977, the Burlington Northern Railroad in the Pacific Northwest required that trainmen and enginemen (T&E) working a road job carry a few rule books: the General Code of Operating Rules (GCOR), the latest edition of the timetable, and two special instruction books which looked more like paper pamphlets (in later years, the three were combined into one). In addition to these books, engineers carried books in reference to the dynamics of locomotives and trainmen carried various literature in relation to train equipment—none of those mandatory, however. On yard jobs, there were a few T&E who carried these items, while some kept them in lockers; but as a rule, most neither carried them or had them in their lockers. Most yardmasters had them available if needed, however some did not.

As the years rolled by, and I went to work at Amtrak, those three rule books we used to carry were added on to. First came the Amtrak Service Standards Manual for Train Service and On-Board Service, which employees also called *the blue book* because it had a blue cover. I would tell people that if they couldn't figure out how to fire a person with the operating rule books, they went to the blue book, and many a time that is just the way it happened.

My last twenty years, I worked about a dozen short stints in the yard on a switch engine or a flagging job; I worked mostly as an Amtrak passenger train conductor, however. I worked the Seattle to Portland Oregon route, the Seattle to Spokane route, and the Seattle to Vancouver, British Columbia, Canada route. The time I spent on those routes was pretty much split equally, all of them at times having tremendous challenges requiring that I reach into my bank of railroad knowledge. I have decided to write what a trip to Canada entailed versus the others, as in my view toward the end of my career it was by far the most challenging route to work. I will relate the routine of a day's work going north, including nicknames of a few coworkers, some of the dry humor announcements I made to the passengers, as well as radio transmissions to coworkers:

I'm not complaining, but by the time I retired, the required rule books and paperwork for a passenger train conductor or locomotive engineer to make a trip from Seattle, Washington, USA to Vancouver, British Columbia, Canada and back was unimaginable. There was the General Code Of Operating Rules (GCOR), the Canadian Railroad Operating Rules CROR), BNSF/Amtrak Operational Differences Job Aid, Rule 83 [c] Quarterly Operating Bulletins British Columbia

South Division, Canadian National West Division Timetable, Canadian National System Special Instructions, Canadian National Regional Special Instructions, Greater Vancouver Terminal Operating Manual, British Columbia Railway Company Port Division Timetable, Operations Standards Updates (OSU's), Burlington Northern Santa Fe Railroad Northwest Timetables (entailing the Seattle, Bellingham, and New Westminster Sub Divisions, AMT-5 Amtrak National Railroad Passenger Corporation for Transportation Employees Book, and the AMT-3 Amtrak Air Brake and Train Handling Rules and Instructions.

As the operating rules piled on over the years, the *Cheat Sheet* came along for transportation employees. In the beginning, it resembled a 4 by 8-inch passenger train route guide, easy to read with station stops, while also showing detector locations. By the time I retired, it had become a 10 by 12-inch double-sided laminated sheet showing an aspect of every operation detail from point A to B relating to safe operations. Having the cheat sheet did not relieve one from having available all the rule books and paperwork as mentioned.

I did come up with a little fun in relation to Canadian rules.

I would catch a coworker off guard, asking them, "Are you Canadian rules qualified?"

"Yes."

Then I would ask, "What is on a Canadian nickel?"

Always baffled, they would ask, "I don't know, what?"

"You don't know what's on a Canadian nickel," I would repeat, as if it was of great importance.

I would pull out a Canadian nickel from my pocket and point to the Queen of England's head and face on one side. "When you get tired of looking at that, you can flip it over and look at her beaver."

The conductor had additional rules and paperwork pertaining to the rifle locker in the baggage car that was a PIA. Special first-aid rules and procedures were required with a specific Canadian government approved defibrillator, first-aid kit, and an ambulance stretcher usually kept in the baggage car. There were rules and paperwork for minor children traveling by themselves; that was often a challenge with parents trying to bend the rules. There were sight-impaired people who needed a good dog; in my later years, there were the emotional support pets that required a doctor's note and Amtrak approval. To challenge a suspect rule violator was deemed a federal offense, so unless the animal bit someone it was going to be allowed to travel. Eventually regular pets were allowed to ride on some trains with many rules associated, such as if the pet was in a cage the owner could place them on a seat next to them, otherwise they were to be on the floor.

There were no mental evaluations required for passengers to ride, as long as they had proper identification, no recent serious criminal arrests, and could answer yes and no questions. Yes, there were the ones who made it through all the jumps and hoops to travel and once they were on board and we were on the way? They became a nightmare to accommodate. The ones who were confused and lost were one thing; the evil ones looking for trouble, however, were the nightmares since to deal with them in the way they deserved was politically incorrect and one could be fired.

We were required to carry a few forms: Report of Near Collision form, Motorist's Failure to Stop at Highway Rail Grade Crossing form, Trespassing Incidents form, Eyewitness Statement form, Environmental Incident Report form, Passenger Incident form, Medical Information and Consent form, Non-Employee Injury Illness Report form, Employee Injury Illness Report form, Non-Employee Personal Statement form, Unusual Occurrence Report form, Operation Heart Saver Employee Responder Report form, Maintenance Analysis Program Equipment Condition Report form, Map 100 form, Talgo Failure Defect form, Private Car Passenger Record form, Pass Abuse Incident Report form, and the Hours of Service Act Reference Manual for Employees Directly Engaged or Connected with the Movement of Passenger Trains or Engines form.

Besides passports and related notarized documents and visas, it was almost unbelievable the many rules, paperwork, and guidelines for passenger requirements to cross the Canada/USA border. This person from this country needed this notarized piece of paper and the other person from this country didn't if they were naturalized before 1959, and on and on. It was f---ing crazy. Both engineers and conductors had to have on person their certified rules card and government issued transportation licenses.

Okay, I am sure I may have left out a piece or two of paperwork, however I think one gets the idea—there was a rule for everything one could think of. In addition to all the rules and paperwork required for making a trip to Canada, our train traveled on and through several different railroad properties with multiple trackside detectors to listen for and many authorities to obtain verbally en route while being prepared to stop and hand copy restrictions or authorities. Not to adhere accordingly in the smallest way to any one of them could result in the crew being pulled out of service and fired. In addition to all the rules and paperwork required for making a trip to Canada, our train traveled on and through several different railroad properties with there being several radio channels to switch back and forth to and being on the wrong one could be deadly.

There was a rule for everything. Rules, rules, and rules on top of rules, all in writing and a few that were not, like the *don't get caught with your pants down* rule. Some of those rules were very trivial pertaining to uniform, hat, and grooming policies. I was reprimanded for wearing my vest while not having my coat on, and reprimanded for wearing my hat in a food service area, although I was never reprimanded for any grooming violations. Nor was I ever caught with my pants down.

In addition to all the required paperwork to carry, there were a few keys essential to have: The Burlington Northern Santa Fe Railroad switch lock key, the Canadian National Railroad switch lock key, the superliner equipment coach door and cabinets key, and the Talgo equipment door and cabinets key. I also carried a 1990s Burlington Northern Railroad switch lock key for locks at Burrard Inlet Junction in Canada and other places lost in time. I also carried various other just-in-case keys, one being a Canadian Pacific Railroad key just in case we were rerouted. I also carried a caboose key and can of hot box powder...*well I did in the '70s, man.*

I also carried a replacement air hose gasket and a Leatherman tool should I in the case of an emergency need to cut, pinch, or screw something. I always had a ruler for measuring the length of ejaculated pistons during an air brake test. I gave up carrying rain gear on account that wearing it got me more wet from sweating than most any rain ever did. In lieu of rain gear, my last ten years I wore or carried a trench coat with a stocking hat in the pocket all year long, and many times it came in handy; several times I offered it to children or ladies in place of a blanket we did not sell or they could not afford. One time during cold weather I used it to cover a badly injured lady whom we had struck until the ambulance arrived. I always carried an extra charged battery for my portable radio and a portable battery charger—until later years when they put chargers on all the trains. I had lockers at crew bases in Seattle, Portland, Spokane, and Vancouver, B.C., Canada and keeping track of the keys or combinations could be a headache...well, I guess you didn't need to know that.

In Seattle, right before I retired, many times we received train orders and other paperwork from the pretty-when-she wanted-to-be T&E clerk, "Tear Ass Terry," then after the morning crew briefing the assistant conductor, usually "Coast Guard Matt," would be driven by Lisa in the company van from the crew base on Holgate Street a half mile to King Street Station to start passenger seat assignments with the on-board chief, who (if I was lucky) would be "Smoky." The engineer, usually Judy, and I would walk across Holgate Street a short distance to our train that was under a building protected by blue flags and derails. I would place my five-pound briefcase entirely full of paperwork needed for Canada (No joke, I've weighed it!) and my personal bag at the conductor's desk in the bistro lounge. The locomotive engineer at this time was checking both the lead head end locomotive and the rear end locomotive, sometimes one end or the other being a unit without a motor used mainly for controlling purposes; they were called *cab cars*, and another way of putting it is that they looked exactly like a locomotive, but without a motor. One of the biggest reasons we had them was so we did not have to turn the train around at final terminals—the engineer could just change ends and commence back the other direction. The ultimate reason we had them was they were much cheaper than a locomotive; however, there were many times when the one locomotive we had failed, so at those times they were worthless. Sometimes there was no rear locomotive or cab car, meaning the train for the return trip from Canada back to Seattle would need turning around, or *wye*, as it's called in railroad terminology.

Okay, the engineer checked the paperwork to the units, making sure they were dated and signed by the appropriate mechanical craft, and if not, radio the mechanical foreman to have someone take care of it. Taking the trip without the required and updated paperwork was a slap in the face of safety, resulting in many locomotive engineers and a few train conductors being temporarily removed from service. I always asked if they checked the paperwork, and many times, I had to do it myself. Actually, there were a few locomotive engineers who would never make it to the rear, trusting me to mount the rear for that deed and a few others.

There were always a few workers on board the train, and often under the train. I would make an announcement on the PA: *This is the conductor. We will be moving the train shortly to the station. If you do not want to go? You have fifteen minutes to detrain.*

Sometimes the hogger, sometimes myself (one or the other), would call to have the derails and blue flags removed, if not already done. I would then walk from one end to the other inside, making sure anyone I came across—coach cleaners, bartenders, or commissary workers—had heard the announcement.

There were Talgo technicians assigned on these trains, such as "Handsome Rick," and finding and conversing with them before moving the train was important. Then I would hit the ground and walk down one side of the train looking for wood chalk blocks or metal skates mechanical workers put under the wheels to keep the train from rolling or anything else out of the ordinary. Then I walked up the other side, observing the same and checking the fuel glass sites, making sure we had ample fuel. From there, I'd check the red rear end marker and call the hogger for a headlight check. At this point, if all workers were clear it was time for a class two air brake test if the class one had already been performed and recorded by Mechanical on the proper paperwork. I would then climb into the rear locomotive or cab car to assist in a brake and amperage test. I would ask the hogger to set up the brakes when ready. The hogger would apply the brakes and I would watch the gauges, while the brakes were applied. If I was on a locomotive we usually did an amperage test, meaning the engineer would throttle a little bit as the brakes were applied and I watched the gauges.

Should Judy be the locomotive engineer, she would always say, "Larry, are you ready for me to shoot you the big load?"

If all was good, I would say, "Good amperage, thanks for the load, Judy. Release your brakes when ready."

Now we were ready to roll one-third of a mile to King Street Station. There was a lot of construction work being done at this time. First we had to get permission from the Amtrak yard flagger, "The Berry Sniffa," on the Amtrak yard radio channel to move the train north toward King Street Station. Before rolling, both the flagger and our crew double-checked with the yard switch crew—one member whose nickname was "Jailbait." After they confirmed that there were no issues with them and the flagger had verified all the tracks and workers were clear for our route, then the okay was given to roll to the north end of the yard. We then had to communicate with the Seattle Terminal train dispatcher on the main line radio channel and receive authority by signal indication to go though a junction point and down the lead track into one of several tracks at King Street Station. By this time, I was on the locomotive with the hogger, which eliminated them having to repeat instructions and authorities to me, Many times, I could not hear very well on the subpar portable radios we were assigned in later years. After receiving permission, but before acting on that signal, we had to talk to a Burlington Northern Santa Fe flagger in charge of the lead and station tracks just beyond the junction, making sure all their workers and equipment were clear. We usually went in the same track, however it was wise to check with the King Street Station agent for any change.

After making it to the station, we could relax *sort of* because buried deep in the blue book there are several *no relaxing* rules. My engineer would drop back to the bistro lounge and along with the Talgo train technician (and sometimes the bistro car attendant, who, if I was lucky, was Eileen) we would enjoy a cup of coffee, juice, or possibly eat some oyster crackers—again, jeopardizing our jobs because there were rules that could interpret that as stealing revenue; should it not be deemed revenue, there was a rule for being immoral—and they got me on that one a couple times.

After ten or fifteen minutes, the passengers in the station were allowed to board with their seat assignments and I would assist passengers into the rear business class cars while the station agent and assistant conductor assisted people into the coach cars and the baggage people loaded bags into the bag car. The Talgo technician would operate the power lift for people in wheelchairs and ones that could not climb stairs and the chief helped where needed. When ready, we would get an *okay to go* wave from the station agent, who in the old days was "The Black Gentleman" or Marlene, and at the end of my career, LaToya, if I was lucky. We would then close up all the doors, and depart signal indication, making sure we did a running air test on departure—not to do so was grounds to be fired.

At this time, there were workers in the King Street tunnel directly in front of us with specific speed limits and routes to follow, as they were revamping the whole railroad between Lander Street about a half mile south of the station and Broad Street about a mile and a half north of the station. We had to talk with one foreman to penetrate the south end of the tunnel and another one right after discharging out the north end.

Okay, after getting out of town there were numerous trackside detectors to listen for and several other permissions and authorities to obtain en route to the great white north, including instructions from yardmasters, train dispatchers (if I was lucky, "Crazy Mary"), and bridge operators. It was very common to have many new temporary speed restrictions to adhere to and several work gangs to communicate with before passing through their limits; missing or confusing one of these situations—even if it did not result in harm—could result in a crew being removed from service and fired. Every now and then, officials (aka "Weed Weasels") would throw up surprise flags as operation tests just as our train approached, further complicating matters. Between Seattle and Edmonds, if all was safe and well I made some fun (to me) announcements, one being at Richmond Beach, where nude men hung out, telling the public that after an oil spill in 1969 the community renamed the beach, "Lube Oil Beach."

Leaving Edmonds toward our next station stop of Everett, I would often make two announcements, the first about the Mukilteo Lighthouse on the left being erected in 1906, and the second, just before penetrating the Everett tunnel: "On the right coming in to view, folks, the Anchor Tavern. It used to have a real anchor mounted on the building, but it fell off during the 1965 earthquake."

Before leaving the Everett station stop, we had to contact the Everett Delta BNSF yardmaster for permission through their yard along the Snohomish River, most crews obtained this permission well in advance of the station stop, while some conductors obtained the permission on the company cell phone and passed it on to the engineer on their portable radio—although some engineers insisted on hearing it on the radio from the yardmaster's mouth.

After leaving Everett and approaching bridge #37 (that used to be named bridge #10) we would call the bridge operator in advance so they could have it lined up to cross the Snohomish River into Marysville There were many other bridges along the route without operators. Every once in a while there were bridge problems and we were governed by rules in the special instructions pertaining to requirements and procedures while taking the switches off power and hand lining the train for the route, important to say the least. As we crossed the Snohomish River, I would mention: "on the left, the Big Boy pole yard at the mouth of the river," and we would continue our trip through Marysville and Silvana, then on to Stanwood, our next station stop.

After Stanwood, we went through Logan, or "4 cylos junction," on past the Conway pole yard that had poles with shaved bark and a couple minutes later arrived just north of the "Three White Balls" monument at the Mount Vernon station.

After departing Mount Vernon, we would pass through Burlington, Bow, Edison, and Blanchard and break out on the saltwater inlet looking at the San Juan Islands and Olympic Mountains, then pass by the Taylor Shellfish Farm in downtown Samish, "the oyster producing capital of the world folks, where they have the Oyster Queen Festival every fall during the harvest moon. If you look closely, you might see someone shucking or gobbling oysters."

We then would go through tunnel number 18 and pass by Dogfish Point and "Tunga Bunga Beach, then Larrabee State Park, through the Chuckanut community, through tunnels number 19 and 20, past "Bird Dung Island," into tunnel number 21 (or more commonly known as the Bellingham tunnel). Come out the other end in south Bellingham's Fairhaven district and roll into the station. "Now arriving What-com county, Squali-cum Bay, Fairhaven Bellingham station folks. If you're leaving us here? Don't forget to get off."

Most trips to Canada were uneventful concerning operations, however not becoming complacent while adhering to the rules and being vigilant at all times was paramount. There was a time when before the signal system was entirely updated when we needed verbal permission from the train dispatcher to run from the South Yard Limits Bellingham to the North Yard Limits Bellingham and from the north siding switch Swift to the USA/Canada border. Back in the '90s and turn of the century, we had very powerful portable radios and I did most of the communication with the train dispatcher.

One day the train dispatcher said, "I'm going to give you both legs of your route today, you ready to copy?"

I repeated back, "Okay from the South Yard Limits Bellingham to the North Yard Limits Bellingham and from the north siding switch Swift to the USA/Canada border," then added, "we got both legs...and everything in between! Is that correct, over?" Hi Yah!

As we left Bellingham, we climbed up the hill and on the left to the west we were overlooking some of the most beautiful scenery in the world as we gazed out over Bellingham Bay, the San Juan Islands, and the Olympic Mountain Range. Fifteen minutes later we would cross the bulging or not-so-bulging Nooksak River and roll through downtown Ferndale on through Custer and at Blaine, Washington we then penetrated the great white north at White Rock, British Columbia, Canada. We reported the time on the radio to the BNSF Rail Traffic Controller positioned in New Westminster, who would communicate our times and estimated times to bridge operators, track foremen, and train dispatchers from other railroads governing routes of junction points we were to soon be passing through.

The stretch of track just over the border there used to be prone to cause harmonic rocking of trains. Speed of train was to be between 13 and 21 mph. If operated outside those speeds, it would cause rocking that had been proven to cause derailments. Old jointed rail was the biggest factor for harmonic rocking, however it was revamped toward the end of my career.

After rolling through White Rock, we called the bridge 69 operator (or at least *I* did) to tip them off we were coming, then we passed through Crescent Beach and came upon Drawbridge 69, renamed 127.6 toward the end of my career; those of us from back in the day had a hard time accepting that, however (in fact, one of my pretty lady conductor coworker friends presented me with a retired *Bridge 69* sign at my retirement lunch). The bridge spanned the Nicomekl River, and that is where we would flip radio channels and call the train dispatcher at the British Columbia Railway Company Port Division in charge of port division for permission and a signal through their territory.

Fifteen minutes later, we would have to flip radio channels just before slipping into Brownsville and communicate with the Fraser River Bridge operator in order to cross the Fraser River. "Ladies and gentlemen, boys and girls, in a few minutes we will be going over the last piece of *clickety clack* track I know of on the mainline. Back in the day, years before my time, when they would lay railroad track, they did so in 66-foot sections while bolting them together with anchor plates, so when train wheels went over the joints you would hear the *click* and a *clack* as in *clickety clack* down the railroad track. In later years, they went to quarter-mile sections of rail and welding the joints together, eliminating any *clickety clack*. There is still lots of *clickety clack* track all over the world, however the vast majority is in rail yards and slow speed branch lines. Coming up here in a couple minutes, we will be on the last piece of *clickety clack* track I know of on the mainline. When you hear the *clickety clack*, we will be fifteen minutes from our last and final station stop of Vancouver, folks."

Then we had to communicate with the Toronto Terminal Railway (TTR ) coordinator for permission to pass Still Creek Junction in order to get to C.N. Junction and then travel the last mile through a maze of yard tracks while usually having to stop to hand line switches along the way, including Burrard Inlet Junction, and finally stopping the train at the end of a stub track at the VIA train station.

We would off-load the baggage from the bag car, lining it up along a fence. Then let the business passengers off, followed by the coach passengers one car at a time. We would then make sure the hand brakes were applied on both ends of the train and get in line behind the passengers and pass through the Canadian Immigration checkpoint. We'd visit a small crew room where we had lockers, call a cab, dodge a panhandler or two, sometimes a drug dealer or hooker, and jump in a Black Top cab. I would always ask the usually English-challenged driver, *how long have you worked for Black Cock Cab?* We would then go to the hotel for a sixteen or seventeen-hour rest. That was a good trip.

Many times it did not happen that way, however, should there be no rear unit or should the unit be unacceptable for being on the lead for the return trip. Some locomotives had paperwork allowing them to be used only in the trailing position for power (producing electricity for the coaches, including the lounge and bistro car); they could hump (or push) from the rear, but there were several reasons both a locomotive or cab car were deemed unacceptable for controlling and safety purposes (for example, no functioning headlight). So the most common reason we would need to wye the train (meaning to turn it around) in order to get it pointed in the right direction for its return trip was that there was no rear unit—the end of the train was a coach car or some other piece of equipment. In this situation, after clearing Customs, instead of getting into a cab and going to the hotel, we got back on the train. We would first communicate with the TTR coordinator and make sure we could come out at C.N. Junction, and from which direction. Then we'd double-check with the C.N. train dispatcher. After receiving authority, we would double-check with the VIA switch crew and advise them of our intention to be on the safe side.

Depending on the crew I was with determined how we would do this move. With an experienced crew, the other trainman and I would get on the rear and have the hogger back the train up a quarter mile through and past the VIA wash track and continue another quarter mile toward the Burrard Inlet Junction, running through rubber switches along the way and stopping to hand line the ones that were not. At the junction where we veered right, the switch or switches would not be lined up for our route and we would stop just short. I would have my partner hop off and line up and then we would shove the train past them, me protecting the point, while leaving my partner there to stop and line things up for our returning route fifteen minutes later. Then my partner jumped on the locomotive and we continued shoving another quarter mile, while I was on the point looking out for switches not properly lined, until we came to the Terminal Avenue Junction (T.A. Junction) with manual crossovers, where we veered right again. If it was lined up, I stayed on or got off and hand lined, got back on the point, and continued shoving again, and when we got past that crossover/junction the train stopped. The other trainman jumped off the locomotive and hand lined it south toward C.N. Junction and jumped back on the locomotive.

We now had the train pointed in the right direction for the return trip, however we still needed to get back to the station.

The hogger pulled the train a half mile down the track, sometimes needing to stop and have the trainman jump off and do a hand job on a switch that was not rubber. If C.N. Junction was lined up, we would get a favorable signal, or if a red we stopped short. The trainman jumped down, walked/jogged/ran one hundred feet to hand line the switch, causing the signal to be red; after hand lining, the signal would turn favorable and we pulled past the trainman standing at the switch and continued about another five hundred feet past the controlling point junction and signal.

I then stopped the train with my portable radio. My partner lined the switch toward the station, the signal turned lunar or flashing red, and we backed up slow to a stop, the trainman hopped on. Then we shoved three-quarter of a mile to the station, looking out for transients and surprise yellow or red flags. In later years, they added a safety stop prior to spotting a passenger train at a stub track, which required two trainmen.

After stopping the train short of the end of a stub track, one trainman would stay on the point with their hand near the emergency brake valve while the other would walk ahead giving the locomotive engineer back up instructions. As an example:

"Okay Miss Judy, you ready?"

"Yes, Larry, I'm ready for the stub."

"Okay here we go, got "The Bag Lady" on the point, I'm on the ground, proceeding, okay Amtrak 470 to back up 200 feet to the stub."

"Roger, 200 feet, here I come"

"Looking good, 150 feet now."

I hear Judy's radio *click-clicks* in acknowledgement.

"100 feet now."

*Click click.*

"50."

*Click click.*

"30...20...10...easy now...that will do. Good spot. Tie her down and I will meet you ladies out front."

Yes, people would ask me, *what exactly is it that you do?*

# Epilogue

*Writing my journey* through life these past three years has been a constant battle between humility and pride—in other words, what to leave in and what to leave out. I truly hope that those of you who may have been offended can find it in your hearts to forgive me. To those of you who were not offended, you are an example of love and tolerance. To all: peace. Yes, this book has to end somewhere, so I will pick up from the "Fatalities" story and my last day on the railroad, after my train struck and killed a human being for the eighteenth time in my career....

After the investigation and release from the coroner and other officials, we continued southbound and the locomotive engineer, Coalition Sniffa, on the northbound passenger train we passed told us to get onto the yard radio channel. When we did, he told us that there was still some DNA on the front of our engine. I had our engineer, "Trench Coat Sam," stop the train in a wooded area before Everett, the next station stop, and I hopped out with a water bottle to clean up the remaining viscera and say a quick prayer before proceeding.

I had not planned for that trip to be my last day on the railroad; however, as we rolled along toward Seattle I recalled that I had been thinking that if I was called into the office again or if I had one more bad trip, I was going to retire. The handwriting was on the wall. The Me Too movement was coming on strong, as well as other humanitarian efforts, and navigating my way through the newest culture without being called into the office would require more energy than this old white boy had left.

I retired.

# Glossary

Angle Cock: Valve at either end of a train car or locomotive that shuts off the flow of pressurized brake line air to the car and to the air hoses between the cars. Not a joke; it is really called an angle cock.

Beans: A lunch break. Often consisting of card games while some washed down their food with coffee, others with spirits back in the day.

Blue Flag: A blue flag or lighted lantern-type signal displayed on tracks or piece of rolling stock. Means that a piece of equipment may not be coupled to. Example being the electrician craft putting up a blue flag on a train for protection while working on, under, or in between. Only the person that put it up could take it down; in later years that rule was changed to a person from that craft could take it down.

Bottling the Air: When air is left in the train brake line system by closing the angle cock, a type of valve, then leaving a train with the locomotive to do other work. Leaving a train with bottled air can be a dangerous situation, as trains have been known to roll away and cause some tremendous catastrophes. When this was done back in the day, a crew member was left behind to protect the situation and should the train start to roll, the crew member could open the angle cock, thus exhausting the brakes into emergency application and stopping the train.

Carried Seniority: When an railroad employee is allowed to use their original hiring out date when changing jobs or locations.

Clear Signal: Or green signal allowing train to travel at maximum authorized speed.

Conductor: Is in charge of the train, crew, cargo, and the passengers on a passenger train. Back in the day, a conductor was sanctioned to perform marriages while on the train.

Deadheading: When a person or crew is transported from one location to another while getting paid. Mostly on passenger trains back in the day.

Dropping Cars: Risky and known to be a deadly train maneuver. There are several reasons for dropping cars, the most common being when pulling a train and wanting to get the car or cars behind the locomotive in a position to be on the other end of the locomotive, then you would make a drop.

Eighth Notch: Most powerful throttle position of the locomotive. Ramming speed.

Engineer: Locomotive operator. Manipulates the throttle and applies brakes as needed.

Foamer: A person who is a fan of anything associated with railroading. Common for railroad employees to call them "foamers" because many become so excited when discussing trains that you would expect them to start foaming at the mouth at any second.

Fusee: Another word for flare or a lighted red stick used for signaling caution or dangerous conditions. Rules require locomotives and cabooses to be stocked back in the day.

Glad Hand: Each end of a train brake pipe is coupled to a "glad hand" connector by an angle or stop cock and a flexible (usually black) hose. The glad hand connectors are slipped together to form a continuous long pipe line stretching from the head locomotive to the rear train car.

Highball: Expressed verbally or by signal, meaning it's okay to operate the train at maximum authorized speed.

Hoghead (or Hogger): Locomotive engineer.

Hot Box: Term used when an axle bearing overheats on a piece of railroad car back in the day.

Hot Box Powder: Powder carried by train crews to sprinkle on and put out a hot box.

Hot Box Detector: Measures the temperature of the journal bearings of a train now days.

Hours of Service Law: 12 hours being the maximum a T & E person could work for the sake of safety. Originally 16 hour law, then 14 hour to 12.

In The Hole: The siding where one train waits to meet another. Different meaning at home.

Load Test: Amperage test on a locomotive standing still. Different meaning at home.

Lunar Signal: Train allowed to crawl past signal, penetrating that block of track and looking out for dangerous conditions.

On Board Service (OBS): Crew members on passenger trains employed to service passengers in various capacities, most not needing supervision from conductors.

Red Signal/Red Block: The signal being red indicates the block of track beyond it is occupied or unsafe to enter; under some conditions the train may be allowed to enter at crawling speed.

Snake: Derogatory term to some, left-handed compliment to others; usually what a locomotive engineer would call a trainman on the ground hand lining switches—as in "snaking around."

Spotting Up: Put a certain car or piece of equipment of the train at an exact location for passenger or freight unloading, including mechanical repair and maintenance.

Stub Track: Stub to some, "tail" to others; track that stubs off a main line track and usually ends at a bumper. Sometimes confused with a tail track, which usually ends at a storage or work facility.

T & E: Abbreviation for Trainmen & Enginemen. Historically, and even today, the enginemen operate the locomotives and the trainmen line switches pertaining to the train's movement. They work together and watch each other's backs. The better they get along, the safer the operations.

Tie Up: When done working, preparing to leave the property by changing clothes and filling in and stamping the pay slip. Usually took longer when overtime was involved back in the day.

Torpedoes (Railroad Torpedoes): Little metal packets with gunpowder-like ingredients. The packets had little metal straps that allowed the torpedo to be attached to the ball of a rail. Torpedoes were left on the rail for emergency situations. For example, in the days when there were no radios or track side lighted signals, a disabled train crew member could lay them out in either direction with red flags well in advance of where they were stopped. The idea was that any train approaching, after running over the torpedo, would hear a loud explosion or see the flag. The locomotive engineer would immediately reduce the speed of the train so as not to run into the disabled train— officially it was called restricted speed. Workers on tracks also used them as well to warn trains that someone ahead was working on or near the tracks. I hired on in 1977, worked forty years, and the only torpedoes my crew ever ran over were during a test by "weed weasels" (as I fondly called trainmasters). Torpedoes were obsolete by 1977 on almost all routes that I worked on, and are now deleted from most rule books.

Whiskers: Seniority term; the longer the whiskers the more time on the railroad. Not to be confused with whisker burns on the Wye.

Wye (or Y): a triangular formation of three railroad tracks that a train can enter at one entrance, travel the route hand lining switches along the way, and come back out where it entered but pointed in the opposite direction. In other words, turning the train around or spinning her on the Y.

Yellow Signal: Also known as an "approach signal." Usually indicates the next one could be a red signal, meaning to slow down and prepare to stop.

*For more definitions, or more clarity on existing ones, contact: Larry Drawdy, P.O. Box 1295, Roy, WA 98580, or ledrawdy@aol. com*

# Acknowledgments

I would like to acknowledge and thank God for my sobriety, resulting in the greatest joys of my life: my wife, our family, our friends, and our health. Without sobriety, those joys would have never been possible, nor would the achievement of writing this book.

The majority of my spare time after retiring these last three years has been spent writing—and has not been exactly what my wife was hoping retirement would be. *Thank you, honey, for your love and patience.*

I have always been a writer, sort of. When given assignments in grammar school, reform school, high school, junior college, and in later years for railroad union and company flyers, my writing was mostly well-received, even with its quirky humor. My mother, in part, was like that with her writing persona. Thank you, Mom!

I would like to acknowledge my railroad coworkers that encouraged me to write a book; you were all inspirational, thank you!

I would also like to acknowledge my nephew, Curtis, son of my loving sister, Denice, with the many flyers he helped me with and also with some of my very first drafts of this book, thank you!

After retirement, when I started writing, most people did not take me seriously, and I needed help. I was at a Christmas gathering with relatives and mentioned that I was writing a book—while getting mostly the *oh, that's nice* reaction, and not much more. My dear brother, Jeffrey, has a daughter, Emily, and her partner, Tyler, seemed interested and we talked. I remember that he studied me as if I was crazy; he heard me out, however, and we struck a deal. I emailed him stories and he edited them while being compensated and doing a great job. Eventually, my eagerness and pace to get a book published did not fare well with his personal life or his job and college courses, leading me to hire a combination professional editor/publisher. Much of the writing in this book has only been slightly altered from his original edit. Thank you, Tyler!

When shopping for a professional established editor, most of the prospects were offended by my material, politely declining. There were a few who expressed interest, but only one who seemed more than just a little bit interested. It turns out that he was an established publisher, as well, and the bonus was him being a rail fan, thus being very instrumental in keeping this book on track and getting it to the end of the line. Thank you, Bryan!

Both my retired judge friend and publisher led me to the gifted entertainment lawyer, Heather Morado. I would like to acknowledge and thank her for the highly professional, detailed review and inspirational report on my book. It is greatly appreciated, really is.

I would also like to acknowledge my good friend Gordon who was the best friend of my brother Darryl, who passed away in 1975. We connected recently and started meeting up for walks and talks that were inspirational in many ways, including the validation of writing this book. Thank you, Gordo!

Another person due acknowledgement is one of my wife's close friends, Kathy, as she reviewed the book before publication, resulting in a few changes, and assuring my wife that all was well and not to worry—*it's not that raunchy*. Thank you, ma'am!

I would also like to acknowledge the pastors and membership from my Lutheran church, notably Judge Darrel, who started the 12-step meeting for sinners, as well as my sponsor, Jim B., and all the friends I made at the meetings—with wisdom honors going to Bill W's bastid son.

I've heard many people say they were going to write a book who never did. That became an inspiration of sorts, as I wanted to be one of the persons who said it and actually did it. Also, many times after stating that I was writing a book, some people responded with some not-so-positive feedback or made fun of me, while most soon changed the subject or ignored me. You were very inspirational, thank you.

Last, but not least, I would like to acknowledge the people who expressed that even if I did accomplish the feat, who would read it? You were my greatest inspiration, thank you, thank you, thank you! May peace be with you.

CPSIA information can be obtained
at www.ICGtesting.com
Printed in the USA
JSHW040843010522
25463JS00001B/2